# Warriors of the Pale
## An Irish Saga

# WARRIORS OF THE PALE

## AN IRISH SAGA

by

Raymond Reagan Butler

SPELLMOUNT

British Library Cataloguing in Publication Data:
A catalogue record for this book is available
from the British Library

Copyright © Raymond Reagan Butler 2006

ISBN 1-86227-341-3

First published in the UK in 2006 by
Spellmount Limited
The Mill, Brimscombe Port
Stroud, Gloucestershire. GL5 2QG

Tel: 01453 883300
Fax: 01453 883233
E-mail: enquiries@spellmount.com
Website: www.spellmount.com

1 3 5 7 9 8 6 4 2

Printed in Great Britain by
Oaklands Book Services
Stonehouse, Gloucestershire GL10 3RQ

# Contents

*To my brother Charles.*

# Acknowledgements

For their professional help I am indebted to the staff of the British Library, and the National Library of Ireland in Dublin, and also to the staff of the Royal Armoury and the Wallace (Armoury) Collection in London. I am also grateful to the Chester Herald at the College of Arms, Melo Lenox-Conyngham of the Butler Society, and Mark Bowyer, the administrator of St Canice's Cathedral, Kilkenny, for their advice. I owe a great debt to Marilyn Corby for rescuing part of the text, and to Ellen Gibbons for putting me in touch with her.

On a personal note I am grateful to David Knowles, Mark Ordish, Stephen Baum-Webb and Andrew Wilson-Jenner for the many ways in which they have helped. A word of appreciation, too, for Kenyon Lilley, who accompanied me on my 'ancestral voyage' to Ireland, Normandy and Norway; and a final acknowledgement to David Grant, for his editing skills.

# A Note on Names

For the sake of consistency I have used the modern equivalents of surnames, both English and Irish throughout my narrative. During the whole
of the period that this book covers the wildly varying spelling of names
can lead to confusion, even in the case of my principal protagonists, the
Butlers. Edmund Curtis, in his edition of the *Calendar of Ormonde Deeds*,
adopts the name *Le Botiller* as convenient from about 1270, but before this
it was spelt in a dozen different ways, and only during the 15th century
did it stabilise as Butler.

To this day the name is written *de* (not *le*) *Buitleir* in Irish Gaelic documents. (This therefore makes it a 'place' rather than an 'occupational'
name, when the name is certainly of the latter category, coming from the
old French word 'bouteiller', meaning either a bottle maker or the servant
in charge of the wine cellar. As such it predates the use made of it by the
founder of the Butler family in Ireland. The earliest record shows a Hugo
Buteiller in France in 1055, and other families bearing the same name,
and recorded in English documents after 1066, can be assumed to be of a
totally different lineage.)

The exclusive use of Latin-Italian surnames at first, and Franco-Norman
ones later, additionally complicates a narrative that is already complex,
and names such as 'de Marisco' or 'de Fraxineto' (ultimately translated
into the Anglo-Norman 'de Mares' and 'de Freigne') were changed out of
all recognition during the medieval period. I have, therefore, settled on
their final French form, if it is still retained into the modern age. (There
were families such as the 'de Burghs' who completely Gaelicised their
name to 'Burke', and similar names of Norman origin are now almost
unrecognisable in their Irish form. With these, I have decided to use the
French names in the earlier period and the Gaelicised names from the time
that they were changed.)

As with Latin-Saxon-Norman English (or, come to that, Scandinavian!),
so with Irish. Ireland was, in fact, one of the earliest countries in Europe
to evolve a system of hereditary surnames, which came into being fairly
generally in the 11th century. The process developed spontaneously as the
population increased and the practice of adding a patronymic to a single

name, or nickname, proved to be not clear enough to single out the individual man. The surname, at first, was formed simply by placing 'Mac' or 'Mc' in front of a father's Christian name, or prefixing the name of a grandfather or earlier ancestor with an 'O'; from 'Ua', meaning descendent. (With regard to the latter, the authors of the *Shell Guide to Ireland* insist the apostrophe that is usually added to the 'O' is incorrect, but I have decided to observe the long-standing usage.) The variant spelling of most Celtic surnames over this period can equally create confusion, and I have modernised them also. I apologise in advance to any Irish reader who may think I have anglicised them to boot.

The same process has been employed with place names. I have used the English translation of the more descriptive Gaelic, and again I apologise if by so doing I have destroyed the inherent poetry in such names. Where a site can be recognised as a modern settlement I have used the present-day name, in order to locate it more clearly.

R.R.B.

## Sources

MacLysacht, *Surnames of Ireland.*
A.D. Mills, *British Place Names.*
P.H. Reaney, *A Dictionary of British Surnames.*

# Introduction

## Surrounding the Pale

Perhaps the most reviled Irishman in their turbulent history is Dermot MacMurrough, King of Leinster, who in the mid-12th century brought the Normans to Ireland, and so opened the gateway to English domination for almost 800 years. Even today, the man is seen as the ultimate villain, although he was at the time, in fact, only acting – or so he believed – in the best interests of his people, by seeking to protect his kingdom from his enemies. Utterly ruthless, it had been by hard fighting that he had gained his crown, and he was as hard pressed to hold on to it.

Yet, in 1152 he made the arrogant mistake of carrying off the wife of one of his courtiers, afterwards casting her aside, even though she had borne him a child. To have abducted her from a powerful lord was audacious enough, but to then abandon her had courted disaster. While the disgraced wife retired to a convent, her outraged husband took up arms against her ravisher, although it took him over a decade to raise a force. For, astonishingly, it was not until 1166 that his army routed that of the King of Leinster, a defeat that would lead to English involvement in Irish affairs for the first time in their history.

Since defeated, Dermot fled to seek assistance from King Henry II of England, an act that would lead to the eventual ruin of his countrymen, as it gave King Henry an opportunity that he had long been brooding over. For he had in his possession a papal bull giving him the pope's authority to invade Ireland in order to reform the Church there; an authority based on a document which purported to subject all Christian *islands* to the pope's jurisdiction (which would later be proved a forgery).[1] So even before Dermot arrived at his court to plead for his help, Henry II had earlier been tempted to add Ireland to his empire, which by then stretched from the Low Countries to the Pyrenees. But, *while she lived*, his formidable mother, the Empress Matilda, who held Ireland to be 'holy ground', had dissuaded him from this action. For the moment, then, King Henry refused MacMurrough any personal help, but he agreed to let him recruit any troops that he could find from within his realm.

The Irish king had little luck in this venture until he encountered Richard de Clare, an impoverished knight, but a man with a martial reputation. Recognising the man's unmatched qualities, and desperate to enlist his aid, King Dermot – notoriously prone to blunders – made the great mistake of promising de Clare, who would come to be known as 'Strongbow', not only his daughter in marriage, but also succession to his kingdom of Leinster. Other equally impoverished Norman knights, realising the wealth that was to be wrested from this unique war zone, were also stirred to volunteer, and Dermot returned to Ireland in their company. Backed by these knights, and a small group of Flemish mercenaries, he managed to survive in the south of his kingdom, until Strongbow could join him with the more substantial army that he was trying to muster.

On 1 May 1169 an advance party of this army, backed by 300 archers, landed at Bannow Bay, near Waterford, to be followed by a smaller party on the next day. By employing a combination of longbow-men and armoured cavalry, a devastating fusion that Irish troops had never before encountered, the Normans swept through their ranks, capturing the important town of Wexford for the Irish King. Other victories followed, but nothing could be consolidated, since the English forces were still too modest in size. And, as other armies would discover, the Irish fought their battles in a way unknown to European armies of that time. 'To fight them is to fight as one beating the air' a later, deeply frustrated, combatant would rail.[2]

Within a year, in response to desperate pleas from a force now so weakened that it was about to be dislodged from Ireland, another Norman detachment arrived at the Bay of Baginbun, a desolate spot where the outline of defensive ditches and ramparts can still be seen. And, finally, to the relief of all, Strongbow himself, with the vast army he had raised, crossed over to Ireland a year almost to the day after the first of his troops had landed there.

The Irish annalists recorded the event, if with their usual poetic inaccuracy: 'The fleet of the Flemings came to Erin; they were ninety heroes dressed in mail, and the Gaels set no store by them!'[3] The Gaels should certainly have set some store by them, for the 'ninety heroes' only spearheaded a much larger army. Yet even after a local Irish force, clad only in linen tunics and armed with spears and short swords, had been roundly defeated by these superbly equipped and brilliantly trained warriors, the vanquished still did not accept the real significance of what was happening. Only Strongbow's Normans saw matters with total clarity, as a traditional rhyme of theirs succinctly expresses, summarising the future tragedy of Ireland:

'At the creek of Baginbun
Ireland was *lost* and *won*.'

Richard de Clare took Waterford within one day, in a bloody attack; and on the same day that he had the substitute 'king' beheaded, he married MacMurrough's daughter, even as the streets ran red with blood. By 21 September 1170 King Dermot, with the aid of his Norman allies, had re-conquered Leinster and taken Dublin, but was also in a position to challenge the neighbouring kingdom of Munster. This was, in fact, the commencement of English inroads into other provinces, as Strongbow's men sought to carve out holdings for themselves.

By the autumn of 1171 Richard de Clare had inherited the whole of Leinster, for his father-in-law had died in the previous May. But by now King Henry II was fully awakened to the danger of having an independent *Norman* kingdom on his western seaboard, and he knew that he had to act decisively to protect his interests there. He embargoed all shipping to Ireland, other than his own, and he prepared to invade, to secure his right to rule Ireland as granted to him by Pope Adrian IV in 1155. Henry moved swiftly, landing at Waterford on 17 October 1171 with a huge and splendid army, intended to impress his English barons as much as it was there to overawe the Irish. With his usual astuteness, he at once declared Waterford to be a 'royal' – that is, an *English* – city.[4]

Realizing that a decisive curb was about to be placed on his ambitions, Strongbow had better sense than to fight such a massively equipped army. Instead he agreed terms with the King, and although he lost everything else, he was allowed to keep Leinster as a fief. Strongbow had also claimed the county of Meath, but King Henry appointed his own man, Hugh de Lacy, as Justiciar (King's deputy) and as Viceroy, and gave him all of Meath to support that position.[5]

In recognising the English King as their overlord, the Irish leaders knew that they had something to gain, if only protection against such men as Strongbow and his ilk. They had not, they must have reasoned, lost any real sovereignty but had simply transferred their allegiance from the traditional High King of Ireland to the 'son of the Empress'.[6] Henry would now attempt to introduce the Church 'reform' demanded by the pope – possibly conformity with the more restrained English observances – to give his actions the sheen of piety.

Six years later King Henry II, seeking a patrimony for his 10-year-old son, Prince John, gave him his Irish possessions, declaring him to be the 'Lord of Ireland' at a great council at Oxford, to the astonishment of most present. Particularly, perhaps, that of his jealous and ambitious brothers; for from being the runt of the royal litter, John 'Lackland' had become the declared ruler of a small kingdom, with all the wealth that such a gift entailed. At Windsor, in 1177, he received the homage of the Anglo-Norman lords then holding land in Ireland from the Crown, although Hugh de Lacy remained in control throughout the remaining years of the Prince's minority.

Yet only seven years after this, while still a minor, the Lord of Ireland sailed for his new domain with a magnificent army, largely to check the ambitions of his father's deputy, who, like Strongbow before him, had developed ambitions that were too independent for King Henry's peace of mind. Hence Henry took what might have been a premature decision to send his son to establish himself in his domain, since the Prince was immature in years, if not in character. (At 17, the Prince was an extremely precocious and a scandalously immoral youth.) But he was still too inexperienced to make any major decisions concerning either civil or martial strategy, and these had been decided for him in advance.

while the overall plan for John's military actions in Ireland bore the hallmarks of his father's practical genius, the man who had closely supervised the administrative detail was Ranulf de Glanville, an East Anglian baron who had made the royal service his career. The most accomplished jurist in England, he had been 'at Henry's elbow' from 1178, and his involvement in Prince John's first Irish expedition would have particular significance for the subjects of this book. It was through Glanville that the first of our warriors, and the founder of the Butler dynasty, also set sail for Ireland, to claim a new inheritance for himself and for his heirs. Service to the prince on the battlefields of Ireland would result in great rewards.

Indeed, almost every combatant who accompanied Prince John on his first foray into Ireland in 1185 received some kind of reward for his services, and these were generally in the shape of acres, with the most important of the land grants going naturally to his closest and most reliable companions. Of these, Philip of Worcester and William de Burgh came into their own immediately, but Theobald Walter[7] – perhaps because he was considered to be still too young, or too unreliable, for such a huge responsibility – at first inherited his lands jointly with his uncle, Ranulf de Glanville. Glanville may even have sent Theobald to Ireland with the express purpose of claiming land there for himself and his own heirs. Though if this is so, it is a tribute to Theobald's business and political shrewdness that, within a decade, he would be in sole control of this immense property.

The extensive and fertile country of Ormond was one of the greatest prizes to be given away, once it had been wrested from the Irish in battle, and Theobald Walter and his uncle Ranulf received five and a half cantreds of prime land in Northern Tipperary.[8] The granting of these holdings was due more to Glanville's usefulness to King Henry II than to Theobald's influence with his son John perhaps, even though Theobald did considerable service to the Prince as he fought to secure the 'kingdom'. Yet the land given to them would become the basis for the entire Walter fortunes in Ireland.

The decision to bestow this land on John's most loyal servants was, to some extent, of course, made to forestall any efforts these men might make to seize it from the Crown in their own name, as had happened with earlier Anglo-Norman invaders from the 1150s. But it meant that this broad margin of what came to be called 'The Land of Peace' – which, moat-like, surrounded the narrow band of land along the eastern seaboard, later to be called the 'Pale' – would serve as a defensive barrier for the latter's protection. The Pale, running roughly from Drogheda in the north to Wexford in the south at its maximum, and perhaps never more than twenty miles in width, was the only part of Ireland to be then wholly occupied by the English.

Importantly, the 'Land of Peace' separated the powerful O'Brien and MacCarthy clans, preventing them from joining together to take on the English intruders. These two perpetually warring families of Thomond and Desmond had remained the greatest menace to the establishment of an English colony on the eastern seaboard, and these two minor 'kingdoms', more than any other Irish factions in the area, needed to be contained.

Yet what was unique about the granting of these great tracts of rich arable land is that they were concentrated within such a small area and along an almost continuous line, so that they formed an almost solid block of fortifications. The estate boundaries of the Anglo-Norman protectors at times connected with those of their co-equals, while the land between them could be easily patrolled. This was a very unusual expedient for the monarch to allow, since it let the barons create a near-solid line of mutual defence, through which they could strike against the interests of the Crown as easily as they could act for them.

From the time of William the Conqueror the fiefs that any great landholder received from the monarch had always been spread over as wide an area as possible, to reduce the possibility of any individual tenant-in-chief establishing his own consolidated power base. The Walter family's extensive holdings in England, for example, held by them for over a hundred years in 1185, were scattered over several counties, precisely to keep their ambitions in check; and so this form of distribution was unique.

But the situation in Ireland was more volatile than that in England (where almost all the huge Saxon estates had been distributed to the faithful Norman followers of the victor of Hastings), and it required a different solution. The larger part of the island remained still in native hands, and most of the new overlords needed to build up a strong defensive front against the continual marauding of this 'Irish enemy' on their borders; an altogether different prospect from dealing with the spasmodic defiance of the long-vanquished Saxons.

The men that Prince John set up as guardians of this borderland could never, however commanding their positions, rest quietly or easily in their new estates; neither then nor later. Limerick Town, for example, which lay on the western edge of the Land of Peace, was dominated by the astute and unscrupulous Donal Mor O'Brien, their implacable enemy. For as long as Donal Mor ruled as the King of Thomond, it would be extremely unwise for any of the new landowners to press their claims too far, or too hastily.[9]

This would be particularly true of Theobald Walter and his dependants, living as they did on the borders of O'Brien's territory, and from whom some of their land had been seized. But equal care had to be taken with Donal Mor MacCarthy, who of all the contemporary 'kings' of Ireland was the most feared – by foreigners and Irish alike – according to the *Annals of Inisfallen*. (The *Annals* make the 'exaggerated and grisly' claim that nine Justiciars of England were slain by this fierce chieftain, who fought twenty-one battles in Munster alone during the English takeover of Ireland.)

By seeking to defend the royal enclave surrounding Dublin, within which English rule would be pre-eminent, John was of course doing no more than following his father's plans, which reveal a consistent policy towards the Irish. But at this stage there was never a detailed blueprint for an Anglo-Norman conquest of Ireland, only a broad strategy which could be adapted to the ever-changeable circumstances, as was shown in the well-judged selection of crucial fortress sites. Neither Henry II, nor his chief adviser Ranulf de Glanville, at this stage, intended a straight conquest of the country.

For King Henry and Glanville – and also for the new 'Lord of Ireland' – that lordship was never more than an opportunity to weld together English settlers and the indigenous Irish in the *name* of the Crown. Critically, at the beginning, this clear objective was threatened more by the restlessly ambitious Norman barons, who had been carving out their own domains in Ireland since the 1150s, than by the Irish nobility. For the latter had still not perceived the full threat to their own prestige by this new influx of warriors.

To begin with, also, there was no noticeable anxiety with regard to the loyalty of the Prince's men, as their immediate future depended upon their master's continued tenure of his Irish 'lordship', for which they, in turn, depended upon the backing of King Henry's armed support. But it was seen as imperative to bind them to the royal cause, and for this they expected further rewards for their loyalty, mostly in the form of larger grants of land. Yet it was also necessary to keep them constantly reminded that, with an armed royal force permanently located within the enclave of The Pale, the Prince's followers could never become as independent of the Crown as had those warriors sent over by King Henry thirty years before. For these men now wielded tremendous power within the baronies they ruled, and they were recognised as a danger to royal interests. Once the new men themselves showed signs of seeking any such degree of autonomy, a royal army would sweep into their lands to restrain their personal ambitions.

In 1185 the first necessity was for an armed force to maintain control over both the conquered Irish and the Anglo-Norman settlers. This was to be supplied by the fighting men who had travelled with John to help him claim his 'kingdom'. So, in return for the land they received, the Prince demanded that this elite should provide him with knights to serve him in whatever battles he would face in the future. All the large fiefs, or 'honours', of the new tenants-in-chief were to be held from him in exchange for military service. But, once having established the principles of that service, the new men were left to the business of securing their properties, or even expanding them, for which they could only rely upon a limited royal assistance.

Prominent among these men was Theobald Walter, the Prince's companion, who would, rather late in life, found a considerable military dynasty. Granted vast tracts of land in Clare, Offaly, Limerick and North Tipperary, the Walter family would fight for centuries to preserve them, holding the borders for successive English kings. Like their fellow Anglo-Norman landowners, they would have to adapt their lives to an economy rooted in the past; and the process of fitting in, and of accommodating their thought and speech to an alien culture would not be easy. The properties they held were for each one of them a danger point, and would remain, for generations to come, military command posts. Ireland outside The Pale would remain an embattled country, although since certain Irish noblemen had been allowed to remain inside the so-called 'Land of Peace', there was also the constant possibility of danger from within.

This would be even truer of the territory held by successive Walters, since they had allowed a few important Irish families to stay on in what had formerly been their ancestral homeland. These Irish tenants – thought at the beginning, astonishingly, to be neither hostile nor subversive; or if so, too weak to ever challenge the newcomers – would prove in time to be an 'enemy within'.

# Notes

1. Stubbs, *Gesta Henrici*.
2. Sir Walter Raleigh (1552–1618).
3. Donovan, *Annals of the Four Masters*.
4. Waterford would remain the most loyal to the English Crown of all the southern Irish cities.
5. Hugh de Lacy would be assassinated soon after John's return to England.
6. Known as the Empress Maud, since her first husband had been the Holy Roman Emperor. Her death in 1167 would release Henry from his promise to her.
7. Gerald de Barri (?1146–?1223), pen-name Giraldus Cambrensis, celebrated for his accounts of travels in Wales and Ireland. Brewer, (ed.) *Expurgantio Hibernaie*.
8. A 'cantred' is a district containing 100 townships. It should be remembered, though, that a 'township' could consist of one street only.
9. *Annals of the Kingdom of Ireland*.

# CHAPTER I

# *The First Butler*

Theobald Walter's family was not strictly of the 'warrior caste', and it is almost certain that it did not cross over to England with Duke William, but followed in the wake of his victorious army. Although a paternal ancestor, William Malet, was said to have accompanied the Normans in 1066, and – because he was himself half-Saxon – had even been entrusted with the burial of King Harold after the Battle of Hastings.[1]

Members of the Walter family were certainly established in England within the next decade, however, for their lands can be traced back to the Domesday Book, the survey of England carried out twenty years after the Conquest. For them to have secured a sizable property in such a short space of time suggests that they must have done the Crown some service, and that presumably of a military nature.[2] Most of the land they held was set in Lancashire, and nine of the sixteen holdings listed there were entered under the ownership of Walter of Caen, the son of William Malet.

Hervey Walter, the grandfather of Theobald, acquired Caen's lands by marriage, becoming Caen's son-in-law about 1130 AD, for he was able to give his daughter Alice a dowry of about 400 acres in Lancashire when she married some sixteen years later. There is a possibility, however, that the Walters themselves were already in place in England long before the invasion, or may not even have been Norman in origin, since the name 'Walter' is actually Germanic.[3] Yet this is a moot point, since as it was also a personal name, introduced into England by the Normans, the family may well have originated in Normandy. Though of whatever nation, the family had clearly held an office of some kind for generations, serving possibly as cupbearers; the proof is in their heraldry.

Hervey Walter would survive his son, who was also called Hervey, and the elder Hervey was said to have earlier campaigned in Ireland during the time of the first invasion of Ireland in the 1150s, although he did not settle there. The younger Hervey died young, perhaps before reaching his thirtieth year, although not before leaving five sons of his own – Theobald, Hubert, Walter, Roger and Hamo. As orphans, they were left in the charge of their grandfather.

All five of these brothers would leave some mark on Norman England, even if three of them did so only by means of making advantageous marriages; with their father setting them off on this course by making a union of considerable importance himself, when he married Maud, a co-heiress of Theobald de Valoines.[4] For Maud was not only excessively rich in her own right, she was also a sister-in-law of Ranulf de Glanville, the most powerful of all Henry II's subjects in the King's last years. Glanville took an avuncular interest in the welfare of Maud's fatherless sons, and the two elder brothers, at least, would always acknowledge his generosity towards them. (There is no doubt that Glanville himself took an especial pride in Hubert Walter's considerable achievements.)

Their date of birth cannot be established with any certainty. It has been suggested that Theobald first went to Ireland with Henry II in 1171, when the King received the submission of all the 'little princes' of that country, and that Henry gave Theobald large possessions there, in consideration of services done for him. It has even been proposed that it was King Henry who made Theobald 'Butler of Ireland', at the same time that he made Prince John 'Lord' of that country.[5] But this cannot be firmly ascertained, and it is unlikely to be true since it would make Theobald at least 21 in that year, considerably older than John, and it is generally understood that the two men met as adolescents in the Glanville household. Besides which, Theobald was never known by the title of his honour until the reign of Richard I, or at least late in the 12th century. If we take it that the first Hervey Walter married in 1130, his son could have not have taken a wife until the mid-to-late-fifties. This would make Theobald, the first born son, though possibly not the eldest child, at the most some ten years older than Prince John, who was born in 1167.

What *is* known is that Hubert Walter, the second son, was seen to be intellectually outstanding from a very early age, and that from adolescence he was so much in his uncle Ranulf's confidence that he was said to have 'shared with him the government of England'. By 1184, he was a Baron of the Exchequer, and a year later he was sent by the King to negotiate with the monks of Canterbury about the choice of a new primate. Described as 'tall of stature, stately in manner, wary of counsel, subtle of wit, though not eloquent of speech' he was 'loyal and resolute, witty and wary'.[6]

There is no comparable description of Theobald; although since Prince John was known to be discriminating with regard to his circle of friends, it can be assumed that Theobald shared some of his brother's intellectual brilliance, or was at least possessed of some of his other qualities. Had he not been personable, he would never have been admitted into the Prince's highly exclusive coterie, since – whatever his many personal faults – John appreciated talent and wit in the men he chose to be his most intimate companions.

2

It has been suggested that Theobald, though, was never particularly close to the mistrustful prince, and had in fact been imposed upon him by Henry II. But it is clear that – until the final years of his life – Theobald was unquestionably attached to John, and at times dangerously steadfast, since the Prince himself proved false to almost all he came into contact with. Although Theobald's own definition of loyalty would come into question at various stages throughout his life. His continued support of Prince John would certainly create problems for his brother Hubert after the death of King Henry II.

That these later complications were largely due to Theobald's stubborn allegiance to the cause of Prince John are irrefutable; and, in the light of future developments, make some sense. He would appear to have always seen John as the more preferable King of England, once his eldest brother Prince Henry was dead and with the second, Richard, having no legitimate heir. He seems never to have considered Arthur of Brittany, then a mere boy, as being a claimant with the better right to the throne.

Moreover, this decision appears to have been reached by hard reasoning, and not simply because the Prince had set him on the way to making a great fortune in Ireland. (John had further given Theobald the castle of Arklow, and 'all the lands pertaining thereto, by the service of a knight's fee',[7] where Theobald temporarily fixed his chief residence and founded an abbey. It is perhaps because of this fief that some historians have claimed a feudal barony for Theobald's descendants, but there is no evidence for this. Although throughout most of Europe, at this period, the rank of baron meant simply any tenant-in-chief of the King who held land by honourable service, and the Walters were certainly of this category.)

Theobald Walter did not return with John when King Henry II recalled the Prince to England after the first, (and unsuccessful), visit to his new possession, since it was Theobald's foremost task to secure his own territory in Ireland. This property, termed an 'honour', was a collection of lands and rights, at the core of which lay farms and manors, yielding great wealth. It was also, of course, a source of power, since this was as much a place of government as a military stronghold. Theobald's first undertaking upon moving in had naturally been the erection of a castle; for it was up to him to prove his fitness for the settling and arranging of his lands, and those of his uncle Ranulf. (His Glanville cousin having been earlier killed in combat in Ireland, he was now perhaps regarded as Ranulf's main heir, and he would already be in full control of their jointly held assets.)

As the most dominant man in the region, he had considerable command over his subordinates, and in himself provided the basis of the social and political lives of his tenants-in-fee. But, as was the feudal custom, he also had complete charge of their livelihoods, since they could not grant away their land, or even sublet it, without his permission. He was able to take their money, in reliefs for example, and through his royally given rights of wardship and marriage, he was even able to make crucial decisions about their future prospects. Yet Theobald's authority was also limited in many ways. Crucially, in the same way that his tenants were completely dependent upon him, he himself could never be independent of the King, (or in his case Prince John); and he was, of course, to a great extent vulnerable to the depredations of the enemy.

At this early stage of his career, still putting his Irish affairs in order, he required all the men he could bring together to defend his lands. Particularly since, in the two years following John's return to England, the Anglo-Normans had been forced to deal with a sudden upsurge of patriotism on the part of the Irish chieftains. (Who had now been fully alerted to the alarming speed and extent of the English takeover, and who were concerned to repossess their lands before they lost them forever.)

In 1187, for example, the castle of Kildare, held by the English, was burned and demolished by the men of Connacht. Apart from the totally unexpected challenge to their presence in Ireland, this was an appalling disaster for the English, since not one defender escaped, and two knights were slain. All were burned alive or suffocated by dense smoke, with the Irish carrying away their accoutrements: arms, shields, coats of mail and horses.[8]

And this was only the beginning, as the Irish began to fight back, however weakly, and they were not always on the losing side. Throughout 1188 there would be a number of retaliatory excursions by the English into Irish territory; but these were mostly just cattle raids and not all of them were victorious. Quite often, in fact, when the Irish pursued the English and engaged them in force, in terrain that was more suitable to their own more irregular methods of warfare, the invaders were defeated, and with great slaughter.

From the beginning, also, the new royal troops were faced with an adversary they could not adjust to, for they often found that their Irish challengers were backed by their own countrymen, resident in this alien land for a generation. Quite early on, one of the leaders of 'the English of Ireland', John de Courcy, made an incursion into Connacht, in the company of Connor O'Dermot. 'Upon which the king of that country assembled all his chiefs, [and they] were joined by Donnell O'Brien, at the head of some [of the] men of Munster'.[9] Since O'Brien had involved himself with the enemy, Theobald Walter would certainly have been forced to act against him, for much of his new domain had been taken from the O'Briens, and such a move on the Irishman's part would have been seen by Theobald as a move against himself. On this occasion many of the English were slain, and those who survived escaped from the county, but without being able to effect any further destruction.

However, in this volatile period allegiances were always flexible. John de Courcy, having earlier backed the Irish against the English newcomers, now

4

changed sides. He plundered Armagh throughout 1189, in the company of his new English allies, which included Theobald Walter's troops, when the tiny kingdom was 'burned from end to end', including the churches. Treachery was frequent, with, on this occasion, the son of an important chieftain being murdered by the English of Dalaradia, 'while he was sleeping among them'.[10] The Lord of Fermanagh was driven from his lordship and fled to the protection of the O'Carrolls; and shortly afterwards an English army arrived in that country, to whom O'Connell and O'Mulrony gave battle, with O'Connor being defeated and O'Mulrony killed.

The henchmen of the King of Connacht, Conor Moinmoy, were said to have killed him at the behest of his own brother, although once again the English were involved in this act of fraternal treachery, since they had originally set the two men against each other. 'Alas for the party who plotted this conspiracy against the heir presumptive of the throne of Ireland!' the chroniclers keened – which would be the first of many such laments.[11] As a great number of people had submitted to Moinmoy as the High King to be, they saw his murder as a particular dishonour. Messengers were sent to his father, Roderic, a former King of Ireland, to offer him the kingdom again, providing that he would avenge his son's murder, and after he had agreed to the proposal, King Roderic took hostages throughout all Connacht.

The Lord of Tirconnell encamped with his forces in Corran, and 'both English and Irish' came to oppose him, without being able to injure him on this occasion. All of them departed without coming to any agreement, and it is significant that throughout this period many Irish sided with the English against their own countrymen. (The enmity that existed between the Irish chieftains being, at this time, greater than their suspicions of the English.) Whether Theobald took part in all these confrontations among the Irish is not known, and is hardly feasible, but it is extremely likely that he participated vigorously whenever the battles took place in the vicinity of his lordship of Limerick, or in North Tipperary.

The situation in his own domain, though, must have been sufficiently peaceful for him to return to England in 1188, to act as a witness to his brother Hubert's charter to West Derham, and he accompanied his Uncle Ranulf to France to attest a charter of Henry II's at Chinon.[12] He was also with John in Normandy on the eve of the King's death in 1189; when Henry, as ever, was still doing all he could for his most loved son, who – even in his father's last days – was secretly making agreements with his enemies. It was said that the news of John's final treachery towards him robbed King Henry of the will to live, and – since the two men were together at that time – one can question the extent of Theobald's participation in John's treason. Henry II, of course, had lived surrounded by traitors, yet both Theobald's uncle and his brother had always been true to the King.

Theobald would have returned to fight the Irish at various times during this period, and he may well have been one of the English lords who refused to help the elderly Roderic O'Connor recover his kingdom of Connacht when it was lost to him in the year 1191. He may also have witnessed the English defeat at the Weir of Anghera in 1192, or taken part in the repulse of the MacCarrons near Kilbeggan, when two of the chieftain's sons were slain.

The English of Leinster were the fiercest of these combatants, committing great depredations against O'Donnell and O'Brien in that year. Their army passed over the open terrain of Killaloe, Walter country, marching westwards until it reached a plain near to the Shannon, where they were opposed by an Irish army of similar size, who slew great numbers of them. Despite this setback, on this expedition, the English managed to erect the castles of Kilfeakle in Tipperary and Knockgrafton near Caher, all of which was close to the Walter region, and Theobald would certainly have taken an active interest in the construction of these two fortifications.

Throughout the 1190s, following royal instructions, he was busy acquiring land for defensive purposes, parts of which he granted to other people, to be held by the service of knights, 'with all liberties and free customs'. Much of it was given to him by the Church, particularly by the Archbishop of Cashel, 'in fee', for which he did homage and service. The Abbot of Glendalough also granted him all the land that belonged to the abbacy, 'to be held by the service of one 1lb of incense yearly, on the altar of St Kevin at Glendalough on that saint's feast'.[13] But not all the land that could be acquired from the Irish came his way, and some of it was disposed of before Theobald could acquire it, even though it would have strengthened his borders. For Prince John, as his overlord, felt free to grant land that lay strategically just outside the Walter domain to others, usually to the Church, and this was always land that had once belonged to the diminishing kingdom of the O'Briens.

Theobald, with more than just an eye to his own future interests, perhaps, attended the Prince whenever he could escape his duties in Ireland, and the only time he spent away from his new lands was with John. This must have taken considerable toll of his purse and his energies, and soaked up much of his spare time, since John – like his father – was an indefatigable traveller, throughout England and the English dominions in France. Passage between the three countries was always arduous, and yet Theobald took every opportunity to catch up with the Prince.

He was certainly with John in 1192, when he received from the Prince the office of 'Chief Butler of Ireland', and he first assumed this style when confirming John's charter to Dublin on 15 May of that year.[14] At the same time receiving a grant of land from the Primate of Ireland in which he was described as *'pincerna domini comitis Moretoniae in Hibernia'*.[15] A description proving that he was appointed as High Butler to Prince John, and chosen by the Prince, using his title of the Earl of Moretain.

Theobald from this time adopted a new seal, to which he added to his family name the style *Pincerna Hibernaie* ('Butler of Ireland') overwhelmed by the honour done to him. Even though it may have been that Theobald had simply been selected for this particular office because his family were by tradition cup-bearers to kings, attending the monarch twice daily; the three cups in their coat of arms testifying to this.

All the same, it was a considerable rise in status, for the *Chief* Butler was a dignitary, not a functionary, being in attendance only at ceremonial occasions, to present his royal master with his first cup of wine. It was also a position of great trust, for in the days when a king's cup could so easily be poisoned, the monarch had to be completely sure of this particular servant's loyalty. In his later days, Theobald was occasionally spoken of as 'Le Botiller', or Butler, and the Latin form of the name, *Pincerna*, would alone come to mean that the person bearing it was a member of his extended clan. From the beginning, other members of Theobald's immediate family would follow his example and they also adopted the name.[16]

Throughout the 1190s, Theobald would go on acquiring land in Ireland, much of which he then invested in others, in the manner of his fellow landholders, thus making vassals of his tenants. Usually to be 'held by the service of half a knight, with all liberties and free customs'[17]. Most of the land that he redistributed had, of course, been taken from the Irish, although not always seized in conquest. Prince John, for example, had granted to the church of St Mary de Sancta Cruce, and the monks of the Cistercian order there, the lands which Domnall O'Brien, King of Leinster, by his charter gave them.

Theobald would enter into similar deals, but mostly with himself in the dependent position, as when the Archbishop of Cashel granted him a fee for his homage and service, for eight carucates of land in the territory of Let, at a yearly payment of a mark of silver. (Interestingly, this land seems to have been taken from, presumably, a renegade Norman, 'Maurice, son of Maurice', and the fitzMaurices – or, as they later became, the FitzGeralds – who would become the Walter family's most obdurate enemies.)

Theobald was in England with John towards the close of 1192, when they visited Nottingham, and where he received a fresh grant of his estate at Amounderness from the Prince. John, going abroad at the turn of the year, then entrusted him with the care of Lancaster Castle, to be defended against the Prince's enemies, presumably because Theobald was already well-established in the county. This is a clear indication that Theobald sided with John in his attempts to seize the English throne from his elder brother Richard.

All of King Henry II's sons were jealous of each, with the jealousy occasionally breaking out in open warfare between them, and all the brothers involved their various factions in their feuds. The death of the eldest, Prince Henry, in 1183, seemed to have ended this strife for a while, but his untimely death had actually only opened up the way to other, fiercer, quarrels. With the death of the second son, Geoffrey, of course, the contestants had been reduced to Richard and John – and, when he came of age, Arthur of Brittany – but Prince John would prove to be the most contentious of all; the most deceitful, and ultimately the most successful.

As he would quickly show from 1187 when, once Richard had been crowned King, he had then left the country for his wars abroad, leaving England dangerously open to John's machinations. (The months between the crowning in September and the new King's departure in December having been occupied in preparing for a Third Crusade, with Richard's envoys scouring England and his continental domains for ships, and his father's treasury being plundered 'for the cause'.[18] All too little for a man who longed to startle his fellow crusaders by the splendour of his armament, and who would have sold London to the highest bidder to raise the money to do so, had it been possible.)

On the death of their father, Richard had received John gracefully enough, granting him many lands and honours (since there were now more to go around), including the entire county of Derby. John had also married Avice, the daughter of William, Earl of Gloucester, whose fabulous marriage portion would be the bulwark of all his wealth. It was perhaps because of John's new affluence that, by the time Richard was due to depart, he began to have second thoughts about leaving his youngest brother in any position of strength.

John was in Wales when Richard I left the country, and the King bound him not to enter England while he was away, rightly suspecting his loyalty; but the Queen Mother Eleanor persuaded him to release John from this oath. Richard did so reluctantly, knowing that it could only be to his detriment, since he had made John so powerful within certain English counties; as he would prove within days of his brother having set sail, for John would always be dangerous to the peace of the kingdom when the King was not there to overawe him. There is equally no doubt, from his subsequent actions, that Theobald Walter was always willingly prepared to abet him – as far as he dared – in his schemes.

Richard I had left almost unlimited power in the hands of William Longchamp, Bishop of Ely, which would also prove to be a miscalculation on his part, for the bishop, whose harshness was only exceeded by his personal extravagance, soon earned the hatred of the people. Seeing this, Prince John began at once to plot against him, seeking to undermine and eventually dislodge him from the chancellorship, with the object of securing his own succession to the throne while his brother was away.

To do this, it was vitally necessary to crush the opposition, and the unpopularity of Richard's chancellor made it easy for John to advance his own interests by placing himself at the head of all counteraction to Longchamp's ministers. In fact, the Prince managed this with such success that Longchamp was forced to quit the kingdom, after the two men had fought in a skirmish outside London. The next day, at a meeting in Old St Paul's, the citizens – who had come out of London to meet John 'with torches and shouts of welcome'[19] – took an oath of fidelity to King Richard, but also to John as his successor. Longchamp, defeated, immediately left the country.

The government then passed into the hands of Walter de Coutances, Archbishop of Rouen, whom King Richard had sent home with secret instructions from his war camp in Sicily. The arrival of Coutances put another check on John, restoring the balance of the two parties, though not for long. John, in pursuit of his ultimate objective, swore to be the King of France's vassal in return for being granted his brother's continental provinces, (and probably England, too.) For the rest of Richard's reign the King of France would use John as a means of troubling Richard's domains, and while Richard was abroad, he would encourage John's subversive activities in England. To seal their compact, Philip even offered John his sister Adela in marriage, but the threat of the seizure of all his castles in England during his absence abroad – plus the fact that he was *still married* – kept the Prince from setting sail to claim his bride.

But even as things stood, John had an almost kingly power in Westminster, while his other possessions enabled him to exert a strong influence on different parts of the realm. As in the days of his lordship in Ireland, he had his own justiciar, chancellor and other officers, who held his courts and carried on the administration, and he kept a royal estate, residing chiefly at Marlborough or at Lancaster. When at the latter he would mostly have been attended by Theobald Walter, as the custodian of the castle, and whose family owned almost half of the county. But Theobald, in his role of butler, would not have served the Prince in any official capacity since his butlership was held only in Ireland. And Ireland it seemed was a responsibility to be either forgotten or temporarily set aside by the ambitious Prince, for everything was to be fought for in England and in his brother's continental empire.

By Easter 1192 news reached Richard in the Holy Land of serious trouble at home, where his presence was absolutely necessary since he seemed in danger of losing his birthright. But it was not until he had arranged a truce of three years with the Saracens that he could set sail for England, and storm and shipwreck then forced him to change his route. Attempting to make his way through Middle Europe, which he was forced to do using many disguises, since he had earlier offended the Holy Roman Emperor and the Duke of Austria, he was captured and lodged in the castle of Durrenstein, where he was held to a colossal ransom.

The news of Richard's captivity came to England from Philip of France, and John immediately demanded the fealty of the barons, who unhesitatingly refused, hoping for the King's return. John went first to France to secure the aid of King Philip, but back in London again demanded that the justices should swear fealty to him, declaring Richard to be dead. When the barons held out, John lost ground rapidly; and by May he was compelled to submit to his enemies, although he made a truce with them at the beginning of November.

Meanwhile John ordered that all his castles in England, and also those that he had taken from his brother, should be put into a state of defence *against* the King's forces; foremost among these being that at Lancaster, held by his faithful Irish butler. This order would not only test Theobald's loyalty to Prince John, it would also put a strain on the relationship between Theobald and his brother Hubert, who was by then the new justiciar, and who remained true to the King who had made him so. When John's courier incautiously boasted of the Prince's ominous instruction, and also of the army of mercenaries poised to arrive in England to back up John's bid to seize power, he was taken to London to be interrogated by the new justiciar. The Council, influenced by Hubert, then declared John to be deprived of all his lands, and even the Pope later excommunicated him; although until Richard was released, John still insisted that he was rightful king. When Richard was finally liberated, a message came from Philip of France: 'Beware, the devil is loosed!'[20]

John fled for France and Philip's protection; and Walter de Coutances was, in fact, still engaged in reducing the castles that had been seized by John when Richard arrived home in 1194, his ransom having eventually been raised. (Largely by Hubert Walter, who had for a short time been with the King in Palestine, and who had brokered a deal with Saladin when Richard had earlier been captured and ransomed in that country.) Coutances captured Marlborough castle, and he received the surrender of Lancaster from Theobald Walter. The capitulation of Nottingham castle completed the reduction of all John's possessions in England, and he was once again – save for his wife's possessions – John Lackland.

The Queen Mother again mediated between her sons, and the brothers were at least partially reconciled, though John was kept in a position of dependence for a while. (In fact John, prudently changing sides, went off to fight for Richard's cause in France, but was put to flight by the French king.) These services to Richard seem to have atoned for his past unfaithfulness; although when John was later accused of further treachery, Richard again seized all his possessions, and the Prince took refuge in his nephew Arthur's dukedom of Brittany; Arthur, following the family tradition of the Plantagenets, now being also alienated from his Uncle Richard.

When the King had dealt with his younger brother, (and his co-conspirators, among them Theobald Walter), he was forced to travel to France, where Philip Augustus had broken into Normandy. So with Longchamp and Coustance both out of the frame, the hugely gifted Hubert Walter, who even as a youth had shown a precocious talent for royal administration, was left to govern England in the King's name. For Richard, deeply indebted to him, had not only made him Archbishop of Canterbury in return for his services to him in the Holy Land, but now offered him the office of Chancellor.[21]

The Walter brothers had long been in conflict over their differing loyalties, but there would seem to have been a genuine affection between them, and Theobald was saved from Richard's wrath, on the King's return, by Hubert's personal intervention. Yet Theobald appears to have possessed a great deal of Prince John's ability to delude others, for it seems that it was largely by his own efforts that he was fully restored to royal favour. With the King not only re-granting him his property of Amounderness, held by a service of three knights' fees, but also awarding him with the town of Preston. (Amounderness being all that country between the rivers Ribble and Coker. The land had been lying waste, but it was now improved and, it was said, 'took up half of Lancashire'.)

The re-granting of Amounderness was only a confirmation of Theobald's former title, of course, but it is unusual in that it was granted to Theobald despite his previous falseness to King Richard. That he was made High Sheriff of Lancashire at the same time is even more astonishing, and it could only have been due to his brother's influence, for Hubert's leverage with the new king was phenomenal. Indeed so trusted was he by the King that when Richard went abroad once more, to settle his differences with the King of France, Theobald's brilliant younger brother then acted as the virtual master of England.

In this capacity Hubert Walter was mainly occupied with the collection of money for Richard's continental warfare, but he also managed to impose his own vision upon English life during the time of his short 'reign', introducing several constitutional innovations that would prove of lasting importance. Scutage (payment exacted in lieu of military service) was raised in 1195, a year which also saw the introduction of an oath 'to keep the peace', extracted from all persons above fifteen years of age. (The knights especially created to enforce this oath later developing into 'justices of the peace'.) Hubert Walter also originated the office of 'coroner' to hold inquests on all suspicious deaths, and he was directly responsible for establishing the Chancery Rolls. A friend of the merchant class, he protected them against the nobles, giving them the right to elect mayors and town councils, in this way virtually initiating civic government throughout the country. He possessed a truly radical approach to feudal politics, although many of his policies, it is true, were based on the principles that he had seen put into action by his uncle, Ranulf de Glanville, in King Henry's time.

Like most successful men in command, he was judiciously generous to those who would best support him, ensuring the trust of powerful individuals by the distribution of important favours. He was also no stranger to nepotism, and his younger brothers benefitted financially from his brief rule. That he did not forget to include his elder brother when it came to handing out this largess, notwithstanding Theobald's treachery towards the absentee King, is indicative of the close family bond between them. In fact, despite having to force Theobald to surrender up Lancaster Castle in the King's name, and the fact that Theobald repeatedly sided with the double-dealing prince, Hubert rewarded Theobald with a number of lucrative offices. He appointed him to be the collector of funds for tournament licences in 1194, was responsible for Theobald being made High Sheriff of Essex, and he made him a Justice Itinerant, with particular authority for assessing the tollage of Colchester, in 1197–8.[22]

Theobald himself seems to have had little influence in English affairs during his brother's ascendancy; but in the brief span of Richard's reign Theobald founded the abbey of Cokersand in Lancashire, among others; for whatever his moral weaknesses, he appears to have been a genuinely devout man. Which is more than can be said for the fiercely ambitious Hubert, who seems to have been a 'career' churchman; or who, at least, had a conflict of conscience between his ecclesiastical and his secular duties. Hubert would have done better, in fact, to confine himself to the politics of the Church, for by the mid-1190s his worldly troubles had begun to plague him, with Prince John's relentless plotting being the least of them.

At mid-Lent in 1196, the London craftsmen, dissatisfied with the way in which the government assessed their local taxes, were on the verge of rising, and this led to a huge scandal created by Hubert Walter. Arrested, the craftsmen's leader, William fitzOsbern, took sanctuary in the church of St Mary at Bow; and, to literally smoke him out, Hubert – acting in his role of Chancellor – had the church set on fire. Upon reaching the safety of the street, fitzOsbern, was seized, quickly tried, condemned and hanged, along with some of his followers; with the clergy horrified at the firing of a holy place by their spiritual leader.[23]

Wearing his ecclesiastical hat, Hubert may have sickened himself by such an extremely irreligious action, but his secular problems continued. An escape from them seemed to come when, soon after he had outraged his clergy, King Richard sent over an abbot of Caen to examine the accounts of all the royal offices of England. Hubert, deeply insulted by this slur upon his integrity, threw up the Justiciarship in disgust, although he quickly withdrew his resignation after the King apologised for his apparent lack of trust in him. Called to the marches to settle a dispute about the true succession of the Celtic Prince of Wales, Hubert took the moment to fortify their castles in the name of the English Crown.

But Hubert's time as the substitute king was drawing to a close, for Innocent III was no sooner Pope than he urged the dismissal of the

Archbishop of Canterbury from the Justiciarship, since he disapproved of priests holding secular office. Hubert, in obedience to the Pope, at once resigned, and he rejoined King Richard in Normandy, where he remained until Richard's untimely death – killed by an arrow, while besieging a French castle.

On the news of Richard's death, there was much disorder in England, since a strong party of barons did not want John as king and did not consider his accession to be a matter of course, (even though Richard had declared him to be his successor on his deathbed). John, still taking refuge in Brittany, was forced to send Hubert Walter home to form a government, with himself as an unofficial regent, until John himself could be crowned. Above all, Hubert was to try to keep the peace among the mutinous barons. In fact the Archbishop himself seems to have changed sides at this point, now backing John against his nephew Arthur, King of England by right of primogeniture. In a strongly worded speech read out in Canterbury and London, Hubert insisted on the right of the *nation* to elect the King against the will of an elite, and so effective was his argument (or his delivery of it) that John was duly chosen. Hubert, as Archbishop of Canterbury, crowned him at Westminster Abbey on 27 May 1199.[24]

On the very next day, though, he set the papal prohibition against himself taking secular appointments at defiance by once again accepting the office of Chancellor. Any love of power apart, he was said to have done this 'for the country's good', since he appeared to be the only person in England who was capable of acting as a check on the new King's rampant ambitions.[25] He at least succeeded in keeping the peace in England whenever John was out of the way.

Theobald, meanwhile, had managed, largely through his brother's influence, to remain High Sheriff of Lancashire, where nepotism also appears to have reigned, for his deputies were his father-in-law and a nephew, Nicholas le Botiller, and with other members of the family taking important civic roles. (Whether these Le Botillers of Lancashire were from a younger branch of Theobald's family is not easy to ascertain, for his three youngest brothers had, like himself, by this time also adopted the epithet 'Butler' to that of their surname. But it is clear that the land they owned was in or around Amounderness, and that the administration of Lancashire was a family-run business.)

Theobald remained High Sheriff until the first year of John's reign, when both he and Philip de Worcester, who had also served the new King excellently over a period of many years, fell abruptly out of favour. The exact nature of the quarrel has never been disclosed, although disputes about money were the usual cause of John's favourites falling into disgrace, but the alacrity with which John struck out at his former friend and ally has the strong aroma of vengeance about it. The new king, of course, had always been quick to take offence, and it may simply have been that he could not excuse his friend for having meekly surrendered Lancaster castle up to his brother, seeing it, perhaps, as a defection to the absent Richard, long before such submission to the former King had been really necessary.

It has also been argued that John valued Theobald simply because he was Hubert Walter's brother; a conclusion that may be based on the grounds that John, when King, promptly took away from Theobald the gifts that he had previously given to him as Lord of Ireland. Although this action is totally consistent with the new King's behaviour towards all his courtiers, for there could never be, in the light of John's pathologically mistrustful nature, any state of complete confidence between the King and his intimates.)

Theobald, dismissed from his base at Amounderness, and further deprived of his jurisdiction as the Sheriff of Lancashire, was dispossessed of much of his English and Irish estates. Hubert – who was still endowed with great power, if only as the Pope's representative in England – could no longer fully protect his brother, although he did what he could to save him from John's temperamental excesses, seeking to effect a compromise.[26] (Which was managed in a remarkably short span of time when one considers John's legendary reputation for holding a long-standing grudge.) Within a year, Theobald would be restored to something approaching favour, but he was still in the – mainly Irish – wilderness.)

The shameful way in which John treated Theobald – who for twenty years had loyally supported his aims – is a typical example of John's arbitrary behaviour, and his lack of generosity towards his dependents. John's decision, soon after his accession, to sell off some of Theobald's lands in Ireland to his new favourite William de Braose, for 4,000 marks, perfectly illustrates his untrustworthiness. Braose, by comparison with Theobald, had done little for the new king over the years of his striving for the Crown, and was, in fact, a brash newcomer to the King's circle. But he was then high in the King's esteem, since he had been the foremost of John's courtiers in urging that he should be crowned in place of his nephew, Arthur of Brittany, who many still regarded as the rightful heir.

Braose, who had accompanied John to France in 1200, had also been granted 'all such land as he could conquer from the Welsh',[27] with the result that he became the most powerful baron in South Wales. But the loss of Normandy to the English in 1204, which meant the loss of most of their French possessions, caused several barons, Braose among them, to involve themselves more deeply in Irish affairs. (Where King John himself, while managing to lose Normandy, had somehow succeeded in imposing stability upon Connacht.)

William de Braose did very well for himself in Ireland, and in 1201 he obtained the honour of Limerick (without the city), for which he agreed to pay 5,000 marks and a rate of 500 per annum. (This was the origin of the misleading statement that John had sold him *all* the land of Philip de Worcester and Theobald Walter.) It is possible that by selling Limerick to him, John may have bought Braose's silence over his part in the suspicious death of Arthur of Brittany; popularly believed to have been murdered at his uncle's instruction.

But, as with William le Marshal, who had served both John's father and his brother with equal loyalty, Braose would later fall from favour with the capricious and vindictive king, who dared trust no one, not even those who were closely bound by self-interest to his service. Marshal was excluded from the English Court for five years, while the rebellious Braose escaped into exile. This fall would come too late to serve Theobald's cause.

Philip de Worcester had escaped the King's wrath, returning to Ireland by way of Scotland, and once on his own territory he recovered it by force of arms. Theobald, though, avoiding a direct confrontation with the King, came to a financial arrangement with Braose with Hubert's assistance, arranging to redeem some of his lands by a payment of 500 marks. As early as 1201, Braose confirmed to him and his heirs five and a half cantreds in Munster, and slightly more land elsewhere. But there was a change of emphasis, since Theobald was now no longer the absolute overlord, and must give Braose the service of 22 knights' fees: '…with the donation of parochial churches, and judgement or trial by water ordeal or fire ordeal, and trial by dual or combat, the said Theobald fitzWalter and his heirs shall hold from the said William de Braose and heirs forever.'[28]

Later, Theobald would purchase more of his own lands from his supplanter, which included the donations of land in Killaloe and in King's County, as well as Tipperary and Limerick. (The five and a half cantreds of land he purchased in Munster must have been a particularly galling negotiation, since the burgh of Killaloe had been one of the earliest of Prince John's donations to him.)

That the King was aware of these transactions is evident, for the grant of Munster had been given before John at Lincoln. He himself had returned to Theobald land that he had earlier given to him, when Lord of Ireland, 'confirmed, by and with the consent of his father'. In the second year of his reign, even at the height of their quarrel, the King had again returned land to Theobald, with a grant that was witnessed by Hubert Walter. Indeed, since Hubert witnessed many of the transactions between the two men he may have been responsible for the King's change of attitude towards his brother, perhaps by persuading John of Theobald's value to his cause across the Irish Sea.

It was a possibility, but only a possibility, that the differences between Theobald and the King lay in the increasing troubles the English were beginning to experience in Ireland, where the English barons were starting to govern as they pleased. And where the Irish, no longer quite so credulous, were taking up arms against them in a more organised way than they had so far done. Meiler fitzHenry, an illegitimate son of King Henry I, who had been on an earlier expedition to Ireland in 1169, had left John's side in France to act as Chief Justiciar in Dublin, for John had few men he could count on to act purely in his name. In 1204 he directed Meiler to build a castle in Dublin, and also to force the citizens to fortify the city.

But there is no evidence of Theobald being in any way less loyal to King John than were any of his other magnates at this time, while there is ample proof that he was more reliable than most, and perhaps John learned to revalue him because of this. It is significant also that John never harassed Theobald's lands while he was in possession of them – as he would do later with Braose and William Marshal. FitzHenry, as John's assessor, would lead an army into the Broase' estates in Munster, an act that provoked the two men to carry on an open war with the Justiciar in Ireland. But it is clear that the King did not wish to completely alienate his former ally. The re-granting of Theobald's lands was often tremendously complicated, and reveal how completely dependent the King was on the *military* might of his Irish landlords.

Typical of these entangled arrangements, a grant of 1201 acknowledges that while Theobald owed to William de Braose the service of 22 knights for land he had been re-allocated in Munster, Braose could not acquire the land and services that a tenant of Theobald's still held of him. The situation could not be changed, and the same services would remain to Theobald and his heirs in perpetuity. In 1205, William le Marshal, independently of the King, granted Theobald the castle of Arklow, (which had earlier been in Theobald's possession), by the service of one knight, and he also granted him a barony in County Kilkenny by the service of four knights.

Quite clearly, however much stripped of his property by the King, Theobald still had some standing at Court, if only among the lesser courtiers. When John allowed Theobald to reclaim his land, it could only have been because he saw that he had need of him in Ireland. Theobald Walter, like most members of his family, had proved to be an excellent administrator, if no martial genius.

On his accession, King John endeavoured to secure a more effective authority in Ireland; and with this end in view he set up a royal administration and courts of law, and sought to make the Church an instrument of state by the appointment of non-Irish, feudal prelates. With the example of the presumption of such rebels as Lacy and Burgh in mind, John also tried to create a new and more subservient baronage, clipping the liberties of the Norman lordships of Leinster and Meath.

If John did quarrel with Theobald on political grounds it may well have been for this reason, as this particular policy aroused much dissatisfaction among the previously uncurbed magnates, who felt their independence was under attack. It actually drove some of them into acts of rebellion, but there is no evidence to show that Theobald was among their number. He was, perhaps, too busy trying to safeguard the property of which he was being dispossessed; a suppliant in 1199, he gave John 80 marks for a plaint of *novel dessein*[29] to be judged by the King.

In fact, Theobald Walter seems to have played little part in the numerous conflicts that followed on from King John's disruptive policies in Ireland, since he appears to have stayed in England throughout much of this period, still perhaps seeking to re-ingratiate himself with the King. That he succeeded in this to some extent is shown by the fact that Amounderness was re-granted to him on 2 January 1202, as *'delicto et fideli nostro'*.[30] And he was certainly in England in 1203, for he is on record as owing King John two palfreys in payment for a licence to return to Ireland. (The fee was still outstanding a year later, when he rendered his account to the Treasury, paying ten marks instead of the horses required. Significantly, the account was sent from his castle at Lancaster, with Theobald keeping a safe distance between himself and John at a time when they were once again estranged from each other.)

While out of favour, numerous complaints had surfaced against Theobald, accusing him of past oppressions, and by 1203 he had decided that it would be more advisable to withdraw to his Irish estates completely. While he may have escaped the baleful influence of King John by doing this, he certainly did not arrive in Ireland at an auspicious time. As ever, battles were raging throughout the country, largely among the Irish; but the most formidable in fact being between the three most dominant Anglo -Norman barons – Lacy, Courcy, and Burgh – and it is very unlikely that Theobald was able to avoid being drawn into their feud.

In 1204, an army of Hugh de Lacy drove John de Courcy into Tyrone, where he sought the protection of the Kindred-Owen, and at Carrickfergus the English of Ulidia slew great numbers of his people. It was reported that Courcy himself was taken prisoner at this battle, but he was afterwards set at liberty, and sought royal permission to go on crusade to Jerusalem. With that feud defused, Walter de Burgh created another martial diversion, which would certainly have involved Theobald Walter since they were connected by mutual self-interest, although Burgh's field of activity was far from Theobald's home ground. He plundered Connacht only; churches as well as territories. This pillaging was stopped only by Burgh's unexpected death, when '…God and the Saints took vengeance on him for that, for he died of a singular disease, too shameful to be described…His entrails and fundament fell from his privy place, and it trailed after him even to the earth. Whereof he died impenitently, without shrive or Extreme Unction, or good burial in any church in the kingdom, but in a waste town'.[31]

Nearer to Theobald's territory, Meiler fitzHenry took possession of Limerick by force, on account of which a fierce war broke out between the English of Meath and fitzHenry's men, in the course of which the son of an Irish chieftain was killed by the rival Irish, 'with many other hurts done among the Englishmen themselves'.[32] It is not known how closely Theobald Walter may have involved his party in these battles, although with the fighting coming so close to his own territory, he must have been prepared, at least, to do battle for his own interests. That is, if he was still alive, since Theobald died in 1205, 'by now far advanced in years',[33] (although in the context of his times this could merely indicate that he lived well into middle age).

As there is confusion about his actual birth-date, it is impossible to state his age at death. His brother Hubert – in 1195 – describes himself as being 'senescent'; but at that period a man who felt he was 'growing old' might well have been only in his early fifties, since few men lived to what we would now regard as a great age. This would put Theobald's date of birth around 1145; but this cannot be the case, for it would make him over twenty years older than King John, who was born in 1167, and the two men are generally thought to have been of the same generation. (They were mentioned as being students together in the household of Ranulf de Glanville.) At the most, Theobald could only have been a decade or so older than John, which puts his birth-date in the late 1150s, and suggests that he was nearing sixty at the time of his death.

Although he had made an uneasy peace with the King, John apparently still felt some animosity towards him, which is made evident by Theobald's decision to take refuge in what was left of his Irish holdings in the last two years of his life. It is made even clearer by his decision to live there in virtual retirement, in which he concentrated upon securing his defences, which might not have arisen simply out of fear of his Irish enemies alone.

He apparently also put his mind with some success to the development of the agricultural and commercial propensities of the territory he had regained and, after a fashion, still ruled, for he appears to have left a well-organised inheritance for his infant son. Among other proofs of this, 50 marks were given to King John for a writ of *morte d'ancestor* in 1205, which touched upon a third part of a cantred in Arklow, of which Theobald was clearly still in possession. That Theobald also remained loyal to the King, despite their separation, is shown by his friendship with Hugh de Lacy, the King's ally, who stood surety for the payment of this money after Theobald's death.

Like most wealthy men of his time Theobald Walter spent huge amounts of money in erecting various ecclesiastical buildings to the glory of God (along with himself, his family and anybody else he thought worthy of inclusion). Yet, in common with his peers, his attitude to the church can only described as ambiguous, since he had expended equally large amounts of money in demolishing other holy places at times of war.

(Churches in Ireland seem always to have been the first to suffer from attack by the Anglo-Normans during hostilities. From the beginning, the 'indecorous' form of Catholicism practiced by the Irish was looked on disapprovingly by the invaders, who saw something primitive, even perverse, in their overwrought observances.)

Throughout his military life, then, Theobald had spent much time and energy in laying waste to church lands in Ireland, and he does not appear to have lost this habit despite increasing age. In a bond certified by the Bishop of Ossary, Theobald was fined 128 marks to be paid for damage to the bishop's church; and Theobald and his men were also excommunicated for a time, because of the lands he had seized from the same church. On his act of repentance he agreed to make satisfaction, but it took the threats of his brother Hubert, as Archbishop of Canterbury, to make him restore the whole of the lands that he had seized.

Yet before Theobald died he would found one of the finest religious houses in Ireland, 'in a fit of piety', and he endowed the prior and canons with over eighty acres of prime farmland for their maintenance. In a charter of 1205 he was granted an area near the town of Clonkin, to found a monastery of the Cistercian order, the Abbey of Owney. There, the monks were to pray for the souls of King Henry II, of King Richard I, of John, the 'Count of Moretain', of Theobald's brother Hubert, of his close friend Adam de Glanville, and of Hervey and Matilda Walter, his parents. (The inclusion of King John as a mere 'count' is, perhaps, a malicious touch that Theobald could not resist.[34])

Theobald had come to Nenagh in County Tipperary about 1200, and he fixed on the town as his chief residence from that time on. Within the next generation a great castle would be built, the foundations of which were undoubtedly dug out in Theobald's time, (and whose fragmentary remains still dominate the little market town). He also built a priory and the hospital of the Augustinian Crucifers in Nenagh, dedicated to St John the Baptist, which he also founded in 1200. Their house was to support 'infirm persons, to have sufficient food and drink, from the cellar'.[35] The canons were to have the power to elect priors, and to create fisheries, and to build mills on the land.

He was also a generous benefactor of St Thomas's church in Dublin, founded to expiate the murder of Thomas Becket, (consistently maintained by the family down the centuries to have been a maternal ancestor of the Walters, although there is little proof of it). Out of his once vast estates Theobald had previously founded a monastery at Arklow in County Wicklow, and an abbey at Cockersands in Lancashire. On his return to Ireland in disgrace, and increasingly aware of his mortality perhaps, he made haste to finish the abbey of Witheny in County Limerick, which he had begun some years before and which he now endowed; and where he was buried.

Theobald was said to have been quite old for the times when he married to start a family, which indeed he was, since he married some time after 1196. But having taken his time he then married astutely, for his wife was immensely rich, Maud Vavaseour being the daughter of an eminent Yorkshire baron.[36] Yet he also fulfilled a Vavaseour legend, since while the men in her family were reputed never to have married a poor woman, the women in it married men who had never 'to bury a wife'. His death complied with this family myth, for Maud was only one in a long line of Vavaseour young widows.

Yet there is some mystery about this union, and even a suggestion that Maud may not have been Theobald's first wife, since he married her at the end of King Richard's reign, when he was long past the age of marrying for the *first* time. In that era the eldest sons of wealthy families were usually married at a very young age, for fear that, as wards of court, they could be disposed of in a disadvantageous marriage by an unfriendly monarch. It seems unlikely that Theobald, as a very eligible catch, would have remained a bachelor for most of his life.

His grandfather was certainly still alive during Theobald's minority, and the old man would have made certain that his heir married well while still a youth, if not a boy; his uncle, Ranulf de Glanville, too, would have exerted himself to find the boy a satisfactory wife. On the strength of a plea roll of 1196, it has been suggested that Theobald had a daughter, Beatrice, by a previous marriage, and it is not improbable. Beatrice was married to a Thomas de Hereford in her father's lifetime, and Theobald was said to have given her a portion of ten knights' fees. Hereford held land in Ely, County Tipperary, under Theobald, whom he acknowledged as his lord. But whether he acknowledged him as his father-in-law is another matter.

His eldest son was also named Theobald, as would be each of the next four Butlers, and they would also perpetuate another family tradition. For even if Theobald had not managed to hold on to his Irish estates in their entirety, he had still retained the office of Chief Butler, which would become hereditary. This would not only be a great office of state, it was also a valuable source of income, for it meant that the Walter family was allowed to level customs duty upon all wine that was imported into Ireland. As this involved the right to about one tenth of any cargo that 'broke bulk' in any port controlled by the English, the Walters would in this way swiftly increase their depleted fortune, as much as they did by marrying well and fighting for the Crown. Both of which they were to do in the next century.

# Notes

1. E. Curtis, *Calendar of Ormonde Deeds*.
2. Ibid. Theobald Walter first appears in the *Liber Niger* about 1166, as holding Amounderness, *per servicium 1 militia*. This suggests that his grandfather was possibly dead by this time.
3. P.H. Reaney, *A Dictionary of British Surnames*.
4. Carte, *The Life of the Duke of Ormonde*. (All references are from the *Introduction* to this work only.)
5. Ibid.
6. K. Norgate, *England under the Angevin Kings*.
7. Carte, op. cit.
8. The Four Masters, *Annals of the Kingdom of Ireland*.
9. Ibid.
10. Ibid.
11. Ibid.
12. W.L. Warren, *King John*.
13. Carte, op. cit.
14. Ibid.
15. Ibid.
16. Ibid.
17. Roger de Hoveden, ed. Stubbs, *Rolls Series, up to 1201*.
18. Norgate, op. cit.
19. Ibid.
20. Ibid.
21. Hook, *Archbishops*. Hubert Walter had been the Chaplain General of the Crusade.
22. Carte, op. cit.
23. Hook, *Archbishops*.
24. Ibid.
25. Ibid.
26. Ibid.
27. Carte, op. cit. Braose is described as being a 'pusillanimous fighter'.
28. Ibid.
29. *Novel Dessein*, derived from Roman Law: means a new amendment to an existing statute.
30. 'One who has sinned against us but is now our faithful subject'.
31. The Four Masters, op. cit.
32. Ibid.
33. *Dictionary of National Biography*; see under Theobald Butler.
34. Carte, op. cit.
35. Ibid.
36. *Dictionary of National Biography*; see under Theobald Butler.

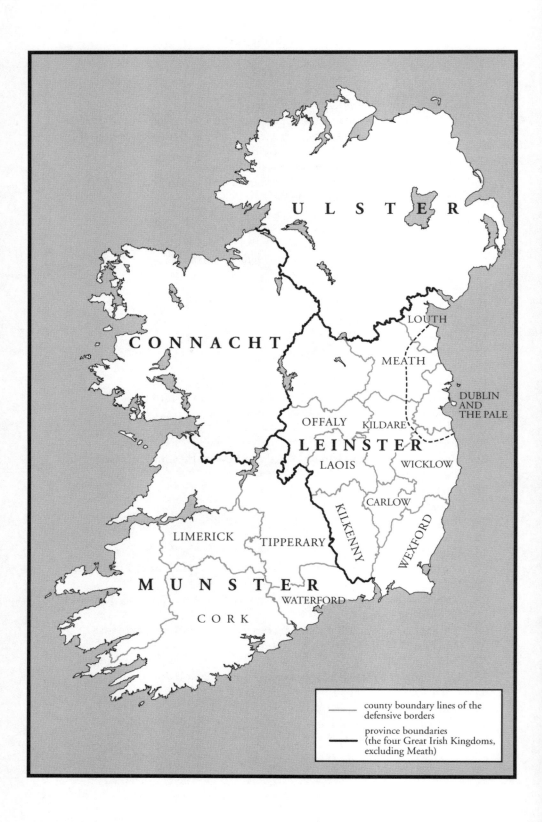

ULSTER

CONNACHT

LEINSTER

LOUTH

MEATH

DUBLIN
AND
THE PALE

OFFALY

KILDARE

WICKLOW

LAOIS

CARLOW

KILKENNY

WEXFORD

LIMERICK

TIPPERARY

MUNSTER

WATERFORD

CORK

county boundary lines of the
defensive borders

province boundaries
(the four Great Irish Kingdoms,
excluding Meath)

# CHAPTER II

## *Getting and Begetting*

The second Theobald was born about 1200, and, as a minor, was made a royal ward. On his father's death, his English lands were seized into King John's hands, and accounted for in the Exchequer. His maternal grandfather was ordered on 2 March 1206 to deliver him up to Gilbert fitzReinfrid, along with his sister Maud and together with all his lands, with fitzReinfrid acting on behalf of King John. Their mother, as a widow, was also 'given up' to her father Robert le Vavaseour, on payment of over 1,200 marks (and two palfreys), although her dower had previously been for a short time in the possession of the King's favourite, William de Braose. Her whole dower, in her late husband's free tenements in Ireland, was restored to her in October 1207, when she married Fulke fitzWarine at the King's suggestion. A dispute arose between father and husband about her lands in Yorkshire, in which fitzWarine got the better of the argument, for he took possession of the manor of Edlington, although this manor and other lands in Yorkshire came back afterwards to the Walter family. The King gave fitzWarine several proofs of favour, although he later lost John's patronage and was divested of several properties.

Her son may have been given into her new husband's charge on her re-marriage; but if this was the case it could have had no happy outcome for the boy, as fitzWarine was one of the malcontent barons who met to plan a revolt against the King in 1215. To punish him the King bestowed some of fitzWarine's lands upon his own supporters, the Pope excommunicated him in that same year, and fitzWarine was virtually an outlaw for a time. In fact fitzWarine became something of a legendary hero in the public mind, roaming through the country seeking forest adventures of the Robin Hood type, robbing the rich and succouring the poor, but one wonders how his new family viewed this uncontrollable dissident. Even in the next reign he would be 'inimical' to the new King, although he would eventually make his peace and found an abbey. But there was a vote of no confidence in him in 1221, when he was not allowed to strengthen his castle.

As the stepfather of Theobald II, he could have brought the boy into disfavour, and it is unlikely that fitzWarine was left in sole charge of his affairs, since a family of such strategic importance required careful guardianship. The great Hubert Walter, who might have been expected to keep a watchful eye on the affairs of his most important nephew, had died a year after his older brother in 1206. ('Now for the first time,' said John, on hearing of Hubert Walter's death, 'I am *truly* king of England'.[1])

By 1214 Maud was under orders 'not to marry any of the King's enemies, nor out of the King's lands', which suggests she was again a widow. But as fitzWarine is said to have lived to a great age and remarried, it is more probable that she was divorced from this pariah. FitzReinfrid had continued in the role of guardian at least until 1214, and appears to have taken his duties seriously, taking charge of the heir's upbringing and education with honour. Like many guardians of that time he could have used his position to his own advantage, for there was no power in law to force him to act honestly, and he could farm his ward's lands to his own profit.

But in August 1214 at least five of the Walter castles were taken back into the King's protection; and these were then put under the protection of Geoffrey de Mares, the Justiciar of Ireland. As another Walter was put into his charge in 1215, it is safe to assume that Theobald was also placed in his care. By 1219 Robert de Mares was the seneschal of 'the heir of Theobald Walter',[2] and so it is possible that young Theobald II was being reared in the Mares's household, since he would have had to enter that of some nobleman to be bred in the knightly arts.

Whatever the case, he seems to have come into his inheritance with his property intact, and to have been properly schooled in his great position. Perhaps because the Walter domain was so vital to the Crown, it was not allowed to fall into disrepair, and a careful watch was kept upon those people surrounding the growing boy. At 17, he was sufficiently in command of his property to negotiate in a civil matter, and as one of the witnesses to this deed was a maternal uncle, one can infer that his mother's family would also have kept track of the management of his affairs. Even though the family had been deprived of the prisage of wines – that is, from benefitting financially from the import of wine – the office of butler remained with them. In many official documents, Theobald II is referred to from boyhood as the 'Butler of Ireland'.

On 2 July 1221 Theobald 'being of full age' paid homage to the King, was given possession of all the English lands that he held from him, and was also given the greater part of his Irish estate. (A third of it continued for almost all his life in the hands of Fulke fitzWarine, who had patched up his quarrel with the royal family, and who seems to have successfully kept a number of other properties from his stepson, at least in Norfolk and Suffolk, where he was charged with the accounts of the sheriffs of those counties for these estates.)

Twenty-one was the age that young men were thought to have the full strength to bear arms; in fact, it was the capacity to fight on horseback that qualified a nobleman. Like his father before him, Theobald had been schooled in all the courtly and martial arts, and when he came into his inheritance and matured, he would do the same for other men's children and keep a band of young knights in his own household. Nobody in his position could live without a retinue of armed men to summon to his aid at a moment's notice, for the expectation of peace was never high.

Like all other inheritors, before he could enter upon his inheritance, he had to pay the King a 'relief', that is a fine or fee for permission to enter upon his father's lands, which had been laid down in 1215 as 100 pounds for a barony, and 100 shillings for a knight. Young Theobald did homage to the equally young King Henry III, 'touching life and limb and earthly honour, in what is honest and profitable, keeping his counsel to the best of his power, saving his faith to God and the ruler of the land'.[3] As Theobald came of age a year after King Henry III was crowned, he would not have been at Westminster on Whitsunday 1220 for the ceremony, but he would have been among the first to pay homage to the 15-year-old King.

The massive castle at Nenagh, whose fragmentary remains still dominate the town, was built around 1217, presumably at the instigation of Theobald II's advisers or at the express command of the English council. Such a fortification was then very necessary, for in 1207 two major wars had broken out among the English of Leinster, with critical repercussions for the people of Munster and the Walter domains. Both of the wars had, significantly, been fought between the Anglo-Normans and not between the English and the Irish; and both had resulted in the two kingdoms suffering severely, with the possessions of the Walter family, in particular, being in great danger; the countryside around them had been wasted. A castle was needed, and so it was built; and it would remain the chief seat of the Walters for over one hundred years.

It was built to inspire fear among natives and settlers alike; a pentagonal fortress, with twin-towered gatehouses on the south-west, strong towers at the north-west and a mighty circular keep on the north-east. This building is the most remarkable structure of its kind in Ireland. Another castle, though much smaller in size, would be built some three miles south-east of Nenagh, which would be granted to the Mares family, when Theobald married his first wife, Joan, a daughter of Geoffey de Mares. Both castles needed a garrison, and Theobald needed help in their maintenance. He also needed an escort for himself and his family as they rode about the land, and so he lived among a huge, inter-knit assortment of servants and soldiers, including several knights. A knight's service to his lord could be taken in one of three ways – on the battlefield, as castle guard, or in escort duty. Some of these knights may well have been relatives, for in 1210, among the knights created in Dublin, before the Earl of Salisbury, an Adam and a William le Butiller are both mentioned. It is evident from this that the first Theobald's immediate relations were not the only Walters to adopt the future name.

Nothing could succeed in stopping the private territorial wars, and Irish or Anglo-Normans rarely took their disputes before the King's Justiciar, to have matters settled peaceably. Throughout Theobald's childhood and adolescence, the wars had continued to rage about him; and not always between the English and the Gaels, but as often between the Irish tribes, or between the English nobles, squabbling over land. King John had sent the Bishop of Norwich to act as Lord Justice of Ireland, and the Pope had excommunicated the entire country because the King had sent a man of God to prosecute a war. Both England and Ireland were without mass, baptism, extreme unction or lawful interment for a period of three years.

Not even King John's arrival in Dublin in 1209, with a great fleet of ships, had done much to halt the carnage, although John had tried to calm his quarrelling subjects, but he seems to have had most success among the Irish. Crodberg O'Connor was one of the many chieftains who made submission to him, and even Hugh O'Neill visited him from his Ulster vastness, although he left no hostages behind as surety for his continued loyalty. John had banished a prime troublemaker, Walter de Lacy, to England, and he levied a considerable army to besiege the town of Carrickfergus until it surrendered, when he placed his own people in it.

In 1210, at a great council of barons, English law was extended into Ireland, and many Gaelic rulers made formal submission. But the King had been forced to return to England without having achieved much, by which time he was experiencing trouble in Wales, and had even greater problems with his disaffected English nobles. Five years later, after these rebellious barons had marched on London and captured the city, he would be forced to sign the Great Charter at Runnymede, in which he recognised the rights and privileges of his barons, church and freemen, and limited his royal authority. Its effect would be also felt in Ireland, for no king thereafter was allowed to forget that this charter had been granted to *all* his subjects. These concessions would extend into Ireland, affecting the later members of the Walter dynasty.

When King John died in 1216, his successor, Henry III, was only a child. The English barons had invited a French prince to be their King in place of John or his offspring. 'The son of the King of France assumed the government of England, and obtained her hostages',[4] among whom might have been the adolescent Theobald Walter, had he not been safely at home in Ireland. But the English nobles soon began to doubt the wisdom of their action and were glad to return to their English allegiance; justifying their change of loyalty by declaring the child should not suffer for the sins of the father. Despite the late King's unpopularity, to the relief of the men who formed the young king's council, John had left behind a strong governmental machine.

Royal power had declined from John's last years, perhaps because of the constant warfare on the Welsh borders, and this continued throughout the regency of King Henry III. The barons were insubordinate, and there were constant endeavours to thwart the Justiciar and set up a state of anarchy. In disorderly Ireland the barons were even less subservient than their English counterparts, and things were going badly. In 1219 matters worsened when Walter de Lacy and a son of William de Burgh returned from England, without the King's consent, and once again both families began to gain real power, particularly in Connacht. Theobald was undoubtedly a fighting man by this time, for in 1220 he paid scutage to the Barons of the Exchequer, in lieu of his military service on King John's last expedition to Poitou, which had been invaded by the French king, Louis VIII. On this occasion he was excused duty by the King's order since he was in Ireland 'on the King's business', and that could only have meant dealing with the mayhem created by the renegade Anglo-Normans.

It was even rumoured that a Norwegian invasion was probable, and that Ireland would be once more at the mercy of the Vikings, although this may have been an invention put about by the English in order to draw the Irish to their side. Meanwhile, they continued to cleverly exploit the perpetual conflicts between the Irish themselves, sometimes assisting both sides at the same time, and acquiring great possessions as they did so, land on which they built strong forts and castles, to defend themselves against the men they had set out to assist.

Much of the warfare was simple marauding, and is so described in the various annals of the time: '…the English of Ulidia mustered a *plundering* army...O'Neill Roe came and took a *prey* from the English of 1200 cows …A *depredation* was committed by the English of Meath.'[5] – the catalogue of such crimes continues from year to year, growing annually. This is not to say that the English did not suffer huge losses – upwards of a hundred men could be slain on these excursions – but with the aid of their castles, the English were acquiring increasingly large tracts of Ireland. By 1215, only a part of Thomond and the whole of Connacht, along with three smaller western counties, remained outside the English 'Land of Peace'.

Walter de Lacy soon joined forces with Hugh O'Neill, the two men together setting out to oppose the English, going to Coleraine, where they demolished a castle, and afterwards entering Meath and Leinster, destroying as they went. Facing up to them the combined 'English of Ireland' managed to muster twenty-four battalions at Dundalk, where O'Neill and Lacy opposed them with four 'great' battalions. This may have been Theobald's first experience of a properly organised battle, even though, from 1220, he had been commissioned to return to Ireland 'on the King's service, by the King's order'. (He had presumably spent his late adolescence in England, familiarising himself with the property he would inherit there.)

But inexperienced as he was, he must have struck his superiors as being a capable soldier, for in 1223 King Henry III committed the custody of Roscrea Castle into his care, Theobald undertaking to restore it to the King whenever he or his heirs should wish to have it back. However the next three years would be peaceful for such English families as the Walters, with the hostilities largely restricted to Connacht and Ulster. Their only anxiety seems to have been the unusually inclement weather. In 1224 the previous year's corn had remained unreaped until 1 February, when the fields were being ploughed, in consequence of the unceasing rain.

In any case, their part of Munster, Ormond, had belonged to the O'Brien kingdom of Thomond, and they were only directly concerned if the clashes involved the O' Briens, or if their lands were threatened. Most of the major battles were between the men of Connacht, Leinster and Ulster, and so the Walters remained for the most part untroubled, unless they were called to join the 'English of Ireland' whenever some major conflict broke out.

As in 1225, when the English of Leinster and Munster forcibly entered South Connacht, where they slew all the people they caught, burning villages and dwellings. 'They came out of envy and rapacity, on hearing of what the other English had obtained in that kingdom. The young warriors did not spare each other, but preyed upon each other to their utmost power'.[6] Women, children and the 'lowly poor' perished as much from cold and famine in this onslaught as by outright killing. The Irish and English of Munster then attacked the sanctuary of the Virgin, St Caelainn, where the English suffered heavy losses. Again, the corn was unreaped until the beginning of February, but this time rain was not the only reason for the long delay.

Theobald, now well qualified for fighting, would have been a member of these warring parties (he was given 50 marks as an advance payment for soldiering in 1227). He might also have been among the 'English of Ireland' who assembled in Council at Dublin, where they had invited Hugh Crobdberg O'Connor and his principal men of Connacht to join them. Theobald may even have been aware of the English plot to take the Irishmen hostage, when Hugh was falsely accused of 'criminal charges', found guilty and apprehended. But William Marshal the Younger, arriving with his forces, rescued him 'by help of his sword and strength of his hand'. Once returned to his kingdom, O'Connor inevitably rose up against the English, 'rushing upon [them], and defeating them'.[7] He plundered Athlone, burning the whole town; and by this means he regained all the hostages that he had been forced to leave in the hands of the English, in return for prisoners.

Yet a year later, O'Connor would be expelled by his own people, and he was killed in the mansion of Geoffrey de Mares, whose guest he was, murdered by an English soldier in revenge for the Irishman having hanged the soldier's wife; for which, the next day, Mares summarily hanged the murderer. Theobald may also have been a guest in the house at this time, for he was by now the widower of Joan, Geoffrey de Mares' daughter, who may have died in childbirth. (This marriage was contracted while

28

Theobald was a minor.) Their descendants would inherit great estates in Ireland and England as a result of this advantageous union.

But the fact that he was married into the Justiciar of Ireland's family would not save him from his father-in-law's displeasure, when Theobald chose to unite with some of the magnates of Ireland against the Crown in 1226. Mares, as Justiciar in that same year, had received the assembled Irish chieftains at Waterford, where they had given him their assurances of loyalty to King Henry. But on setting out for Dublin, he was told that William Earl Marshal, with the assent of Theobald le Butiller, was about to oppose his passage, 'with all the force of Leinster'. (The reason for Theobald's brief rebellion has never been disclosed.) Mares did eventually arrive in the capital, to hold a great council, where all but four of the King's subjects rendered oaths of loyalty to him; and he found Theobald in attendance at the meeting, but unwillingly. On being asked to also take the oath, he excused himself, asserting that he could not part with custody of the castles committed to him by the Earl Marshal. It soon became clear to Mares that Theobald had, notwithstanding his oath of fealty, fortified the castle of Dublin, with a force against the King. In fact, all his castles had been fortified against the Crown.

Four disloyal Irish chieftains had banded together, and Theobald appears to have joined their ranks in sympathy, under the influence of a colleague of William the Marshal. In fact, Mares reported, they had been 'so wheedled' by him 'that they cannot be reconciled from their conspiracy'.[8] The Justiciar could not obtain delivery of the King's castles; 'they fortify them more each day', and he particularly wanted to take over the castle of Roscrea, since his son-in-law 'had so misconducted himself in regard to the King'. Mares wrote to King Henry III, informing him of Theobald's strange obstinacy, declaring that although he had been married to his daughter, and 'has by her a son', the Justiciar would 'of the King's will deprive him of all the lands which he holds in Ireland...The King need not fear the wickedness or craft of his Irish enemies, or others; all these will Geoffrey root out.'[9] In September the King ordered Theobald to deliver up the castle of Roscrea to his father-in-law.

This attitude was totally in keeping with Mares's reputation, since he was an able royal servant, but of a somewhat sinister character – to the Irish especially. He was a man who had risen from nowhere, for nothing was certain about his parentage, except that he was a nephew of the Archbishop of Dublin; a fact that may have accounted for his rapid rise to wealth and power in Ireland. Dominant in the south of Munster and Leinster, he had received large grants of land from King John, and when war broke out among the English of Leinster, the discontented lords had looked upon him as a leader.

He had long established himself within the Walter lordship of Ormond, and was twice associated with them by marriage, since Eva de

Bermingham, their kinswoman, was his wife. When Theobald was 19, Mares had absented himself from Ireland, having taken the Cross and received safe-conduct to make pilgrimage to the Holy Land, and Theobald had married into his family when Mares returned to Ireland and was once again firmly in power. Indeed, during the absence of the Justiciar, William Marshal, Mares had charge of the country, and he carried on a number of successful wars.

That Theobald should have been allied in marriage with such a dominant man was entirely consistent with his family's viewpoint at that time, since it was their method to extend their influence steadily, and without warfare where possible. In an ambitious age, marriage was the simplest way of acquiring unearned wealth, and hard bargains were often struck. The aim was to make the estates sufficiently large to enable the holder to provide for his other children without endangering the heir's position. Mares was often impatient with the compromises by which the Walters adapted themselves to the Irish world of north-east Munster, but marriage alliances and legal agreements was their preferred method of operating.

Mares must certainly have totally approved of Theobald's choice of a second wife, since Rohesia de Verdon was the only daughter and the heiress of Nicholas de Verdon, the last male representative of an old Norman family. The possessors of large estates in middle England, Alton Castle was their principal residence, and they had also acquired considerable estates in Ireland, in the county of Meath. Rohesia was one of the greatest heiresses of her time, although none of her wealth would directly benefit the Walter family. After her marriage, she would insist upon retaining her family name and arms, and these would be handed on to her sons; and through her Theobald would be the forefather of the Lords of Verdon. For Theobald's children by her disdained the name of Le Butiller (which Theobald had begun to use in 1221) and preferred that of their mother.

Rohesia herself seems to have been reluctant to marry in the first place, and in fact it needed the King to persuade this proud woman to do so. In 1225 Henry III had personally requested her to marry his 'beloved Theobald le Botiller', an entreaty she could not ignore. Since Henry was a man of refined mind and cultivated tastes, that he should have befriended Theobald, and sought a profitable marriage for him in this way, suggests that Theobald was a man of like tastes.

The marriage was, in any case, short-lived, for Theobald died in 1230, a little short of his 30th birthday, dying in the same year that William the Marshal transferred to him all the lands that Marshal had by charter in the tenement of Gowran, a place that would come to have a particular significance for the Botillers. But Theobald would die in France, where he had joined the forces of King Henry III in Brittany, in May of that year. In 1227 he had received an advanced payment of wages for military duties in Ireland, and in 1230 the Exchequer ruled that Theobald should 'have peace' regarding the debts exacted from him by that department 'so long as he shall be in the King's service in parts beyond the sea'. The French King had marched a large army to Angers, in order to shut the English out of Poitou, but King Henry had managed to get his men into Gascony, which they had also come to relieve. Since Henry III had neither military ability nor diplomatic skills, the expedition had been a failure, and one from which Theobald Botiller did not return.

However he died – from a wound in battle or some soldier's sickness – Theobald must have died before July 1230, perhaps in Gascony, for in that month the King ordered that his widow Rohesia should be given her dower, taken out of her husband's lands, first taking from her the usual security that she would not marry without his consent. She herself would die in 1247, having founded a convent for Austin canonesses on her Leicestershire property five years earlier.

Since the third Theobald took homage from King Henry III in 1244, he was probably born around 1223. A year after his father's death, the King granted to his brother Richard, Earl of Cornwall, custody of the Walter inheritance, both in England and Ireland, 'until the full age of the heir'. At the same time, the Seneschal of Leinster was also ordered to take possession of all the lands that had been held by the late Theobald from William, the Earl Marshal, as these it was judged, belonged to the King. (The Justiciar, Maurice FitzGerald, grandson of 'the Invader of Ireland', although a vassal of the Earl Marshal, had laid waste to Marshal's lands at the instigation of the King, or his councillors.)

In 1232 the Earl of Cornwall sold custody of Theobald's lands and heirs to Richard de Burgh, who would become the boy's father-in-law, and Theobald's father was referred to in these arrangements as the *former* Butler of Ireland. (By a mandate of June 1225, issued by King Henry III, William Marshal had been directed to seize the county of Connacht and deliver it to Richard de Burgh, making him the virtual ruler of that vast area.)

Throughout Theobald's minority, Ireland continued to be torn apart, particularly Connacht, which was given back to Hugh O'Connor by William de Burgh, 'the great Lord of Connacht', for the grant of that kingdom to his son Richard was seen as a 'shameful act'.[10] William himself had English royal antecedents, being the son of Isabel, the natural daughter of King Richard I, and the widow of Llewellyn, Prince of Wales. As Richard de Burgh became the father-in-law of the third Theobald, this is the first introduction of a royal line into the family's history.

In 1234 Richard, the son of William Marshal, 'having rebelled against the King of England', landed in Ireland and marched through Leinster, and the English of Ireland assembled to oppose him, on behalf of the King. They engaged with Richard Marshal and killed him, at the same time taking prisoner Geoffrey de Mares, Theobald's grandfather, 'who had been bribed to this desertion'. But a year later his future father-in-law would assemble an expedition against the Irish, and among the 'illustrious names' was that of Walter le Botiller, Theobald's uncle, thus helping to wipe out the disgrace of Mares' betrayal.

This expedition was very much a Munster affair, for their light armed infantry was an essential part of this force. Not content with burning the town of Roscommon and the magnificent church at Elphin, the marauders assailed the abbey of Boyle and encamped within its walls. Here, they carried away 'all the goods they could finger', even to the apparel of the monks, 'stripping the friars very irreverently of their habits in the midst of their cloister'.[11] They also took a great prey from a more appropriate adversary, Cormack MacDermott, 'which was then generally called the "prey of preys"'. (Later, other English nobles would be repelled by this act of sacrilege, and sent back what they could retrieve to the monastery, paying for what they could not.) Yet on their return to Thomond they, too, ravaged the country they passed through.

It was a foretaste of what was to come, for throughout the next few years the Irish of Connacht and Munster held frequent pitched battles against the English, 'fighting manfully', with the English cavalry, 'clad in armour', usually overcoming them. The men of Connacht would then make peace with the English and offer them hostages, but it was the people of Munster who suffered most, for the Connacians, having returned to Connacht, would leave the countryside desolate 'for the English'. In reply, the English would then send their forces against the Connacians, plundering them at will, and carrying off great spoils in the vessels supplied to them by their Irish allies.

Some of these battles were partly fought at sea, the English boats being filled with 'a numerous army of troops, of well-armed and mail clad soldiers'. The English killed 'many of the inferior sort', and their army chiefs only ordered the slaughter to cease 'in honour of the Crucifixion of Christ'.[12] The English then devastated Umallia, both by sea and by land, taking a prey from all those followers of King Felim O' Connor who were granted asylum after they had expelled him from Connacht. On these forays, they constructed wonderful engines of war, with 'great art and ingenuity'; although no one left any description of what these might have been.[13] But their excursions were as deadly for the civilian population as for the military: the people were left without food, cattle or clothing, 'and the country without peace of tranquillity'.[14] The English were not alone, though, in creating this misery, for the Gaels were themselves plundering and destroying one another.

The Botillers, however, managed to prosper from these continuing hostilities. In recognition of their skill in keeping the enemy at bay, and of the mastery by which they controlled their own borders, the Archbishop of Dublin granted sixteen estates to the family between 1228 and 1255. Land had come to them from elsewhere, too, the most important being the villages of Paulstown and Gowran, particularly the latter. At the intersection of four major roads, it was of strategic importance as it commanded the ancient route through the bogs and forests of the Leinster-Ossary marches.

From as early as 1235 Theobald, although only aged about 12, was known as the 'Lord of Gowran' and the men who fought in his name were apparently much feared. In a grant of land conveyed by a relative, Richard Pincerna, the grantee is promised that 'should the Lord of Gowran – or any other – take his land by force, the grantee will restore an equivalent portion in a fitting place.'[15] (Confusingly, the family was at this time still undecided about the correct style of the family name; they appear quite often in the documents of the time as 'Pincerna', the Latinised form of the surname Butler.)

In 1241 the Lord Justice, Maurice FitzGerald, mustered a great army with which he marched into Roscommon, when a small party of Irish overtook them, slaying many. In the following year, the Lord Justice would raise another army, comprising *all* the English of Ireland, and this time he had marched to Tirconnell in pursuit of Teige O'Connor, who had fled to the Kindred Connell. Theobald III would certainly have served in this army, even though he was not yet of age.

However, he was considered old enough to marry, for he did so in that same year, 1242. His father in law, Richard de Burgh, granted to him 'in free marriage with Margery, his daughter', the manor of Ardmayle, to 'hold to them and the heir of the said Margery'. If Burgh could not guarantee it, he would assign another manor at Kilfeakle for forty *librates*[16] of land; but if there was more land than agreed upon, it would remain to the grantor; and if less, Burgh would assign forty *librates* of land nearby. He also granted his son-in-law more land, paying 100s sterling. This was a relatively uncomplicated arrangement for marriage portions at this period, for much harder bargains were struck in that particular market. But that Theobald III married from a position of strength is shown by the standing of his wife's family; now among the most important in Ireland. After 1215 the law provided that an heir could only be married to one of his own degree.

By the time Theobald was into his twenties, the spasmodic campaigning in Ireland was not his only concern, for in 1243 King Henry III mustered another immense army in England to oppose the King of France. He sent ambassadors to summon the English of Ireland to his aid, and among the many who answered the King's call went Richard de Burgh, who died on the expedition. If Theobald did not accompany his father-in-law on this occasion, it is almost certain that he joined the English army in Wales two years later, when aid was once more requested of the English in Ireland. Henry's Irish allies ravaged Anglesey, laying the country waste and bringing the Welsh to a state of near-starvation.

In 1247 Theobald may have been among the many barons summoned to London by Henry III so that they might be present when the gift of the Blood of Christ was brought from Jerusalem and taken in solemn procession to Westminster Abbey. But when Maurice FitzGerald led an enormous army back into Ireland, Theobald would have returned in its ranks; along with John le Butiller, 'of the King's household', who was to be retained for the army, and paid 20*l* a year while he remained on active service. It was to the King's advantage to have as many Botillers in Ireland as he could muster, and another member of the family, Geoffrey, was ordered to exchange his acres in England for the land of Robert de Blunteston that bordered on the Botillers' property in Tipperary.

The Kindred Connell and the Kindred Owen were assembled against this great army, and the Irish defended themselves ably at the ford of the Salmon Leap, until confused by a trick that was played upon them by the English cavalry. The English, not being allowed to pass, decided to send a large body of cavalry down river to cross at another ford, unseen by anyone. The Kindred Connell knew nothing of this move until they were attacked in the rear by a large troop of horsemen, and surrounded on all sides they were picked off where they stood. Many of FitzGerald's forces were also slain or wounded, with others dying in pursuit of the Gaels as they fled before them. The country was afterwards plundered.[17]

Turlough O'Connor kindled a new war against the English of Connacht in which many English were killed and the Irish went on a rampage, until they, in turn, were attacked by the English of Carra, when Turlogh left the country, as he had not equal forces. 'The English of Connacht had not for a long time experienced such a war as was waged against them by the royal heirs presumptive. There was not a district or cantred in their possession which was not left undevastated.'[18] These campaigns were carried out at a great distance from their own domain, but the Botillers had an interest in their outcome as they were now married into the de Burgh family, and the Connacht lowlands had been parcelled out among the liegemen of that family.

That the Botillers did take part in warfare far from their own possessions is shown by the presence of John 'Butler' a year later, when the Connacians again rose up against the English, and Butler was one of the men listed in the army that marched against them, helping to plunder the country 'north and south'. In that same year, the Lord Justiciar led another army, at an even farther distance, this time into Tyrone, against O'Neill. According to the *Annals of Insifallen*, this expedition was organised by no less a person than Theobald Botiller, who was the Lord Justice in 1248, at the age of 25. This time, though, there was to be no confrontation, for the Kindred Owen held a council in which they decided that, as the English had the advantage over them, it was held advisable to give them hostages and make their peace. On this expedition, the English erected a bridge over the Bann River and a castle to protect it.

This was possibly Theobald's last act, however, as he died in that year. Like his father before him, he was buried in the monastery of the Friars Preachers at Arklow in Wicklow, which King John had granted to his grandfather. In August his young widow Margery gave security to the King that she would not marry without his licence. He caused her dower to be assigned to her out of her husband's lands. They were said to have had a younger son, who settled in Lancashire.

The next Theobald was also a minor at his father's death, being 5 years old, and Peter de Bermyngham was the custodian of his estates, 'doing pleasure of all the lands and castles which belonged to Richard de Burgh and Theobald le Butiller in Ireland. Peter, when ordered, 'shall account thereof'.[19] But his accounting could not have been satisfactory, for in 1250 King Henry granted John fitzGeoffrey, the Justiciar of Ireland, 'all the ploughs in the lands which belonged to Theobald le Butiller, with all the corn sown in these lands, according to its sworn value.'[20] De Bermyngham was mandated, as the custodee, to give possession of all the land and castles whereof he had custody, including those in England.

In 1252 FitzGeoffrey owed the King 1,000*l* for custody of the 'land and marriage' of the heir of Theobald le Butiller, which he paid off at 500 marks a year. Geoffrey de Geneville had the custody of the lands in 1253, and three years later fitzGeoffrey would again be given supervision of *all* the boy's inheritance, for a fee of 3,000 marks, for which he had to render 500 marks yearly to the King. Theobald's mother, Margery, must have been considering re-marriage as early as the year of her widowhood, since in 1248 the King granted her a licence to marry whom she pleased, for a fee of 500 marks.

The English civil war of the 1260s seems to have had few political repercussions in Ireland, even though many of the great absentee landlords of Irish estates were heavily involved. Their allegiances should perhaps have been reflected in Irish political life, but there is no evidence to support this, and the most serious disturbances in Ireland at this time were domestic.

The only occasion on which the constitutional crisis in England had any effect in Ireland was in the summer of 1265, when Simon de Montfort, the leader of the extreme baronial reformers, attempted to deprive Prince Edward, the King's eldest son, of his rights in Ireland. (Edward had been created Lord of Ireland in 1254.) Letters were sent announcing that the Prince had forfeited his rights and should no longer be obeyed. But by this time Edward had joined the lords of the Welsh marches, who continued to hold out against Montfort and the English government and, in the event, Anglo-Irish loyalty was not put to the test. For Montfort was killed at the battle of Evesham in August 1265, and the ultimate defeat of his party saw the full restoration of King Henry III, and an end to any effective opposition. Prince Edward was also back in the ascendancy, and Theobald le Butiller, now 19 years old, had fought alongside him at the battle of Evesham, along with his uncle, John le Butiller.

Only three other Butlers seem to have done any kind of military service during this period, though they were not of knightly rank. In 1242, Walter le Butiller was in receipt of 100 shillings, 'in the King's gift', to buy a palfrey, and a year later he was with the King in Gascony, being granted 10 marks for his expenses. In neither case was his actual occupation revealed, although he is twice referred to as 'brother'. In 1244 he was a sergeant of the Count of Flanders, but this was almost certainly a civilian post, perhaps clerical, for he negotiated the purchase of corn from the merchants of Bruges, to be sent to the King on the island of Olerum. In 1262 one Henry le Butiller was paid the arrears of his wages while in the garrison of the Tower of London and the castle of Rochester; his specific post is not revealed. Hugh le Butiller had been a sergeant of Joan, late Queen of Scotland, King Henry's sister; but again the office may have been purely ceremonial.

John le Butiller was an attorney in 1267, and Ralph le Butiller was given money for his expenses as a clerk. Bartholomew le Butiller was the keeper of the King's manor and parkland at Guildford, and had been for some years, since in 1267 he was paid 2*d* daily for keeping the same, 'as he used to in times past'. But the most important role that any Butler played outside Ireland was, significantly, to do with the importation of wine; throughout the 1240s Michael le Butiller was the acknowledged buyer of the King's vintages. He and his wife lived in Winchester, and seem to have been worked out of the customs house at Southampton. Other Butlers around the country seem also to have also been concerned with the buying and selling of wine, and perhaps this is connected to the fact that the fourth Theodore had been re-granted the prisage of wines in Ireland that had been taken from his great-grandfather.

Many Butlers in England would often be on the wrong side of the law, and none would profit to the same extent as those who made their mark in Ireland. Indeed the only English member of the family to attain a status comparable to that of his Irish relations was William le Butiller, a former Sheriff of Lancaster, who in 1260 was selling off the stock of the King's larder in those parts on the King's orders. Which suggests that he, too, played some ceremonial part in the general provisioning of the King's household.

The roles the English Butlers played, though, were largely in civilian life, and most of them were salaried officials. Even when they owned land, for which they paid knights' fees, they preferred to pay scutage in lieu of military service. Their lives were very different from those of the relations they had left behind in Ireland, being closer to the clerical interests of their earlier ancestors.

Back in Ireland, the Irish themselves were, however tardily, beginning to learn from their invaders. In the early 1250s, the self-styled High King of Ireland began to employ armies of mail-clad foreign mercenaries, the so-called 'gallowglasses', from the Scottish kingdom of Argyll and the Lordship of the Isles. These men were to receive estates by way of payment, and this importation of Hebridean fighting men would come to form an appreciable element of the Gaelic speaking population. From 1258 Irish resistance would quicken, for in that year two important Irish chieftains both acknowledged the ancestral claims of Brian O'Neill to the High-Kingship of Ireland, by which they firmly repudiated the English pretension.

Partly as a result of this, a fresh war broke out between the English and Conor O' Brien, who also acknowledged the Irish overlord, during which the English burned many street-towns in Galway, 'and much corn'. Two years later an army of Thomond, commanded by Sir Gerald FitzGerald, would be led against O'Brien and 'the chiefs of all his people', and the English were defeated with the loss of at least one *puissant* knight. FitzGerald would also march an army into Desmond, to be again defeated by the Irish, with the loss of eight barons and five knights, and 'countless numbers of English common soldiers'.[21]

A 'very great army' was mobilised against the Irish (and against Felim O'Connor in particular) in 1262; but the Irish backed away from this confrontation, and a peace conference resulted, without either side giving pledge or hostage. Another army of the 'English in Ireland' went into Desmond, where each side did do battle, when both the English and the Irish suffered great losses, without either gaining a clear advantage. When the Anglo-Normans were not fighting the MacCarthys they would be attacking the O'Connors, but when they were not campaigning against the Irish they were assaulting each other. There were deadly 'discords' between the Geraldines and the Burghs, 'which wrought great bloodsheds', and these clashes were, perhaps, of greater importance to Ireland than were the wars against the Irish.

Disturbances arose out of a notorious incident on 6 December 1264, when the Earl of Desmond captured Richard de RuCapella, the Lord Justice of Ireland, along with John de Cogan and Theobald le Butiller, committing them to prison in a consecrated church, 'to the outrage of the pious'.[22] While the Geraldines held Theobald captive, Walter de Burgh attacked and seized the Geraldine castles and manors in Connacht, and widespread disorder followed, tantamount to armed conflict.

In fact, so serious was this situation that Geoffrey de Geneville assumed control in the absence of the Lord Justice. He prepared Dublin Castle to withstand a siege, and in the south, the citizens of New Ross decided also to enclose their town. The alarm of the government in London was such that they asked the Archbishop of Dublin to take over the Irish administration, being mostly afraid that a rebellion by the Irish nobility would reactivate the King's problems with his English barons, which were still smouldering. The Archbishop was commanded to take castles by force, and then to supply them with munitions.

So by the late spring of 1265, a civil war was raging in Ireland. However, the Archbishop was later able to mount an expedition against the Geraldines, and he was successful in persuading the dissidents to travel to Dublin under a safe conduct, where he brought them together long enough to make peace. The magnates who were present swore to abide by this declaration, and by the early summer Richard de RuCapella was once more at the head of the government, and Theobald le Butiller was back at home.

'Friendly meetings and hostile expeditions' characterised the years between 1263 and 1270, when in that year a general war broke out between the English and Irish of Connacht. Otherwise, the Irish chieftains took no advantage of the disunity between the Anglo-Normans, but instead they aided their enemies by continuing to quarrel among themselves. Conor O'Brien the Lord of Thomond, his son and randson were slain by a kinsman, Dermot O'Brien, in a bid for the lordship. Brian Ruadh, another son of Conor O'Brien, inherited that mantle, but in 1270 this chieftain would turn against his occasional allies, the Butillers, committing great devastation against them.

And the O'Briens were not the only challengers; Hugh O'Connor would be killed by Thomas Butiller in 1271, and Henry Butiller, the Lord of Umallia, was slain by a son of Conor Roe O'Connor a year later. Maurice fitzMaurice, Justiciar of Ireland, led an expedition against Brian Ruadh O'Brien in 1272, with great success, since he 'took many hostages and obtained sway over the O'Briens'. A year later another expedition would be mounted against the O'Briens, for which the Justiciar borrowed 86*l* 19*s* from the citizens of Dublin, which they asked the King to repay in 1275; the Justiciar was aided by Theobald le Butiller on this undertaking. Four years later, they again led an army against O'Brien, who was taken prisoner and beheaded. But a little while later fitzMaurice was himself besieged in Slow-Banny, and reduced to such straits that he had to give hostages for his life and to yield up the castle of Roscommon.

But throughout this constant armed conflict, the Butillers continued to amass large properties, and again this land was widely distributed. An estate was granted to them by Edmund le Brun near Dublin; Nicolas de Valle gave Sir Theobald the estate of Rosiat, 'with the chief messuage', for which Theobald paid a penny yearly at Easter. The Lord Justice granted him land near Locker, 'by service of eight marks yearly rent' (to be paid again at Easter, 'with a pair of white gloves and a penny'). Nearer home, Robert Talebot returned an estate in the parish of Monsea, Lower Ormond, 'which he had the donation of Theobald'. He also received the manor of

Tankardstown, and Sir Nicolas de Dunheud granted 'Lord' Theobald Pincerna and his heirs forever, 'of all his lordship, and rent of 6d', along with 'all homages, services, etc'.[23]

Property also came to him from the Church; the prior of St Edmund of Athassell 'and convent' renounced a claim to Theobald, Butler of Ireland', of all the houses, buildings and closes which had been managed by John de Hakerford, the farmer of their church. Theobald also acquired land in Portraine, for which he must pay a yearly rent to the Archbishop of Dublin 'at his Court of Swords'; and the Abbot of the Holy Cross let a farm to him, which lay alongside his lordship of Ardmayer.

Yet Theobald seems not to have been simply content with acquiring land in the normal manner; he was, at times, prepared to take the law into his own hands and to indulge in the odd violation. A letter patent of Prince Edward, witnessed on 24 January 1270, pardons Theobald and his tenants for various transgressions:

> Edward, eldest son of the King of England, to all his lieges and bailiffs of the Land of Ireland, etc. Whereas Theobald Walter, Butler of Ireland, and his men and tenants in the counties of Tipperary and Limerick, were accused of several robberies, felonies, receiving of outlaws and other malefactors, and many other transgressions and forfeitures committed in the land against our peace. Whereas the said Theobald came before Lord Robert de Ufford, our Justiciar of Ireland at Athassel on Wednesday next after the Feast of St Lucy, Virgin, in the 54th year of the King our father, and made a fine with us of 500*l* payable at our Exchequer at Dublin, for himself and all his men and tenants, both English and Irish, in the said counties. For which fine as far as concerns us we have pardoned him and all his men of all robberies and felonies, etc., as above, up to the aforesaid day, and have granted them our firm peace, provided that in the future they conduct themselves faithfully in our said land.[24]

War broke out in that same year, between O'Connor and Walter de Burgh, Earl of Ulster. The Earl assembled the chiefs of the English in Ireland, and marched into Connacht. Turlough O'Brien came to the assistance of O'Connor, and he was slain at once by the Earl, 'mindful of their past enmity'. The Connacians came up against the English at a ford, where they 'poured down upon them, horse and foot, broke through their van, and forcibly dislodged their rear'.[25] In this onslaught, nine of the chief English knights were killed, among them John 'Butler'. Immense spoils were taken from the dead men, consisting of arms, armour and horses. Afterwards, Brian Roe O'Brien turned against the English, and 'committed great depredations against them'. A year later the Butillers would take their revenge, when Hugh O'Connor was killed by one Thomas Butler, and in 1172, the Irish would retaliate, when Henry Butler, the 'Lord of Umallia', was slain by a son of Conor Roe O'Connor.

In that same year, Edward I was made King over the English, on 6 November. Born in 1239, he was tall and handsome, in the Irish sense being in every way worthy to be a king, for his 'nobility, personal shape, and heroism'. With a programme of wars ahead, the new King, from the beginning of his reign, vigorously encouraged young men to become knights, and the tournament became an accepted part of the social scene. He seems to have encouraged a deliberate archaism in which such milestones as the conquest of Wales and Scotland could be regarded as Arthurian adventures, and all the idealistic males of this generation would have been caught up in this romantic view of war. The King was fond of recreating the Round Table, and certain members of the Butiller family were happy to sit at it.

Walter de Burgh had died in 1271, after a short illness, and a year later Theobald was given custody of his lands, which had been held by King Edward, 'being waste after the Earl's death'. Edward, who was then at Cashel, gave his consent, and 20 marks were to be allocated annually to Theobald for custody of Burgh's castle. More land came to him in 1273, when Walter de Barri granted him all his lands at Cross-patrick for 200*l* sterling.

In 1273 Maurice FitzGerald led an army into Thomond, where he took hostages and 'obtained sway' over the O'Briens, 'subduing the whole country', for which he borrowed 100 marks for the expenses of the campaign, 86*l* of which came from the citizens of Dublin, a sum they resented paying, and which they asked the King to repay in 1275. This was Butiller territory, and Theobald aided FitzGerald in his offensive against his recalcitrant dependants.

In 1276 Theobald did homage to King Edward I for his lands in Lancashire, which were a welcome addition to his financial position, for he was by now also in debt to Jews as well as to Italians. He was not compelled to make a renewed payment to the former, by order of the King; yet two years later Theobald would be pledging his land in Lancashire for the payment of debts, and there would be another 'plea of land' in 1277. The Treasurer of the Exchequer at Dublin granted Theobald permission to pay 900*l*, due from him at the rate of 100 marks yearly. In the complicated manner of the time, when Peter was robbed to pay Paul, they also granted him 400 marks, to be allowed to him yearly out of the 900*l*, to recompense him for his release and quitclaim of the advowson of the church at Kirkeham, County Lancaster. 100*l* was also allowed him for 'his damages by reason of him taking Castle Conyn, in Ireland, into the King's hands'. Clearly, the Butillers preferred to endanger their lands in England rather than in Ireland, when it came to the non-payment of debts. Or perhaps they were so ordered to do, since it was more important for the estates in Ireland to be properly protected.

The wars went on about them, some being fought if not on their door-step, then in their own backyard. In 1275 there was a great victory over the English in Ulidia, where 200 horses and 200 heads were counted, 'besides the plebeians', and O'Brien, the Lord of Thomond, was captured by the son of the Earl of Clare in 1277, 'despite their mutual friendship'. The O'Briens were one of the three great Irish families, the descendants of the magnificent Brian Boru, whose greatness gave them pre-eminence in Munster, of which they were frequent kings. The relationship between them and their overlords, the Butillers, was always difficult, and Theobald may have assisted the Earl of Clare's son in his deceit. However, the tables were turned on the Clares the following year, when O'Brien's son defeated the Earl, burning the church 'over the heads of his people'.

But the four years following were relatively peaceful, and during this period of calm Theobald took advantage of it, being often in England, in attendance upon the monarch. In 1276 King Edward notified his bailiffs that Theobald, 'about by the King's licence to proceed to Ireland' had given power to the Earl of Warwick 'to make attorneys for him in all pleas and plaints in the King's courts'.[26] Yet whenever possible, the Butillers stood aside from the disputes that continually broke out around them, even when they involved their own dependants. However, in 1281–2 100*l* was paid to Theobald for his expenses and those of his men-at-arms in the 'King's army, whom he had led against the King's enemies in Thomond'. A further sum of 128*l* 16s 2d was set as stipends for his household and retainers.

Meanwhile other land was steadily being acquired, some of it now coming to the family from beyond their own borders. Philip de RuCapella granted Theobald and his heirs many acres in Omany, land taken from the O'Kellys in Connacht, and also the manor of Bray, near Dublin, 'paying to the King of England and other chief lords the accustomed services'. Such arrangements, of course, were not permanent; the manor of Bray had earlier been granted to Sir Fromund le Brun 'for his life', and the re-sale came about only because RuCapella owed King Edward 600 marks sterling.

The Butillers were also granted land in Tyrmany, another of the King's cantreds. This consisted of the baronies of Athlone, some in Roscommon, some in Galway, and some west of the Suck in Killian. (A barony was a territorial division next in order of size to a county, each county comprising from five to twenty baronies according to the extent of the individual province.) Theobald also held land of Walter de Lacy, that family being among the richest in Ireland. The Earl of Ulster (and Lord of Connacht) granted him two townlands and half of his land in Oleychath, along with the township of Achethdoyne and the half-township of Corbaly for a term of ten years from Easter 1282. But again, there were preconditions: the Butillers would lose their title to the land if the Earl or his heirs should wish to inhabit that land again, or build a house there. More conventionally, Matilda de Mares granted land to Theobald, to be held in fee with homage and the sixth part service of a knight. For other land, 'Sir' Theobald or his heirs would do the chief lord, Lord of Bruary, service of the tenth part of a knight.

In 1285 Theobald himself went to war, and by order of the Chief Justiciar of Ireland was paid 104*l* 12s. 9d for the wages of constables, servants and vassals who had accompanied the Justiciar on an expedition led by him into Thomond, 'against the King's enemies'. He died in that same year – at a relatively advanced age for a first-born Butler – but in his last year he was still claiming land from different sources. At Ardmayle, the prior of St John's church at Kilkenny convent made a unique compact with Theobald. If his monks ever appropriated that land, Theobald could enter and hold the same forever. The deed was signed in August, and Theobald was dead before the year was out.

He left eight sons and two daughters by his widow Joan, the granddaughter of Geoffrey, Earl of Essex, the Justiciar of England. The King ordered a dower to be assigned to Joan, when she made the usual promise to the King in Ireland that she would not re-marry without his licence.

With so many sons to inherit, not even the vast estates already accumulated in Ireland could suffice to accommodate them all, and so some of them had joined the Butillers of an earlier generation to seek their fortunes back in England, even though Theobald appears to have provided adequately for all of them, without making inroads into the Irish property. Most of his sons were 'in the King's eye', if not in attendance at court, but one or two of them rose high in his service. In 1279 Adam le Botiller was commanded to examine the treasure chests of the Jews, 'lately condemned, fugitive, or converted to the Christian faith'. (The year before, King Edward had caused all the Jews throughout the kingdom to be arrested on charges of clipping the coinage. In April 1279, he had 267 Jews hanged in London, and he altered the specie.[27]) Adam's area covered a wide remit: Winchester, Bristol, Hereford, Gloucester and Worcestor; when he died, two years before his father, he was the tenant of the abbey of Evesham. Like his mother in Ireland, Adam's wife, Margery, was assigned a dower, upon her taking an oath not to re-marry without King Edward's consent. Other widows, too, were taken into the King's protection. William, who was 'tenant in chief' of Wemme, near Shrewsbury, also died before his father in 1284. His wife, Angharetta, received a dower. As did Eleanor, the widow of John le Botiller, also of Wemme. These royal orders were considered to be important enough to be witnessed by Edmund, Earl of Cornwall.

Theobald himself retained his hold upon his English estates, for which he had done homage to King Edward I in 1274, and two years later he had pledged his lands in Lancashire for payment of debts. A year later there had been another plea of land, and the King had allowed Theobald to pay off 900*l* at the rate of 100 marks yearly. But he had also granted 400 marks to be allowed Theobald annually out of the 900*l* for his release and quit-claim of the vacant benefice of the church of Kirkeham, in Lancashire. He was also given 100*l* for the damages he had suffered when taking Castle Conyn in Ireland 'into the King's hands'.

But the Butillers were heavily in debt, and even Theobald's widow found herself in a financial predicament. An account was taken in Dublin, on 28 June 1287, between Bendimus Payne, citizen and merchant of the Society of the Riccardi of Lucca, for the society, and Geoffrey de Roilly, knight; and Henry Laffayn, clerk, attorneys of Theobald's widow, Joan le Botiller. She had borrowed in excess of 340*l* from the Italian bankers, for a variety of expenses: her transport, food and luxury goods, grain, wages, and even the cost of her husband's grand funeral.

Like many of her family and dependants she had previously been in debt to the Jews, and now she was further in debt to the rapacious Italians. They had begun to arrive in England and Ireland in great numbers in the early years of the reign of Henry III, gradually supplanting the more amenable Jewish financiers. By the first years of the reign of Edward I, few Anglo-Norman families were compelled to make restitution to the Jews, but five years after her husband's death Joan would still be paying off this enormous bill to the Italians. Even the fact that two years earlier she had inherited two manors and two hamlets in England could not alleviate her situation. She needed to give power to her attorneys in London to receive all pleas and plaints in England, for she was allowed 'by licence' to remain in Ireland, along with her daughter Matilda.

In 1290, her son would also be in trouble, but this time with the Justiciar of Ireland, when he was fined 100 marks for not proving his age before the judiciary. He would have been about 17 at the time of his father's death, and automatically became a royal ward, with his lands seized into the King's hands. He had, in fact, done homage to the King on 18 February 1289, at which time the warring O'Briens had taken advantage of his absence to ravage his lands, which were still 'in the King's custody'. In that same year his mother had entertained the Keeper of Ireland at Nenagh. The Keeper was on a survey of land, 'so that justice might be done at all and the King's dignity be everywhere maintained',[28] an assurance that was clearly impossible to sustain in the light of the O'Briens' incursions into Butler territory.

Theobald had to show cause to have full possession of the land that had fallen to him by his father's death, 'so that he should not come to the King of England to demand such seisin of him'. The judiciary found that Theobald had come of age, which puts his birth at around 1267, and they allowed him to have possession of his family estates. He petitioned to have them before the gathering of the Easter rents, but the Escheater confirmed that no writ had been taken to him until after the festival, and the rents had

43

been kept for the King's use. His castle of Dorz was delivered to William le Marshal, upon security that if the castle, while in his custody, were taken or knocked down, all Marshal's lands should remain in the King's possession until Dorz was handed back in its former state. The castle *had* been taken and knocked down, to the 'great damage and destruction of Theobald's lands', and he therefore requested the King to restore it, as 'He can have no profit of his lands until his castle is restored'.[29]

He also wanted the prisage of wines in the King's cities in Ireland, on the same terms that his father and his ancestors had enjoyed, they having been entitled to take from each ship 'arriving with wine' one hogshead before and one hogshead behind the mast, paying to the King 40s each hogshead. In his formal application, Theobald V claims: 'He and his ancestors had been butlers in fee to the King, and hence the Surname'.[30] The Escheator agreed that Theobald's father had died in possession of this franchise, but he did not know by what warrant. The matter was to be looked into.

Theobald further held land of the King in Bray, County Dublin, 'by the service of finding an armoured horse at the gate of the castle of Dublin when the King's service is summoned'. The Treasurer of Ireland had converted this service into the payment of money, 'that is to say 40s'. No money, however, had ever been given, no demand of money made, and 'his ancestors have ever rendered the service in the form aforesaid'.[31] Theobald also wished to do the same, and the Treasurer wanted to know his reason for making the demand.

Another son, the sixth, Walter, inherited the castle of Dorz at his father's death, which he later committed to William le Marshal, to be kept in the King's name, a condition of this being that if the castle should 'decay or be thrown down', the Marshal should repair it at his own charge. As a surety of this, the Escheater of Ireland took over the Marshal's lands in Tyringlas. The Earl of Ulster also argued that these lands belonged to him, by reason of the 'grant and gift' of William le Marshal. He petitioned the King to have the lands delivered to him, and the King agreed to this, providing that the Earl would find the money to repair the castle. If not, he would have to come to an agreement with Theobald le Butiller, son and heir, concerning it.

Theobald V still had his financial problems, although all of them were due to claims upon his late father's estate. He acknowledged in 1293 that he owed 560 marks, to be levied in Ireland and County Lancaster, and conceded that his father had owed the executors of Queen Eleanor's will 1000*l*, to be levied on lands and chattels in Ireland. He was allowed by the King, by his 'special grace', to pay this off at the rate of 100 marks per annum, payable at the Exchequer of Dublin, until the debt was discharged (possibly because at this time he was 'under the King's protection', for three years, since he was in Ireland on King Edward's service). Theobald promised that he would find the security to pay the sum at Dublin, on the terms agreed upon, and he made a recognisance for this at the King's Exchequer in England.

But even after this date, the last Theobald would still be paying off the debts of his late father, in Tipperary and Connacht. As late as 1296, he would have to pay 60 marks for possession of his lands in Lancashire, and in 1298 the King would be writing to the Treasurer of the Dublin Exchequer, directing them to levy from the lands and chattels of Theobald le Butiller in Ireland. They took 100 marks for the seisin of his lands.

The fifth and last Theobald came into his inheritance either shortly before or soon after his 22nd birthday in 1290. By that time the main part of his Irish inheritance would spread in an almost straight course across Ireland, from Arklow on the eastern coast to the mouth of the Shannon, forming a collective fortification along that line. Although the Butlers had played no major role in the bloody hostilities that had bedevilled the past century, they had successfully strengthened their own position; and at the very least that part of Ireland south of their holdings could be militarily defended. This had been achieved both by design and by accident.

For the fifteen years that Theobald would head the family, warfare would continue spasmodically, as it had done throughout his minority. Most of it was at some distance from his lands, but the O'Briens had 'ravaged the lands of Theobald le Butiller, in the King's custody'[32] in 1289. The next four years, however, would be relatively peaceful; that is until the FitzGeralds took the Red Earl of Ulster prisoner in 1294, and all of Ireland would be 'thrown into a state of disturbance'.

Ulster was only released through the power of King Edward, when 'good hostages of his own tribe were received in his stead'.[33] (Such was the level of assimilation that many Anglo-Norman families were now seen as tribal groups to match those of the native Irish.) Payment was made to Theobald for expenses he had incurred when raising an armed force in the mountains of Leinster during the disturbances, and for 'remaining there for some time, on account of the war aforesaid'.[34] These troops consisted of light horsemen and 'footmen'. Later, he would be recompensed for the money he had also laid out to freight ships for that same army.

Some members of the Butler family were also involved on the FitzGerald side during the disturbance, if only as sympathisers. In 1295 Peter le Butiller stood surety for John, son of Thomas, a knight, accused of the abduction of the Earl of Ulster, and 'certain other crimes and trespasses committed in Ireland against the King and his Peace'.[35] John was bound to find twenty-four 'mainpersons', each having at least 100 marks yearly of land in fee, upon his return to Ireland, and Peter le Butiller was one of only three that he had so far found.

Theobald was present in the Irish parliament of 1295, when the 'great lords of Ireland' were called together by John Wogan, the Lord Justice, and Theobald stood fifth in the roll of honour. That he was given no territorial designation on this occasion suggests that the office of Chief Butler of Ireland carried with it the status of baron, at least. In January 1296 he was one of twenty-eight men 'requested' to be present with horses and arms on 1 March, prepared to set out on the King's service on his invasion of Scotland. (With thirteen competitors for the crown of Scotland, King Edward hoped to bring that country as much under his authority as he had Wales.) Theobald had been enjoined to do so by the Justiciary of Ireland, to whom the King had ordered the men to 'give credence' and to do what the Justiciary should order on the King's behalf.

Theobald, in company with the Lord Justice, the Earl of Ulster and other important magnates, went over to England early in spring, and were nobly entertained by Edward I on Whitsunday at a solemn feast in the castle of Roxburgh. King Edward himself proposed to be in Ireland at this time, although instead he chose to make an incursion into Scotland later in the year, when he forcibly removed the coronation stone of Scone, transferring it to Westminster Abbey.[36] The English ravaged Scotland, 'both territories and churches. They killed many priests, besides women and persons not able to bear arms'. Theobald V accompanied King Edward I throughout the whole of this expedition, 'when all the forces of Scotland were reduced'.[37]

Others of his extended family also made themselves useful to the King in his other struggles. In 1294 Thomas le Butiller set out for Gascony in the King's service. Thomas, who had a manor and park at Badminton, Gloucestershire, sought redress from two 'Normans' who had trespassed, 'breaking the said park', during his absence. In 1297 John le Butiller guarded Agnes of Valencia, the King's kinswoman, as part of her retinue, when she went abroad. In 1298 the King acquitted William le Butiller of Wemme of the payment of three knights' fees in the army of Wales, because William's kinsman Ralph had been with the King as part of that army.

Four years of peace would follow King Edward's incursion into Scotland, in all three countries, and the Butler concerns would once again be domestic and legal. Joan la Botillere and the Earl of Ulster were the co-heirs of an inheritance in the English Home Counties, and the quarrel that ensued concerning it lasted for some months, with Ulster complaining that Joan had received more than her fair share. Joan, a sister of the Earl of Surrey, was also distrained in 1299 for not going to do homage to the King for the manor of Shyre in Surrey, which was held by the Earl in knight's service. King Edward gave it to her nonetheless. In that same year, she was given other knights' fees and advowsons; seven knights in all.

But the last Theobald was in possession of his rich heritage for fifteen years only. On May 14 1299 the 'illustrious baron' died at Turvey. He was unmarried and without issue and he was buried in his great-great-grandfather's abbey at Wothney.

As with any conquest – even this partial takeover – it had brought disaster to the old aristocracy. The years between the first Theobald and the last had seen a vast transfer of property, perhaps the largest in recorded Irish history, for virtually a whole upper caste was now displaced.

Again, as with the Norman Conquest of England, the incoming warrior caste had expected to enrich themselves, and their first objective had been to take military control over the land, notably by building castles at strategic points and making certain that they were well secured. Nowhere had this been better accomplished than in the Butler domain, where a consolidated lordship had been created in key positions. The east-west boundaries not only kept the Butler country free of serious Irish attack; it also secured the vital line of communication to the eastern seaboard. Alone among their Anglo-Norman partners the Butlers throughout the 13th century had not acquired most of their land through armed conflict, but because of this they had not torn the fabric of their family apart. At the beginning of the 14th century, they would be in a much stronger position than that of their chief English rivals, and the coming century would be one of the most memorable in their long history.

# Notes

1. Carte, *Life of the Duke of Ormonde.*
2. Ibid.
3. Ibid.
4. K. Norgate, *Angevin Kings.*
5. The Four Masters, *Annals of the Kingdom of Ireland.*
6. Ibid.
7. Ibid.
8. Carte, op. cit.
9. Ibid.
10. The Four Masters, op. cit.
11. Ibid.
12. Ibid.
13. It is hard to imagine exactly what these new-fangled 'engines of war' could have been since the Anglo-Normans did not need to use siege towers or battering rams against an enemy so lacking in walled defences.
14. The Four Masters, op. cit.
15. Carte, op. cit.
16. *Librates,* a piece of land worth one Medieval English pound per year.
17. The Four Masters, op. cit.
18. Ibid.
19. Hoveden (ed. Stubbs) *Rolls Series.*

20. Ibid.
21. The Four Masters, op. cit.
22. Ibid.
23. Curtis, *Calendar of Ormonde Deeds*.
24. Carte, op. cit.
25. Ibid.
26. Ibid.
27. T.F.T. Plucknett, *The Legislation of Edward I.*
28. Ibid.
29. Curtis, op. cit.
30. Ibid.
31. Ibid.
32. The Four Masters, op. cit.
33. Ibid.
34. Carte, op. cit.
35. Curtis, op. cit.
36. Scone is the site of a Pictish capital, and the stone was effectively the throne upon which medieval Scottish kings were crowned.
37. The Four Masters, op. cit.

# CHAPTER III

## *The First Earls*

Edmund, who succeeded his brother, was the second son of the fourth Theobald, and he had already proved that he had inherited the family's flair for organisation, for he had long shared in the running of the Butler domain. When the 2nd Earl of Ulster burst upon Connacht, plundering monasteries and churches, it had been left to his nephew, Edmund Butler, to negotiate any form of peace. From about 1290 Edmund had received grants alongside his elder brother; and in 1295 King Edward I 'under his seal of England' gave him twenty-five towns in the land of Omany for the whole of his life, at a rent of 125*l*, 'paid to us yearly.' '…We wishing to do special grace to the said Edmund for the laudable service which he has done and will do for us in the future.'[1] Castle Grace was also granted to him, by service of a knight's fee.

Edmund did homage to the King in 1300, receiving possession of all the lands that his brother Theobald had held at his death, in both countries. Edmund himself granted land to another brother Gilbert in 1302, for which Gilbert was to do royal service for this land, as often as it would be 'proclaimed for all service, exaction and demand'.[2] The grant was given at Nenagh, but significantly the property itself was in Connacht, in which province the Butler family had begun to make some inroads, largely due to the influence of their grandfather Richard de Burgh.

But it was always more important to ensure the family's security by placing their own kinfolk in areas of danger that were nearer to home. Edmund's nephew, Sir John le Butiller, was given land near to Gowran, to be granted, in turn, to his son Nicholas at his death. Because this land was so strategically important to the Butlers, it was further ruled that if Nicholas failed to produce an heir then the land would pass to another brother William. Failing that, to other brothers, for it must not go beyond the influence of the immediate kinsmen, as not even distant relatives could be trusted. If all the brothers and their offspring died without issue, the land would return to Edmund's line.

Edmund's importance in Ireland to the Crown was quickly recognised. As early as 1301, when the truce granted to the King of Scotland by Edward I was about to expire, he was one of the men provided with a strong force of men-at-arms, 'in order to proceed vigorously with war'.[3] In 1302 he was commanded to assist at a parliament that was called in Ireland, where he is named 'Edmond le Botiller'. (The use of the office as a surname, as with his brother Theobald, again signifying that he was of the baronage.)

In 1303, when a huge royal army crossed over into Scotland, under the direct command of King Edward, the 'red' Earl of Ulster and many of the English of Ireland went, with a great fleet, to assist the King. On this occasion Edward took many cities, and 'gained great sway over the Scots'; but perhaps because of his youth, Edmund was not a part of this assembly. But in 1304 he was definitely recognised as being 'of full age', for he went in company with the Earl of Ulster to Dublin, with a sizeable band of men-at-arms, 'ready to come to the King in his service in Scotland'. (The Earl of Ulster creating thirty-three knights in Dublin Castle for this purpose.) All the Irish barons, including Edmund's relations, were set to attend King Edward on his invasion, but it was unanimously agreed by the council at Dublin that both Edmund and his uncle would be of more use in Ireland, 'in aid of the King's other subjects of those parts'.[4]

Which was undoubtedly true, since there were greater disturbances than ever within the realm in this year. But the King at first resented Edmund for appearing to withdraw from his Scottish enterprise, and as a punitive measure he put a stop to the granting of the conveyance of the lands of Edmund's mother, who died about this time. But when the King learned that Edmund had been fully prepared to join him in Scotland, and was informed of the reasons behind Edmund's absence, he immediately turned over to him all the lands in England and Ireland that were his by right of his mother's recent death. 'As a show of special favour' Edmund was to go to the King before Whitsuntide, to do homage for those lands. In that same year, John Butler, was also given land in Ireland, 'for good service rendered in Scotland'.[5]

By the following year, Edmund had advanced so far in the King's favour that he was made the Keeper of Ireland, with the style of *Custos Hiberniae*, and throughout his life he would frequently hold this post. Seven years after first receiving it, when the Justiciar of Ireland, John Wogan, returned to England, Edmund was by letters patent appointed to govern the country as his lieutenant, but he refused the office because he thought that it 'insulted his honour', having previously been the Chief Governor.

In 1305 the 'robbers of Offaly' burned the town of Ley and laid siege to its castle, until driven back by the combined forces of John FitzGerald and Edmund Butler. In 1307 the same Irish of Offaly besieged the Butler castle of Cashel and took the town, although they afterwards invested the castle. They were routed, with the siege being again raised by Edmund Butler, who was then Deputy of Ireland.

He would often act in concert with John FitzGerald (commonly called fitzThomas), who was by then his father-in-law, and Edmund may also have assisted FitzGerald in earlier encounters with the Irish, for these were years of great confusion in Offaly and Kildare. Ley, the FitzGeralds' chief stronghold, had previously been taken and burned in 1284, and the castle of Kildare was captured in 1294, with 'the country round laid waste by bands of predatory Irish and English'.[6]

A large number of the Roscommon English were slain by O'Kelly, the Lord of Hy-Many, at St Cuan's ridge on the Clonback River in Galway. Three Irish chieftains, allies of the English, were taken prisoner at this battle but were later released after making a full restitution to the inhabitants for the burning of their town by Edmund Butler. Although, a year later, when 'a thunderbolt came from heaven',[7] falling on to the monastery at Roscommon and destroying the building along with several friars, there was a popular belief that divine retribution was responsible for the catastrophe.

In 1308, a year after England had a new King in Edward II, there would be fresh outbreaks of civic disturbance in Ireland after Conor Roe O'Brien was slain by the 'Black English' (that is, by new settlers from England, who were arriving in ever- increasing numbers, and usually accompanied by substantial armed forces). All Irish magnates were expected to raise a force to deal with these eruptions of popular anger, but the Butlers seem to have stood apart from them during this time. But they did make their own particular arrangements with the colonists, offering them protection from the Irish, with these deals being always of a financial nature.

So, too, were many of the agreements the Butlers came to with their peers, although in some of these cases they were themselves buying a similar sort of protection. A compact of Palm Sunday 1308 being a typical example, in which Sir William de Burgh agreed to take two vallates of land, 'and the liberties appertaining to the same' in part payment for Edmund being excused from supplying a military retinue that would be under Burgh's charge. (For this Edmund agreed to render yearly one pair of gilt spurs or 12d at each feast of St Michael, while Sir William undertook to answer – for himself and his men – for any further trespasses that might be committed against the Butlers.) This contract is interesting in that it also reveals how strongly the family protected their tenants. For an Irish farmer already occupied the land on a lease from Edmund Butler, and Sir William – in accepting the terms – was to 'assure' this dependant that the lease would be continued, '…unless by law or right he shall be expelled'.[8])

Not that the Butlers could avoid military action, or wished to do so, especially when their possessions were threatened by these flashes of violence. In 1308 Edmund was in England to make his homage to the new King, where he was knighted for his previous services to the Crown. But he returned to Ireland at once in 1309, when his presence there was necessary, and he could not then hold back from taking part in the numerous disturbances that were convulsing the country. English superiority in weaponry, battle strategy and tactics may have helped to keep them almost invincible for the past century, but the Irish were now managing to win many important battles despite the odds against them, wresting back control.

In 1311 William 'Burke' (formerly Burgh) led a huge army into Munster, against the Earl of Clare's men. Clare was defeated in the battle fought, and Burke pursued the enemy with his typical ferocity until Clare's people turned and closed around him, taking him prisoner, although he had still been the victor in the battle. This blood had been shed in, or near to, Butler territory, and the Anglo-Normans were not the only threat to their peace in that year, for when a war broke out in Thomond between the MacNamaras and the O'Briens, it also involved them. MacNamara was defeated, and was in fact killed on the battlefield, with both armies suffering immense slaughter, but the victory was an empty one for the O'Briens, when their king was afterwards treacherously murdered, and a lesser O'Brien elected in his place. A year later, the Butlers would acquire the castle of Knocktopher, as a further line in the defence of their domain against this particular sept, for of all the Irish clans living within their rule, the O' Briens were the most to be feared

When Edward II came to the throne in 1307 the future had looked very bright for England, for there was a new generation of young men gathered around a King still in his early 20s, all of them on the threshold of their careers. But unfortunately Edward had lost no time in antagonising the men he most depended upon, and he had swiftly elevated his unpopular favourites to unsuitable positions.

Piers Gaveston, a Gascon adventurer and the most detested of these intimates, had been briefly Lord Lieutenant of Ireland in 1309, sent there for safety by the King when faced with an armed intervention by his nobles in parliament (all of them seeking to have the favourite ousted, or even executed). To the surprise of many, Gaveston had proved to be a successful and competent military governor in Ireland, his time there marking a new attempt to deal with the 'mountain Irish', who by then threatened the environs of Dublin, so that it was no longer safe to leave state money outside the protection of the castle walls. (It had to be escorted to the Exchequer under guard from the safety of the castle each morning, and back again at the close of day.)

Gaveston made a big impression on the Irish, not only because of his extravagance and generosity, but also through his achievements in safeguarding English assets. The favourite proved also to be militarily ambitious, and having once satisfied himself that the danger in Ireland was contained, he set about arranging for a large expeditionary force to sail for Scotland. And among the most important tenants-in-chief designated to accompany him was to be Edmund Butler, who received two hundred Irish pounds from the Lord Lieutenant to defray his expenses in this endeavour.

Matters, in fact, ran more smoothly in Ireland under the favourite than went well for his master in England. Within a year of Edward's accession the lords in parliament declared that their loyalty was due to the Crown rather than to the King's *person*, and in 1310 they forced Edward to appoint a committee to reform the government, on the principle that the law was superior to the King. Edward was forced to assent to their demands, but the capture and murder of his favourite Gaveston (who had injudiciously left his stronghold in Ireland) brought no resolution to the situation. For Edward was now as completely opposed to his barons as his grandfather and great-grandfather had ever been, although neither side was strong enough to crush the other. By 1312 the government of England was in a state of paralysis.

But while the reforming baronial party was in partial control in England, an attempt had already been made to provide better government in Ireland, where the King's party had less sway. In August 1312 Edmund Butler was installed as an interim Justiciar, and – according to the Chronicle of Dublin – he quickly enjoyed spectacular success against the Irish in Glenmalure. Repressing the repeated excursions of the O'Byrnes and the O'Tooles, he attacked them so ferociously in their own fastness in Glendelorie that they were forced to submit in order to avoid utter destruction. His achievement afterwards in 'quieting' the Irish was apparently so complete that he was said to be able to progress from one side of his country to the other with only three mounted men as escort.[9] He continued in government as a permanent Justiciar, and in the next year, on Michaelmas Day, he dubbed thirty knights in the courtyard of the castle in Dublin, all of whom were pledged to serve him personally.

Yet the times were increasingly threatening, and the Butlers now not only acquired new fortresses they also went about expanding the private army that they had been assembling for some years. Every Anglo-Irish magnate at this period aspired to have an army of his own for his personal protection, and in this Edmund was no different from his peers, although perhaps he proved more capable than most at conscripting men and keeping them occupied. Most Anglo-Norman lords by this time had begun to give preference to Irishmen in the ranks of these armies, and Edmund also seems to have subscribed to this partiality. (Largely because his English tenants were reluctant to 'endure' his 'quarterings' – that is, the allocation of accommodation to military personnel – but the Irish were happy enough to do so since it was traditional among them.) The decision to favour the Irish as recruits would eventually, of course, act against the interests of the magnates, since it would lead to a decline of the English in their ranks.

However, Edmund Butler did conscript Englishmen where he could, as in 1314, when as the 'Lord of Carrick', he enlisted the lightly armed soldiers of one of his tenants, and those of the English farmers in his domain. Adam de la Roche was one of several men who 'bound himself to

Sir Edmund's service, and to take up his arms', but he was one of the few Anglo-Normans to do so. All, naturally, swore to 'abide with him as one of his men in counsel and deed against all men save our Lord the King'. But they also swore to refrain from attacking certain men in particular, these men then being temporary allies of the Butlers, 'against whom by homage he [Edmund Butler] ought not to carry arms'.

The military contract between Edmund and Adam de la Roche seems almost modern in its terminology, and the agreements with his Irish conscripts must have been just as crisp:

> So that when the said Adam is summoned by Sir Edmund to come to his aid with his force, the latter shall bear the costs of leading Adam's force in the parts of Wexford until he comes to wherever Sir Edmund be, and until he returns to his house and abode in the parts of Wexford. And if Adam come to Sir Edmund by his command, and in no other manner, that then when he has come where Sir Edmund is, he shall be received at the cost of the latter with five draught horses on each occasion. And for the receipt of arms aforesaid, and for his sojourn, Sir Edmund binds himself and his heirs and executors to the said Adam in 100 marks sterling of pure debt, to be paid at certain terms, viz. 20 marks at Michaelmas next to come and 20 marks at Easter next ensuing, and so from year to year and term to term, until the said 100 marks be fully paid.[10]

Both men witnessed this indenture (which was written in French), with the men using their interchangeable seals.

Such contracts were essential in the warlike conditions of Ireland, and in fact the situation was to worsen in that same year. For the greatest threat to the whole of Anglo-Norman Ireland came in May 1315, when a great fleet landed in Antrim, commanded by Edward Bruce, the King of Scotland's brother. King Robert I was said to have sent him to find a kingdom for himself; but it is just as likely that Robert saw it as an opportunity to create a Scottish-Irish-Welsh alliance, after their first great victory over the English. (Unlike his father, King Edward II had dealt disastrously with the Scots. In 1314 he had been humiliated at the battle of Bannockburn, and the Scots were now raiding English border country with impunity.) Here, in Ireland, was an opportunity for them to open up a second front. But whatever the motive, Edward Bruce came to Ireland with about 6,000 men.

One result of this new incursion by the Scots in a territory they had not been expected to invade proved to be the suddenly apparent prowess of Edmund Butler. When it was evident that the invasion of Ireland was being prepared, Edward II sent a special envoy to Dublin to discuss the situation with the magnates. Letters of credence were addressed to prelates, nobles and the Commons of Ireland, enjoining them to 'hear and assist the Justiciar and his fellow officers', and Edmund Butler was named as that Justiciar. Particular letters were also addressed to twenty-two Gaelic chieftains and sixty-three bishops, abbots and town magistrates, bearing the same charge.

Throughout 1315 Edmund rendered such 'good and laudable service' to the King that he was granted further lands in the county of Tipperary. But even when the intentions of the Scots became known, the decisive interval had been badly spent, and there was little that Edmund could do to alter matters; the arrival of the Scots was a storm that burst upon an unprepared state.

The Scots invaders in Ireland began by 'committing great injury' to the Earl of Ulster's people and to the English of Meath, despite the fact that the Earl had mustered a large army to oppose them. Since the Earl of Ulster was Edmund's uncle he would have gone to his defence, but within months, Bruce had driven the English out of Ulster, and believed that he had made good his claim to the Irish monarchy by this triumph. Indeed, some Ulster princes, regarding him as being of their own ancestry, did then urge him to take the crown, with one of them even renouncing his hereditary right in Bruce's favour, and Bruce accepted their proposal.

He was prematurely crowned as the King of Ireland, in the open air on a hill near Dundalk, on May Day 1316, in the presence of many Irish allies. The 'red' Earl could not back away from this challenge, and he and Edward Bruce immediately did battle, at which Ulster was defeated and taken prisoner. Thereafter Bruce ravished Ireland with such great effect that English power quickly shrank to a narrow territory around Dublin.

Edmund, as the Lord Justice, now assembled an immense army in Leinster and Munster, to oppose the Scots (and their Irish allies). His father-in-law's estates had been laid waste by Bruce's forces, but at Arscoll, county Kildare, the invader was met by the combined armies of three leaders, with each of their armies outnumbering that of Bruce. But the captains of these three armies – John FitzGerald, Edmund Butler and Arnold le Poer – were at variance as to the best tactics to pursue, and the Scots gained an easy victory. Half a year later, John FitzGerald would be created Earl of Kildare (in England), by a patent dated 16 May 1316; but before he could return to Ireland, to deal with the arrival of the Scottish King himself, bringing reinforcements, the new Earl died suddenly, though of natural causes. FitzGerald had been one of the most unruly of Irish barons, but at one time or another he had under his control no inconsiderable part of the island; that he was never made a Justiciar is perhaps due to the fact that he had never been entirely trusted.

The Scots in Ireland marched south, early in 1317 (although once Robert I had returned to his kingdom, Edward Bruce remained at Carrickfergus, calling himself the King of Ireland). Bulls were issued by the Pope, for the purpose of detaching the Irish clergy from the Bruce's cause, and to warn them against inciting the people against the King of England; and a public excommunication was pronounced against those who persisted in this course. Not that this appears to have affected the situation overmuch. John Barbour in his patriotic poem *The Bruce* alleged that Edward Bruce defeated the English forces in Ireland on nineteen separate engagements, in which he had not more than one man against five.[11] He also maintained that he was in a 'good way' to conquering the entire island, as he had the Irish on his side and was in possession of Ulster, and would have succeeded had not his fortunes been marred by his 'outrageous pride', (which was a sound assessment, as would be later shown).

The English advanced to Dundalk, to be joined by the Earl of Ulster, who had been released after the payment of a huge ransom, and had then raised another great force in Connacht. The Scots retired before this formidable array, and they would surely have been cut in pieces had not the old feuds between the Burkes and the FitzGeralds broken out again when they met up with each other. The Scots, faced with such a formidable array of armed might, departed the field; at which the English army separated, instead of uniting together, and only the Earl of Ulster went off in pursuit of the Scots, chasing them as far as Coleraine in the north. There, with his forces greatly depleted, Ulster was inevitably soundly defeated.

But from the time the Scots had landed in Ireland the Irish had been encouraged to break into open rebellion, which they did throughout Connacht, Munster, Meath and Leinster. Bruce, encouraged by their rebellion, and strengthened by new forces that he had sent for from Scotland, marched into Meath and Kildare, burning and spoiling all before him.

Edmund Butler again opposed the Scots in Kildare, where he had managed to bring the nobles of Leinster and Munster together, along with their followers. Combined, they made a numerous army, but the dissension that had earlier split the English once more broke out, with the army dispersing in disorder, without doing any kind of battle. It was only for lack of provisions that the Scots retired back to their base of Ulster on this calamitous occasion.

Edmund used an interval of peace to call a parliament in Dublin, at which he again tried to reconcile the great men with each other, and to concert measures for carrying on the war. The necessary steps were taken, and Edmund thought it best to deal with what he saw as the weaker Irish enemy in Leinster before going on to tackle the more organised forces of Edward Bruce. Having routed the O'Mores, who had ravaged the county of Leix under the protection of the Scots, he then attacked the O'Byrnes and the O'Tooles, who had once more risen in arms, burning Arklow, Newcastle, Bray, 'and all the villages adjoining'.

Edmund defeated the Irish completely on 16 April 1316, soon after which Roger Mortimer was sent over from England to act as the King's Lieutenant, displacing Edmund, although he continued to do battle, using his own followers. He made a great slaughter of the Irish in the two engagements he had with them: with one encounter near Castle Dermot and the other at Ballylethen, when over 400 Irish died in these actions.

Seeing the Irish in disarray from the English onslaught, Edward Bruce then invaded Meath. Roger Mortimer at once gave battle, and was as immediately defeated at Kells in December; owing, it was said, to the treachery of the Lacys, who now openly joined Bruce. They had guided his troops into the midlands, and they also brought over to his standard no fewer than seventy of the foremost gentry of Meath, along with four Gaelic chieftains, all of whom were the Lacys' clients or dependants.

After Christmas 1316 Bruce invaded Kildare, where he overthrew the royal forces under the command of Edmund Butler and John FitzGerald on 26 January 1317. To secure their advantage, Bruce reinforced his forces from Scotland, and advanced towards Dublin at the beginning of 1317 with an army of 20,000 men. The citizens of Dublin, frenzied with fear at the approach of the Scots, had made the Earl of Ulster their prisoner, hoping perhaps to offer him up to Edward Bruce as a peace offering, and neither Edmund Butler nor the new Earl of Kildare were successful in gaining his release.

The Scots, though, inexplicably made no attempt to move into Dublin, but instead marched southwards into Butler territory, carrying on to Cashel and Nenagh, wasting the county of Tipperary as they passed through it. Edmund's forces, combined with those of Kildare, drew on 30,000 men to fight the Scots; but both leaders were held back from confronting them by Roger Mortimer, who had sent for a larger force from England and wished to hold off until their arrival. Once arrived at Youghal, he had sent to tell Edmund that he should do nothing until his appearance on the battlefield; and by obeying him Edmund lost the initiative.

As the Scots progressed through Butler country, the town of Kilkenny was largely left alone as the invaders moved towards the Shannon River, although they caused a terrible destruction to property along the way. Bruce hoped to link up at the Shannon with the Irish of Thomond, and possibly those of Desmond as well, but he had no time at hand for lengthy sieges, and so he ignored the walled towns that he could not take by storm.

An account of John of Patrickschurch, a clerk of wages to the army of the Justiciar, enables us to follow Edmund's path as he moved rapidly through Munster raising men. From 24 February, when he went to Cork for this purpose, to 17 April when his hastily assembled troops assaulted the Scots as they were crossing the Bog of Ely, Edmund remained in touch with the enemy without actually bringing them to do battle. For a time, he had as many as 920 paid fighting men at his command: 220 men-at-arms, 300 hobelars, and 400 men-on-foot. But the Scots army was too formidable, and Edmund, even with this crack force, hesitated to meet it in the open.

It is clear that if Bruce had succeeded in his plan to link up with Donncherel O' Brien he would have been able to press on with the business of conquest. But instead, he found Donncherel's great rival, Muirchetack O'Brien, waiting for him across the Shannon with a formidable army, ready to give battle to his enemy's ally. Now it was Edmund who suddenly held the advantage, and there was little the Scots could do except to retreat. From the vicinity of Limerick they moved through Kildare and into Meath, reaching the safety of Ulster on 1 May 1318.

But in the autumn of 1318 Edward Bruce proposed another descent upon Leinster, and to prevent this movement the colonists mustered a huge army. Bruce's chief advisers counselled him against coming to an engagement with a force so numerically superior to that under his own command, but the Scottish Prince haughtily declined their advice, and neither would he wait for reinforcements. As a result, the Scots were not long in possession of the field, for they were thoroughly routed by Lord John Bermyngham at Dundalk on 14 October 1318.

'King' Edward Bruce was killed in this encounter, along with 20,000 of his men, while the rest were put to flight. Bruce's corpse was found on the field, with that of his slayer stretched out upon it; quarters of his body were set up as trophies in all the chief towns of the English colony in Ireland, and his head was presented to King Edward II in England. Barbour insisted that it was not Edward Bruce, but a devoted follower, who had worn his armour on the day of battle, but whoever's the corpse, the result was a complete triumph for the English. Any hopes of an independent Celtic monarchy (albeit one to be headed by a Scottish king), were dashed with this defeat:

Edward Bruce, destroyer of the people of Ireland, in general both English and Irish, was slain by the English through dint of battle and bravery at Dundalk, with many other Scottish chieftains slain. And no achievement had been performed in Ireland for a long time before, from which greater benefit had accrued to the country than from this. For during the three and a half years that Edward spent in it, a universal famine prevailed to such a degree that men were wont to devour each other. Some people were so pinched with famine they dug up the graves in churchyards and boiled the corpses.[12]

Even allowing for the exaggeration of the annalists, there can be little doubt that the Scottish invasion had further added to the general misery of the people; and there is no question that the Bruce episode had shaken the whole Anglo-Norman colonial fabric. Many inland towns and settlements were destroyed forever, while huge areas had been recovered for Gaelic civilization; a fact well demonstrated, nine years later, by the restoration of the MacMurrough kingdom of Leinster, a realm that had been in an indeterminate state of ownership from 1171. (From about this time, too, the militarisation of the native Irish along more English lines would proceed with rapidity. Irish chiefs and their officers, at least, would go into battle wearing armour and helmets, and they would also start to build their own castles in imitation of the invaders, made of stone and timber, and built to last. They would also take up the custom of hiring heavily armed mercenaries, the gallowglasses of the Hebrides.[13] Fortunately for the English the Irish did not just turn their new expertise against them exclusively; instead, they used these troops to fight out wars with each other, with twice as much ferocity as they wielded against the 'enemy from overseas', thus weakening their effectiveness.)

In 1315 King Edward II had decreed that, because of 'the good and laudable service rendered to us by our beloved Edmund le Botiller of Ireland', he had granted him more land in the county of Tipperary. Somewhat confusingly, he goes on to say that he had decided upon this award, influenced by the request of 'our beloved cousin, Thomas, Earl of Ormonde and Ossary, Treasurer of our Kingdom of Ireland.'[14] Yet both these two earldoms were as yet to be created, and the identity of Thomas, and his kinship to King Edward, is not known. But the letters patent conferring the earldom of Carrick upon Edmund *Butler* (the first official use of the modern name) were granted on 1 Sept 1316.

In the main medieval kings were extremely cautious about creating earldoms, and by the time that Edward I died there were only eleven of them, two of whom played no part in strictly *English* affairs; one of them being Edmund's near-kinsman, the Earl of Ulster. Of the other nine, seven of them were all younger men, of King Edward II's own generation, and Edmund would not have been included in this group, being slightly older. But the men who held this singular honour were an extremely select group, their political influence matched only by their status and wealth.

Politically, though, since these honours were solely at the discretion of the King, there was always some danger to him in their creation, as Edward II had already discovered when he conferred the earldom of Cornwall on his friend Piers Gaveston. But clearly Edmund's elevation to an earldom was acceptable to the leading magnates of the kingdom, and it was seen to have been a well-deserved reward for his substantial work in Ireland.

The patent for the earldom was written in the usual style of licences of that age, and Edmund chose as his title that of his township of Carrick on the fast-flowing Suir. The town, between Clonmel and the pre-eminent port of Waterford, had belonged to the Butlers for a long time and had grown increasingly important, although its castle was not built until 1309. His decision to choose this name over that of his other strongholds was never explained, and although Edmund would be so-styled for the rest of his life, he seems not to have used the title much. His son, too, would accept the title with a strange indifference, and become better known by another.

The Dublin Chroniclers say that it was because the English leaders in Ireland had quarrelled so continuously among themselves that the invading Scots had been allowed to advance as far as they had, which was true. Edmund Butler had certainly found it impossible to hold these Anglo-Irish agitators in check; and now, as he had earlier failed with Burke, he failed with two other great magnates, Maurice fitzThomas and Arnold le Poer. The death of the Earl of Ulster, fitzThomas's father-in-law, had seen the beginning of new feuds.

But when these leaders reached Dublin, disconsolate at the singular triumph of Lord John Bermyngham over 'King' Edward Bruce, Edmund persuaded them to put their seals to a solemn declaration in which they swore to defend the English King's rights in Ireland, a condition of this statement being that if they 'failed in their loyalty', their bodies, lands and chattels were to be forfeited, and they must also give up hostages to the King, 'for the fulfillment thereof', with these captives held in Dublin castle 'at the King's pleasure.'[15] During the next few years, payment for the upkeep of these vital hostages figure largely on the issue rolls of the Irish Exchequer and in the records of the King's Wardrobe.

The Butler family was as much involved with Church matters as with warfare at this period, both in their own interests and in those of the state. Between 1312 and 1320 a number of instruments in Chancery deal with the advowsons of churches in the area of Ballygaveran, made between Edmund and the Prior of Kilmainham, under the Great Seal of Ireland. But the Butler interest in religion also had a political tinge, for many priests were active in Irish power struggles. In 1317 the Pope issued a decree from Avignon against the clergy in Ireland, who were said to be fostering rebellion against Edward II.

These priests, it was claimed, were 'withdrawing' the Irish people under their charge from obedience and fealty to 'our dear son, Edward, King of England' [16], and a main weapon in their ecclesiastical armoury was the wholesale giving of absolution for acts of homicide, arson, sacrilege, robberies and such crimes committed by their people against the King's name. The clergy were urged to desist from inciting their flocks from making war under threat of excommunication, 'to be pronounced on all Sundays and feast days, with ringing of bells and quenching of candles'.[17] Edmund was one of the great lords who were charged with helping to carry out this decree, which was done with uneven success. One certain consequence of priestly intervention in the political arena came with an uprising in the Butler authority of Ely in 1318, when a great victory was gained over the English, and Adam de Mares, a relative by marriage, was among the many slain.

As a family man, and a man now deeply conscious of his heritage, Edmund – as with most of his peers – was also engaged with the spiritual welfare of himself and his descendants, and even that of his predecessors. In 1320 he commissioned the prior and brethren at the monastery of Gowran to find four chaplains, 'suitable and sufficient', of the church of the Blessed Virgin Mary, to celebrate mass there every day, and to pray for the souls of Edmund and Johanna, 'formerly his wife'. They were also to pray for the 'ancestors, heirs, issue, brothers and sisters of the said Edmund, and the charge of the said hospital, St John of Jerusalem in Ireland, forever'. Provision was made for their places to be filled whenever one of the priests died, or became 'insufficient', with a fine paid to the Butler family for any failure to do so. In return, Edmund undertook to protect the prior, the clergy and their tenants, 'in all places where they may personally be against all men, saving the Lord King'.[18]

This was a necessary commitment since King Edward II was rapidly proving to be the most divisive and unpopular monarch since King John. From about 1312 there had been a growing opposition to 'the Lord King' and his half-brother, Thomas, Earl of Lancaster. But it had also hardened against a second unpopular favourite, Hugh le Despenser the Younger, who had succeeded Piers Gaveston, murdered by the King's enemies. Hugh, with his father, also called Hugh, tried to build up a royalist party, with the result that the three men now partly governed England and Ireland through their malevolent influence over the King.

Lancaster, in particular, was so politically inept that he had virtually brought all administration to a standstill, and Hugh le Despenser the elder, a violent man, had pursued a land-grabbing policy in South Wales – always a dangerous area – that had alienated most of Edward's courtiers. While Despenser did not aim at establishing a royal tyranny, there were so many objections to his policies that most magnates, by voicing their protests, were suspected of disloyalty to the Crown. But for a time, the Despensers were all-powerful, with no bounds to their greed.

The atmosphere of distrust surrounding the King and his 'government' extended into Ireland, and the Earl of Ulster was imprisoned, while most Anglo-Irish grandees were forced to leave hostages with the Crown. '...Rumour played with the good name of even the greatest', and even the Butlers were, for a time, among those who were mistrusted. In 1320 the King had to publish a formal declaration, 'to clear the fair name of Edmund le Botiller, who has been accused of having assisted the Scots in Ireland, that he has borne himself well and faithfully towards the King'.[19]

Robert de la Freigne was the steward and surveyor of the Butler lordship at this time, and the Ormonde deeds show that under his management the family consolidated its position, slowly building up their properties. But, as with the master's family, that of his servants was 'warfare all the way', particularly for the Earl's right-hand man, who was expected to aid his master in his military campaigns as well as in domestic matters. Robert, it seems, was as able in one discipline as in the other.

His son, Fulk de la Freigne, was in fact 'a man devoted to war and the military life from boyhood', and he was also held in high regard by Edmund Butler. But not all of the members of the Freigne family were as devoted to the Earl's cause. Robert's father was killed in 1320 by Edmund's mercenaries – that is, by the men who were paid by his own son – and so he must have been fighting in alliance with the Earl's enemies, although whether English or Irish is not known. (The Gaelic Irish would kill his grandson, Sir Fulk de la Freigne in 1349, and the death is again a mystery, brought about by 'trusting too much in treacherous promises'. The Earl had rewarded Fulk's loyalty with a knighthood some fourteen years before.)

Yet with the Scots driven out of Ireland, and the kingdom quieted, Edmund himself went over to England in 1320. Both he and his wife, and his heir James, had earlier taken a vow to go on pilgrimage to the shrine of Saint James at Compostela, but the whole family had then been absolved from this holy obligation 'on account of the [continuing] wars between the English and the Irish'.[21] As this particular pilgrimage was regarded as having been abandoned for purely political reasons, the Butlers' expenses for the holy undertaking – computed by the Treasury – were paid into the 'Holy Land Subsidy'.[22]

Another reason for the aborted journey, though, may have been the state of the first Earl's health. He was forced by ailments of one sort or another to remain in England for over a year, unable to go on pilgrimage for his soul's sake or to return to Ireland for more material reasons, and he died in London on 13 September 1321. By now, it was thought traditional for all the heads of the Butler lordship to be buried 'at home', and so his corpse was carried over into Ireland, where, on St Martin's Eve, he was interred at Gowran.

He had married Joanna, the daughter of the John FitzGerald who became the 1st Earl of Kildare, and by her he had two sons, James, who would inherit, and John (who died in 1336). His only daughter, Joanne, would innocently create new complications for the Butler family when she married the second son of the Roger de Mortimer who had been sent to Edmund's assistance against the Scots. Her husband, Edward, was the brother of Roger de Mortimer, the 1st Earl of March, the lover of King Edward II's Queen, who together would soon come to play a sinister role in English history, and a significant one in the career of Edmund's heir.

In 1321 the Escheators of the English in Ireland were ordered to take into the King's hands the late Edmund Butler's estates in Ireland. A year later, his young son, James, was sent to the King in England, under safe conduct, to be his ward.

By the time of James's birth, the Butler family had grown powerful enough to have their firstborn held as hostage to the King; and, at the age of 12, James was such a captive in Dublin Castle. But by the time he reached the age of 20, he had the protection of the King, since he was then about to join Edward II overseas. Throughout his minority the Butler lands had been under a renewed threat from the Irish of his region, with the armed force raised in his name suffering a memorable defeat from Brian O'Brien in 1322. A year later his guardian, Lord John Bermyngham, aided by the English of Ireland, marched a sizeable army into County Longford, against Donnell O'Farrell, where many of the English fell in battle.

In 1325 the O'Brien clan was fighting among themselves, on Butler territory, with the young Earl being powerless to act against them personally. But in that same year, although he was still technically under age, the King took his act of homage, which suggests that the youth was either very precocious or that the government was in a panic. James would appear to have been removed from his guardian Bermyngham's charge, either to release the new 'Earl of Louth' for wider service, or because James was thought to be ready for his adult responsibilities.

More than any of his co-equals, James received many gifts from Edward II in their short acquaintance. But the most remarkable favour the King granted him was to give him, despite his not having come legally into his inheritance, a licence to marry the woman of his choice, for the sum of 2,000 marks.

This must have been to reward him for the valiant work that he had already carried out in the King's name in Ireland, but it was even so a singular honour. It could not have pleased Edward, though, that James would then fix upon the King's own niece, Eleanor de Bohun, for his bride. However dominant his family in Ireland, James was no proper match for the eldest daughter of the seventh daughter of Edward I, even if that princess had herself married beneath her royal station. (Despite the fact that Eleanor's father, the Earl of Hereford, was one of the most eligible men of the time; then Constable of England, and among the richest grandees in the country.)

But the King, recognising James's extreme importance to his plans for Ireland, even though the youth was still relatively untried on the battle-field, gave his consent, and the young couple married in 1327. The King even persuaded the Earl of Hereford to grant them, as a wedding present, two manors and a bailiwick of the Forest of Hay in County Hereford. But when James was of age, or at least had livery of his lands, he would have to wait until the next reign for a writ in relation to the prisage of wines for all Ireland, in which James's rights were set out, 'and the dues thereon to be paid'.[23] He would then also be made Keeper of the King's Weirs at Limerick.

However, it may have been that King Edward's consent to James Butler's marriage with his cousin was never actually needed, as they were married in the same year that Edward was deposed. It may even have been that the King was coerced into agreeing to their union by the man who later deposed him, since that man, Roger de Mortimer, would have had a particular reason for such a marriage. Mortimer, a once-trusted favourite of King Edward II, and at one point his guardian, had for many years been his open enemy. Appointed to be the Lieutenant of the King, with all the royal castles in Wales entrusted to his keeping, he had ruled Wales like a monarch from 1307 to 1321; his love of regality had never left him, and now he was King of England in all but name. As such, he could easily have 'persuaded' the ineffectual Edward to consent to such a match, since it would have served his own purpose.

For Edward II had been in danger of losing the crown he so ineptly defended long before the time of James Butler's marriage, and by 1327 he was no longer in control. The Queen, who not only loathed the Despensers but also feared them, had gladly left the country on an embassy to her brother, the King of France, taking with her the heir to the throne, in order to escape their machinations. There, in the spring of 1325, she had met Roger Mortimer, newly escaped from the Tower of London, where he had been imprisoned for acting against the Despensers. A close connection had been formed between the outraged Queen and the abused courtier, and Mortimer quickly became her chief adviser.

When Isabella refused to return to England she had been outlawed by her husband, after which she and Mortimer plotted to overthrow the favourites from the safety of France. But as her brother refused to support her, the couple, by now lovers, left for the Low Countries in search of backing. There, once Mortimer had arranged for the Prince of Wales to be betrothed to Philippa of Hainault, men and money were provided, and a bold scheme planned for the invasion of her husband's realm.

In September 1326, a year before James Butler's marriage, an invading army led by Roger Mortimer and Isabella, the 'She-Wolf of France', had entered England. Putting out a proclamation against the Despensers, she had successfully routed the father at Bristol, putting him to death as a common felon on the town gallows, and when Hugh Despenser the younger also capitulated to her his head was sent to adorn London Bridge. King Edward II, who had retreated before her steady advance, was captured in a daring coup.

The chief men of the realm had soon deserted Edward, including his own brothers, and among them many Irish magnates; with England being made free of his cronies and his disastrous favourites, after which events moved fast. In January 1327 Edward II was constrained to abdicate in favour of his son, and the new king, Edward III, assumed the government by order of his mother in opposition to his father and was crowned at the expressed desire of a parliamentary council of England. But even though the deposed King was now their captive, his embittered wife and her insecure lover felt they could not allow him to live, and so he was murdered in Berkeley Castle.

After the Mortimer coup in England, when very few English nobles stood up for the humiliated King, political alignments in Ireland also became less clear cut, and the Butlers were among the many to be involved in further factions. James Butler, although his family would remain loyal to the Crown for most of their history, was in no wise different from his self-seeking equals, despite being married to the King's cousin-german. He, too, sought to establish his independence.

The proof of this is borne out by a meeting, held at Kilkenny in July 1326, at which James (still Earl of Carrick) was present, and at which the conspirators agreed to rise up against King Edward II, to assume control of Ireland. The most bizarre aspect of a badly laid plot was the decision to crown James Butler's relative, Maurice fitzThomas, as the de facto *King of Ireland*. FitzThomas was perhaps considered the most logical choice among other possible candidates since he was of royal blood himself, his father having also married a cousin of the King.

In reality, the plotters were determined to share Ireland among themselves, in direct proportion to the contribution that each man would make to the quest for conquest. This plotting was a straight response to events in England that were leading to the deposition of Edward II, and that their conspiracy came to nothing did not make the possibility die away.

Later plots to make fitzThomas King of Ireland occasionally surfaced in the next few years, and these involved powerful Gaelic as well as Anglo-Norman lords. There was even talk of restoring the old provincial kingdoms under a fitzThomas high-kingship, and with the years the fitzThomas dynasty would always incline more and more towards the beguiling Gaelic culture.

Whether or not the Butler family campaigned for Maurice fitzThomas's bid for the Irish crown, they definitely supported him throughout 1327, in his private wars against the powerful Arnold le Poer, who had gravely insulted him. And from the time that James officially came of age, he engaged with his Geraldine uncle, the Earl of Kildare, in his quarrels with the Burkes and Poers. Besides his keenness to fight off the Irish, James at once plunged into the brawls between the Anglo-Norman lords.

He certainly assisted Kildare against the Poers, driving their army – along with that of their allies the Burkes – into Connacht. The Viceroy tried to intervene but civil war followed, causing widespread devastation of lands and castles, and the government in Dublin was rendered powerless by this disorder. Poer was eventually forced to leave the country, but the tide of the fitzThomas fortunes also turned, and that of the Butler's along with it. So much so that James and his associates were forced to beg the King's council to travel to Kilkenny, where they had taken refuge in the castle, so that they could be cleared of plotting 'evil against the King's lands',[24] petitioning that they had only acted to 'avenge themselves on their enemies'.

Such an open declaration of the barons' right to conduct private warfare among themselves could never have been made in a period of strong rule, and the Irish nobles in general took every advantage of the chaos now rampant in England, both before and after the King's deposition. In 1328 fitzThomas – who had craved the King's pardon at Kilkenny – would again collect a strong army against Poer, who had returned with forces of his own, to mount a fresh challenge to his old enemy, and once again the country was in turmoil. At this time, too, the 'speckled disease', or the 'pied pox', raged throughout Ireland, and it 'took away persons both great and small'.[25]

1328 was another disastrous year for Ireland, and James's former guardian, John Bermyngham, Earl of Louth, 'the most vigorous, puissant, and hospitable of the English in Ireland',[26] was treacherously slain by his own people, the English of Oriel in another fierce quarrel between the Anglo-Norman lords. Killed with him were a great many 'worthy English and Irish men', among them 'as great a minstrel as the world has ever heard'.

A great army led by William Burke then turned into Butler lands, when – assisted by the O'Connors and O'Brien, the King of Munster – this army fought against one of James Butler's vassals, Brian Bane O'Brien. With no appreciable help, it seems, from his overlord, O'Brien defeated the invaders, with the loss of eighty people, 'chieftains and plebeians'. Within months though another war would be raised against O'Brien, although this was also defeated. The English, however, sustained a great defeat from a chieftain called MacGeoghenan. One hundred and forty men were slain in this contest, among them several distinguished knights.

But these grim events in Ireland led to James Butler being singularly rewarded by the new regime in England, when he was created the 1st Earl of Ormonde on 13 October 1328, a year after the murder of King Edward II. In November he had a grant made to him of 10*l* a year, the annual rent of the farm of the city of Waterford, to be held by him and his heirs as the *Lords of Ormonde*. Soon after, in consideration of his recent marriage into the King's family, he was pardoned of all the arrears in the fine of 2,000 marks, by which he had paid for the liberty of marrying as he pleased.

There can be little doubt that the earldom was really the gift of Roger Mortimer, who ruled England in the young King Edward III's name, and it may be that the regent Mortimer's particular interest in the Butler family lay in James's sister Joan, who had married his brother. But the preservation of the status quo in Ireland was also one of Mortimer's main concerns, for he had been in the country in 1308 fighting for his wife's magnificent inheritance; and for that of his own in Leix, which had come to him from his grandmother.

In the August following the creation of the earldom of Ormonde, the never-to-be–trusted fitzThomas was made the Earl of Desmond and received the County Palatinate of Kerry to support the honour. Throughout this uncertain period, it was clearly the policy of the rebel government in England to give earldoms to the more important leaders of the English colony in Ireland. The new regime needed all the allies it could recruit and both James Butler and fitzThomas were probably given their peerages to secure their compliance, if not their valuable services to the illegal Mortimer regency. The 15–year-old King Edward III was perhaps coerced into giving both titles, since although he was ruler in name his mother and her lover were rulers in fact. But the regent, ruthless and greedy, had quickly proved to be no better than the men he had driven from power, which meant that a new opposition to his regime was slowly building up, and he needed all the allies he could find. James's second earldom could well have been as much a bribe as an honour, for Mortimer needed strong men in Ireland.

When he came to reflect on it, however, the Ormonde earldom must have been as equally acceptable to Edward III, since he later renewed the grant, along with the regality and liberty of Tipperary, made in November 1328, although it appears to have been afterwards taken back into royal hands for a brief span of time, 'by virtue of a certain ordinance lately made by King and Council'.[27] This came shortly after the King had overthrown the 'regent' in the sequence of extraordinary events that followed soon after James had been ennobled.

In January 1329 Roger Mortimer had to put down a rebellion against his illegal government, which was led by the brother of King Edward II; and in March 1330 the new King's uncle was again caught plotting against the regime and was summarily executed. That this was done at the express command of Roger Mortimer was clear, and for the young and inexperienced Edward III it seems to have been the last outrage. In a carefully planned and daring coup at Nottingham castle, in October 1330, he brought about the arrest of his mother and her lover in a brilliantly realised seizure. Once taken up, Queen Isabella was placed in a comfortable captivity, while her lover was swiftly executed; and Edward III, now 18 years old, proclaimed that he had taken over the government.

As the sole royal power, he could have easily reversed the dubious honour granted to his cousin's husband, but he would seem to have quickly recognised Ormonde's worth to him. 'Now, at the petition of the Earl, and on account of his kinship with him, the King renews the grant as amply as before.'[28] In fact he not only formally renewed the honour but he also personally 'girded him with the sword', which was a singular recognition of his value.

Why the Butlers dropped the earlier title of Carrick, which had been truly royally invested, in favour of that of Ormonde is an interesting point. Ormonde is fourth in the rank of earls created in Ireland while Carrick actually comes second, after the first creation, the earldom of Ulster. So James Butler in point of fact chose to demote himself in the matter of precedence, in order to choose a more impressive name. It was, perhaps, because James had married a member of the royal family that 'Carrick' – as the name of a mere manor – was probably thought to be too modest, whereas 'Ormonde', as an extensive territory, had a more unmistakeable air of grandeur to it. As a title, it was on a par with the English 'shire' earldoms of Derby, Leicester or Worcester.

In fact the new Earl of Ormonde, as the husband of the King's cousin-german, procured still more considerable advantages; particularly with the grants of regalities and liberties of Tipperary, and the rights of a Palatinate in that county, even if the first grant was for life only. Whatever English titles his family possessed were as nothing compared to his earldom, for the grant of the Palatinate gave him almost royal powers, including the right to try all treasonous activities within the semi-regal territory, when the forfeitures of those condemned went to Ormonde, who could try all causes; except in four cases: namely arson, rape, forestall (a law applying to the King's hunting grounds), and treasure trove. This ruling was common to all the palatine counties of Ireland.

But within a year, Edward III would issue orders to seize all the palatinates back into his own hands, when the near royal status of their possessors became a cause of friction between the other great lords of the kingdom, and also the 'source of infinite mischiefs to the people'.[29] Then, perhaps in consideration of the new Earl's family connection to himself, King Edward decided to restore the palatinate of Tipperary to James, alone of all of them, which was done by letters patent. Initially this was again only a grant for life, but six years later the King would grant it in fee to each of James' heirs, making it hereditary.

The many natural disasters that affected Ireland in the Middle Ages could not halt the general bloodshed and only marriage could unite the warring clans, with the Burkes, FitzGeralds, Bermynghams, fitzThomases and Butlers being by this time all interrelated by marriage to dangerous degrees. This had come about partly because of their relative isolation and the smallness of their society, but also because the inordinate amount of baronial feuding that took place often made marriage a convenient device of reconciliation. Such tactical unions were the direct consequence of a way of life that was essentially the making of war at the behest of the King, although a side effect of this was that the warriors were also able to increase their own power and importance by making such marital partnerships.

Such inter-marriage was also, of course, a way of uniting the Anglo-Norman forces against the constant harrying of the Irish (whose own families were often as intricately linked in a solid network of matrimonial alliances). Certainly, without this kind of bonding between the great English families, a victory such as that of the MacCarthys over the FitzGeralds and the English of Munster in 1327, when many of their knights were slaughtered, would have been much worse. Had the FitzGeralds acted alone, their entire house could have been wiped out.

Yet despite these domestic affiliations, relationships between the Anglo-Norman families were never easy. In the early days of his lordship, James Butler, regardless of his family connections, seems to have been caught up in a destructive series of feuds with his peers, which were in many ways more unmanageable than his frequent affrays with the Irish. It was only after he had dealt successfully with the Burkes and the Poers, and when James had re-allied himself with the new Earl of Ulster (whose father had died in 1326), that he could turn his full attention to dealing with the Irish. And when, in 1330, the MacGeoghans again raised a disturbance in Meath, they were only routed in two savage engagements because Ulster and Ormonde acted together.

The 1st Earl of Ormonde, in fact, was forced to pursue a complicated factional course throughout the first years of his earldom; for it would appear that he was in some way still bound to the policies of fitzThomas, who was again creating havoc in Ireland. In 1330 the renegade Earl of Desmond had, for a change, been dutifully helping the Viceroy of Ireland in his battles against the clans of Leinster, when 10,000 men followed his standards, among them some of Ormonde's henchmen. But he had soon renewed his quarrel with James' recent ally, the Earl of Ulster, which placed Ormonde in a sensitive position; for with whom should he side? The problem was only resolved when the Justiciar shut up both Desmond and Ulster in prison.

However, Desmond, captured at Limerick, soon escaped, and was at liberty long enough to resist the next Viceroy, Anthony de Lucy. He refused to attend the Dublin parliament of 1331, although he appeared before it after it had been transferred to Kilkenny, where he swore an oath of faithfulness and was pardoned. The English government, distrusting him with good reason, seized him once more at Limerick in August, and shut him up in Dublin Castle. But after eighteen months' imprisonment, fitzThomas was liberated after the Three Estates had petitioned for his release, and when the greatest lords in Ireland (among them, Ormonde) bound themselves under heavy penalties to be sureties for his continued good behaviour.

FitzThomas swore before the high altar of Christ Church, Dublin that he would attend the next parliament and be faithful to the King. In that same year, 1333, he broke his leg by a fall from his horse, which curtailed his activities considerably, and perhaps kept him more trustworthy than would have been the case had he been in full health. In 1335 he would serve under a new Viceroy, d'Arcy, in an expedition of Edward III's against the Scots.

But the year 1333 had marked another grave blow for the English in Ireland (and for the Butlers in particular), when the 'brown' Earl of Ulster was murdered in the course of a family feud. Since he had no male heir, the title to his wide possessions passed to an infant daughter, and this left the earldom of Ulster leaderless against the northern Irish. Their great hour would come in the time of the next Earl of Ormonde, but their resurgence began with the death of James Butler's closest ally.

The Gaelic order in fact was making a spectacular recovery, for almost the whole of the west of Ireland had been won back to their speech and ways; and even in the midlands, despite the best efforts of such families as the Ormondes, the Gaelic tide was on the turn. The O'Kennedys of North Ormond went on to have notable successes against the English within the Butler boundaries.

Outsiders, too, moved into their territory, when a great army, composed of both English and Irish combatants, was led by the Connacians into Munster in 1334. A party of this army burned a church, in which 180 people had taken refuge, among them two priests, and none of which escaped the conflagration. James Butler took men in pursuit of these arsonists, but there is nothing known about the outcome. In 1335 the Earl would conduct a successful campaign against the O'Byrnes in County Wexford, and the following year would see him in action against the O'Mordhas of Leix, whose chieftain had succeeded in rallying considerable forces of the Gaelic Irish of Munster and Leinster to his support. But the last years of James's life were relatively peaceful, and his relationships with his Irish tenants were undeniably more settled than were those of his peers.

An agreement 'concerning all preys, homicides and other transgressions', made between the Earl and the O'Kennedy's may be typical of others that he had made with different vassals. In this one, 'made on either side up to the present', the Earl granted to O'Kennedy, 'and those of his nation', a sizeable amount of land, for which they would pay rent annually to his exchequer. He also granted that 'the said Irish' should make no suit at assize or county court, but that they should petition and appeal at the court of Nenagh, 'during the four years until they shall have come to make complete peace with the men of the Marches'.[30] A steward, acceptable to both parties, should attend the court 'as often as is necessary'.

If it was found 'by inquisition' that any of O'Kennedy's men had 'done damage' to the Earl or his 'betaghs'[31] they would atone twofold, with Ormonde to have half the fine and the wronged person the other. Equal justice was to be done to the injured Irish on the part of the English. But if O'Kennedy himself was found 'by inquisition' to have harmed the Earl or his people, he would atone threefold, with again half to the lord, and half to the injured English, 'as above'.

O'Kennedy could not be arrested in person for any damage carried out by his men, but the Earl's sergeant would levy a fine upon him, unless 'before the Lord's departure' he had given his word on oath to make atonement. (Ormonde was clearly envisioning a period of time to be spent out of Ireland at this juncture, which may have prompted the writing of the agreement.) Further, O'Kennedy was pledged to serve the Earl in his army, 'as he was wont to do to him and his ancestors, and to make war upon such English or Irish as shall rise against the Lord'. Similarly it was agreed that if any of the Earl of Ormonde's men, whether English or Irish, slew O'Kennedy, or any of his men 'by treachery', the body of the traitor was to be handed over in place of the body of the slain, 'if he can be found'. Compensation was to be levied and paid to the kindred of the slaughtered man, and the killer was to 'have no peace from the Lord forever, without the consent of O'Kennedy and his kin'.[32]

> ...For the full observance of all the above, the Earl and O'Kennedy, each for himself and his men, have found pledges, namely the Archbishop of Cashel, etc., who shall make war upon O'Kennedy or his men if they violate these terms. Further the Lord grants to O'Kennedy and his brothers, as far as he is concerned, all the lands from Belacharri to the [river] Shannon. Paying therefore to the lords of those lands as much rent as three on the side of the English and three to the side of O'Kennedy as agreed upon.[33]

The agreement was signed at Nenagh on 5 March 1336, and in it James refers to his 'land in Ormond, among the Irish'. (Which suggests that he early recognised his vulnerability, for the land given to the Kennedys was uncomfortably close to Nenagh, which was still a base for the Butler family.) In a later indenture, James is not called O'Kennedy's 'lord', and the lands granted are the Irishman's own, as formerly held by him, but now ratified by the Earl.

The military services rendered in return for grants of lands to the 'Irish nations' were of such frequency, and were so standardised in their form, that they could only have been renewals of a relationship that was already well established. The agreements were always solemn oaths, sworn on gospel books and saints' relics; they even carried the sanction of excommunication for any violation of them. In addition to these sacred oaths, of course, those who signed were also required to give up their son, or sons, as hostages to their word, and this particular enforcing of an agreement was a common feature (and a very Irish solution). 'He is no King,' as one law text had it, 'who has not hostages in fetters'.[34] But a ruler's status was higher, or so the poets thought, if he had no need to take hostages at all, for this shows how truly dreaded he was. For the ordinary run of chiefs, and for Anglo-Irish barons, the taking of hostages was a sure way of ensuring that the agreements would be honoured.

In 1336 James founded the friary of the Minorites at Little Carrick in Waterford, where John Clyn, the originator of the *Annals of Ireland*, would be its first guardian. In that same year he also founded a Franciscan monastery at Carrick-on-Suir, where his father had built a castle in 1309. In the next century the Butlers would go on to largely create the town of Carrick, the sleepy heart of which today remains much as it was. In the next century it would be a strategic site, commanding access west to Clonmel, and south-east to Waterford.

Throughout the rest of his life, James would continue to hold the prisage of wines, and he remained in charge of the King's fisheries in Ireland, 'at the customary rent'. But in July 1338 the prisage would be granted to the King's Clerk, as a reward 'for good service in Ireland', since the prises of wines were then in the King's hands, as the 1st Earl of Ormonde was now dead. The King's Clerk was only to hold them until the heir's lawful age, and he was to be held accountable to the Exchequer at Dublin during this time. The royal widow was also to be safeguarded. On 12 June 1338 King Edward declared to all his bailiffs and lieges in Ireland:

> Know that we have taken into our protection our dear cousin Eleanor, formerly wife of James le Botiller, late Earl of Ormonde, and all her men, lands, rents and possessions. And so we command that ye maintain and protect and defend the same Countess and her men, etc., not inflicting upon her or permitting to be inflicted any injury, wrong, loss, grievance, and if any wrong should have been done to them ye shall without delay have it amended. We also forbid that anything be taken from the corn, hay, horses, carts, wagons, victuals, or any goods or chattels of the same Countess, against her will, or [of] that of her men and sergeants in the said lands of Ireland.[35]

Four years later King Edward III would grant to his kinswoman the wardship of land near Naas, to be held for her son, and a year after that she would be given the keeping of two castles (including that of Nenagh), and three manors in Munster, to hold for him. Later, manors and lands in Leinster would also be put under her control. Once again the heir to the Butler possessions was a minor and the immediate future would be particularly hazardous for him, since the first James left only one son, and a daughter, Petronella. She would later marry Gilbert, Lord Talbot, which would bring her into the mainstream of the English nobility, but also create a new range of problems for her brother, the 2nd Earl of Ormonde.

From the later years of the reign of Edward I onwards the emerging importance of the Butler family had become evident. In the previous century, unlike other Anglo-Irish dynasties, they had shown no signs of dying out, even though minors were a constant in the family succession. All five Theobalds had been the eldest sons of eldest sons. Edmund had been the only break in this tradition, and yet with him the family began to strike a deeper root. The grant of the first and second earldoms, together with the large grants of palatine power, and the hereditary prisage of wines, would establish them completely in the next generation.

Up to the reign of Edward III, their power had been mainly in Tipperary. Here, their English rivals, and Irish chieftains such as O'Kennedy, often caused their territory to recede to the southern half of that county, but their overall claim to the lordship of Tipperary would never be renounced. In County Kilkenny they had held at first little more than the manor of Gowran, while in Carlow and Wicklow their fiefs were widely separated from each other, but within a century they had expanded their holdings enormously. The next event of real importance would be the acquisition of Kilkenny Castle and the rich lands that went with it; and this splendid acquisition would be brought off by the next earl, who would be called the 'Noble Earl', in deference to his royal descent.

## Notes

1. Curtis, *Calendar of Ormonde Deeds*.
2. Ibid.
3. Ibid.
4. Ibid.
5. Ibid.
6. The Four Masters, *Annals of the Kingdom of Ireland*.
7. Ibid.
8. Curtis, op. cit.
9. Carte, *Life of the Duke of Ormonde*.
10. Curtis, op. cit.
11. John Barbour (1320–95). One must allow for poetic license in his account.
12. The Four Masters, op. cit.
13. Some Irish chieftains would retain such men until as late as the 16th century.
14. Curtis, op. cit.
15. Carte, op. cit.
16. E. Curtis, *History of Medieval Ireland*.
17. Ibid.
18. Curtis, op. cit.
19. Ibid.
20. Ibid.
21. Carte, op. cit.
22. The Holy Land Subsidy was a fund created for the furtherance of a new Crusade.
23. Curtis, op. cit.
24. Carte, op. cit.
25. The Four Masters, op. cit.

26. Ibid.
27. Curtis, op. cit.
28. Ibid.
29. Carte, op. cit.
30. Curtis, p. cit.
31. 'Betaghs'; possibly from the Gaelic *beathach*, meaning 'beasts'?
32. Curtis, op. cit.
33. Ibid.
34. The Four Masters, op. cit.
35. Curtis, op. cit.

# CHAPTER IV

# *The Noble Earl*

The 2nd Earl of Ormonde, born at Kilkenny on 4 October 1331, was 7 years old at his father's death, and he appears never to have been known by his father's title of Earl of Carrick. In 1338 the 'Escheators of the lands on both sides of the Trent' were given orders touching the estates in England of the late Earl of Ormonde, which were to be returned to the Exchequer. Both the 1st Earl's lands and the office of butler were back in the King's hands 'due to the minority of the son and heir of James le Botiller', and they were to be held until 'the lawful age of the heir'.[1] (Which does show that the office of butler was by then seen as an inheritable one.)

The older part of the estate the adolescent Earl was due to inherit was somewhat depleted. An inquisition held in 1337, on the death of the 1st Earl of Ormonde, shows how the English were losing ground in the county of Ormond itself, which had been widely enfeoffed early in the Conquest. At Nenagh the land surrounding the five-towered castle was let out to farmers, but the Irish had thrown off the Butler yoke in the northern parts of the county and the petty towns were already starting to decay. Less money was now being sent to the lord, 'and nothing in time of war'[2] (an almost perpetual state of affairs), because of the growing strength of the Irish, and their intimidation of the tenants.

For a century and a half the O'Kennedy clan had been fairly quiescent under their guarantees with the Butlers, and this would continue until as late as 1336. But eleven years later their chief would feel assertive enough to raid Ormond and drive out the English settlers from the lands around Nenagh, and even to burn the town. Butler control of it seemed threatened, although the 2nd Earl would not lose Nenagh for good until his 36 year, and then only because he was to choose another site as his base.

The Ormondes were, of course, still possessed of more land than most of their fellow magnates. As we have seen, Eleanor, Countess of Ormonde, was given the wardship of the small garrison town of Naas in County Kildare, to be held for her son. A year later, she would receive the keeping of the castles of Nenagh and Moialuy, and three manors in Munster were also to be held for young James. To these were added the keeping of all castles, manors and lands in Leinster alone, and simply by evaluating the

75

property held by the dowager countess (a fraction of the entirety), it can be seen how extensive were the increasing grants of land to the family at this period.

But others would also be given control of the heir's considerable estates, and the boy would become the ward of two powerful men in turn. For a payment of 2,300 marks to the Crown, the Earl of Desmond, a relative, was awarded command of all the Ormonde castles in Ireland.

> To hold with reversions, liberties, franchises and all other profits of old belonging thereto, until the lawful age of James. With marriage of the heir, and forfeiture if the heir refuse to marry. Notwithstanding any commissions of the said wardship of marriage to Eleanor, late the wife of the said Earl, which the King hereby revokes, and so from heir to heir.[3]

The wardship was granted at an unusually late date to Desmond, nearly seven years after the death of James's father, and it is possible that the young Earl was left to the care of his mother during that interval. He was taken from her at the time of her second marriage to Sir Thomas Dagworth, after which the boy was placed in the care of Sir John d'Arcy, which suggests that the King was unhappy with Desmond's running of the Ormonde estates during his guardianship. D'Arcy was an altogether different proposition, a totally reliable servant of the Crown. He had served in Scotland under King Edward I, and had been the Sheriff of three English counties before being appointed Lord Justice of Ireland (which, in 1341, would be granted to him for life). He was also a Steward of the King's Household and held the grant of Constable of the Tower of London. His own lands lay chiefly in England, and he was generally styled Lord Darcy of Knaith, to distinguish him from an older branch of his house.

The second guardian appears to have taken great care with his new stepson's property, but it would seem that others – mainly the higher servants – had mismanaged the inheritance. In 1338, a year after the 1st Earl's death, his chief steward Fulk de la Freigne was suddenly arrested and imprisoned, along with his son Oliver, in Kilkenny Castle; and this action was taken by Eustace de la Poer, the Seneschal of Kilkenny. The exact nature of their crime is unknown, although perhaps is not hard to guess at when one remembers the authority they possessed as administrators of the estates. Both father and son escaped from prison on this occasion and 'lived to fight another day'; and that day was not far distant, since a fierce war broke out in Meath less than a year later, between the Irish and the English.

The next four years would be relatively uneventful for the Butler family, or indeed the Norman lords generally, for the wars that were fought spasmodically on their borders were usually between the Irish themselves. As often as not these were brought about by the system of inheritance peculiar to the Irish, when the beneficiaries had to literally fight for their legacies. An extreme example of this occurring when the Lord of Thomond died in 1343 and the lordship was assumed briefly by a challenger to his title. This man was only banished after some strenuous fighting, with the rightful lord, Brian O'Brien, being recognised by the chieftains of Thomond, who afterwards submitted to him.

Fulk de la Freigne, long-established as a steward to the Butler family, was made Seneschal of Kilkenny in 1344, despite the scandal of his previous imprisonment, and he remained in that position for a number of years. But even as Seneschal, he remained the Butler's most valuable servant, and in 1348, while the Earl of Ormonde was in England, he would have complete charge of his lands, having apparently completely re-established himself in their favour. (It is possible that his previous confinement had been due only to Poer's personal animosity towards him.) It would appear, in fact, that the affairs of the Ormondes were managed so well by Freigne during his time in full control, the family could still wage war successfully during the Earl's absence.

For the campaigning never ceased. In 1346 the Ormondes successfully attacked the O'Carrolls, the O'Mores, 'and those Anglo-Irish of Ely O'Carroll who supported them'.[4] Nenagh, which had been captured by the Irish, was retaken from them, and a stronger guard was put into the town. The English settlers were restored to their homes and lands, and the Gaelic Irish of the district were reduced to their former obedience, 'which everyone had thought impossible'. (Fulk de la Freigne even forced the Irish to rebuild the town walls they had destroyed; and, by the payment of cows and hostages, to buy themselves back into their 'former state of docility'.) The Irish would later have their revenge.

An ill-devised plan of King Edward III's Viceroy in Ireland, to replace all the old Anglo-Norman settlers with men born in England as ministers in the Irish parliament, produced an instinctive and terrible dissension between the two groups. Of the many magnates to rebel against this imposition, the most important was Maurice FitzGerald, who took the lead in the struggle. (FitzGerald was also a stepson of Sir John d'Arcy, James Butler's guardian.) He refused to attend the parliament of October 1341 at Dublin, and to further protest against the plan he collected a great gathering of the nobles and townsfolk of English blood at Kilkenny. This assembly sent a long complaint to the King against the policy of his viceroy, and they denounced the incompetence and greed of the 'needy men sent from England without knowledge of Ireland'.[5] But the Justiciar, Ralph d'Ufford, persevered in his policy.

When the Earl of Kildare again absented himself, in protest, from the parliament of 1345, Ufford treated his nonappearance as a declaration of war. He invaded the rebel peer's territories and captured two of his castles, where he promptly hanged the leaders of the garrison. He then sent a young knight to the Earl with two writs, one of which summoned Kildare on an expedition into Munster, the other being a secret warrant for his arrest. The inexperienced knight, afraid to seize such a powerful man on his own ground, enticed him to Dublin (where he was arrested while sitting in Council at the Exchequer). The grandees who had previously acted as sureties for the fealty of Kildare in 1343 were ruined by Ufford's insistence upon their forfeiture when the Earl reneged on his oath and, as a result of the Justiciar's resolute action, many other nobles abandoned fitzThomas in alarm. When captured, fitzThomas was imprisoned and stripped of his estates.

Ufford died in office, on Palm Sunday 1346, but fitzThomas only benefitted from his death by being given a respite and a safe-conduct, and he was only restored to King Edward's favour when he went to fight alongside him at the Siege of Calais in 1347. But his pre-eminence was never in question; he was the foremost Irish noble of his time, and he always acted as the spokesman for the Anglo-Irish party, which aspired to practical independence. He felt himself Irish enough, and strong enough, to take for his third wife the daughter of the Prince of Thomond. His son Gerald would later marry into the Butler family, with the two bloodlines, already intermixed, being further interwoven. But this last marriage would be a blatantly political alliance between two equal houses; and it is one that reveals the almost princely state these Irish families now kept.

During the last years of the minority of the 2nd Earl, life continued as normally as it could for the Butlers. But their domestic arrangements were by no means untroubled, with many of the problems stemming from a long-running quarrel with the Church; the 1st Earl's decision to construct a monastery in honour of his wife, the Lady Eleanor, being the prime cause. This project had been abandoned only because James Butler had died before the building could be completed and before he could obtain permission from the Apostolic See. All attempts by the family thereafter to obtain a licence and finish the building resulted in a series of humiliating setbacks for them. As it had been agreed the Friars Minor of Ireland could take up residence in this monastery, once it was finished, the family was at odds with both the ecclesiastical and secular powers over its construction. Their failure to complete this prestigious project affected the Ormondes in two ways, since not only did they wish to appear as pious as their rivals, but the donation of a religious house was one of the most powerful *political* statements an aristocrat could make at that period.

Such ambivalent thinking is foreign to us now, but other attitudes of the time are similarly strange to us, and much of what constituted conventional life then seems abnormal to our modern sensitivities. This is particularly true when it comes to the question of marriage, for the marital contracts between most noble families of the age approached a near-incestuous nature, but had become almost commonplace by this period. Young James Butler's marriage to Elizabeth d'Arcy in 1346 was certainly in this category of extreme interrelation, requiring a papal dispensation at the King's request, since the bride and groom were related in the fourth degree of kindred.

Then, too, it was widely accepted that both males and females could be married long before they had reached an age that we would recognise as mature. The second James Butler was certainly not an adult when he took a wife, for in that same year a grant was made to the bride's father, John d'Arcy, of the wardship of *all* Ormonde lands in Ireland. 'To hold until the lawful age of the heir, rendering yearly at the Exchequer of Dublin'.[6] At the same time 1,000 marks were awarded to D'Arcy by the Crown 'for good and long service, which he will pay at the Exchequer Michaelmas next, following by equal portions of the marriage of James, son and heir, a minor in the King's ward'.[7] D'Arcy, it would seem, was being rewarded both for his services to the Crown, but also for marrying his daughter into a powerful family.

And once again a guardian appeared to have taken advantage of his unique position to acquire a rich and powerful son-in-law while being in charge of his ward's fortune. But James Butler was less vulnerable than most, being almost of age when he married, and certainly old enough to withstand any undue pressure. Besides which, D'Arcy would have only temporary control of the Ormonde properties, for it was little more than a year later, on 24 February 1347, that the letters patent acknowledging James as the rightful earl were published.

> ...Edward, King of England, etc., to whom all these presents shall come, greeting. Whereas we have of late our special grace taken to fealty of our dear cousin, James le Botiller, son and heir of James, late Earl of Ormonde, defunct, who held of us *in capite* for all lands and tenements which the same Earl his father held of us in chief, and have rendered and ordered the same to be delivered to him, notwithstanding that the same James, son of James, is under age, even as we are given to understand from the Rolls of our Chancery, we wish that the said James, son of James, shall have all the aforesaid lands and tenements, with all other things belonging partly to his heritage, together with the office of Butler in the Land of Ireland. And thus, by these presents, we make known to all concerned. *Teste* Lionel, our dear son, Guardian of England.[8]

James Butler's father-in-law, also known as 'Le Pierre', presumably because of his stone-like disposition or obdurate expression, came of a modest Lincolnshire family that had gained some prominence in the service of the Earl of Pembroke. He had long served King Edward III in a menial position, holding a number of indifferent posts under the Crown until being elevated to the Justiciarship of Ireland. But by marrying James into his family D'Arcy knew that he was strengthening his own prestige, since James, as a blood cousin of the King, would immeasurably enhance his status in Irish society.

Natural catastrophes rather than human strife created most wretchedness in 1349 when a great plague raged throughout Ireland and thousands fell victim to the strain. But as the Gaelic order was making something of a recovery, they also added to the general misery for the English; and here, the most notable Irish successes were won by the O'Mores of Laois, the O'Connors of Ely, and the O'Kennedys of North Ormond. But by 1351 the Irish were once again playing into the hands of their enemies, bringing about their own ruin by their own actions. The grandson of Brian O'Brien, who could be called a hereditary enemy of the Butlers, was 'treacherously slain' while one of his kinsman killed sixteen of the Clan Keogh in revenge, 'despoiling them of their lands and cattle'. Life returned to normal for the Irish feuding families, and any advances made by their earlier successes were swept aside by their inability to remain unaligned.

Ironically, being Keeper of the Peace (*Custos Pacis*) – an impossible task – was the most characteristic Anglo-Irish office of this period; an almost routine duty for earls, magnates, seneschals and the higher gentry, and James Butler would soon be asked to perform this function. In England, the role of such men had already evolved into that of a primarily judicial one, but in Ireland – inevitably, in view of the volatile nature of the people – the essentially militaristic aspect of the 'keeper's' function persisted. They assessed arms, mustered local levies, acted as commanders in the field during the incessant border warfare, and attempted to negotiate ineffective truces. The Ordinance of Kilkenny, drawn up in 1351, made it obligatory for every Irish county to have four keepers, drawn from 'the most substantial of the county', and it clearly defined their duties. Quite simply, the very survival of the colony depended upon their individual abilities.

King Edward III was anxious for the 2nd Earl of Ormonde to assume his obligations, even before coming into his majority, as is shown by an extract from the King's 'letters patent' of 6 July 1351:

...Edward, King of England, etc., to Thomas fitzMaurice, Earl of Desmond, greeting. Whereas of late we, for the good service done to us and to our father, Edward, late King of England, by James le Botiller, now defunct, whom we created Earl of Ormonde, and for the better maintenance of his state of honour as Earl gave and granted him for the whole of his life the regularity and other liberties with knights' fees and all other things whatsoever which we had in Country Tipperary. (Four pleas alone excepted, etc.) We, wishing that our dear cousin and liege, James, son and heir of the said Earl, may becomingly hold the name and honour of Earl of the said place, by our special grace we have given and granted to the said Earl, etc., the said regularities and liberties, etc., saving the four pleas mentioned above. To have and to hold for the remainder of his life, in the same manner as his father, late Earl, held by the same virtue of our grant thereof by our letters patent to him make. We therefore command you to be intendent and respondent to the said Earl of Ormonde in those things which concern you by reason of the regularity, knights' fees and other liberties now granted to him, according to the tenour of these our letters patent.[9]

Although not yet 21, the young earl apparently took his duties seriously, and he began by giving grants of lands to those he wished to draw to his side, among them two lordships and their appurtenances to Adam fitzPeter and the 'heirs male of his body, lawfully begotten'. Further grants were given to his own relatives, chiefly to his cousin Thomas, the son of his father's brother. It was essential that James, not yet fully in control of his inheritance, should surround himself with men on whom he could rely. At his age it is doubtful that he had much experience of field warfare, but he must already have been familiar with local skirmishes. He may even have taken part in a fierce encounter of 1351, when the O'Mores defeated the English of Dublin and 240 combatants were killed in the skirmish.

The warfare of two centuries had shown that the rights of the Irish chieftains could not be completely extinguished, and so the great Norman lords had begun to enter into elaborate treaties with them. The Irish leaders for their part – once it had been formally admitted that they were 'free of blood', and equal in noble status to the 'foreigners of Erin' – did not refuse to make bargains in which they admitted to the overlordship of the 'nobler of these foreigners'.[10] Absorbing this lesson early, the new Earl of Ormonde at once proved that he was particularly adept at treating with the Irish, acting towards them in ways that were wise beyond his years. (Either that or he was extremely well advised, and absorbed the counsel attentively.) This is most clearly shown by a treaty made in March 1354 between himself and an Irish chieftain, when he was barely into his maturity. Apart from being an extremely resourceful agreement, it is strangely modern in its legal terminology.

This indenture made between James le Botiller, Earl of Ormonde of the one part and Alan O'Maghra of the other. Witness that the Earl has granted to Alan 'Les Rathyns' in Clandonoal for the term of 16 years, beginning at Christmas in the 28th of Edward III of England, to the end of 16 years fully completed. Rendering in the first year 40s of silver, half at the feast of St John the Baptist [24 June], and the other at Christmas next following. And in the second year, four marks of silver; and in the fourth year six marks of silver; and afterwards the said Alan will pay yearly to the Earl or his heirs and assigns six marks per annum to the end of the term. Moreover, Alan shall reply to all the duties touching the said Earl. To have and to hold for the said term as long as he shall faithfully bear himself to the Earl and his liegemen. To which agreement the earl and Alan have set their seals alternatively. Given at Nenagh.[11]

A similar treaty made at Nenagh bound one Donough MacNamara to serve the Earl and his heirs 'in all his affairs with all his power, against all whomsoever for the life of the said *donatus*. At his own cost in his marches, where he can return [within a few hours], and elsewhere in Ireland at the Earl's cost'. In return for this, MacNamara was to receive his father's lands in Thomond, then held by the Earl, in lease. 'Rendering and doing therefore yearly whatever four lawful men [lawyers], two named from each side, elected *ad hoc*, shall ordain'.[12]

Another agreement for 'retinue and military service' was made at Clonmel, between James and one Oliver Howell. In it, Howell agreed to serve the Earl 'for all of Oliver's life, with all his power' and this service was to be rendered both in war or peace. Howell was to mainly discharge his duties within County Kilkenny, 'and the marches of the same wherever they lie', but he was also to make himself available for action elsewhere throughout the whole of Ireland. He was to bring as his contribution to the Earl's forces: four men-at-arms with horses fitted out, twelve hobellers and forty able footmen and kernes when 'reasonably summoned', and he was to be prepared to strike against all, save the King and his heirs, *and the Earl of Desmond*. As with his other dependants, all costs were to be borne by Ormonde, unless Howell was in a position to return to his home easily, and he would receive payment for his retinue of 100 marks of silver. 'Ten marks payable at once, and at Michaelmas next following six marks, and at Easter next six marks, and so from year to year at the same term six marks, until the whole 100 marks is paid'.[13]

If the Earl failed in his payment, 'the said Oliver' had the right to quit his service 'according to the terms, until he shall be satisfied in the matter'. But Howell, in turn, granted that he and his heirs would restore to the Earl all his losses if he failed in his service. It was also allowed that Howell would receive military arms from Ormonde 'for certain other lords, when they shall be prepared', which indicates that Howell was expected to recruit other men for the Earl's cause.

But perhaps the most important of all the treaties made between the Earl and his Irish dependants was the contract he entered into with Rory O'Kennedy, the 'chief of his nation [in Ormond]'. The indenture was made on 16 May 1357 at Cashel, when they met together 'wholly and unanimously' to agree a peace pact between them as the Earl set out for England.

All offences done to Ormonde in his absence were to be 'amended' by O'Kennedy and his men; and eight men, four to be chosen from each side, were to decide on the restitution. If the eight could not agree in all things, they were to choose 'by their common assent' another competent person, and the judgement by five each of the two parties would be bound. For whatever trespasses had taken place between Rory O' Kennedy and his men on the one side and the common (English) people on the other, satisfactory pledges were to be delivered into the Earl's hands. Moreover, O'Kennedy was bound, according to the 'form of peace made between them, to be obedient and respondent to the Earl.'[14] If any of his people infringed the 'said peace' in any way, O' Kennedy was to restrain and punish the transgressors according to the counsel of the Earl. The Earl and his men were also bound to assist O'Kennedy in the punishment and restraint of the wrongdoers, but their transgressions were not to be charged against O' Kennedy if it happened that he was unable to punish them. Otherwise he was bound to be faithful 'according to the effect and force of former indentures and tenour of this indenture'.

Ormonde himself was bound, as he was O'Kennedy's overlord, to go to his aid 'for the sake of justice' against all that opposed the Irishman 'in matters of peace'. In return, O'Kennedy, 'now and forever' firmly pledged on the Gospels to do all that was contained in the indentures, and this oath was very solemnly made in the presence of the Archbishop of Cashel, the Bishop of Killaloe and many great men of the land.

Significantly the Earl also promised that whenever O'Kennedy came to him (for whatever reason), he 'would not make him his captive' – that is, act treacherously towards him, a common practice of the English – and this promise also applied to the Irishman's sons and followers. As with every other dependant, O'Kennedy swore to serve the Earl 'all his life, in all matters, against all whosoever', and the customary arrangements were made about payment; at O'Kennedy's own cost in the marches of Ormond and Ely, and elsewhere at the Earl's expense. In return for which, he was given land, on which he would pay no rent. Other land was his on similar terms, but for which he would pay 'what four lawful men of the Earl's lordship of Ormond, according to their valuation, think the said lands ought to pay or can pay yearly'.[15]

But not only the Irish promised to serve him 'in peace and war'. An indenture made between Ormonde and his kinsman Sir Richard de Burgh follows much the same lines, with Richard meeting his own costs if he could return to his own estate within that day, and the Earl meeting the outlay if he could not. In this instance, Ormonde paid out 100*l* in silver for Sir Richard's loyalty, 10*l* payable within a month and 10*l* payable at the next Easter, with payments thereafter of 20*l* per annum, at Michaelmas and Easter, until the whole sum was paid. Ormonde himself promised to aid, protect and maintain Richard in all his just quarrels, 'as a lord ought to maintain his knight or vassal, as long as Richard shall keep the peace and fealty to the Earl'.[16] Any of Richard's horses killed in the Earl's service would be replaced. At Carrickfergus, the Earl agreed that another kinsman, Geoffrey le Poer, should make his retinue on the same terms.

From the wording of these sealed agreements, it is clear there was a difference between the agreements made between the Earl's Irish and his Anglo-Irish dependants, with the latter being granted much more pronounced favours than the former in return for their loyalty. But perhaps the strangest indenture of all was that made between the Earl and Geoffrey Roth Purcell and one O'Kathyll, in August 1356. For in it the two men subjected themselves to his lordship only 'until the coming of a certain true heir of the Purcells', another lord, but of *Irish* extraction; and until this event they would only be bound to the Earl for the lands they held 'at the time'. This, more than any other such deed, reveals the essential fluidity of such arrangements.

In it Ormonde agreed to 'correct all the defects between them in his own parts, regarding all the trespasses done to him' since it appears they had previously been in contention. Furthermore, the two men would not be accused or 'disquieted', or 'held to answer for trespasses of any of the name or nation dwelling within "Les Purcells",[17] or any subject of their own adjacent'. The Earl also pardoned them of all their trespasses against him; for which pardon they paid him fourteen cows, 'eight at once, and six at Michaelmas next'.

The Earl of Ormonde was not, of course, only duty bound to provide men and arms for the King, for in his case there was always the ongoing matter of customs duties to be levied. Edward III wrote to the Justiciar of Ireland in December 1355 expressing his concern over the report that both Irish, as well as English merchants, were refusing to pay 'our right prise of wine due to us, as the merchants of England pay it'.[18] The King wished that all matters concerning custom duties on wine should be dealt with in Ireland 'by our Butler there, or by his deputy, and answered for', since he wanted his faithful subjects in Ireland to be treated according to the laws and customs of England.

He commanded that this should be carried out, with Ormonde given new powers if necessary. 'That ye permit the right prise of wines there, now and in the future, both of tuns and pipes, according to the rate of tuns, to be taken by our Butler or his deputy, compelling merchants and others who refuse the prise to payment thereof.'[19]

This command refers not only to the Butler prise of wine, but also to the much more complicated 'royal' prise of wine, which had been settled by the merchants of the 'Nova Custuma' in 1303 at a rate of two shillings per tun. Fifty years later the wine merchants preferred to give the monarch one tun from a small cargo and two tuns from a large one (of twenty tuns or over).

It was also during this time that English inquest and jury procedures were adopted in Ireland as the King had requested. In a compact of 1356, for example, provision was made for a panel of four men, two drawn from each 'nation', to settle responsibility for offences against the Earl of Ormonde; and should a casting vote be needed, a person acceptable to *both* sides was to be chosen. This was only one of the many legalities brought into the country from England; and while the English legal system might have seemed to the Irish to be in many ways superior to their ancient Brehon law, there were singular differences that would have struck them as astonishing.

Not least the fact that, for the payment of a fee, a man could be *pardoned* of all felonies (save arson, rape, forestall and treasure-trove), by an over-lord such as the Earl of Ormonde or his equal. One could rob a church or commit a murder and be pardoned for it; or even be acquitted of a robbery and murder together; and such 'penances' were, in fact, often enacted at various courts throughout Tipperary. In one extraordinary case, the theft of four horses, 100 farm beasts, 1,000 sheep, 100 pigs 'and other goods', was pardoned for a payment of 20 shillings.[20] Even Ormonde's own relatives paid fines to the 'Lord Earl' for peace.

The death of Maurice fitzThomas in 1356, followed soon after by the death of his eldest son, produced great disturbances in Munster. This was because the remaining heirs were two brothers, the eldest of whom was mentally retarded; a condition that could not be tolerated in a society where the wholeness of a man's wits was essential to the well being of his dependants. There was a strong movement among the late Earl of Kildare's followers to set aside the idiot Nicholas in favour of his more competent younger brother Gerald; and to appease the disputants King Edward III granted the younger son the lands of his brother. He also granted Gerald custody of the rightful heir, although he could not pass on his title, which came to the inadequate Nicholas by right of primogeniture. But this singular grant was made even more surprising by its being conditional upon Gerald marrying Eleanor, the daughter of the Earl of Ormonde, who was then Justiciar of Ireland. The girl herself was still an infant, but in this way the King made sure that one of his most dependable servants, Ormonde, was allied to perhaps the most rebellious Anglo-Irish family in the country.

In March 1357 the Earl of Ormonde made Thomas Talbot constable of his castle of Arklow, for the term of twelve years, for which Talbot received 20*l* of silver, and all the other fees pertaining to his constableship. And the said Thomas agrees to keep and guard the castle, safe and secure for the use of the Earl, and to return it (unless it be besieged, which God forbid, by Irish enemies of the Lord King or other adversaries of the English) in the sufficient state in which it now is, and at the end of the said term to surrender it to the Earl or his heirs.[21]

This appointment was the first to be made between the Ormondes and a member of the Talbot family, now their in-laws, but who would prove to be a dynasty that would play an increasingly malign role in the lives of the Earl's descendants.

In June 1358 James Butler travelled to England, and it is evident from a number of indentures made at the time that certain Irish leaders throughout his lands were taken into custody, to be held as a security measure, during his absence. One contract drawn up between Ormonde and the chieftain, Edmund O'Kennedy, promised Edmund his release upon the Earl's return to Ireland, with a singular provision that the Irishman should pay the Earl, *before he could be released*, 100*l* in money or in kind. For the surety of this payment he was to give his brother as a hostage if he could not satisfy the Earl with any other sort of security. Besides which, for the sum of 200 marks, he was to deliver up his six sons and the two sons of his brother also, as hostages for his 'good and loyal bearing'.

He was further ordered to attend the Earl's (liberty) court, 'as in ancient times was the custom'; and he was to attend the Earl whenever he went to war, 'with all his power in his marches at his own cost'. To recompense him for this, when 'outside his own area', he was guaranteed 100 horses and sixty men on foot, at the Earl's expense. But in more peaceful circumstances, he himself in return for land would account to the Earl of Ormonde for 40 horses and 120 men on foot.[22]

With regard to the Earl's own security, if any of O'Kennedy's men trespassed in the seignory of the Earl, the chieftain was to give them up within fifteen days, or pay 5*d* for each man. (Of this, the Earl retained 4*d*, with one penny going to any party who had been injured due to the unlawful entry.) But the agreement was not all one-sided, for if any Englishman trespassed against O'Kennedy the violated man was to be given title to the culprit's worldly goods. But O'Kennedy was also to ensure that his 'idlemen'[23] should never invade Ormonde's tenants, 'unless he be in aid of the county, for one night only, which may be found'. In the case of any trespass against himself, he was to complain to Ormonde's Seneschal, and if that failed, or the official did not requite him, he was approach the Earl upon his return to Ireland, who 'undertakes to do him right'.

Strangely, both men were in England at the time they interchanged their seals on this document, which was made out and signed at 'La Vacherie' in Surrey, in the presence of 'Dame Eleanor, Countess of Ormonde', the Earl's mother. The seal on this agreement is defaced, as no doubt the agreement was itself in good time; but it is highly indicative that, even though both men were away from their homeland, the Irishman should still be made a prisoner by the Earl. Such measures were always necessary in order to keep a chief's followers inactive back in Ireland.

Other O'Kennedys would be well rewarded by the Earl, and apparently served him faithfully enough, particularly when it came to taking his side in battle. One Bernard O'Kennedy, 'Captain of his Nation', was given two caracutes of land in the grange of Nenagh, 'for his good and laudable services done to the Earl in the parts of Leinster'. Such generosity was, of course, always conditional on the Irishman continuing to bear himself 'faithfully and well to the Lord King and the Earl'.

The Earl of Ormonde was now the greatest of the resident nobles in Ireland, even if his cousin Mortimer possessed more land, and James Butler was one of the most trusted of all the King's officials. His royal descent, naturally, as well as the personal service he had done the King, commended James highly to the favour of Edward III, from whom he received many grants of land. In September 1358 he was made the 'Guardian of the Peace' for the whole of Munster, 'to deal with those of the English and Irish nations who are confederated to destroy the faithful people of Munster, and to usurp their lordship by conquest'.[24] The King's faith in his cousin was in stark contrast to the lack of trust he felt for Ormonde's other relative the Earl of Desmond, who – as leader of the 'Patriot Party' – was by now vociferously asking the English to keep their hands off Ireland and to let the Anglo-Irish magnates rule in their stead.

James Butler was made Justiciar of Ireland on 15 February 1359, and granted supernumerary powers by the King.

> Know that we, confiding in your wisdom and fidelity, have given you by the tenour of these presents the power to remove sheriffs, constables, bailiffs and all other ministers whatsoever in our land of Ireland, whom you have found unsuitable in their places, by council and advice of our Chancellor and Treasurer of Ireland, as often as need shall be and for our greater advantage you shall deem fit. We do not wish, however, that Justices or Barons of the Exchequer, or our other Ministers in the said land, whose offices have been granted them by Letters Patent under our Great Seal of England, shall under pretext of this present power given by us be removed by you from their offices.[25]

The King also gave Ormonde the power to receive the peace and fealty of all, both English and Irish, who were, or had been, rebellious or hostile to the King, and he could issue pardons to them, by 'counsel and advice of the Archbishop of Dublin'. He could also draw up letters patent under the Seal of Ireland, but all fines and reductions were to be retained to the King's use. As an amplification of the Justiciar's powers, the Archbishop of Cashel possessed the authority to impose ecclesiastical penalties on the offender and on all his lands, for example, when a hostage was not given up on demand.

In 1359 the Earl, as Justiciar, made a very important treaty with Murtagh O'Brenan, in which the chief swore to serve him against Irish foes and English rebels, and to keep the peace himself, receiving for his loyalty five marks of silver yearly. But the new relations of the Gaelic chiefs with the hated 'middle nation' were not simply based on profitable treaties between the two parties, they were also based on the system of 'fosterage' (or promotion), and even on marriage, although this latter was at variance with the law. So far, the heads of the Geraldine and Butler families had married only English or Anglo-Irish wives, but from the middle of the 14th Century they began to give their daughters liberally to the Irish chiefs. Joan, a daughter of the 2nd Earl of Ormonde would marry the chief of the O'Carrolls of Ely, which gave the Earl some essential respite from his family's previous enmity with that disorderly clan.

On 18 April 1359, Ormonde was made Viceroy of Ireland (as well as retaining the office of Lord Justice) and after a short absence in England – when the viceroyalty was held by Maurice fitzThomas, Earl of Kildare – he was again appointed in March 1360. It was, as always, a delicate position to uphold, and with most antagonism towards him coming, predictably, not from the Irish but from his Anglo-Irish peers.

A perfect example of this is the agreement, made soon after his appointment as Viceroy, between himself and Sir Richard de Burgh. In this (not untypical) document, Sir Richard undertook that neither he nor his dependants 'would inflict any injury, loss or damage upon the Earl of Ormonde, by way of revenge *for any action of law* [my italics] made by the Earl against De Burgh and other felons'.[26] (That is, they would not seek to punish him for punishing them!) They were solemnly pledged 'in the name of the King' to give 'aid and council always to him, etc., forever, against all save the Lord King'. Sir Richard deposited 1,000*l* in silver as a pledge for his dependants' 'good behaviour'. Similar contracts were made with the Irish, and early the next year, William O'Carroll, 'son of Rory, Captain of his Nation', would be delivered as hostage, for the same undertaking.

Ormonde had inherited a thankless task, for between 1352 and his taking over the role the state of Ireland had grown steadily worse. So much so, in fact, that King Edward III resolved to send his second son, Lionel of Antwerp, as Governor, believing 'that our Irish dominions have been reduced to such utter devastation, ruin and misery, that they may be totally lost if our subjects there are not immediately succoured.'[27] A great gathering of the English landholders in Ireland had been assembled at Easter, and they had been strictly commanded not only to provide soldiers, but also to accompany the Prince on his mission to defend their estates. On 1 July 1361 Lionel was appointed the King's Lieutenant in Ireland, having first been made a Knight of the Garter. He landed in Dublin in September 1361, with a body of 1,500 men, supplemented by those of many great landowners, who – as ordered – provided an extra army. The Prince was also accompanied by his wife, Elizabeth, the only daughter of the 3rd Earl of Ulster, who had brought her husband a lavish marriage portion of great parts of the west and north of Ireland. She was undoubtedly the greatest Irish heiress of her day.

(To make more certain of this tremendous inheritance, the King had appointed Ralph d'Ufford – a gallant soldier who had fortuitously married Elizabeth's widowed mother, the Countess of Ulster – Governor of Ireland in 1344, when the marriage had been first proposed. To make the situation even clearer Prince Lionel himself was created Earl of Ulster, and all proceedings connected with his wife's vast inheritance were afterwards always transacted in his name. They had been married in 1352, but due to the parlous state of Ireland at this period, very little of Elizabeth's heritage was really in the hands of either bride or groom.)

The young Viceroy displayed some vigour at the beginning of his term of office, but he achieved nothing of real importance; perhaps because he depended upon the wrong men for advice, and he did not sufficiently trust those who were better qualified to understand his unruly domain. The best example of his approach is in the way that he provided for his own safety, which he did by prohibiting 'any man born in Ireland' from approaching his army. As a result, he lost 100 of his mercenaries when on an incursion into unfamiliar terrain, and he 'was soon glad to rely upon the aid' of the Anglo-Irish lords that he had previously spurned.

He was also capable of huge errors of judgement about the native Irish; and he was inclined to grossly mistreat them, as when he treacherously made the King of Leinster and his heir apparent his prisoners while they were his guests, they afterwards dying in custody. In retaliation against this huge offence against a fellow monarch, the King of Connacht led a great army into Meath in 1362, which he 'triumphantly desolated by fire'. They burned the church at Kilkenny, and fourteen other churches in towns where the English had garrisons. Doing 'the English many injuries before returning [to the safety] of their homes'. [28] The Earl of Ormonde, although he would never himself have committed an error on the scale of Lionel's, was forced to take retaliatory action on the Prince's part, and in return slew 600 of MacMurrough's men at Teogstoffin in County Kilkenny.

In February 1362 King Edward strove to strengthen his son's hand by reiterating, with even greater emphasis, the orders of the previous year to the possessors of the Irish estates, forcing them to increase their contributions of men to the Prince's cause. On 13 November Lionel was created Duke of Clarence – a title derived, not from the Irish county Clare, but from a village in Suffolk, which was also an inheritance of his wife. The dukedom was a gift from his father, not to add further loftiness to his status as Viceroy however, but simply to celebrate the King's 50th birthday. Lionel was not at home to help celebrate his father's anniversary, but remained in Ireland, where his salary was doubled and his armed forces increased. Outside the line of duty, which did not detain him much, he busied himself with works 'agreeable to him for sports and other pleasures, as well within the castle of Dublin as elsewhere'.[29] Following a very narrow line of duty he 'made inquiries into the rights of chartered towns and carried out many expeditions against the Irish',[30] but whatever successes he had in that direction, his triumphs were marred by the untimely death of his wife, who left an only child, a daughter.

(In 1368 this girl, the Princess Philippa, would marry Edmund Mortimer, the 3rd Earl of March. Edmund, who was a cousin of the Butlers, was himself descended from the youngest son of Edward III and was also a great magnate, with wide lands and influence in the Welsh marches. As she had the strongest claim to the throne, if the rights of primogeniture were set aside, Philippa would ultimately transfer her claim to her husband's line, the house of York, and this would have considerable consequences for the English and Irish aristocracy, the Butlers among them. All would be forced to take sides in the civil war that followed on a Yorkist challenge to the Crown.)

Lionel was absent from government between April and December 1364, when the Earl of Ormonde acted as his deputy; and when Lionel again returned to England a year later his place was taken by Sir Thomas Dale. (It would seem that, however loyal or competent an Irish lord, an Englishman was still to be better trusted.) While in Ireland, the Duke's main concern seemed to be that of regaining possession of his dead wife's estates, but he only succeeded in getting into his hands a small part of the coast of eastern Ulster. More publicly, Clarence's constant efforts to rule only through the Englishmen that he had brought to Ireland in his retinue led to great quarrels with his Anglo-Irish lords; although his father, in an effort to unite both factions in the wars against the native Irish, did his best to appease the opposing parties.

Lionel, with an unfounded distrust of the Irish establishment in Dublin, had the exchequer transferred to Carlow, and he spent 500*l* in walling that town, which would later prove to be yet another blunder. The Earl of Ormonde in the meantime made every effort to be of service to the Duke, and while Clarence may never have relied upon him entirely, he still made good use of him. The castle of Kilkenny, in Butler territory, if not yet owned by them, soon became known as the 'Court of Lionel of Antwerp'.[31]

Even so, Ormonde, like most Irish magnates of that period, seems to have been playing a double game with the English, for on 24 April 1365 King Edward pardoned him of 'all seditions, trespasses and felonies done by him against our peace of Ireland', of which he stood 'indicted and accused'.[32] As 'the deaths of William de Burgh, lately Earl of Ulster,

Walter de la Hyde, Sheriff of Meath, and John de Scottoun [were] alone excepted' in this pardon, Ormonde's offence would appear to have been in directly challenging the King's – or more probably Clarence's men – in some manner, a challenge that must have led to a battle between his men and theirs, in which they died. William de Burgh, of course, had been Philippa's grandfather and the source of Prince Lionel's great fortune, and whatever the nature of the violations committed against him by the Earl of Ormonde, even if he was the King's cousin, they could not be over-looked. However, there must have been a further extension to Ormonde's offences, for he was also pardoned for

> ...all confederacies, *champerties* [illegal bargains], allegations, oppres-sions, extortions, excesses, deceptions, etc., whatsoever done by him in our land of Ireland, and have granted him our firm peace. Provided that he shall stand to right in our Court if anyone wishes to plead against him there, and that in future he faithfully bear himself towards us, our heirs, and ministers, and towards our faithful people.[33]

This pardon was signed at Cork, and attested by the Duke of Clarence; but the exact nature of Ormonde's offence is not known. If he had perhaps sided with the rebellious Anglo-Irish leaders, it must have been a tem-porary aberration only, for the Ormondes were the natural leaders of the English Party among the colonists.

Along with the Earls of Kildare and Desmond, the Ormonde family, at least for the present, continue to be loyal – or, in the first two cases, at least semi-loyal – to the traditions of English law and government, where a century before their ancestors had been totally staunch. But of these three, the one earldom to remain most faithful to the English tradition would be the Butlers. If only because at this particular period, having lost some of Upper Ormond to the Irish in various encounters, they had been generously compensated for their losses by the King with more land in the south and east.

Early in Lent 1366 the Duke of Clarence held a memorable parliament, at his 'court' in Kilkenny Castle, the great aim of which was to pass an enact-ment that became notorious as the 'Statute of Kilkenny'. This misguided plan was, in fact, King Edward's own, and it would produce terrible dissension among the Anglo-Irish. For by a series of minute restrictions and prohibitions the object of this act was to prevent the tendency to inter-mixture between the 'English by blood' (those born in England) and those English of Irish birth, a situation that was thought to be rapidly destroying the basis of English rule (and which was also 'withdrawing English set-tlers from English [notions of] English civilisation'). Distinctions between the 'English by Blood' and the 'English by Birth' were as far as possible to be removed.

As a piece of legislature designed to prevent the colony from succumbing to Gaelic influence, it was quickly seen to contain decrees that were unworkable, being 'full of that penal spirit which kept the Irish in a state of warfare within the English Pale for centuries after'.[34] The statutes were, in fact, a clear admission that the island was divided into three parts: the country of the 'Irish enemies', that of the 'degenerate English', and the Anglo-Norman 'land of peace', which was not simply a geographical demarcation but also a patriotic partition. It would now seem that four-fifths of the island were abandoned to the 'Irish enemies' and the 'English rebels', though the feudal titles to them, ostensibly owned by Anglo-Irish lords, were never surrendered by the interested parties.

This unenforceable legislation created at Kilkenny was the last – if not the main – important act of the Duke of Clarence in Ireland. Weary of an unrewarding task, he returned to England in November 1366, declaring that he would never return of his own free will; and his role, unsuccessful as it was, marks an epoch in the history of English relations with Ireland. Significantly, the government was handed over to the 4th Earl of Desmond, and Gerald FitzGerald succeeded the Duke of Clarence as Justiciar of Ireland in the same year that this highly charged piece of legislation was passed.

As an appointment it was an open confession of weakness by the Crown, since Gerald was known to unofficially repudiate the Kilkenny Statute, and he stubbornly carried on his father's policy of amalgamation with the native Irish, which it had been Lionel's chief object to prevent. The following period of Gerald's rule was, as a result of this contradiction, exceptionally turbulent for all concerned. A great meeting had also to be held at Kilkenny to induce another rebel, Bermyngham, to live in peace with the government, and the Exchequer had to be removed back to Dublin from Carlow, where it had become increasingly exposed to Irish attack.

Under the escalating menace of Irish expansion, many more English were leaving the country, and it was reasoned that if the growing exodus of English out of the 'land of peace' could be brought to a halt, some kind of balance might be attained. So, to counteract this tendency, the Irish Parliament proclaimed the Absentee Act in 1368, when it was decreed that all who held land in Ireland, and who lived there, should be compelled to defend their estates in person; or if they could not do so, to supply efficient deputies.

In a further attempt to force the absentee landlords to return, to hold and populate, or at the least to garrison their vast estates, it was ordered that all those in England 'of whatever rank' who had lands in Ireland, should hereafter reside upon them in person. They were to return, with their families, or men-at-arms, before the following Easter; and in default of carrying out this order, they were to be summarily deprived of all their lands, lordships, possessions and inheritance. There is, however, no evidence that this sweeping demand was ever firmly applied, or that it led to any considerable re-establishment of the absentees; or, indeed, that it checked any further exodus of the Anglo-Irish.

The law prohibiting intermarriage between the two nations proved equally unworkable, for such marriages were never properly suppressed. Indeed they became so mundane – at least at an aristocratic level – that many leading men were referred to as being 'both Gael and Gaul' whenever their bards wished to praise them. It was increasingly seen as no dishonour for Anglo-Irish aristocrats to marry their daughters to an Irish chieftain or his heirs; although to marry her to a vassal, or even to a lowly Irish landowner, was quite another thing of course.

In 1369 Sir William de Windsor succeeded FitzGerald as Justiciar of Ireland, with the English government recognising, at last, that they had given power to the wrong man. Almost at once the English of Munster suffered a great defeat at the hands of Brian O'Brien, Lord of Thomond, near Nenagh, who had less fear of the new Justiciar than he had felt for the deposed one. The Earl of Desmond himself, along with 'an array of the chiefs of England',[35] was taken prisoner during this encounter, and the remainder were cut down 'with an incredible slaughter'. O'Brien's victorious army plundered the area and torched the city of Limerick, while many of its most important inhabitants were captured for ransom.

This was one of the greatest victories ever won by the Irish of Munster, with one of their chiefs taking over the wardenship of the devastated city. But the English 'acted treacherously towards him' and he was swiftly murdered, mourned by the chroniclers; 'a lamentable treatment of the son of a chieftain.'[36] A year later Windsor led a small expedition to effect Desmond's release, but in 1372 O'Brien was again in arms and threatening the city of Limerick. Between these two events, Brian O'Kennedy, Lord of Ormond, was 'treacherously slain by the English', with his heir dying at his side.

The Burghs were also once more giving cause for concern. In February 1372 the King wrote to the constable of Dublin castle, where Richard and Meyler de Burgh were in prison 'for divers treasons and other crimes done to us and our people'. They were planning to procure their freedom by way of a bribe to the Lord Lieutenant, which was a practice that was to be stamped out, according to instructions from the King, '…unless you hear otherwise from us'.[37]

In 1374 the O'Farrells went to war with the English, and a fierce and sharp conflict took place. Then in 1375 MacMurrough, King of Leinster, was treacherously slain by the Anglo-Irish, 'among whom he had often before spread desolation'. But if the English had hoped to destroy Irish ambitions by his death, the reign of his vengeful son, Art Oge MacMurrough, with its widespread attacks on the fast dwindling 'land of peace', presented the

English with a crisis of even greater magnitude. So great, in fact, that the new King of England, Richard II, would feel impelled to voyage to Ireland in order to deal with it in person.

Art Oge MacMurrough was not acting alone. Elsewhere, a great victory was won by the O'Neills over the English of Downpatrick, where the King of England's deputy, Burke, and others – too many to be listed – were slain in the conflict. The MacTiernan clan, too, marched against the English, 'with all their forces'. (Although ineffectively, since one of their own people betrayed their encampment for a bribe. The English, surrounding them, beheaded the chieftain's two sons on the spot, along with twenty-five other prominent men.)

In 1377 Nenagh Castle was besieged and taken by MacBrian of Arra, in whose hands it remained, and the O'Kennedys recovered much of the baronies of upper and lower Ormond. Perhaps the inability of James Butler to protect his birthright can be put down to the fact that he had pressing duties elsewhere at this time, since he was again made Lord Justice in July 1376, an office in which he would remain until the first year of Richard II, who was crowned King of England on 21 June 1377.

The earl had, as always, been kept very busy by his duties. Irish Exchequer rolls were searched by the new king's accountant, and afterwards arrears of 500*l* were paid to Ormonde for the money he had personally loaned to the war-fund, with 50*l* also due to him as a reward for military service 'in the King's war'. Another (undisclosed) payment was made to him, for a grant he had made to Tyrelagh O'Brien, 'Captain of his Nation', to maintain against O'Bren Shramagh, 'the King's enemy'. In that year, the renegade Earl of Desmond, now released, was once again at odds with Richard de Burgh, and the private armies they had raised were creating havoc within, and without, the individual territories of these two unmanageable warlords.

Ormonde, too, was extending his privileges by maintaining an even larger standing army, but now astonishingly comprising mostly Irishman. An indenture, signed at Cork in July 1377, had William More McBreen of Narlagh, 'Captain of his Nation', agreeing to do military service with the Earl, 'against all men, English and Irish, the King excepted'.[38] But unlike his Irish peers, the Earl had raised these men primarily to serve in the English cause.

In June 1378 Art Oge McMurrough claimed to be the rightful King of Leinster, and swiftly accumulated a huge following of disaffected men.

...There being confederated and allied with him all the Irish of Leinster, and several others, as well as Irish and English rebels of Munster. With a great number of men, on horse and foot, supporting him with intent to destroy the said parts of Leinster, and to make a general conquest of the lieges of our Lord the King there, had wickedly risen in open war. ...To resist and overthrow this wicked design, and to save the said parts, it was ordered that the said Justice should retain from time to time as many men-at-arms, archers, hobellers and footmen, in addition to the armed men included in the commission of his office, as seemed to him good and necessary for resistance of the said enemies.[39]

The government sent about 300*l* to Ormonde, in part payment for an addition to the standing army. But Ormonde, seeing that the Irish were about to descend on his men, and realising that there was little in the King's Irish treasury for mounting a resistance with the troops at his command, was forced to retain a certain number of men-at-arms at his own expense, for which he had already loaned King Edward III 254*l* for their wages. He had every hope of being repaid, but this had taken some considerable time, since he could not be paid from Dublin 'owing to the poverty of the treasury there'. Eventually, in the next reign, he would receive 1,000 marks 'in full payment and satisfaction of all sums due to him. Five hundred down, and 200 per annum for two years'.[40]

Other debts were also repaid, including the wages of 120 men-at-arms, knights and squires, plus 200 archers, all dating from the last years of King Edward III's reign, and. James was to receive 'the rewards of war usual in English war'. (That is, whatever his men could plunder from those he defeated). The war-fund was to be repaid with a deduction of 500*l* for that advanced by the late King, and at the same time, it was decreed that the Earl should have twenty men-at-arms, 'with horses caparisoned'. He should also be supplied with 'sufficient shipping for his passage by sea out of the realm of England, and return for the same retinue, with their horses and men, at the cost of the said King'. Ormonde was further advised by the King's council that if any soldiers of his retinue (born and raised in England) 'should quit his company for lack of payment, he could replace them with suitable persons, English born in Ireland, for whom the Earl should have allowance'.[41]

The treaties between the Earl of Ormonde and some Irish chieftains at this time show from their seals that the Gaelic commanders by now made the same use of their family crests, armorial bearings and written charters as did the Anglo-Normans. And a remarkable feature of these treaties is that the chiefs simultaneously recognised both the King of England and the Earl of Ormonde as their *equal* overlords.

Above all, the 'agreements of retinue' and suchlike indentures for military service and vassalage made between the Earl and his dependants are also interesting because they show that warfare of one kind or another had now become utterly routine in Ireland. They also demonstrate that a similar system to that of the hated 'livery and maintenance', which had long afflicted England, was now to be found in Ireland. In these agreements, the proviso 'Saving always against the King' is general, but the growing power of the Irish 'kings' is illustrated by the increasing self-determination of men such as Art Oge MacMurrough and Brian O'Brien.

In 1380 Sir Edmund Mortimer was sent to Ireland with great powers as Justiciar. Most of the Irish nobility went to pay court to him, and after the Lord of Iveagh, one of the greatest Irish chieftains, was treacherously taken prisoner in Mortimer's house while doing so, the Irish stood in much awe of such a dangerously duplicitous man. 'Seeing themselves at his mercy, they resolved not to cultivate any [further] familiarity with him'.[42] He later led an army into Ulster, destroying many fortresses and towns, including a number of ecclesiastical buildings; but he died prematurely of natural causes in 1381, less than a year after taking over control. Which meant that he had not sufficient time in which to effect any great changes to the country's administration.

This was a year in which three other important people also died: the Irish 'Lord of Ormond', his wife, and his son Philip. The Irish lord had ruled for more than nine years, generally to the benefit of the Ormonde family, and it was perhaps as a result of these deaths – all of them presumably unnatural – that the Earl of Desmond was appointed to 'repress the malice of the rebels' in Munster (where no Justiciar dared venture to show his face after the death of the Earl of March). At this time, Desmond is generally described as the chief upholder of the King's cause in Munster; and yet, perverse as ever, his policy was still to set English law at defiance and to adopt Irish customs. There is no doubt that Desmond wholly sympathised with the native Irish, and he was said to excel all of the English in his knowledge of the Gaelic language, poetry and history.

On 24 January 1482 Roger Mortimer, the 4th Earl of March, was appointed Lord Lieutenant of Ireland, an appointment that was due entirely to hereditary influence, since he was still a child. The experiment of an infant Viceroy was soon seen as the fatuity that it was, with both magnates and commoners protesting against a parliament being held in his absence, and the powerless boy was quickly superseded, for Ireland was once again facing a new menace, but, this time, not one of human making. In 1483 Edmond Oge, son of Sir Edmund Butler, and Joanna, daughter of the Earl of Ormonde, and wife of Tiege O'Carroll, the Lord of Ely, died of the plague, along with thousands of others who also succumbed to the disease, which raged throughout Ireland for two more years.

During this time, the Earl of Ormonde also passed away, although not of the plague. He died on 18 October 1382, in his castle of Knocktopher, and was buried in the cathedral of St Canice, Kilkenny, then in a stage of reconstruction. (The lofty bell tower had collapsed in 1332, bringing down much of the choir and one of the transept chapels. Completed in the 13th century, this building displays a magnificence that is far beyond its actual size, due to its unity and purity. Rich in carvings, the church would become the repository of many striking Butler effigies over the next few centuries, after the next Earl had bought Kilkenny Castle.)

On Ormonde's death, the Escheator's accounts name among his vast possessions, titles and perquisites, the 'liberties and regalities of County Tipperary'. Since Nenagh was now lost to the family (or had been made insecure through the revival of the O'Kennedy clan), Clonmel, in southern Tipperary, would become the palatine capital. The Ormonde butlership had not become fixed or hereditary in the family until this century, but it was finally granted to them for good in 1355. The rate was then one tun from each cargo of nine tuns, and upwards to twenty or twenty-two tons, or their value, (forty shillings each), from a cargo of twenty upwards.

The 2nd Earl, the 'Noble Earl' – so-called in reference to his royal descent – had served King Edward III well, not only in the wars in France, where he took part in the battle of Crecy, the first decisive battle of the Hundred Year's War, but more notably in the wearying wars in Ireland. Yet though his achievements were hugely important, the summit of political and military influence in that much-troubled country would be attained by his son, the 3rd earl, and by his grandson, the 'White Earl'. These two men, by means of frontier alliances with both Irish and Anglo-Irish clans, would extend their influence well beyond the borders of their lordship.

## *Notes*

1.  Curtis, *Calendar of Ormonde Deeds*.
2.  Carte, *Life of the Duke of Ormonde*.
3.  Curtis, op. cit.
4.  The Four Masters, *Annals of the Kingdom of Ireland*.
5.  Carte, op. cit.
6.  Ibid.
7.  Ibid
8.  Curtis, op. cit.
9.  Ibid.
10. The Four Masters, op. cit.
11. Curtis, op. cit.
12. Ibid.
13. Ibid.
14. Ibid.
15. Ibid.
16. Ibid.
17. An area owned by the Purcell family.
18. Curtis, op. cit.
19. Ibid.
20. Ibid.

21. Ibid.
22. Ibid.
23. 'Idlemen': Irish gentlemen as opposed to workers.
24. Carte, op, cit.
25. Curtis, op. cit.
26. Ibid.
27. *Dictionary of National Biography* (under 'Lionel of Antwerp'.)
28. Ibid.
29. Ibid.
30. Ibid.
31. Ibid.
32. Carte, op. cit.
33. Ibid.
34. Ibid.
35. The Four Masters, op. cit.
36. Ibid.
37. *Dictionary of National Biography* (under *Lionel of Antwerp*.)
38. Curtis, op. cit.
39. The Four Masters, op. cit. 'Hobellers' were light horsemen, literally 'hobby-horse' men.
40. Curtis, op. cit.
41. Ibid.
42. The Four Masters, op. cit.

# CHAPTER V

# *The Shrinking of the Pale*

As with most of his forebears, the third James le Botiller was not of age when his father died in 1382. William fitzWilliam, the Escheator of Ireland, charged his accounts with the issues, rent and profits of six manors and four baronies of the late Earl, along with a moiety of three other manors. These went with the liberties and regalities of Tipperary; and, very significantly, he received the prise wines of all the ports and places near the sea, as well as cities and towns, as other places in the realm of Ireland[1] (except for the prisage of Cork, and half the prisage of Waterford). All this, of course had been returned in to the King's hands, with the rest of the estate, at the second James's death. However, an accepted part of the prisage had already been assigned to the new Earl's mother, for her thirds or jointure; this is apparent in that, after young James came of age, she then resigned to him 'all her dower, except her share of the prise wines'.[2]

The third James, who was born in the early 1360s, had achieved his majority by 1384, for on 16 November 1384 the new King, Richard II sent letters patent to Phillip de Courtenay, Lord Lieutenant of Ireland, and to the Chancellor and Treasurer.

> Wishing to act graciously to our dear cousin James le Botiller – son and heir of James le Botiller, lately Earl of Ormonde, defunct, who held of us in chief – who is now full of age, as is shown by various inquisitions taken after his father's death and returned unto our Chancery in England – we have granted to the said James that he, who is now in our land of Ireland, for the safeguard of the same, may enter our realm of England and come and do homage to us for the lands and tenements which were his father's and to sue for the same lands and tenements out of our hands as the custom is, and may make his stay in the same for various purposes, until the said James shall return by our command to the said land of Ireland, notwithstanding any statutes or ordinances … or any order of ours made to the contrary, etc.[3]

A year earlier his mother had formally renounced her claims in Ireland to her son, with the exception of four estates 'and all her other lands and tenements in Fyngall in County Dublin'. Interestingly, in her quitclaim, she refers to herself by her maiden name, Elizabeth d'Arcy, although retaining the title of Countess. It is also interesting that this quitclaim was given at Kilkenny, and not at the castle of Gowran, which was built in the young Earl's minority, and which was his usual residence. This suggests that he had even then some stake in Kilkenny Castle, which he was to purchase from Sir Hugh Despenser, and which would afterwards become his chief seat. Nevertheless, because Gowran was for the most part his usual residence until he bought Kilkenny Castle, James was known as the 'Earl of Gowran'. (As some other Earls of Ormonde would come to call themselves the 'Earls of Tipperary', either because Ormond and Carrick lay in that county, or because they had the regality of that County Palatine).

Irish politics of this period were, as ever, inextricably entangled with those England, and although successive English kings had neglected the country over the generations, to further their aims in France or Scotland, King Richard II took a renewed interest in the country (as time would show, to the disadvantage of Ireland). The conditions there had given the new King anxiety from the beginning of his reign, and within a few years of his coming to the throne, the turbulent septs of Leinster were harassing the Pale. Art MacMurrough had assumed the Irish royal title, with the result that Anglo-Irish families were now departing for England in large numbers. Edward III was said to have drawn 30,000 marks a year from Ireland, but it was costing his grandson that much to maintain it.

By the mid-eighties the idealistic young King had begun to build up a party of confidantes devoted to himself and to his policies, but these policies were to quickly prove unpopular. From the beginning, Richard's main ambition was to discontinue the wars in France – set in motion by his grandfather, Edward III – and he worked hard to achieve this aim, but with the natural result that the men who had most profited from King Edward's wars, either through gaining wealth or acquiring prestige, would come to detest him. Above all, most 'patriotic' Englishmen hated the idea of a peace that could not be settled with an outright victory.

Richard's nobles were also indignant at being set aside in favour of men whom they thought of as being less worthy than themselves, or certainly less valorous; men such as the Earl of Oxford, who was created *Marquis* of Dublin in 1385[4] (the first of such in British history a marquess ranking above an earl and below a duke). One year later Richard would further outrage his courtiers by investing De Vere as the 'Duke of Ireland', the intention being for the new Duke to first conquer the country then hold it as his lordship. At 24, De Vere would be only the second duke outside the royal family in England, although few thought him deserving of the honour.

Richard was too arrogant and high-spirited ever to submit quietly to opponent's demands, but he was chronically short of money and his enemies were powerful and ruthless; and these included members of his own family, who were prepared to take up arms against him. In 1387 the King's youngest uncle, the Duke of Gloucester, together with two other peers raised a considerable army against him, with which they defeated Richard's forces. The victors then caused a parliament to be summoned in February 1388, to exercise power in their name, and which earned the epithet of the 'Merciless Parliament'. Many of the King's supporters – particularly the despised favourites – were executed, exiled or gaoled and for a time Richard was impotent against his enemies. These men, who were known as the 'appellants', once firmly in control of the government, were swift to reward themselves and their friends with money, honours and appointments.

But within little more than a year Richard was able to reassert his regal authority, and even to recapture the lost affection of his nobles. For the appellant lords quickly alienated many of their former supporters by the extreme way in which they conducted the business of government, and by their increasing greed. Heir political and military incompetence, too, had allowed the Scots to inflict a severe defeat on the English at the battle of Otterburn in 1388. This extravagant and incompetent regime, in fact, had cost England a great deal, and with little to show for it.

Once he regained control of his government Richard's enemies may have hoped that he would discredit himself again by tactless and high-handed actions, in the same way that he had done in 1386, when he had – in the self-willed manner of his great-grandfather, Edward II – raised his favourites too high. But the King made no attempt to recall his exiled friends, or to undo the work of the 'Merciless Parliament'. He did not even exclude the appellants from his council, with the result that domestic affairs in the years from 1389 to 1397 were fairly calm, and this gave Richard the opportunity to reassert royal authority in Ireland. He believed that a successful intervention there might also revive the Crown's authority at home, and in 1394 the King went to Ireland to try to arrest the decay of English power, (power that was then in the hands of the 3rd Earl of Ormonde, who was only a few years older than the 27-year-old King). However, James Butler was, as yet, virtually untried when it came to the exercise of his authority. Indeed, until the advent of the King into Ireland, the acquisition of Kilkenny Castle, on 4 September 1391, had been his most considerable achievement. Which is not to decry that pacific coup, for by its purchase, the Earl had greatly increased his military power base, since Kilkenny was the ancient capital of Ossary and in itself was a fortification. Moreover, not only had Ormonde acquired the impressive castle that dominated this incomparable town, but he was also in possession of the immense property surrounding it, the extensive 'mills, dovecots, lands, tenements, meadows, weirs, waters, fisheries, and all their appurtenances which he has there'.[5] With this also went the borough of Rosbargon, with its mill, two manors, a sergeancy, tenements, advowsons and knights' fees in sixteen other boroughs.

All these had come from Hugh Despenser, who had married Eleanor, the sister of Gilbert le Clare, Earl of Gloucester and Lord of Kilkenny, and it was by right of this marriage that Despenser had got a share of the liberty of Kilkenny. In a document of 12 September 1391 he instructed his tenants and men, 'both free and villein, and all others whom it concerns in Ireland', that he had granted the castle to Ormonde, and he commanded them to be 'intendent, obedient and respondent to the Earl, his heirs and assigns'. His vast and important property cost Ormonde 1,000*l* of 'lawful money' to purchase, which along with royal service 'in County Kilkenny and the parts there' was in excess of twenty-five knights' fees.

But in his haste to acquire this hugely important acquisition Ormonde had been forced to seek a pardon from King Richard II for entering into his new possessions without a royal licence, although the warrant granting it was given quickly enough. Richard could not afford to alienate his most influential nobleman in Ireland, for despite his lack of years, Richard recognised the young Earl's value to him. It was, in fact, as much for his grasp of the Irish political situation as for his fluency in Gaelic that the King selected James Butler to be his chief adviser and go-between during his first expedition to Ireland three years later. As Richard himself said, he was 'unwilling that the said Earl or his heirs…should by reason of the above [the taking over of another man's castle with royal permission] be in future times ever vexed or molested by us or by our heirs'.[6]

James had been made Lord Justice of Ireland in July 1392, and from the first he proved as popular with the Irish as with the King, and for much the same reasons. As he understood the everyday problems of the community and spoke their language fluently, he could interpret for the King's counsellors. Furthermore, as a brother-in-law of one of their greatest chieftains, Taig O'Carroll, he was trusted more by the people than were most other English-imposed executives, who lacked these vital links.

Yet despite his important connections he would retain his sense of 'Englishness', and prove himself ruthless in pursing the King's opponents of creating great confusion among the 'Irish enemy'. Soon after becoming Lord Justice he routed the MacMoynes, who had entered Kilkenny with a force that was strong enough to inflict huge damage on Ormonde's troops. In the same year, though, Ormonde had suffered a humiliating defeat, when the 'King of Tyrone' led a great army against the English at Dundalk, where he 'acquired great power over them on this occasion'. (This was the time which Tyrone famously, in a chivalrous gesture worthy of the 'Arthurian ideal', personally slew an English captain who had been engaged to meet him in single combat.)

In this same year, Ormonde's much loved sister, the Countess of Desmond, died, 'after the victory of Penance'. Not only was she mourned by people generally, as 'a bountiful and truly hospitable woman',[7] she was much lamented by her brother since she was the last mediator between himself and her quarrelsome husband. From this time onwards the quarrels between the two families would grow increasingly bitter, coming to a climax in the time of the next Earls of Desmond and Ormonde.

James continued as Lord Justice until Michaelmas 1394, when King Richard landed at Waterford and proceeded to hold court in Dublin. The Anglo-Irish had been asking the King since 1392 to make an appearance in Ireland (an endeavour in which the Irish parliament was enthusiastically backed by Roger Mortimer, 4th Earl of March, heir to the earldom of Ulster – if only to bring about the recovery of *his* Irish lands). But the King, whose various alliances with European powers and an abandonment of all English ambitions on the continent had led to a greater harmony in that political area, was only now free to restore order in his most unmanageable dominion. He and his advisers were also aware, of course, that he badly needed the prestige of some military, or diplomatic, triumph, to impress his magnates at home, and of all the urgent affairs of state, those of Ireland cried out most loudly for a cure. It was time to reassert royal authority there.

Richard, although too sensitive and artistic to make a good medieval prince (he would, perhaps, have made an excellent Renaissance king), seems to have deeply felt the shameful lack of support by successive English governments for his champions in Ireland. His predecessors seemed always to have neglected that country in order to further their imperialist aims in Scotland and France, so that by now the royal authority in Ireland was hardly even nominal beyond a small area around Dublin. The royal lordship had certainly decayed throughout the English-held parts, but a successful intervention by his forces might revive the Crown's authority (not only in Ireland, but in England too, where the King's prerogative was being increasingly questioned).

Richard was also grieving the death of his wife, Anne of Bohemia, whom he had truly loved; he was seeking further distraction, and martial matters might just fill the void. The English parliament was equally anxious to see the prestige of England restored *somewhere* overseas, since Richard's calculated decision not to continue his grandfather's war with France, in order to claim the French crown, was seen by them as a setback for English ambitions. They accordingly voted a generous subsidy 'for the recovery of Ireland', to make up for the shame of retreat in Europe.

The King crossed the Irish Sea, having already made his first mistake even before setting sail by leaving his incompetent uncle, the Duke of York, in charge of England. He would then make a second mistake, on his arrival in Ireland, by putting a temporary end to the tenure of an extremely able Lord Justice. (However, James Butler would soon prove his value to the King in many other ways, since the monarch was a stranger in this part of his kingdom). Richard arrived with several English lords, many of whom owned estates in Ireland but who had never had any real contact with the country. Yet the King hoped, with their compliance, to swell the ranks of his Irish peerage.

Richard II was the first English king since John to visit his Irish dominion; and the truth was that MacMurrough's reign of terror had presented him with a crisis of such magnitude that he had felt compelled to resolve it in person. Such widespread and continuous assaults on the dwindling 'Land of Peace' could no longer be ignored, and the guarding of the Pale was a continuing drain on royal resources. So the King arrived in force, with a fleet of '200 sail' and an army including 30,000 archers and 4,000 men-at-arms – a stunning exhibition of strength which easily procured him the ready submission of all the Irish princes and chieftains, at least for the time that his army remained in their country.

Richard's cousin, the Earl of March (and Ulster), in Ireland 'to get his rents', keenly desired to be restored to his Irish lordship and his vast inheritance. In 1393, when he had done homage to the King, his power in Ireland was still merely nominal, for Irish rebels had long since devastated his estates. But now, among the chieftains who would submit to King Richard was the O'Neill, the real ruler of March's titular earldom, and this would mean the restoration of Mortimer's rights. If not, the Earl had brought with him enough men to contend for them by force of arms, and when Roger Mortimer came over with Richard he was himself attended by a huge following, having raised his own troops.

He brought them knowing that he could not depend upon the King's forces to help him, but King Richard could not have been entirely happy in the company of this second army, which seemed to bolster that of his own. The King had been well advised from the Anglo-Irish side, and he had come as much to make terms with the native prices as to make war on them. Indeed, in a letter to the O'Neill, despatched before he set sail, the King had promised to do right and justice to every man. But first he had to march upon Dublin and make an imposing display before the Leinster rebels.

There was little if any fighting, for the presence of the English King and his imposing force overwhelmed even the most refractory Irish chieftains. But there were a number of considerable local demonstrations against the English during Richard's descent upon Ireland, among which, the King of Leinster was the most active in his efforts to wreck whatever remained of English unity, since formidable as the King's forces were, MacMurrough refused to be overawed. Within days of the royal party's arrival, he had led his much smaller army against them with astounding success, most spectacularly burning the magnificently walled town of New Ross before the King's own eyes, 'with its houses and castles'.[8] He carried from the wreckage gold, silver and hostages, but sensibly retired to his forest refuge before he could be assailed by the combined might of England and their Anglo-Irish forces.

The English, out of necessity, retaliated immediately. Ormonde mustered an equal force to that of MacMurrough and marched into Leinster to 'spoil it' burning the town of Gailine to the ground as well as the territories of the O'Kelly's, 'the most fertile district in Leix'. Both Ormonde and the Earl Marshall attacked the Leinster chief in 'the woods and wilds under Mount Leinster, where MacMurrough had his forest fortress of Garbhcoill'.[9] But they experienced humiliating failure, being unable to draw the Irish from out of their refuge.

Afterwards, Ormonde returned to his base, but the protests were not yet over. The son of the King of Leinster took up arms against King Richard, 'and numbers were slain by him', although he went in the end to make submission to the King, 'at the solicitation of the English and Irish of Leinster'.[10] The son was detained a prisoner at the request of the Earl of Ormonde, acting as Lord Justice, but he was afterwards freed, although others were kept back in custody as a guarantee of the Prince of Leinster's renewed loyalty to King Richard.

Richard himself went to Dublin early in November, where the four Irish 'kings' of Meath, Thomond, Leinster and Connacht were persuaded to visit him there, and while there to recognise his sovereignty. Richard stayed at the castle until the end of January 1395; and it was in Dublin, while treating Art Oge MacMurrough as the leading rebel, that he evolved a general plan for the pacification and recovery of Ireland. Very much simplified, it reads:

A.   The Irish chieftains, except for MacMurrough and his Leinster vassals, were to surrender lands they had 'usurped' from England, and to swear a double allegiance: one to the King, as their liege lord, and the other to the Norman earls, to whom they owed simple homage as their suzerains. In return, they were to be confirmed in their 'Irish lands' (that is, *in the territories they had managed to hold on to since the Conquest*).
B.   The rebel English would be given a general pardon.
C.   A definite 'English land' was to be created on the eastern coast, east of a line drawn from Dundalk to the Boyne, and down the Barrow to Waterford. In this newly created 'English Pale', grants were to be made to any (new) English immigrants, with the intention of colonising the area anew.
D.   In order to carry out the latter plan, the warlike Art Oge MacMurrough and his followers must be *compelled* to quit the lands of Leinster.[11]

To his uncle, the Duke of York Richard wrote:

There are in the land of Ireland three kinds of people; the wild Irish, our enemies; the Irish rebels; and the obedient English. To us and our council it appears that the Irish rebels here rebelled because of the injustice and wrongs practiced upon them, for which they have no [redress], and unless they are widely treated and given hope of grace, they will most likely ally themselves with our enemies.[12]

The King was actually quite sympathetic towards the 'degenerate English', but it was, in fact, the 'Irish rebels', or Hibernicised English, who were the true danger to the state. Richard also determined upon an action that no other king or viceroy had thought of undertaking since the Conquest, and this was to admit the minor kings and primary chiefs of Ireland to full legal status under the Crown. 'In token of his grace' in this matter he substituted the leopard flag of England for that of the arms of Edward the Confessor, a saint most venerated by the Irish, and it did in fact make a compromise flag of sorts.

As a result of Richard's enlightened attitude, four of the principal kings of Ireland 'came to the obeysance of the King of England, by love and fayreness and not by batayle nor constraynte';[13] but there also followed a remarkable series of submissions attested by legal instruments. Richard himself renounced all intention of conquest, and the Irish generally, under their natural leader O'Neill, decided to make a national act of submission, such as their ancestors had formerly sought in vain to make to the English 'Lord of Ireland'.

During the first months of 1395, Richard II received the Irish princes in person. Submissions were made province by province and those Irish of royal blood were treated as suzerains over their 'urrighs'.[14] The King, as Lord of Ireland, and Mortimer, as the Earl of Ulster, received the homage of the northern chiefs, except for Turloch O'Donnell, who 'stood aloof', as did his vassal, Maguire. Among those who went to the King to make submission, was MacWilliam Burke, who 'received great honour and lordship'; and most remarkable of all perhaps, was given 'chieftainship over the *English* of Connacht'. The submissions were all in Irish, rendered into English by interpreters, and recoded in Latin. Brian O'Brien did homage to the King in a room of St Thomas's abbey, Dublin, his interpreter being the Earl of Ormonde, who did the same service for others, in *'lingua Hibernica bene ereditus'*.[15]

Turlogh O'Brien, on the other hand, refused to conform, and waged war with the English King both in Munster and Leinster, and he afterwards plundered and burned the county of Limerick. But more Irish chieftains went to the King's house to make submission than offered warfare, and many of them were content to accept English honours. Four of their greatest chieftains, who styled themselves 'kings', after being prepared and instructed by the Earl of Ormonde, and having performed their vigils in Christ Church, were on the next day, 25 March 1395, knighted in the same church by King Richard II. Later that day, 'in the robes agreeable to their state' – whether as kings or knights is not made plain – they ate with him at table'. (However there is no evidence to support the story that

Ormonde gave Froissart 'an amusing account of his experience in instructing "kings" in the usages of civilised society'.)[16]

Finally, even Turloch O'Donnell submitted to King Richard II, at another imposing ceremony attended by five bishops and three earls. This submission was of the greatest significance of all, since O'Donnell had the power to do homage on behalf of seven 'nations' and four other chieftains; although another important capitulation would be that of the chiefs of Upper Ormond, who submitted as vassals of their Earl'. Seven more Irish chieftains submitted at Kilkenny, on 25 April 1595; and, so far, the terms were seen as being honourable to the Irish. But the men were, in effect, only promised the 'Irish lands' that they already held; or, at least, these were the only lands they unequivocally secured. The response of the 'degenerate English' was nothing like the general and generous one of the native Irish. Six, though, did submit and were 'received back to grace'.

In a last ceremony, on 1 May 1395, on the King's ship *Le Trinitée*, in the port of Waterford, three of the most notable rebels came on board and were created knights by the King, and presented with arms and armour. They were, apparently, not entirely overwhelmed with the honour, answering proudly that it was their custom for every chieftain's son to take up arms at 7 years of age; and when the ceremony was over, 'they departed, having asserted in a dignified aloofness the tenacious traditions of their race'.[17]

Yet Richard, despite his reasonable attitude towards the Irish who submitted to him, at the same time pursued an active military policy against his more unwilling subjects. It was certainly on his instructions that a party of his own people set out on a predatory excursion into Offaly, although they were not to get their own way in this matter. An Irish chieftain, who had not sworn allegiance to the King, pursued them to a point where they could only turn to fight, and when they did so the Irish had the best of it, with great numbers of English slain and sixty horses taken from them.

Another of the King of England's party, under the control of the Earl Marshal – Roger Mortimer, Earl of March, who had since been appointed Lieutenant of Ulster, Connacht and Meath – set out upon a predatory excursion into the province of Ely (which was Butler territory). But here again his men lost out against the Irish, with O'Carroll's people killing many of their best soldiers when they came up against them; and again taking many of their strongest horses, which was always the best indication of a successful encounter.

Richard was compelled to return to England at the news of a fierce Lollard attack upon the Church, when 'swearing to hang them all unless they recanted, Richard hastened home'.[18] His stay in Ireland had lasted for just over seven months – a visit too short to enable him to subdue the Irish by force but long enough for him to arrest the decay of English power in the country. The expedition was useful, too, in helping Richard to build up his military forces, especially from his own estates. He had come to realise that if he was not to be constantly at the mercy of the private armies his English magnates had mobilised while fighting in the French wars, and still retained after peace had been declared, he must raise an army of his own; moreover, one that must be kept on permanent notice in England. The troops of this new army, the King's men-at-arms and his archers, all of which had been raised in Ireland, were distinguished by a badge on which was emblazoned a white hart.

Richard sailed for England on 15 May 1395, and before he went he made several extensive grants of land in Leinster, with the intention of creating a new group of landlords there. But in doing so, he diplomatically left out the acres that bordered those of the Earl of Ormonde in these new grants. With the exception of Leinster, though, the settlement of their affairs was considered to be a triumph for the Gaelic chiefs who had attended upon him, since it almost amounted to a division of Ireland between them and the hated 'middle nation'. True, whatever they had usurped they would have to surrender, and MacCarthy, O'Kennedy and O'Neill must admit the Earls of Desmond, Ormonde and Ulster as their mesne lords, to negotiate between them and the 'Lord of Ireland'. But after such binding instruments – if they were actually ever observed – no further doubt existed that they had received full legal status for their lands and their captaincies.

Leinster however was a different matter. The chiefs there would not think of giving up the 'fair hills of their hereditary province' to a people as belligerent as they themselves, and King Richard's high hopes of a lasting truce came to little here. The much-loathed Anglo-Irish parliament, with its French and English speech, its feudal peers and 'bourgeois' commons, was not a place where such Irish could ever have felt at ease. Nor would they ever feel truly safe there; and in this respect nothing had really changed.

Indeed upon the King's departure for England, after even more chieftains had made submission to him, the O' Byrnes immediately rose up in arms against the Earl of March, who had been left as the King's representative. March, together with the Earl of Ormonde, immediately retaliated, wasting the O'Byrne lands in Wicklow and seizing their castle. MacMurrough, too, soon broke faith with the King (never having seen him as a lawful sovereign), and he would not adhere, he said, to a promise 'extorted by fear'. So, in the event, MacMurrough still held on to Norragh and refused to depart. The English of Leinster then attempted to make him a prisoner by means of some unspecified treachery, in which they were unsuccessful; for he escaped from them 'by the strength of his arm, or by his valour, so they were not able to do him an injury'.[19]

O'Kennedy, the Irish 'Lord of Ormond', died in 1936, having proved himself an implacable enemy to the English lords of that same name. Others were there to take over his enmity, and a triumph was gained by one of them, O'Toole, over the Irish and the 'Saxons' of Leinster, in which the English were 'dreadfully slaughtered', and six score of their heads

**1.** Bannow Bay, county Wexford, where the Anglo-Normans landed in 1169. The ruined church in the distance marks the site of an abandoned Anglo-Norman settlement.

**2.** Perkin Warbeck, who used Ireland as a base for his claim to the English throne.

**3.** Sir John de Botiller (d. 1285). The fact that he has his legs crossed signifies that he had been on a crusade.

*Above:* **4.** A knighting ceremony, mid-13th century.

*Below:* **5.** Death of Simon de Montfort 1265.

**6.** Castle building, 13th century.

**7.** Tomb of Piers Butler, who became the 8th Earl Ormonde upon the death of Thomas Butler in 1515

**8.** Battle of Towton 1461, the bloodiest battle in the Wars of the Roses. Chroniclers record that the snow-covered terrain was turned crimson by the bloodshed.

**9.** An Irish soldier of the 13th century.

**10.** Boys training to be knights.

**11.** Irish warfare: cattle raiding.

**12.** The Irish Exchequer was first set up in 1200 and a Chancery followed in 1232.

**13.** Prisoners.

**14.** 16th-century Irish apparel.

**15.** An Irish warrior fells a sacred tree.

**16.** Sir Henry Sidney arrives in Dublin, 1581. He first went to Ireland with Lord Deputy Thomas Radcliffe, 3rd Earl of Sussex (his brother-in-law) in 1556. He succeeded to the post himself in 1566.

**17.** Irish chieftains submitting to Sidney.

**18.** The Earl of Desmond murders an English Deputy.

**19.** An Irish soldier contrasted with an English soldier, *c.* 1600.

**20.** Effigy of a knight, County Kilkenny.

**21.** Ormonde Castle, Carrick-on-Suir, acquired by the Butler family in 1315. All that survives today dates from the 15th century or later.

**22.** Ormonde Castle. The manor house was built by 'Black Tom' Butler, 10th Earl of Ormonde *c.* 1600. Although the style is relatively common in England, the manor is the only one of its kind in Ireland. It is said to be the birthplace of Anne Boleyn.

**23.** Kilkenny Castle. The first Norman tower was built on the site in 1172 by 'Strongbow' Richard de Clare. The castle became the base of the Butler family after James Butler, 3rd Earl of Ormonde, bought it in 1391.

24. Kilkenny Castle. The castle was damaged during the Cromwellian conquest and remodelled in the manner of a chateau by James Butler, 12th Earl and 1st Duke of Ormonde, when he returned from exile.

*Above:* **25.** Roscommon Castle, a royal fortress, was erected shortly before 1300. The insertion of large, mullioned windows in the late 1500s rendered it less formidable as a military fortress.

*Right:* **26.** Effigy of Edward III, from his tomb in Westminster Abbey. Although a decisive ruler in his maturity, the fact that he was crowned too young to govern enabled the regent Roger Mortimer to ensure that the new earldom of Ormonde was granted to James Butler.

**27.** Ross Castle, Killarney. Built in 1269 by the Lord Justice of Ireland, Robert de Ufford, the castle passed back and forth between Anglo-Norman and Irish hands.

It was badly damaged by the Cromwellian forces in Ireland in 1652 and fell into disrepair after a fire in 1690.

**28.** Oliver Cromwell (1599–1658) at Westminster.

were carried off for exhibition before the victor. Besides this he acquired a vast number of prisoners, along with the spoils of their armaments, horses and armour.

James Butler's brother-in-law, the Earl of Desmond, also died in this fatal year, 'after the victory of Penance' – though it was in his bed, and not on the battlefield. He was esteemed as 'a cheerful and courteous man', who excelled all his English peers (and many Irish scholars) in his knowledge of the Irish language, poetry, history and other learning. Popular with Irish and English alike, his only absolute enemy appears to have been his brother-in-law, James Butler. Desmond's successor, his son, drowned in the Suir, not long after assuming the earldom.

The Earl of March had remained in Ireland, in order to wage vigorous war against various Irish septs, yet this did not bring any notable results – indeed at times it only resulted in humiliating failures. The chieftains, O'Byrne and O'Toole, combined to give a battle to the English, and the Lord Lieutenant, backed by Ormonde, made war on their integrated army, engaging them in battle at Kellistown bear Carlow. This proved to be a more fatal encounter for the English than most, since the Earl of March's force was overwhelmed, and the Earl himself, wearing only the linen dress of an Irish chieftain, was slain on 10 June 1398. (He had been so keen to identify himself with his Irish subjects that he assumed the Irish dress and horse trappings, and being conspicuously brave he had rashly rushed on, far in advance of his followers. Unrecognised by them in his Irish dress, he had been instantly killed and torn to pieces.[20]

Many English were slaughtered in that action, but the Earl's death would prove to have disastrous consequences, for his own family as well as for the King of England, who had long accepted him as his heir, should he himself fail to provide one. The name of Mortimer, 'to which Ireland had been so fatal' (Roger would be one of three of his family to die there), was reduced to one young son, Edward, and a daughter, Anne. The boy was far too young to be considered as a possible monarch, and so it was that, 'in an obscure Irish battle died the heir to the throne of England, and the King's right-hand man against his baronial enemies'.[21] His death would also provoke Richard II into undertaking his last fatal expedition to Ireland.

In that same year there was a plague within the English Pale, and in the following year Henry O'Neill led an army against the English, after which a great number of them were expelled from 'his' province of Ulster. O'Neill's two sons later went on an excursion against the English of Dundalk, when the English assembled to oppose them and routed their army, taking Donnell, Henry O'Neill's son prisoner and killing most of his men. Donnell O'Neill was sent to England as a hostage in the following year, after his people had refused to pay his ransom (or, more possibly, could not raise it at the time, since he was ransomed from England as late as 1400).

In England matters were coming to a crisis point, and King Richard called up the army he had assembled in Ireland to back him in the moves he planned to make against his recalcitrant nobles. By 1397 the King felt strong enough to strike back at the enemies he had suffered for so long and three great earls were arrested and charged with treason. Appealing to a parliament greatly intimidated by the menacing presence of his 'white hart' retainers, the commons executed, imprisoned or deprived his opponents, and the house was then adjourned to meet again at Shrewsbury, one of the strongest centres of Richard's military power.

From the safety of Shrewsbury, Richard II took his final revenge on all those who had defied him earlier in his reign, and he declared illegal all the acts of the 'Merciless Parliament'. To stress this change of policy, he also rehabilitated the old defenders of the royal authority as far back as the executed Despensers. In Ireland, only a few of the Butlers had any need of this act of rehabilitation, but many of their powerful Anglo-Irish enemies were placed on an offenders list, to the immense satisfaction of the Ormonde family.

Shortly after the extraordinary parliamentary session was held at which King Richard snatched back power, he also seized an opportunity to exile his cousin, Henry Bolingbroke, not wishing to face the might of the House of Lancaster, of whom Henry was the acknowledged leader. When Bolingbroke's aged father, John of Gaunt, died in February 1399, the King forbade Henry to enter into his inheritance, and then extended what had initially been a simple banishment into permanent exile.

This extraordinary blunder by the King turned the greatest magnate of the realm into his bitterest foe. Furthermore, it unsettled the propertied classes in the process; for if a prince could be debarred from his inheritance by an arbitrary decree, were any man's possessions safe? The magnates were all the more unnerved because Richard II, having tasted success, began to make himself even more unpopular with the politically powerful classes. Exercising a strict control over local government, he used more authoritarian courts of law, demanded ever larger loans, and issued blank charters, later to be filled in as he pleased.

With a total belief in his divine right to rule, and elated by his success, Richard II never realised how slender were the foundations of his royal authority. He had a fatal incapacity to judge situations or to gauge other men's thoughts, but despite this lack he must have thought he had so effectively cowed his subjects that he might safely cross the Irish Sea. Consequently, he chose this critical time to yet again leave his unhappy kingdom for Ireland – this time to avenge the death of his heir, Roger Mortimer. He went despite warnings of a coming catastrophe in England, although before leaving London he made his will, in which he expressly provided for the possibility of his being drowned at sea or slain in Ireland.

Filled with fury and despair at Mortimer's death, King Richard declared that MacMurrough had forfeited his lands, which he then bestowed on his illegitimate half-brother, the English Duke of Surrey, whom he appointed as Lord Lieutenant of Ireland and sent over in advance of his own party. Surrey landed at Dublin in October 1388, and his task was to prepare for the 'Second Coming of the King'.[22]

As Richard was childless, despite two marriages, his heir presumptive had long been officially recognised as Roger Mortimer, grandson of Lionel, second son of King Edward III. His cousin's death now left Mortimer's son, a boy of 6, between Henry of Lancaster and the succession to the throne, and so any decision by King Richard to leave England at this critical juncture carried within it the seeds of fatality. But the King, who had loved his cousin, even while suspecting the nature of his ambitions, needed to avenge the death of Mortimer and to 'vindicate the royal majesty against Ireland',[23] and so a fresh army was raised for that purpose. It would prove a calamitous decision, for Richard not only went to Ireland at the wrong time, he again appointed his incompetent uncle, Edmund, Duke of York, as Regent of England in his absence.

King Richard II landed at Waterford on 1 June 1399. He was accompanied by upwards of a dozen peers and bishops, and he carried with him the royal regalia and his personal treasure. The last reigning monarch to visit Ireland in the Middle Ages, this improvident step would prove to have far-reaching consequences for him as King, although neither of his two campaigns in Ireland would have any long-lasting impact on that country. On this expedition he included John Lovel. Perhaps his best fighting commander; he was a confirmed supporter of the king and had been retained by King Richard 'for life' in 1388.

From Kilkenny, the whole English army marched against MacMurrough, 'suffering terribly in the trackless hill country on the borders of Carlow and Wexford'.[24] Jean Creton, a French esquire, left a vivid description in verse of the misery of Richard's army in the dense woods of MacMurrough's country, where his knights had no food for days on end. As had happened previously the Leinster King could not be 'drawn to battle', and so Richard pressured to send the Earl of Gloucester to meet him. MacMurrough, rejecting all ideas of pardon and submission, declared himself to be the rightful King of Ireland, asserting that it was 'unjust to deprive me of what is my land by conquest'.[25] (This meeting between Gloucester and MacMurrough, along with his 3,000 men in some unnamed glen in Leinster, gives us a graphic picture of the times and the extravagant character of the Irish, both in appearance and manners, as reported by Jean Creton.)

Later, negotiations having inevitably failed, the two sides fought each other; with the 'large, handsome Irishman, dressed – in flamboyantly colourful costume – and mounted as his ancestors were',[26] charging on horseback against the serried ranks of mail-clad English knights. On this occasion the knights came off worse, for though they may have been the heroes on the battlefields of 14th century Europe with their well-shaped – even formalised – tactics, they found that they were useless in the face of the guerrilla warfare they encountered with the Irish.

Richard, recognising this, returned to Dublin, proposing to renew the campaign in autumn, when the trees were leafless and MacMurrough could not rely upon their camouflage. He was said to have intended crowning the Duke of Surrey as the 'King of Ireland'[27] to express his contempt for Irish pretensions. But as a proper reply to what he saw as a victory, MacMurrough demanded a peace treaty with reservation, and when King Richard, who had reached Dublin on 1 July, heard this 'he paled with anger, offering 100 marks for Art MacMurrough, alive or dead'.

Richard swore that he would burn the Irishman out of his forest stronghold, and he consequently marched his troops back to Waterford. But there, the news of Henry Bolinbroke's illegal return to England reached him. Henry had in fact arrived in England at the same time as Richard had reached Dublin, and by now he was in full march upon Bristol, where the troops raised in the king's defence were displaying no readiness to be led against him. With his realm of England in the gravest danger from his most dreaded challenger, Ireland must suddenly have seemed to Richard to be the least important of his problems.

Yet between them, the king and his best commander managed to inflict considerable damage on the King of Leinster, who 'was mightily weakened and brought low',[28] when he was overtaken by the English of Leinster and Meath although there were huge losses on both sides. Despite this, the English king's lordship of Ireland collapsed, even as his authority in England was foundering, and royal ascendancy was not to be fully restored for over a century. From 1399 to 1534 the effective authority of the English Crown in Ireland was hedged into the little Pale, outside of which Gaelic kings and Norman magnates ruled the land. A succession of these magnates, among them the Ormonde Butlers, would nominally represent the King in Ireland, but they increasingly behaved as though they were independent princes, which by then they very possibly believed to be the case.

The last truly undeniable King of England sailed for Milford Haven on 18 August 1399, to meet his tragic fate. Art Oge MacMurrough may have suffered defeat in his own country, but he was to enjoy a peculiar form of triumph abroad. For having first brought about the death of Roger Mortimer, the true heir, by delaying Richard in the wilds of Leinster, he had let the ambitious usurper Bolingbroke into England and had wrecked the unity of that country for the next 100 years. (Although, according to Bolingbroke's own testimony, he had returned from exile with no intention of seizing the throne, but had simply re-entered England to recover his ducal inheritance.)

He was, however, warmly welcomed by the northern lords when he landed at the port of Ravenspur on the Humber, and he acted throughout with such speed and skill that Richard's incompetent lieutenants were quickly out-manoeuvred. When the king returned from his ineffectual visit to Ireland, Bolingbroke and his followers had cut a swathe through England, gathering adherents all the time. By the time that Richard reached Gloucester, Henry stood at the head of a substantial army (perhaps 100,000 strong). Even the two men who had served the king best in Ireland, Mowbray and Lovel, deserted to Henry Bolingbroke on their return to England, and when Richard reached Conway he found only a small band of supporters waiting for him.

From Conway, he could have escaped by sea, either to return to Ireland, or even to sail to Gascony; but instead he spinelessly delivered himself up into Henry's hands (having previously declared that the Duke of Lancaster 'should die a death that would make a noise as far as Turkey'[29]). A surprising detail in this story is that Bolingbroke's son, Henry – later King Henry V – of whom Richard was apparently genuinely fond, had accompanied him to Ireland, and had even been knighted by him during the visit. (Young Henry's battles in Ireland were rehearsals for the ones that would later bring him fame.) It seems not to have occurred to the embattled king to use young Henry as a bargaining counter, or as a hostage, although the youth had been sent to the castle of Trim for safekeeping.

Having rejected advice to cross at once into North Wales, with such a following as he had shipping for, Richard had returned to Waterford and conveyed the bulk of his army over to Milford Haven, sending a trusted commander to raise Cheshire and North Wales. Deserted by most of his men, he was taken prisoner at Flint and tricked by Bolingbroke into signing the document of abdication, although he did not resign his crown to his cousin Henry, but rather placed it on the ground, resigning it to God. (It had already been settled by parliament that Richard's second cousin, the boy Roger Mortimer, was the true heir, and it may be that Richard surrendered his crown so cravenly because he believed it could not legitimately pass to his greatest rival.)

However the warm greeting of the northern lords echoed by that of the Londoners, and the need for a powerful individual of unchallenged status among the nobility overrode all other factors. England needed a ruler who would restore confidence and unite a government that had gone to pieces as a result of Richard's excesses. This was no time to install a minor on the throne, and so Bolingbroke became Henry IV of England in September 1399. By the acclamation of parliament he was crowned on 13 October.

Yet throughout what remained of 1399 the Irish administration hesitated to amend the new seal of the usurper, waiting to see, perhaps, if he could establish his position before transferring their loyalty to him. The new king, of course, was too occupied with matters at home to concern himself much with Ireland, even though, from early in his reign, the Irish chieftains began to regain land at an alarming rate. The Anglo-Irish were pushed back to an even narrower coastal strip around Dublin, and the Butlers, although their lands were by now someway to the south of this Pale, would become more predominant in securing these borders for the king. In May 1400 King Henry IV appointed Ormonde as chief commissioner to inquire into 'certain seditions'.

But the Butlers themselves may have attempted to undermine the authority of the state during these first critical months of Henry's reign. A message sent to England by the guardian and council of Ireland, at the end of 1399, reported that the English septs (les nacions Englois), 'who are rebels in all parts of the country, such as the Butlers, Le Poers, Geraldines, Berminghams, etc., are not amenable to the law. And though they wish to be called gentlemen, they are in truth nothing but sturdy robbers'.[30]

It was not a good time to be in the service of the King of England, of *any* King of England, and not simply because of the commotion in that troubled kingdom. Life in Ireland for officials in the English service was growing increasingly hazardous. Even the collectors of customs duties, appointed in 1400 'for all ports of Ireland', were now permitted to use deputies, on the grounds that 'the administration of these offices ... could only go by sea, and this with a force of fencibles'.[31] The lack of communication was such that the Mayor of Waterford was excused from taking his oath of office in Dublin because of the dangers in journeying there. In June 1400 it was claimed that both city and county were being harassed by the attempts of Lord Poers and other rebels, and many dared not go outside their town 'on account of the dangers, and the peril to their lives'.[32]

Other Munster towns faced similar problems, being 'surrounded and hemmed in by enemies and rebels'. Henry IV, 'at the instant supplication of our dear cousin, James le Botiller, Earl of Ormonde',[33] representing the tenants of Imokill in County Cork, 'both temporal and spiritual', granted the townsfolk a special dispensation from labouring outside their walls, where they were a prey to the Irish rebels. They must only answer when the King's Lieutenant, the Justiciar, Chancellor or Treasurer, came within the county, and then only upon the King's writ, or the mandate of the Lieutenant. Henry commanded his officers not to 'molest' the citizens because of this situation.

From the beginning of Henry IV's reign, money – or rather the lack of it – was the main problem, although the King had ambitious plans for Ireland (as he had also for Guienne, the last English-held part of the old empire in France). He had ordered a great programme of expenditure to be undertaken in these two countries, and his Treasurer did his best to carry it out. Yet because of the continual demands on his expenses – for the most part made by the King's own family – finding the money for these grand schemes became impossible. As the treasurer wrote to the King, at the end of 1401:

For truly, revered lord, there is not in your Treasury at the moment enough to pay the messengers who are to bear the letters which you have ordained to be sent to the lords, knights and esquires to be of your council…unless loans are resorted to by the aid of your gracious power and of my lords of your council.[34]

An expedition against the Scots in July–September 1400 had been a very costly one, and the escalating harassment by the Irish chieftains was a growing drain on expenses. In fact, only one part of Ireland remained relatively quiescent at this period; for the relations between the Gaelic Irish and the Butlers, at least with in the confines of the Ormonde domain, were less out of control than those outside their borders during this difficult year.

There are a number of examples of contracts drawn up between the Earl and his Irish liegemen. On 20 January 1401 O'Brennan, head of his nation, or sept, 'became the faithful man' of the Earl of Ormonde, paying him six marks yearly, 'at or before the Feast of All Saints, as a token of his homage'. In the case of O'Brennan or of any member of this family committing trespass on the Earl's people and tenants, or of the county of Kilkenny, then the offender was to pay the Earl for double the value of the 'said trespass…Which in Ireland is called keyn or ardkeyn, etc.'[35]

The new king, while still trying to stabilise his realm in spite of the various attempts to dethrone him, quickly realised the extent of James Butler's worth. Ormonde was made Constable of Ireland in the third year of Henry IV's reign, according to the patent rolls of that year, and in the next year he was also appointed deputy of that office (during which term he was ordered by the usurper to adjourn an exceptionally boisterous session of the Irish parliament, then discussing the dubiety of Henry IV's right to the English crown). But to make an uncertain situation even more unpredictable, a hasty decision by King Henry would lead to a state of tremendous political confusion for the Anglo-Irish when he raised his second son to a position far beyond his capacities, and gave him control of Ireland.

Henry's most urgent problem was in finding men that he could trust for the more sensitive positions within his government, and as a result he had to depend too much upon the members of his own family, and his sons particularly, even though they were still immature youths. On his father's accession to the throne, Thomas of Lancaster, born in 1388, had been made the Seneschal of England, despite being too young to discharge the office adequately. Yet only two years later, in the summer of 1401, he was also made Lord Justice of Ireland for three years, for which he had to have the guidance of two wardens in order to carry out his duties effectively.[36] He crossed the Irish Sea in November, arriving in Dublin on the 13th. A council met at Christmas, and took Thomas for a journey down the coast to 'assert his authority', but with no notable success. The difficulties of the English government in Ireland were very acute, and a boy lieutenant simply added to the cares of his guardians.

As always with Ireland, money, or the lack of it, was the major problem. In 1401 there was a special grant made by the local communities, in which magnates, nobles, clergy and commons are mentioned as taking part. But subsidies had to be reinforced by a further grant to enable 800 foot soldiers to be maintained. These were paid to receivers appointed by the Lieutenant.

Appointed on 1 May, with a salary of 12,000*l* per annum, Prince Thomas secured so little in funding that by the following February many of his captains had already deserted him, and others were threatening to follow suit because of the non-payment of their wages. By August 1402 he was reputed to be, 'so destitute of money that he has not a penny in the world. Nor can [he] borrow a single penny, because all his jewels and plate, that he can spare of those which he must of necessity keep, are spent and sunk in wages'.[37] Even members of his immediate household were considering abandoning him because of his poverty, and he was shut up in the town of Naas with the council and a small retinue (who dared not leave him for fear of the harm that might have befallen him).

The Prince was not helped by the attitude of his permanently sparring Anglo-Irish allies, and the Earl of Ormonde, perhaps the most loyal of King Henry's Irish nobles, was occasionally called away to deal with sporadic domestic conflicts. In 1401 he had sought to secure his flank by a marriage alliance with Theobald Burke of Clan William in County Tipperary, whose territories were strategically situated between his earldom and that of his greatest rivals, the Desmonds. (It is significant that by agreeing to this alliance Ormonde was stepping across the Anglo-Irish divide in a sense, for by this time the Burkes – formerly the De Burghs – had become almost completely Gaelic, and the treaty speaks of the Burkes 'and others of their nation'.) Under the marriage terms Ormonde, 'for [the] fostering [of] the good love and accord' between the two families, gave his daughter Elizabeth to Theobald Burke. In return, Burke undertook, 'to aid the Earl in all his wars and disputes and those of his people, saving only more ancient friendships and the claims of justice'.[38] Burke does seem to have honoured this undertaking when a minor war broke out between the Earls of Desmond and Ormonde in 1402, and the two MacWilliams brothers went to the assistance of the latter.

The marriage of Theobald Burke to Elizabeth Butler required a dispensation from the Holy See, which was obtained by Theobald at his own cost. Her dowry, too, was more substantial than usual, comprising 240 cows, 120 in hand, and the other half by Michaelmas; and the Earl also gave Theobald Burke a gift of forty stud horses, all evidence of the importance he attached to this union. In return, Theobald gave his new wife a manor house, with all its lands; and, more importantly, he granted her 'free passage for all merchants, carriers and tradesmen, coming and going as far as [the city of] Limerick'[39] (a freedom of movement that would be more useful to her father than to his wife).

It soon became obvious that Ireland could not be governed by a mere stripling, and on 1 September 1403, it was decided that Thomas of Lancaster should return to England although he nominally remained the Lieutenant of Ireland, which was to be now ruled by deputy, Sir Stephen Scrope. Having sampled the peculiar nature of campaigning in Ireland, the 15-year–old Prince would be given a wider experience of warfare in Glamorganshire and Normandy; and when he returned to Ireland, in the early days of the next earldom of Ormonde, he would be battle-hardened, and more fitted for command.

But his removal from Ireland in 1403 made little impression, and it was the absence of his mature and experienced deputy Le Scrope, when he was forced by circumstance to return to England, that was the more marked. In March 1404 the now politically seasoned Earl of Ormonde was offered the office of Justiciar, but it was an honour that he vigorously sought to avoid. In a strongly worded petition to the King, he asked to be excused responsibility on the grounds that he could simply not afford it, since he had already incurred heavy expenses during his government service with the two previous monarchs. The Irish treasury was now so feeble and reduced that it could offer him little assistance, and he therefore requested the Lords of the Privy Council to urge the King to make new provisions for Ireland, provisions that would allow him to be discharged from duty.

Henry IV's response – phenomenal for so impoverished a king – was to grant an unusually generous subsidy, through the Irish parliament, which helped to tide the Earl over the emergency, but which left the fundamental problem unsolved. The subsidy was granted to Ormonde as 'soldier and governor of the wars', rather than as Justiciar, so that the grant would not set a precedent, but which meant that no account was ever rendered at the Dublin Exchequer. It was also granted to the Earl on the important condition that he renounced the system of coigne and livery for as long as he remained Justiciar.[40]

Unable to withdraw from the office, Ormonde was again made Constable of Ireland in 1405, in the absence of Sir Stephen le Scrope, and in April of that year he held a parliament at Dublin, where the statutes of Dublin and Kilkenny, and the Charter of Ireland were confirmed. (The commons had not been summoned since 1394. There were twenty-six constituencies in all, fourteen counties and twelve towns at the maximum, but it is unlikely that the fifty-two members ever fully assembled at any one time. At this period, membership of the Commons house seems to have been little valued, and the difficulty of getting the right sort of candidate was pronounced, a problem that would surface more dramatically in the time of the next Earl.)

During his time as Justiciar, Ormonde's triumphs were more military in origin than political. Most spectacularly, he had a number of triumphs when repressing the Scots and Welsh in their renewed depredations upon the Irish coastline, and – even more impressively – he returned their outrages tenfold by making astonishingly successful retaliatory assaults upon their own shores.

The third Earl died, still in possession of the unwanted office of Lord Justice, in Gowran, on 7 September 1405, in the sixth year of the usurper Henry IV's reign. In his lifetime the Butlers had come dramatically to the forefront of Irish history, and James himself was known as 'the head of the chivalry of all Ireland'.[41] The 5th Earl of Kildare was elected Lord Justice at Ormonde's death; and in the same year as his father's passing the Earl's second son, Sir Richard Butler, known as 'Hardfoot' was killed by an Irish rival. Almost certainly encouraged by the Earl's demise, Art MacMurrough, 'King of Leinster', was encouraged once again to wage war against the English.

James married a daughter of Lord Welles, and had two sons, James IV and Richard, to whom King Richard II had been godfather. He had also two illegitimate sons; one of whom, Thomas le Botiller would become the Prior of Kilmainham, and who, despite his calling, was a 'very martial man'. (He, too, would serve as Lord Justice of Ireland from 1408 to 1409, and he appears to have held little truck with the religious vow of chastity, since 'several good families of gentlemen in the counties Kilkenny and Tipperary sprang from his loins'). The other illegitimate son, James le Botiller, alias 'Goldie', was the ancestor of the lords of Caher (created barons in 1542), and from whom other gentry of Tipperary and Waterford were descended.

The third James built the castle of Dunfert in County Kilkenny, and in 1386 he had founded a house of Friars Minors at Aylesbury, Buckinghamshire, England. Up to the end of King Edward III's reign, Butler power had mainly lain in County Tipperary, but here the revival of Irish chieftains such as the O'Kennedys had caused the territory to recede to the southern half of that county, though the Butler claim to the overlordship of Tipperary was never renounced.

The great event in the family fortunes had been the acquisition of Kilkenny Castle, along with its rich acres, which the Butlers continually improved and increased. For up to their coming into its possession, the liberty of Kilkenny, like the other lordships of Leinster, had by 1390 become little better than an absentee business, and a mere right to collect Irish rents, a situation the Butlers transformed once they had gained legal title to the estate. In one of the most remarkable transfers of feudal property ever recorded, Hugh Despenser had surrendered all his lands and ownership in County Kilkenny to the 3rd Earl of Ormonde, and Kilkenny would remain the capital of the Earl's successors until the 20th century. It can truly be said that the Ormondes derived their main strength from this fertile and compact county.

The 3rd Earl, during the reign of Richard II, seems to have been the leading Irish magnate in the southern part of the country. It was largely upon him that the King relied during his visit to Ireland in 1394–5, not least to bring the Irish of East Munster to obedience. Here is considerable evidence to show that Ormonde had great personal influence with the Irish chiefs, that he spoke their language well, and was regarded on all sides as a 'wise and gallant cavalier'.[42]

# *Notes:*

1. Curtis, *Calendar of Ormonde Deeds.*
2. Ibid.
3. Ibid.
4. Ibid. De Vere was presumably styled 'Marquis' from the French 'marchis', literally meaning 'Count of the March'. In modern usage, it is always spelled 'Marquess' *(Oxford English Dictionary).*
5. Carte, *The Life of the Duke of Ormonde.*
6. Curtis, op. cit.
7. The Four Masters, *Annals of the Kingdom of Ireland.*
8. Ibid.
9. Ibid.
10. Carte, op. cit.
11. Creton (ed. Webb) *History of King Richard II.*
12. Ibid.
13. The Four Masters, op. cit.
14. *Urrighs:* his personal escort or bodyguards.
15. Carte, op. cit.
16. Froissart, *Chronique.*
17. The Four Masters, op. cit.
18. Creton, op. cit.
19. The Four Masters, op. cit.
20. Ibid.
21. Carte, op. cit.
22. Creton, op. cit.
23. Ibid.
24. The Four Masters, op. cit.
25. Ibid.
26. Creton, op. cit.
27. Ibid.
28. The Four Masters, op. cit.
29. Creton, op. cit.

30. The Four Masters, op.cit.
31. 'Fencibles' were men who took military service purely in defence of their homeland (A.J. Aitken, *Oxford English Dictionary*).
32. The Four Masters, op. cit.
33. Carte, op. cit.
34. Kygngeston ed. *Expenses Rolls* (Camden Society).
35. '…keyn and ardkeyn': more a matter of 'unlawful entry', or even simple poaching, than any act of invasion.
36. Nicolas, *Proceedings Privy Council.*
37. Ibid.
38. Curtis, op. cit.
39. Ibid.
40. 'Coigne' was a system adopted from the Irish, by which military personnel were billeted upon private families, an exaction demanded as a right by Irish chieftains. 'Livery' meant not only provisions or clothing for retainers, but also provender for their horses.
41. Four Masters, op. cit.
42. Ibid.

# CHAPTER VI

# *The White Earl*

King Henry IV granted to his 'dear son' Thomas custody of all the castles, manors, lands, rents and possessions, together with all their appurtenances. They had belonged to James le Botiller, the late Earl of Ormonde, because the new earl was under age, and the estates had therefore reverted to the Crown. This was undeniably the strangest of the Butler successor guardianships since Thomas of Lancaster was himself then only seventeen years old. But he was to hold James Butler's inheritance until 'the full coming of age of the heir, together with the marriage of the same'.[1]

As was customary at that time the immature Earl was expected to marry young and to breed early, as is revealed in the next clause:

> If the said heir die before he reach full age, with his heir still under age, then Thomas shall have custody of the next heir, and marriage of same, without disparagement, and so from heir to heir until one of the said heirs come of age.[2]

The Prince was to provide sufficient maintenance for him, to keep the houses, closes and buildings on all his castles and manors, 'without waste or destruction', and expected to, 'discharge all burdens due from the same, as long as he shall have this custody.'[3]

The document was officially sealed on 2 October 1405, and a year later James 'fitzJames' le Botiller was given a whole township in County Waterford 'to have and to hold of him and his heirs of the Church's Lords of the Fee, etc'.[4]

In March 1406 Thomas of Lancaster was confirmed as Lord Lieutenant of Ireland for a term of twelve years, giving him full power. He was to receive a salary of 7,000 marks per annum, but (as in his previous viceroyalty) the money was not forthcoming; and by 1411 the amount owed to him would exceed 5,000 marks. Thomas did not take to his duties at once, as he wished to hear parliament regulate the succession to the throne; but the parlous affairs of Ireland required a royal presence, and so he sailed on 2 August, landing at Carlingford and proceeding directly to Dublin. There his first act was to arrest the Earl of Kildare and his sons, and his next step was to make a raid in Leinster, during the course of which he was wounded. Thomas, at 18, had developed a keen taste for the battlefield and a great capacity for risk-taking.

Stephen le Scrope, who was Thomas's deputy, was due to leave for England the moment that Thomas arrived in Ireland. Henry IV suggested that the absent deputy should be replaced by a suitable substitute. And astonishing as the decision to make his immature son the chief governor of his most volatile dominion had been, King Henry's choice of his deputy would be even more extraordinary, since this proxy would be his 'dear cousin', James le Botiller, Earl of Ormonde. Yet more astonishingly this plan was accepted without noticeable protest by the Irish parliament; and so it came about that a youth still unable to enter into his inheritance was made second-in-command to the callow adolescent who controlled both his fortune and the destiny of Ireland.

However Thomas was not able to control James Butler's fortune for long, for soon after taking custody of Ormonde lands they were put into other hands. A patent dated Dublin, January 10, Henry IV, reads:

> Wherein the King with the consent of Stephen le Scrope, knight, deputy to his son, Thomas of Lancastre, Steward of England and Lieutenant of Ireland, and of his Council there, at the request of James le Botiller, Earl of Ermon [sic] and to his use of profit, grants to Robert Habrick and Nicholas Stokes, the *custodian* of all the castles and manors of Nenagh, Roscre, Thurles, Ardmaile, Milton, Cathydrunesse, Inchcoyne, Balybothy, Carrick-MacGriffen, Grenagh, to be held by them until full Age, without paying anything hereout to us, for the better government and sustenation thereof, etc.[5]

Clearly, the Prince was having difficulty tending to his ward's property while supervising the government of Ireland; although it is evident from the wording of the patent that the young Earl himself desired a change of guardianship.

Looking at the heavy responsibilities with which the fourth James was entrusted it is apparent that he was mature beyond his years, even though he was still politically unfledged, for it cannot all have been due to nepotism. That he was more than capable is shown by the ease with which he held on to office during Scrope's absence and also by the extraordinary powers he was accorded. He had the authority to keep the peace and to, 'chastise and repress all, both English and Irish enemies, who rise up against us,'[6] and the Irish clergy were commanded to be 'intendent to the new deputy', but whether this was a royal or an archiepiscopal order is not clear.

Of all the Ormondes to that date the fourth James had received the best education and was seen as a 'man of good parts' even in youth. Extremely precocious, he was famous as a master of learning. As most noblemen of that time were unable even to write their own name this was rare enough, but the fact that he was so young was astonishing. James was noted for the 'refinement' of his education, and his castle-seat at Kilkenny was the centre of a flourishing Anglo-Irish culture with a particular focus on literature. His ancestors had shown a taste for books in the native script, and James was known to be strongly Gaelicised. Like his father he was as fluent in Irish as the best of his bards, and he was probably the first of the Anglo-Irish lords to appoint a *brehon* [7] to his service, although it was most likely that the majority of his tenants were of English descent.

James Butler was also a great patron of scribes and he was fortunate with the skillful capabilities of the men who worked for him. For the period in which they were working, the books they produced were stunning. Each writer was a virtuoso calligrapher, with the sumptuous initials of the various 'Books of Hours' he commissioned merging the sophisticated foliage patterns of contemporary European artwork with the traditional Irish 'mosaic' backgrounds. The contents, too, for the period, are no less remarkable, as they also blend English and Irish themes.

Yet despite his love of the arts and his patronage of them, James was actually no less martial in character than any of his predecessors, which would be shown by his early advances into the field. When as a youth he accompanied Stephen le Scrope on an invasion into MacMurrough's territory, he was as energetic in his routing of the Irish and the capture of important prisoners as the best of his companions. He had also marched to Callan with a great expedition, surprising the rebels, defeating a whole force, and leaving 800 corpses on the battlefield. It was, perhaps, the reports of these military excursions that had been enough to qualify him for the highest employment at government level, even before the law deemed him to be fit to run his own estates.

The commission that made him Lord Deputy in 1407 reads:

...during the absence of Stephen le Scrope, knight, deputy to the said Thomas of Lancastre, taking notice of the said Earl's being then the King's ward, and his wardship being granted to the said Duke, as hath been said before.[8]

This young governor astonishingly held a parliament in the following spring at Dublin, in which the statutes of Kilkenny were confirmed, and a charter against purveyors was enacted.

Prince Thomas was an ardent soldier but he proved an untrustworthy leader, although in fairness he was dealing with many undependable allies. An early mistake had been to have taken the Earl of Kildare prisoner, when Kildare had gone to meet him in all expectation of being received with honour, although Thomas may have been badly guided in this. But he had quickly compounded his first miscalculation by leading an army composed of the 'English of Dublin' into the county of Leinster, where he again treated his captives unscrupulously. Nor can all his later blunders be simply put down to immaturity, for he had had time to grow into his role before he was recalled to England by news of his father's grave illness. Henry IV, who had suffered a stroke in 1405, was now convinced that he was dying, and government in England was passing into the hands of the Prince of Wales.

Little was heard of Thomas during 1410–11, except for some reports of his riotous conduct in London. James Butler appears to have also been in London at this time, and he may even have been one of the Prince's rampageous companions, for he later made a collection of reminiscences in which he refers to the Prince's behaviour during this period. These recollections, for the most part political meditations that predate the contents of Machiavelli's book *Il Principe* by almost a century, deal with matters such as the duties of a Prince and the law of arms (although they have nothing of the amorality of the Italian's political philosophy). A vital contribution to the history of the early 15th century, they found their way into *The Latin Life of Henry V* by Titius Livius, whose patron was the 7th Earl of Ormonde. They contain a plausible account of Prince Henry's dissension with his father in 1411, and the stories of Henry's wildness as a youth – robbing his father's receivers, striking the Chief Justice, and so forth – can only have been observed at first hand.[9] Both of the royal brothers had a mad streak in them.

Thomas was made Duke of Clarence in May 1412, and then given command of an army that was headed for France, where, like his eldest brother, he would within a year become a hard-bitten leader, with useful experience of campaigning under extreme conditions. Of the two brothers, although Henry would prove the finer commander, Thomas more resembled a soldier.

That there was a deep friendship between Prince Thomas and James Butler is made plain from various sources, and James was also part of the notable force that went with the Duke of Clarence to France. James took with him ninety lances and 270 archers, all bound to five month's service with the Duke, with the knights paid 2s daily, the esquires at 1s.6d and the archers at 9d for the first two months. Afterwards they were to be rewarded 'according to what the lords of France should pay'[10] (presumably through the tradition of ransoms). James was at that time still under age, but he quickly acquired a reputation as a fearless knight, and he would earn his spurs in the French wars.

The force landed, captured three major towns, and passed through Anjou to the neighbourhood of Blois, afterwards entering the duchy of Orleans, and marching through Sologne to the valley of the Indre. By which time the French dukes were anxious to buy the English out, and arranged to pay them 150,000 crowns, which was later raised to 210,000 crowns, payable at a later date, when no ready money was forthcoming.

Clarence asked for 120,000 crowns, of which he received some 40,000 as a down payment, together with a valuable gold crucifix, 'with a ruby in its wounded side'.[11] He also received another gold cross, in which was embedded one of the nails from the Crucifixion. Clarence then passed on to Gascony and wintered at Bordeaux, preparing to fight for the recovery of English territory in the south. It is not known how much James Butler received from the French, or whether he accompanied Prince Thomas to his winter quarters.

In any case King Henry IV's death in 1413 cut short any possibility of further campaigning by Clarence in France, and compelled him to return to England. There, the new King, Henry V, immediately stripped him of his Irish authority, although he remained on good terms personally with his brother, despite rumours to the contrary. Henry deprived his brother of the government of Ireland because, it would seem, he had a more urgent need of him in his battles on the continent. Yet if Henry V had turned his attention to Ireland, instead of pursuing his dream of conquering France and wearing the French crown, the resulting history of the English in Ireland would have been very different.

A much stronger leadership was now needed in Ireland, where the colonials were under increasing pressure from the Irish. Their particular scourge, MacMurrough, waged war against them repeatedly, in which he was largely, and humiliatingly, victorious. The O'Connors also carried on continuous guerilla tactics, plundering and carrying off large amounts of spoils with them. The English, to defend themselves against their 'Irish enemies', had been increasingly forced to raise their own private armies of 'kernes, coynes, hobelers and idlemen'[12] in defiance of the 1366 Statute of Kilkenny. This had permitted noblemen to maintain such forces only in the border areas (and at their own expense). Attempts to stamp out this abuse had seen little success, since the government itself was often forced to resort to this expedient as a means of supporting its troops.

Yet the English parliament still made strenuous, but unavailing, efforts to suppress these private armies. A petition of 1410 demanded that any Chief Governor, or any others, who put 'any manner of coyne or livery upon the King's faithful people should be treated as traitors and open robbers of the King and his subjects'. The official reply to this, that the former statutes on these matters should be observed (but with no way of enforcing them) can have brought little satisfaction to the petitioners.

James Butler 'proved' his coming of age in 1411, and he was in England when he sent for the livery of his lordship, doing homage and fealty to the King. He had shown himself to be a youth of unusual talents, for at the time he was restored to his possessions he was still deputy to the now displaced Thomas of Lancaster, having been so for the past four years. In appreciation, he was given various royal grants in recognition of his services in the wars of Ireland.

Throughout the first half of the 15th century, the area under direct control of the administration declined proportionately as increasing territory passed into the hands of 'Irish enemies' and 'English rebels'. The town of Carlingford was probably the outer limit at the northern extremity of The Pale, while south of Dublin the port of Wicklow lay among the King's Irish enemies, and most notably the Byrnes' sept. By 1416 these places were too distant to obtain any aid from the colonists, and one could not travel far to the south of Dublin without entering hostile territory. Inland, the frontier was a constantly shifting line, but the balance of the advantage clearly lay with the Irish. Kilcullen town, a mere twenty miles south-west of Dublin, in the rich green pastures of the Curragh, was burnt by them early in the century. While in Meath, the town of Drumconrath could only hold a market once a week through 1412, because its position on the border had led to frequent torching.

In August 1413 the Earl of Ormonde returned from England to Ireland, 'for the defence of the same', in the company of the equally young Earl of Desmond, with 100 men-at-arms and 460 archers between them. But it is more likely that Thomas of Desmond was using this opportunity to recover the rights of his earldom as well as to relieve the English of Ireland, for two years earlier he had been expelled from his own estates by his uncle James. The *Annals of Ireland* put it that, 'The Earl of Desmond came to Ireland with many Englishmen to devastate Munster', but whether James Butler returned with Thomas for the same purpose is not stated. As it came about, the uncle proved too strong for the nephew and took him prisoner after their first armed confrontation.

The Irish surrounded the town of Naas in 1414, when a grant was made for its defence by the Dublin government, yet the English still appeared to be losing control. Then, in the November of that year, John Talbot, Lord Furnival, the new Lieutenant of Ireland, landed at Dalkey, and his arrival gives another insight into the desperation of the English government. Despite being a brilliantly unconventional soldier – one who would later gain his greatest fame on the battlefields of France – he was then only in his mid-20s, and still relatively untried.

However within a few months of his arrival he had brought many septs to submission, and had even managed to capture Donal MacMurrough, the scourge of the English. As with those who preceded him, his foremost problem remained a lack of proper funding and he himself, appointed at a reduced salary of 4,000 marks for the first year and 3,000 per annum thereafter, had difficulty in obtaining even the first payment.

His greatest success at this time was, perhaps, the deliverance of the rightful Earl of Desmond from his rival's custody, and the Irish Assembly praised him for it, since the young Earl's false imprisonment by his uncle had led to extreme destruction in the county of Munster. But even though he had been set free, Earl Thomas could still not 'recover his ground', and he returned to England to plead his case at Court. Whether the Earl of Ormonde had played any part in the 'great labours and costes' of his deliverance is not recorded; but to judge from his subsequent actions, he seems rather to have inclined towards the wicked uncle.

A subsidy was collected in County Meath during 1415, for the expenses incurred in raising an army of 5,000 horse and foot soldiers, which had been brought to the midlands to campaign there for thirteen days. Both the Desmond usurper and the young Earl of Ormonde were equally involved in the assembly of this army, since they were together fighting the menace presented to Meath by the Irish, but outside of these emergencies, each tended to steer clear of the other. Ormonde, though, seems to have realised that the older man was the best person to control the Desmond territory at a perilous time. Despite their mutual links with Dublin both earls also tended to rule their territories as autonomous units, with as little interference from Dublin – and each other – as was possible in the circumstances. As a result of this way of operating, both men would come to dominate the politics of Munster throughout their equally long lifetimes.

For this same reason Ormonde only ever reluctantly collaborated with the new Lord Lieutenant, since one cause of the simmering resentment he persistently bore towards John Talbot was his constant interference in the internal affairs of the Ormonde lordship. James was particularly rankled by Talbot's regular attempts to support his state-licensed troops by levying coigne and livery from the Ormonde tenants. James, like most Anglo-Irish lords, occasionally used such exactions to maintain an army, although in statutes that he himself drew up for his lordship, he attempted to regulate their imposition. But it was one thing for a landlord to tax his tenants in this fashion, and quite another for such resources to be tapped by the Chief Governor, particularly one who proved as personally hostile to him as did Talbot. For this reason when Ormonde himself was Chief Governor, he had always made efforts to avoid the use of these irregular impositions outside his own territories as a means of supporting government forces.

The fourth Baron Talbot, a kinsman through marriage to the Butlers, was Irish to the extent that he had succeeded to the honour of Wexford, inherited through a mutual ancestor of both families. He was in many ways a radical, even an extremist, and had been imprisoned in the Tower of London during the Lollard panic, which came soon after the accession of Henry IV, although he never expressed any personal sympathy with the followers of the religious reformer Wycliffe. Soon released by the new King, Henry V, who was quick to recognise his military talents and qualities of leadership, Talbot had been sent to Ireland, once he had sufficiently shown his loyalty to the new regime.

In Ireland he lost no time in engaging the Irish, and a successful expedition he commanded against the Men of Leix in 1415 led to a strengthening of the position of Athy. Here, the repair of the bridge and the erection of a new fortification in 1417 gave the inhabitants a greater security than they had known for thirty years, and for the next seventeen years it would remain, 'the great fortalice and key town of the area'.[13] But such advances were few in the beginning, and they did little to compensate for more serious losses elsewhere.

Talbot was apparently popular at first with the Anglo-Irish, although complaints of misgovernment by some of his officers soon surfaced and were reported to the King. He also quickly ran into debt, and a former squire of King Richard II accused him of withholding certain Irish revenues, for which he held a royal grant. There may have been some truth in this, for so acute were his financial problems that he had to interrupt a very vigorous and largely successful campaign in 1416 to return to England seeking payment for what was owed to him. The failure to secure an adequate reimbursement forced him to pass on his debts to others.

Talbot was called away to the French wars of Henry V in 1419, during which he would hugely distinguish himself in various battles, but when he left Ireland one chronicler castigated him for his failure to pay what he owed for victuals and other necessities. In 1421 it was reckoned that his debts 'amounted to a great summe', and his critics accused him of having committed, 'several great and monstrous extortions and oppressions...against your [the King's] said lieges', including taking their goods and chattels 'paying them little or nothing therefore, by which your said lieges in that part have been greatly injured and impoverished'.[14]

Talbot had left his brother Richard as deputy in his place; and Richard, who was also the Archbishop of Dublin, would become an outright opponent of the Earl of Ormonde when his authority was taken from him in favour of the Earl, with the enmity lasting for several years. Another brother, Sir Thomas Talbot, would also cause considerable outrage when he arrested the Earl of Kildare, who had expressed his dissatisfaction with the way they had mismanaged several affairs, particularly the handling of a quarrel between Walter Burke and Thomas Butler, Prior of Kilmainham. The latter was a half-brother of the Earl of Ormonde, and Kildare was Ormonde's father-in-law. This quarrel was probably a part of the larger Ormonde-Talbot feud, but if, as one report stated, Kildare was at that time planning to seize Richard Talbot and replace him as Deputy-Governor, the arrest had ample justification.

Subsequently, Kildare and his associates were brought before the English Council, and part of the evidence in the case against them was a copy of the *Modus*, found in their possession. This tract, a summary of the procedure of parliament, contained the radical suggestion that *elected* representatives of the shires had a more important part to play than that of unrepresentative nobles and high churchmen, at least in the granting of taxes. The book had considerable influence in any political crisis in the

England (or Ireland) of the late Middle Ages, since it persuasively argued that elected spokesmen would speak, 'for the whole community, whereas magnates spoke only for their own interests'. This was an argument that would come to haunt the Earl of Ormonde within a few years.

He was, however, in France throughout this fracas, serving with King Henry V in Normandy at the successful siege of Rouen; but he was made Lieutenant of Ireland in 1419, and he landed at Waterford in April 1420. Almost at once he was plunged into the freakish conditions of Irish discord, with the first example coming from his own family. Two of his cousins had opted to settle a purely domestic quarrel by the warlike solution of single combat, with the result that one of them died on the field and the other was carried off wounded; it was left to Ormonde to condemn the cousin who survived.

Faced with even more inflammatory instances of civil lawlessness, James tried to maintain a general peace throughout the country, holding a Council and summoning parliament to meet on St. George's Day. But he himself had added to civic confusion when, on 4 April 1421, he sensationally allied himself to the usurping James of Desmond, procuring him recognition from the Crown, conceding that James would be a stronger partner than his nephew, the legitimate earl. Fortunately, in the interests of peace at least, Thomas FitzGerald, again ousted from his estates, would soon die in France, where he was seeking to establish a reputation, to be buried in Paris, which left his uncle in legal possession of the earldom. In December, Ormonde appointed the new Earl as 'Guardian of the Peace' in three counties and the 'Cross of Kerry'. In the meantime James Butler was forced to travel to Ulster to suppress an uprising, where he successfully overran the territory of three rebellious Irish chiefs.

In May 1422, a party of the O'Mores attacked a number of Ormonde servants, killing one of them and besieging 200 more, most of who fled for refuge to the Abbey of Leix. The Earl immediately invaded O'More's country, and pulled off a tremendous coup at the Red Bog of Athy, since he defeated an army of great strength with a much smaller party of men. Not only did he relieve his own men, besieged in the abbey, he also 'spoiled and burnt' the rebel lands for four days, until they sued for peace and made submission.

This was not his only triumph at the time. Another chieftain, MacMahon, was also 'destroying all before him in Urgal';[15] but the Earl, on the way back from his expedition against O'More, turned aside to take on MacMahon's troops, and soon forced them to come to terms. He brought off many such martial exploits in the course of his government, but he was even more successful when it came to civil matters. The arrangements that were made between the Dublin government and the Earl in 1420 famously worked to the satisfaction of all concerned throughout a two-year term of office, primarily because Ormonde (by injecting a fair amount of his own money into various projects) was able to generate considerable mercantile revenue within Ireland itself.

The Irish parliament must have been well satisfied with the 4th Earl of Ormonde, for not only did he raise funding from outside sources, he also promised to make due payment for anything that was required out of his own capacious pocket, should the government in England let them down. As security against non-payment by the Crown, for example, he pledged the rents from his own lands as an insurance against any outstanding debts at the end of his term of office. Thanks from the State were also conveyed to him because he had abolished the 'bad, most heinous and unbearable custom, called coigne'.[16] It is however doubtful whether this was a genuine achievement; it was a practice that had been treasured for so long by the Irish chieftains that all previous attempts to get rid of it had proved futile.

Edmund Mortimer, 5th Earl of March, was appointed Lieutenant of Ireland in May 1423. Regarded by many as the true heir to the throne, he had astonishingly proved remarkably faithful to the first two Lancastrian kings. He had taken part in Henry V's last expedition to France, and had probably been present at Agincourt; while at King Henry's death he had been appointed as a member of the Council of Regency on 9 December 1422. But he had quickly come into conflict with the new king's uncle, the Duke of Gloucester, and was sent out of the way to Ireland, where a chronic confusion was growing worse. After his arrival, March – as his father had done in King Richard's time – concentrated less on dealing with the complications that bedevilled Ireland generally, but busied himself in negotiating with the Irish septs that held almost all of his lands in Ulster. Said to be 'severe' in morals, and surnamed 'the Good' by reason of his humanity, March might have proved a fine Lord Lieutenant, had he not been cut off suddenly by contracting the plague, dying within a year of his arrival in Ireland. Since he left no family and his brother had predeceased him, the male line of the March dynasty was made extinct, while the Mortimer estates went to Richard of York, the son of March's sister Anne. Now recognised as the Earl of Ulster, Richard would come to play his own part in developments in Ireland within a few years.

Not surprisingly, in view of his previous success, Ormonde was re-appointed Lord Lieutenant after the sudden death of the 3rd Earl of March. A return was then made to the pre-1420 financial arrangements, when money had to be found to support the Lord Lieutenant from Irish sources only, and for the next twenty years all English viceroys would be required to hold office under similar terms. It is clear that the office of Lord Deputy had begun to exert a strong attraction to the Anglo-Irish magnates, despite the obvious risks, both financial and political. James Butler, for one, was certainly willing enough to pay off the debts incurred by holding the office, which contrasted starkly with his father's reluctance to undertake the chief governorship in 1404. However to justify such reluctance, it is possible that it was simply due to the 3rd Earl's knowledge that the position was only a temporary assignment and therefore he would not have had time to establish himself or to recoup his losses.

The 4th Earl was to hold the office three more times during this period, and he accepted it in 1422 despite the refusal of the English administration to treat him with the terms that he requested. By this time it is obvious that the power and prestige attached to this semi-royal office far outweighed the costs involved in its exercise, and the addition of the King's delegated authority to his own palatine powers made Ormonde a formidable figure. Some of the charges that were later made against him may well have been the result of fears that he was becoming too powerful, and more importantly too independent of royal control.

From the beginning it was made clear that there would be checks upon his control over his officers and administration. His power was not absolute, since he was forbidden to dismiss either his Chancellor or his Treasurer, and at times even the Chief Justices and the Barons of the Exchequer were exempted from his supervision. His conduct was also subject to review by the English Council and, from 1423 onwards, the royal patents and appointments specifically stated that were a Lieutenant or his deputy to do anything 'unlawful', the Council in England was to 'correct and reform the matter'.[17] The numerous appeals that were to be made to the English Privy Council in the course of the impending Ormonde-Talbot dispute would confirm its role in this regard.

Two events of extreme importance affected James Butler's first period of office. In April 1421 he lost a valued friend and protector of sorts, with the death of the Duke of Clarence at the battle of Bauge. This proved to be the first real setback for the English in their French wars. The two men had been close from boyhood and they shared much in common, not least a talent for soldiering. However, Clarence had not always served James's interests well, since at least two of the royal grants that came to James in youth were given in consideration of the 'waste of his estate during his minority'.[18] It is always possible that the Duke, constantly hard pressed for money, had dipped into the Ormonde fortune while he had custody of their lands, in order to help offset the financial straits in which he found himself in 1402.

The second catastrophe came within a year and a half of the loss of Clarence in battle, with the news of Henry V's premature death, at the age of 33, in August 1422. This totally unforeseen departure from the European stage by *the* major player of the age would have a profound effect on the political evolution of three countries, leading to civil war in England as well as unrest in Ireland and Wales. Henry's will was perfectly straightforward when it came to personal matters, but the plans he had arranged for the governance of France and England and, by association, that of Ireland and Wales, would quickly lead to anarchy. The warmongering adventurer Henry had allowed himself too little time for the realities of kingship in his brief and militaristic reign, and he had not lived long enough to consolidate his triumphs. He left one son, then a babe in arms, and since the magnates almost unanimously rejected Henry's proposal for the regency, England would suffer as a consequence. This too would have a knock-on effect for England's more vulnerable dependencies. Moreover after Henry's death, his brother, the Duke of Bedford, would lead the English in France to continue extending their conquests. Naturally, all this had to be paid for, which meant that Ireland would once again be neglected financially.

In 1422, Ormonde called upon the Earl of Desmond to come to his aid against two of his most uncontrollable enemies, Calvach O'Connor Faly and Meyler Bermyngham, 'then designing to make a final conquest of Meath'.[19] James of Desmond – now the undisputed Earl and a great force in the land – came with 5,000 horse and foot, which was paid by state subsidy. He was also rewarded with the Constableship of Limerick Castle, and 50*l* annual rental out of the city.

In 1426 Ormonde was again made Chief Governor 'by the style of Lord Lieutenant' for two years, although in August of that year he 'surrendered the sword' to Sir John de Grey. The situation at this point was extremely complicated, for Ormonde's powers had been restricted to those of Lord Justice since the re-appointment of a Royal Lieutenant: the sudden death of the Earl of March in 1425 had meant that John Talbot, having recently returned to Ireland from service in Normandy was able to reassume the position.

Talbot was at first triumphant against the Irish in combat. His bravery had already been assured by his valiant fighting for the English occupying forces in France, particularly at that 'second Agincourt', Verneuil, and his acceptance of the Order of the Garter in 1424. In addition he had been rewarded with the title of 1st Earl of Shrewsbury. Using the brilliant skirmishing techniques that he had developed abroad, Talbot surprised and held to ransom a number of northern chieftains who had gone to Trim for an interview, and he obtained the promise of some to abstain from preying on the Anglo-Irish. But Talbot's reign as Lord Lieutenant was short-lived, and he gave the place to Ormonde in that same year, for in March 1427 he would accompany the Duke of Bedford back to France. Ormonde may have hoped at the very least to be free of his malevolent influence. But this was not to be, for Talbot's brother, the Archbishop of Dublin, maintained the same pressures.

Ormonde, as Lord Lieutenant, also made vigorous war against the Irish, with his most famous fight being at the Red Moor of Athy in 1420. However his rule as Lieutenant, between 1420 and 1422, was shaken by his great feud with the Talbot brothers and also by the 'English interest' against himself and the Home Rule party, where the meetings of parliament were the main field of battle. In 1421, the Archbishop of Cashel and the Bishop of Cork were accused of having 'Irish hearts' (the Archbishop had an Irish name) and it was reported that he had made attempts to become the 'King of Munster'. Both men were certainly activists for the Gaelic side and some part of James Butler may have sympathised with them, but if this was true he was certainly up against the 'English interest', who strove hard to put the anti-Irish statutes into force.

Shortly after the accession of the infant Henry VI in 1422, the long-standing quarrel between these two powerful kinsmen reached a climax, with the English in Ireland divided into armed Ormonde and Talbot factions. Each charged the other with paying blackmail to Irish chieftains, and one of Talbot's last acts before leaving for France was to denounce James Butler as a traitor to the Royal Council, accusing him of treason and of 'setting the laws at naught and favouring the Irish enemy'.[21] It was true that Ormonde, having failed in an outright confrontation with O'Connor Faly, had afterwards allowed him to impose 'black-rent', which was an illegal act; and there may have been similar examples.

The Patriot Party, in a vigorous defence of Ormonde, had sent a declaration of 'the Community of the Land of Ireland' to King Henry V in April 1421. In it they attacked Talbot as a failed leader, listing his 'late, monstrous oppressions' and praised Ormonde as a model viceroy. They had begged the king to come to Ireland in person, and they made 'many and bitter complaints',[22] but by then Henry V was in France, pursuing his dream of a dual monarchy.

Some of the grievances of the Patriot Party were undeniably on the right lines, such as the inequity of those English lieges, born in Ireland 'of good and gentle families', being no longer received at English Inns of Court on account of their birthplace. Or that more people, from landowners to labourers, were now forced to leave Ireland as a result of 'being laden with the charges of wars',[23] (those of King Henry V in his bid for the French throne). Money, they also argued, should be coined in Ireland as it was in England. Their most urgent request had been for the king to visit their country, to see for himself how it was being destroyed by his 'Irish enemies' and by 'English rebels'. 'If the king himself come not, the land is lost!'[24] But the king they addressed was a dying man, and when Talbot raised these matters in the English Council, they were dismissed as being no more than the same 'dissensions, commotions, lawsuits, scandals, and intolerable evils' with which the Mother Country was itself now ridden.

The new Council of the infant King Henry VI, however, dealt sharply with the accusations of treason against James Butler and with the consent of parliament legal proceedings against him were stopped in October 1423. The findings were unsatisfactory to Ormonde, since they were not based upon the true facts of the matter, but upon the kinship of both parties to the king along with his fears of 'scandals and inconveniences which might result in both countries'[25] should the accusations be pursued. (An interesting point to note is that in the same parliament the Commons petitioned the Crown for the 'redress of grievances of certain individuals of Herefordshire who had been carried off with their goods to Goodrich Castle [his main residence] by Talbot and others, and held to ransom'.[26] Talbot had to find security to keep the peace, and a judicial enquiry was promised.) Fortunately for Ormonde he was not the only rival with whom Talbot quarrelled, since he had carried on a fierce dispute for precedence in parliament with another of his kinsmen. Rather confusingly, during his dispute both parties had called themselves the 'Lord of Wexford', although Talbot was in actual possession of the town.

Edmund, the 5th Earl of March and Ulster, had been a man of 30 when he became Lieutenant of Ireland in 1423, and most people of the time thought that he 'would have been a very great personage, had not his unaspiring nature made him a man without a party'.[27] Many, in fact, considered him, as the great-grandson of Lionel of Clarence, to be a truer heir to the throne than the infant Henry VI. But his name only bore weight in Ireland, where – as the Earl of Ulster – he was the 'Lord of the English of Ireland', and a more royal personage than any man of England (that is, any Lancastrian claimant) was considered to be.

When, in February 1424, he had arrived in Ireland, with the maintenance of 5,000 marks per annum, no-one, it was thought, had been so fitted to reconcile all Irishmen. When he held the Court of his Liberty at Trim, all the great men of the north came in to do homage to him, if only as the Earl of Ulster. And when Mortimer died suddenly of the plague in 1425, it was to the consternation of most people.

It was thought particularly unfortunate since Talbot was at once made Justiciar, he being still in Ireland. Although, showing his usual tactical brilliance, he immediately marched west to complete the submissions of the chieftains, after which, leading men were brought to Dublin, where they entered into indentures of fealty. But Talbot did not last long, being commanded again to surrender his office to the Earl of Ormonde, who received the final submissions of the chieftains, from April 1425 to July 1427 (on terms very similar to those agreed by King Richard II in 1395).

James Butler retired from office at the end of July 1427, and the acts of the Irish parliament under his successor, the hated Archbishop of Dublin, are largely punitive measures that have a draconian dreariness about them. It was decreed that serving-men and labourers leaving Ireland without a licence should be arrested, and nobody could sell corn, iron, salt or victuals to the 'Irish enemy' without leave. Penalties of treason were affirmed against those who practiced coigne and livery, or entered into marriage, fostered, or even 'gossiped' (communicated) with the native Irish. It was forbidden to entertain, or to let land in the border country to 'Irish rhymers and others, outlaws and felons who come with their *creaghs*[28] into the Land of Peace called the Maghery.[29]

Any of the successful measures that had been initiated by the Earl of Ormonde were not to be repeated, and the Justiciars who followed him, due to increasing neglect by the English government, would have a hard time raising the necessary investment to withstand the mounting offensives of the Irish. Even when it came to the matter of their salaries, the Lord Lieutenants could only procure an ever-decreasing percentage of the revenue collected within Ireland, while in London the English Exchequer did not pursue its aim of exercising a closer supervision over Irish revenues. Thus any attempt to make the Irish nobility contribute more to the costs of their own government and defence was ultimately bound to achieve very little. (The old feudal system of exacting payment from a vassal in place of his military service survived as a method of raising levies in Ireland long after it had disappeared in England.)

Sizeable arrears would have to be remitted by the Dublin government to the city of Cork because of the huge losses they had sustained through the invasion of the rebel Irish forces. It would come to the point where the citizens could not pay the 'fee farm' of 80 marks due to the Crown since all the money raised had been spent on paying tribute to the rebels, exacted from the townsfolk as they entered and left their own walls. It was claimed in 1427 that Cork was the 'only place of resistance in these parts', and the Mayor successfully petitioned the King for custody of the castle, on which the security of his city depended.

The Irish parliament of 1428 made a general request that all the Lord Lieutenants and their deputies who had held office under the kings Henry V and Henry VI should be paid what was owed to them for themselves and for their soldiers. These debts were by now considerable; and their non-repayment had led to considerable complaints from the populace, since they had been forced to provide for the troops. The Archbishop of Armagh complained that the soldiers lived on the people, 'not paying for horsemeat nor manmeat'.[30] The Lieutenant's purveyors also helped themselves liberally to corn, hay, beasts and poultry, 'and all things needful for their household. They paid nothing, but offered tallies'. 20,000*l* was owed to the people, despite the fact that the Lieutenant had great subsidies and tallages granted him. '…and all this the poor husbandry bears and pays for, and the war on the other side destroys them.'[31]

The Irish parliament of 1428 was very pro-Ormonde in outlook. Because he had proved to be one of the best Governors of recent times, they requested that he should stay in place more permanently. For it was true, as they pointed out, that the frequent changes in both the Lieutenancy and the Deputyship had been to the disadvantage of the colony, and they petitioned that no changes should be made in future, for so long as the conduct of the officials was satisfactory. The Irish magistrates' answer to this, much as they admired Ormonde, was to underline the Lieutenant's dependence upon the Crown, and they claimed that Parliament's request was illegal, since it attempted to circumscribe the power of the (then seven-year-old) king.

In a further petition of that year, the Irish parliament alleged that the charges against the Chief Governor, unfounded and unsubstantiated, were motivated by 'malice and ill will', and had been brought before the English Council without any prior investigation in Ireland. It suggested that in future, such accusations should always be notified to the Council in Dublin, to be examined in a Grand Council mustered in Parliament there. Much the same suggestion had been made in the previous century; an ordinance of 1357 had laid down procedures not unlike those that were now requested for dealing with false accusation made in England against offices of the Irish administration.

However the pro-Talbot faction now opposed any such restriction on the access of the English Council, claiming – perhaps not unreasonably – that the truth would never be discovered if the charges were to be submitted in Ireland first. They argued that 'those who are sent to Parliaments and Councils are chosen not for the good of the king and his lieges, but at the will of the nobles and magnates'.[32] This fear that any charges against the Chief Governor would be smothered by the Irish Council and Parliament seems to be been shared by the English government; and complaints from unofficial sources continued to come before the English Council throughout the rest of the century.

The most constant of these pleas to come before the English government was that Ireland should be under a peace and truce by 'special word', since the seas around the country were now being 'scourged' by Bretons and the Scots, and even the Spanish were beginning to menace the coastline. What was required, they insisted, was that the English should send a new Lieutenant with 'sufficient goods and men'; or else that some great man 'of the king's blood'[33] should come to their defence. But England had been almost bankrupted by their wars in France, which they were then losing, and their government had neither money nor men to spare for Ireland. Though, in fact, one member of the royal family was in Ireland in 1433, when the new Duke of York (who was also the Earl of Ulster by inheritance) went to look into his estates.

York however was having his own problems. In August 1435 he received a pardon under the Great Seal of Ireland for having intruded into the area of Ulster still held in dower by the widow of his uncle, the late Earl. York was now the most powerful English nobleman in Ireland. The English government recognised this and and fearing the strength of his influence there, took the measure of designating him to become Regent of France, upon the death of the king's uncle, the Duke of Bedford. It was an elevation made simply to remove him from this dangerous new sphere of influence. But that year the Irish rebels dominated Carlow, and a report states that 148 castles 'and other fortified positions' had been lost in the previous sixty years. In fact the losses in this key area had severed the line of communication between Dublin and the outlying parts of the colony in Kilkenny and Tipperary. To some extent the English nobles could only survive by becoming as Irish (if not more so) than the Irish. The Butler lords, and particularly the 4th Earl of Ormonde, allowed some Anglo-Norman traditions to become intermingled with Gaelic practices, blurring the distinctions between the two. To hang on to their increasingly endangered properties, the Butlers – alongside their Anglo-Norman cousins – reluctantly identified with their 'subjects' when it came to matters of local administration.

Some of this empathy may also, of course, have had a purely financial basis, for the noble families – along with the townships – were always keen to avoid paying their royal dues. But it is a fact that the area under effective English control contracted considerably during the first half of the 15th century. The basic reason for this decline was the government's inability to put sufficient military forces into the field for long enough to achieve any lasting expansion, or even the stabilisation of the frontier, and the lack of money was the major factor behind this failure.

The inevitable results of this administrative parsimony had been apparent from the earliest days of the Duke of Clarence's Lieutenancy at the beginning of the century, where he had been the victim of the system of financing adopted by the practically bankrupt Lancaster government in its early years. But penny-pinching alone cannot completely account for the continuing neglect of Ireland; during the reigns of Henry IV, V and VI money was found for other purposes, notably the prosecution of the wars in France. It has to be acknowledged that the Irish question was simply too low in importance for English priorities.

In 1441 Ormonde was appointed Deputy Lord Lieutenant and had the revenues of the See of Cashel granted to him for ten years; but he continued in this post only until William Welles came over in 1442, as deputy to his brother, Lion, Lord Welles. In the year following, Ormonde was again made Lord Lieutenant when Welles's time in office proved undistinguished, and yet fresh attempts were made to remove the Earl, now the acknowledged leader of the Anglo-Irish.

His most persistent enemy, the Archbishop of Dublin, aided by the Irish Chancellor, induced their parliament of 1441 to transmit charges against him by the Treasurer of Ireland. He had been accused in 1440 of having had members of his own household elected as Knights of the Shire and hand-picked for parliament, so that it might be the more completely under his control. The charge was also made against him that he had Gaelic Irish illegally elected to parliament for the same reason; but now they added old age and senility to their charges, describing him as being 'too old and unwieldy, and he cannot even defend his own lands'.[34] He had never been completely absolved from the charge of treason brought against him earlier, and the discords between him and Lord Talbot and his brothers had become so inflamed that it was generally thought 'no suit touching the other can have due process in Ireland'.

Ormonde, having been appointed Lieutenant in February 1442, the charges against him, returned under the Privy Seal, were tried before the Irish Council at Trim on 5 June 1442. However the Home Rule aristocracy was too strong for the Talbots' Unionist faction and the Council repudiated the charges, denying that parliament had ever desired them to be drawn up. Ormonde's enemies then accused him of intimidation, declaring that the Clerk of the Rolls had recorded the acts at Trim 'for drede of his life of the seide earl'.[35] Ormonde was summoned to England to answer these later charges, but being cleared again, he returned in triumph.

At this period the Assembly remained essentially a colonial body, despite King Richard's attempt in 1395 to include Irish lords within it. The Gaelic Irish were unqualified for election, although very occasionally an Irish bishop or abbot might attend the sessions, but without actively participating. Parliament remained largely an irrelevance to the 'Irish enemies', although they did take advantage of their exclusion from it to launch attacks upon the property of the English who did attend, during their absence from their home ground. 'In which time the Irish burned all that stood in their way, as was their usual custom in times of other parliaments.'[36]

It is possible that Ormonde did attempt to manipulate the elections of knights in the shires in the early 1440s. But if this was so, it probably owed less to his desire to overwhelm the Talbot faction inside parliament than to a fear the Commons might begin to act independently of his administration. The continual feuding between the two men was softened, if not exactly settled, by a marriage between one of Ormonde's daughters and a son of Talbot in 1444. Yet friction remained between them – evident, for example, when Talbot charged Ormonde with willful disobeyance of many of the directives sent to him from England. As this happened to be true, James's only defence was to indicate the practical difficulties of trying to enforce unpopular Crown rulings inside Ireland, thus explaining his need to often take an independent line.

However, the settlement of 1444 meant such issues were temporarily placed in abeyance and Ormonde obtained a licence to be absent from Ireland for several years, without incurring the penalty of the statute of Richard II, touching upon absentees. He then managed to procure a royal licence for his great ally the Earl of Desmond to act in his stead. Desmond was 'to appear in the parliaments of the Great Council by proxy, whenever he could not appear in person; and to acquire the lands and rents held in chief of the King by any tenure whatsoever'.[37] Ormonde made sure that the English government heard of Desmond's magnificent work in keeping King Henry's title from his 'Irish enemies and rebels' in four counties.

Astonishingly, despite receiving the licence to depart, though, Ormonde continued in government until the arrival of his most feared opponent, John Talbot, Earl of Shrewsbury.

In 1444, King Henry VI summoned Ormonde to appear before the English Cabinet, to explain his conduct in the light of yet more accusations. Before leaving Ireland, the Earl, in order to refute any charges against him, assembled a great council at Drogheda, where his leadership was eulogised by the Speaker of the Commons, the Bishop of Cork, two lords, and the vassals of the Earl of Desmond. (A 'great council' was often a favourite substitute for a true parliament, but in any case a man such as Ormonde could easily dominate either of the assemblies. The more dominant lords usually divided the offices of state among their dependants, and they generally took into their hands the prerogatives of the absent monarch.) Ormonde's decision to mount a prior defence in Ireland was an unusual move, although an astute one, since it gave a clear message to the King's councillors at Court: find unfairly against the accused and they would be facing strong opposition from his adherents. And so, having taken the precaution of organising his defence on his home ground, the 'game old Earl'[38] arrived in London to fight his chief accuser, the Prior of Kilmainham, Thomas FitzGerald.

The earliest official use of the word 'Pale' occurs in 1446–47, when an Irish leader promised 'to carry nothing out of the English Pale contrary to the statutes'.[39] But the concept of a geographically defined limitation on English authority in Ireland is clearly present in a report of 1435, which gloomily records that the king's 'land of Ireland is well nigh destroyed and inhabited with his enemies and rebels'.[40] So much so that little was left to the English in the lower parts of the counties of Dublin, Meath, Louth and Kildare, the lands 'that join together', though scarcely thirty miles in length and twenty in breadth, 'as a man may surely ride or go in the said counties, to answer the king's writs and to his commandments.'[41]

Some of the summary of 1435 may have been a calculated exaggeration, in order to persuade the adolescent King to go to Ireland, to see for himself just how parlous the situation was. For it was undeniably true that the previous thirty-five years of relentless conflict had seen an increasing fragmentation of the colony, and that outlying areas could only be visited by administrators when they were accompanied by a sizeable military force.

Fifteenth-century England's preoccupation with the dynastic wars in France played into the hands of the Irish potentates on both sides of the divide, although perhaps more observably among the Gaels. Most of these spectacular manifestations of Irish resurgence were in the north, where political recovery went hand in hand with a religious revival, exemplified by the Observant movement. This campaign was at first favoured chiefly by Augustinian, Franciscan and Dominican friars, who could strictly follow the movement's rituals and ceremonies; but it was the Gaelic lands which first and most widely adopted the Observant forms. Among the old Norman families, by now speakers of English and Irish rather than the French of their ancestors, the counterpart of the Gaelic religious resurgence was the secular Home Rule Movement.

This development had first manifested itself as far back as 1326 when – or so his enemies alleged – the over-ambitious Maurice FitzThomas engaged in the first of the many conspiracies to make himself King of Ireland. But from the Earl of Ormonde's viceroyalty of 1441–4 onwards, it was the Home Rule party that mostly ruled Ireland, controlling its parliament and sharing the offices of state, with its leader exercising the prerogatives of the 'Lord of Ireland'.

In March 1445, long after the English had been expelled from France, John Talbot sailed to Dublin to govern the country for the third time, being created the 'Steward of Ireland' on 17 July 1446. He rebuilt Castle Carberry to protect his lands in Meath, and he captured several Irish chieftains, again using the techniques he had perfected in France. He also enacted several laws, among them the bizarre edict that those Irish who 'would be taken for Englishmen' should not 'use a beard upon the upper lips alone', and should shave at least once a fortnight. He had long lost any popularity with the Irish, who were of the opinion that 'there came not from the time of Herod anyone so wicked in evil deeds.'[42]

Ormonde certainly continued to suffer from his enmity, and on Talbot's return to Ireland he quickly accused the Earl of treason for a second time. This was presumably the stock charge (made by both sides in the Ormonde-Talbot feud) that each camp had been guilty of complicity with the 'Irish enemy', since relations with the Gaelic Irish was still governed by the 1366 statutes of Kilkenny. This was certainly so in both cases, for the strict segregation set out in that detested measure could never be properly enforced. The king, recognising this, quashed the latest accusation against James Butler.

Richard Talbot, Archbishop of Dublin, Ormonde's other great enemy, did his best to revive the charge of treasonable activity, but other bishops and several peers gave a full testimonial of the Earl's invaluable services to Ireland. Yet Talbot persisted, and Thomas FitzGerald, Prior of Kilmainham, a dependant of the Archbishop, was sent over to London to renew the accusation. This time, for some reason, the renewed charge was given more credence, and by a grotesque sentence of the Earl Marshal, the elderly Ormonde – then temporarily imprisoned in the Tower of London – was ordered to do trial by 'single combat' with the Prior of Kilmainham at Smithfield. (The Prior himself having to be instructed in the correct method of duelling for this contest by a Cockney fishmonger!) Various other clergymen, however, prevailed upon the King to forbid this 'ungodly combat', and Henry VI again interposed in the matter, 'and would not suffer it to proceed'.

To put an end to these accusations, the King also saw fit on this occasion to have a complete examination into the cause, manner and circumstances of the accusation. From this it was adjudged 'by clear testimony of several of the nobility and other persons of credit, as well as by undoubted evidence in writing, that the charge arose purely from pique and malice, and therefore all proceedings against Ormonde were to be cancelled'.[43] The decision was confirmed by letters patent, of 20 September, 27 Henry VI, and afterwards enrolled in the Chancery of Ireland. The judges found that the Earl of Ormonde was 'faithful in his allegiance, meritorious in his services, and whole and uncontaminated in his fame'.[44] King Henry further ruled that nobody else should dare 'on pain and indignation' revive the accusation, reproach Ormonde's conduct, or to 'throw a blot on his character', and that the accusers were 'men of no credit, nor should their testimony be admitted in any case'.[45] To the Archbishop of Dublin's mortification, a writ recapitulating all this (which had to be attested by the Archbishop himself), was sent to the magistrates of Limerick and other cities, 'to cause the proclamation to be made thereof all over the kingdom'.

It was to the relief of most in Irish government that, at the end of 1447, Talbot resigned the reins to his brother Richard, and, in July 1448, was sent as Lieutenant of Lower Normandy. (Talbot was said to be a Hotspur, owing his reputation more to dash and daring than to true military genius.[46]) His son, John, who became the 2nd Earl of Shrewsbury, was appointed Chancellor of Ireland in 1446, and he appears to have shared much of his father's character. Fortunately for the Ormonde family, he was killed while fighting on King Henry's side at the battle of Northampton in 1460. A partisan of the Lancastrian dynasty, this was the Talbot who had been married to Elizabeth, James Butler's daughter. Despite the fact that the two men had been the bitterest of enemies in Ireland, they had still found it provident to seek a marriage alliance between their two families. Nevertheless, this did not diminish their mutual antipathy towards each other, or do much to mend their differences.

The 4th Earl of Ormonde was at that time about sixty years old, described as 'unwieldy and unlusty to labour, a great grown man of flesh'.[47] The last years of his life were spent, as had been most of his middle years, in military operations in Ireland. Having spent so much of his energies in attempting to keep the King's subjects under control, he had at least the satisfaction of living long enough to see 'the good government of Richard, Duke of York', who arrived in Ireland in 1449.[48]

Richard is described in the *Concordia*, which recognised him as the heir apparent, as 'the right high and myghty Prince Richard Plantagenet, Duke of York'. He had adopted Plantagenet as a surname to emphasise his dynastic claims, and to express the superiority of his descent in the blood royal over his Lancastrian cousins. He had been Lieutenant in France until 1445, an office he had hoped would be renewed since it gave him an overseas power base of sorts. However, never popular with the Lancastrian faction at Court, he had been banished in September 1447 into a 'kind of honourable exile' by sending him as Governor to Ireland for ten years, although he remained in England until 1449.

Before leaving England Richard insisted that during his office he should receive all the King's revenues in Ireland, without being asked to give any account of his use of them, and this stipulation was astonishingly agreed to, so anxious were the royal family to see him depart. Had the Lancastrians been forewarned of his popularity among the Irish, they might have thought it safer to send him back across the Channel. His appearance in Ireland in the summer of 1449 was greeted 'with great glory and pomp'[49] and the wildest enthusiasm.

Richard's stay did not bring forth many notable achievements: the fortunes of the colony were certainly not advanced by his presence. Yet he did manage to carry out a successful expedition into the O'Byrne's country, where he compelled their chieftain to swear allegiance – and exacted a promise from him to learn the English language besides! On 16 October he opened a parliament at Dublin and held another at Drogheda, where 'important acts were passed', but beyond these activities he did very little to impose himself or English rule upon the Irish.

It was not all straightforward acclamation and sycophancy, however; he would need money urgently when four Irish chiefs and a number of 'English rebels' revolted against some minor ordinance of his. This would reveal the vulnerability of his position; for without adequate funding he could not keep the land in subjection, and the home government, troubled at that time with rebellions of its own, was in no condition to supply him with money, men or arms. Yet the Duke won widespread personal popularity among the Anglo-Irish, and the links he established with the leading families were to endure for four decades. His second son, born at Dublin in the year following his arrival, was afterwards known as George, Duke of Clarence, and both the earls of Ormonde and Desmond stood as godfathers to the boy.

Sadly, James Butler's advanced years meant that the Ormonde bond with the house of York was one that could not last. The two men did however reach a vital agreement even though shortly before York's departure from Ireland in 1450, the two men had reached a vital agreement. In this unusual compact the aging but still energetic Ormonde agreed to serve the Duke in peace and war, for an annual fee of 200 marks, with the most significant part of the arrangement being that Ormonde undertook to serve the Duke in England as well as Ireland. So strong, in fact, was the bond between the two men at this time that York chose James Butler to act as his deputy in his absence.

It is possible that the Duke of York had never planned to stay long in Ireland, but he simply used his stay there to gather strength, and to seek outside support. In Ireland, he constantly promised (or threatened, as the royal councillors saw it) to return to England, to live on his 'poor livelihood', and he was finally forced to keep his word, in order to re-establish himself at Court. He crossed over to Wales in 1450, in spite of orders from London to prevent his ships being victuallised. Denounced as a traitor by the King's councillors, and held responsible for recent disturbances both in England and Ireland, gangs of men were set to waylay him on his journey to London. However he continued his progress, accompanied by 4,000 armed men, and was said to have 'beaten down the spears and walls in the King's chamber'[50] in order to gain entrance and secure an audience.

Ormonde's final campaign was in 1452, a campaign which gave the lie to the earlier charge that he was too old and weak for the task. In the space of six weeks he traversed the country from Limerick to Ulster, enforcing submission on a number of midland and northern chieftains before confronting Henry O'Neill on his own territory. This last encounter was largely on a family matter; for Ormonde made the Ulster leader put away his cousin Edmund Butler's recently widowed daughter, to take back his lawful wife – who was also Ormonde's own niece. That he succeeded is a striking demonstration of the power which a great magnate such as Ormonde, with numerous connections among both Gaelic and Anglo-Irish families, could bring to the office of Chief Governor.

During the campaign, the Earl broke down the castle of Owny and took the castle of Leix from the O'Dempseys, which then permitted him to pass to Airem, where he rescued a member of the Bermyngham family, who was imprisoned there. Ormonde then burned Airem in retaliation for the townspeople's offence, and from there he proceeded to Offaly, where the O'Connors sued for peace. At Annaly, the O'Farrells also signed a peace pact, promising him whole herds of cattle as the price for obtaining it, and in the county of Longford he demolished the castle of Barry, destroying the greater part of the harvest as an added punishment. From there he marched to the plain of Maine in County Cavan, where the O'Rileys sued for peace, acceding to all the Earl's conditions. In County Louth, the MacMahons gave in to his demands.

After other, lesser, victories, the Earl marched to the town of Atherdee in the county of Louth, where he died on St Bartholomew's Eve, 23 August 1452. (An omen was popularly believed to have occurred before his death, when a part of the Liffey River dried up for a two-mile length.[51]) The promises of 'peace' that he procured through his remarkable last journey: 'in half a fourth of a year' inevitably became 'null with his death', there being no such thing as a lasting truce in the country he had fought for so long to pacify. He was buried in the church of the abbey of St Mary in Dublin. A lover of history, antiquity and heraldry, he left some of his English lands to endow a college of heralds. His secretary, James Yonge, an academic of note, dedicated to him his English translation of the *Secretum Secretorum*, which deals with such issues as prudence, justice, fortitude, temperance, chivalry, the king's title to Ireland, and other themes. Yonge wrote that English was the Earl's 'modyre tongue', and he had done his best to make his Irish dependents love it as much as he did himself.

James was married twice. His first marriage was to Joanne, the daughter and heir-general of the Earl of Kildare. She had died, childless, in 1430, and was buried in London, her husband being at that time abroad with the King in France (where he was a witness of the young Henry's double coronation as King of England and France). The Earl wasted no time in looking for a second wife, and he soon married Elizabeth, the widow of Lord Grey, (for which he had to seek a pardon under the Great Seal for this union, since they were kindred). Elizabeth was a daughter of Lord Bergaveny, and by this 'second bed' he had three sons; James, John and Thomas. Elizabeth seems to have died as soon as she gave birth to the last of her children, for she is not mentioned in her mother's will, which was dated 10 January 1434, and left 'more bequests to her relations and servants than usual'. Lady Bergaveny[52] had been enormously rich in her own right, and the fact that she had overlooked her daughter, for whatever reason, did not dissuade her from being spectacularly generous to Elizabeth's sons,[53] who would all become Earls of Ormonde in turn.

## Notes

1. Curtis, *Calendar of Ormonde Deeds*.
2. Ibid.
3. *Calendar of State Papers, England.*
4. Ibid.
5. Carte, *The Life of the Duke of Ormonde.*
6. Ibid.
7. 'Brehon': an Irish lawyer.
8. *Calendar of State Papers, England.*
9. Shakespeare made good use of these reminiscences when he came to write of Prince Hal's escapades in *Henry IV*.
10. Carte, op. cit.
11. Ibid.
12. 'Kernes' were lightly armed foot soldiers (usually Irish peasants).
13. Carte, op. cit.
14. Ibid.
15. The Four Masters, *Annals of the Kingdom of Ireland*. (Urgal has long since disappeared from the map.)
16. *Calendar of State Papers, Ireland.*
17. *Calendar of State Papers, England.*
18. Carte, op. cit.

19.  Ibid.
20.  The Four Masters, op. cit.
21.  *Calendar of State Papers, Ireland.*
22.  Curtis, op. cit.
23.  Carte, op. cit.
24.  *Calendar of State Papers, Ireland.*
25.  *Calendar of State Papers, England.*
26.  Ibid.
27.  The Four Masters, op. cit.
28.  'Creaghts' were possible the wounded (or criminals who had been branded).
29.  'Maghery', like Urgal, has long since vanished.
30.  Four Masters, op. cit.
31.  Ibid.
32.  Carte, op. cit.
33.  Ibid.
34.  Ibid.
35.  *Calendar of State Papers, Ireland.*
36.  Carte, op. cit.
37.  Ibid.
38.  Ibid.
39.  *Calendar of State Papers, Ireland.*
40.  *Calendar of State Papers, England.*
41.  Carte, op. cit.
42.  The Four Masters, op. cit.
43.  *Calendar of State Papers, England.*
44.  Ibid.
45.  Ibid.
46.  Talbot (1388–1453) became one of England's most famous generals. He was said to have waged war honourably, and was a valiant man. De Maupoint, *Journal.*
47.  Carte, op. cit.
48.  Ibid. (Richard, Duke of York, 1411–60.) For the question of 'high treason' against him, see *Liber Hiberniae*, vol. 3.
49.  Four Masters, op. cit.
50.  *Calendar of State Papers, England.*
51.  The Four Masters, op. cit.
52.  Lady Bergavenny was the first wife of Edward Neville, first Baron of Bergavenny (or Abergavenney), whose family can be traced to John of Gaunt. This may help explain the singular adherence of the Ormonde family to the House of Lancaster.
53.  James Yonge flourished c. 1423 when he wrote the *Secreta Secretorum*, perhaps the only important work of any length to have been written in the English of the Pale.

# CHAPTER VII

# *The English Earl*

James, the 5th Earl of Ormonde, was the first in the succession who was not left a minor when he came into possession of his father's estates, being about 32 years old at the 4th earl's death in 1452. This James Butler was also rich in his own right, since he had inherited a considerable fortune from his grandmother, Joan, the widow of Lord Bergaveny, who left an enormous amount of property in six English shires. It was to go to his sons in succession, if he died.

Even before he came into his English and Irish inheritance, the new Earl was singularly honoured, being no more than a boy of six when the four-year old King Henry VI knighted him at the 'Parliament of the Bats' at Leicester in 1426 (so called because the nobles who attended were forbidden to wear swords, and consequently armed themselves with bats). At age eight James proudly wore the King's livery complete with gold collar and was one of the three noble boys who resided with the child King at Court. One of the others was to become his life-long enemy: the 17-year-old Richard, Duke of York.

James may also have been subject to the authority of the King's governess, a near relation of the Ormonde family, Lady – or Dame – Alice Butler, whose status was comparable to that of a chief officer of the household (and who was one of the few people allowed to physically discipline the boy King). Given a salary of 40*l* per year, she was so successful in the post that she would be awarded that same sum as a life pension. Her chief function was to instil in the young King the virtues of courtesy, discipline and all things necessary for a royal person, and her 'rule' lasted until 1428, by which time, James was serving as a page in the retinue of the Duke of Bedford, the king's uncle and heir to the throne, then Regent of France.

In many ways James missed out on the normal schooling of a boy of his rank at that time, with its emphasis on the martial arts and 'knightly demeanour' at the expense of scholarship. But his experiences in France during the occupation of Paris, throughout the period known as the 'Dual Monarchy',[1] must have been a more than adequate substitute, since he had gained command of his own men-at-arms by 1441, when he also attended Richard, Duke of York. This was on an expedition to France, when the duke was made regent after Bedford's death. It is notable that the Duke of York was generally regarded as the heir to the English throne at the death of King Henry VI's last Lancastrian uncle, Humphrey, Duke of Gloucester in 1447. Richard of York was also, as Henry's heir, a claimant to the French crown since the English now held the kingdoms of England and France, with Henry VI crowned King of both.

Despite one of his relations becoming Captain of the Bastille during the English occupation of Paris, Sir James Butler himself appears to have made little impact as a soldier during his time in France. However his career was to flourish on his return to England. There James would remain for extensive periods of time and he was the first of his family to consistently neglect his duties in Ireland. Undoubtedly this was because the time he spent in England became increasingly more rewarding, resulting in his steady rise through the hierarchy of the court. He was in addition granted the lucrative sheriffdoms of Cardigan and Camarthen for life, as well as being a member of numerous royal commissions. The most important of these commissions was in 1444, when he accompanied the Marquess of Suffolk to fetch Margaret of Anjou from France, for her marriage to Henry VI.

There can be little doubt that without the efforts of this formidable queen the conflicts in England, from 1455 to 1485, when the houses of Lancaster and York struggled for the throne, would have foundered from the beginning. King Henry VI, with his periodic fits of madness, was congenitally incapable of fighting for his kingship, and even in his saner moments proved generally unfit to rule. From the commencement of his reign – the triumphalist character of his father's monarchy being forgotten – many people in England had begun to question the right of the Lancastrians to the throne. But from the year that Henry VI first displayed the signs of his hereditary madness, in August 1453, the country at large was more than ever divided in its loyalties, although, in this year, a considerable number of courtiers deserted to the Yorkist side. And it was at this time that the King's advisers considered it prudent to send the Duke of York to Ireland, as Lieutenant, rather than to let him stay in England as a focus for discontent.

Sir James Butler, however, was one of the few who steadfastly supported the Lancastrian interest, and it is perhaps because of this loyalty to them that he avoided Ireland, where the majority of his peers supported the opposing party. In the face of rising opposition to the royal family James did what he could to help their cause, though he lacked the English title that would allow him to take his place in the House of Peers to pursue their interests further. However this matter was rectified when, in July 1449, during the lifetime of his father, he was created a peer of England as the Earl of Wiltshire, by a patent bearing the date of 8 July, Henry VI. (Wiltshire was one of the few counties, incidentally, in which the Ormondes did not have any sizeable estate.) With the right to vote in an English assembly the new Earl was called to parliament in that year, to become a 'trier of petitions'.[2]

By the following year Sir James Butler had accumulated further honours, and he was appointed as one of the commissioners to whom custody of the Castle at Calais, with the Tower of Rysbank and the marshes of Picardy, were committed for five years. This was a strategic position of marked importance, for it was during his tour of duty in 1450 that the French artillery annihilated the last English army in Gascony, and only Calais was left of all the English dominions in France. However Wiltshire's duties on the continent were cut short by the violent events then taking place in England, where the men of Kent were under arms, led by Jack Cade.[3] This rebellion broke out in 1450, with the rioters protesting mainly against the government's incompetence and financial oppression, and they occupied London for three days.

Hardly had this uprising been suppressed when the Duke of York returned from Ireland, without permission from the King. In fact, he had taken advantage of a clause in his indentures that allowed him to return to England in an emergency (the Cade rebellion making the perfect justification), although his motives for doing so appear to have been very mixed. In a letter he wrote to his brother-in-law, York revealed that he dreaded failure in Ireland believing it would destroy his reputation in the same way that the growing failures of the English leaders in Normandy were firmly putting an end to their careers.

In 1451 the new Earl of Wiltshire was made Lord Deputy of Ireland in the absence of the Duke of York, and in the next year, after the death of his father, he was upgraded to viceroy by a commission granting him the office for ten years. Yet the glittering rewards to be found at the English court still presented a seductive pull for the Earl of Wiltshire, and he could never quite throw himself wholeheartedly into his Irish duties. Arguably the longevity of his father and his domination of the Irish scene during James's lifetime may have often made him feel redundant in Ireland, therefore influencing his decision to spend most of his life in England. It is indeed true that both of his brothers were also drawn to life in England rather than their Irish birthplace.

James Butler's first real clash – outside the schoolroom – with the man who would prove to be his bitterest enemy came in September 1451, when the Duke of York intervened on his own initiative to settle a dispute in Somerset that led to an armed confrontation, in which quarrel Wiltshire sided with the opposition. The origins of the disagreement remain obscure, but it is unlikely that the Duke of York's intervention had anything to do with his earlier enmity towards Wiltshire, for at this stage he had left the Earl's English father to act as his deputy in Ireland. Since his return from there, in August 1450, York had 'acted consistently as an upholder of good government',[4] and James Butler, too, was anxious to prove his reliability. As now for when the Earl of Devon marched across the country with a substantial force to bring Wiltshire to battle, James Butler departed the scene in dutiful answer to a summons from the King at Coventry.

He was in attendance on Henry during most of the King's tours of the country throughout 1451, when the nobles who had broken the peace were judged. Yet at Coventry, in September of that same year, Wiltshire himself was imprisoned at Berkhamstead Castle for taking part in a quarrel of the Duke of Somerset's (the Duke of York's most powerful royal enemy at Court, and one of the King's strongest supporters). But only a year later, their mutual animosity would flare into the open when James was one of the lords sent to extract York's right-hand man from the sanctuary he had taken in a royal chapel, and to take him to confinement in Westminster Palace. York's man was to be questioned there with regard to the role he had supposedly played in preparing his master's supposed armed rising of 1452.

In that year, Wiltshire had again taken part in what would be the longest royal progress of the reign. The King's entourage was very substantial, with fifteen lords and six judges in his train, and James Butler was prominent as one of the lords to head the commission while the Duke of York was conspicuous by his absence. Understandably so, since the judicial sessions at Ludlow, in the heart of York's country, were held principally to try the Duke's followers accused of rebellion in London, Kent and the Welsh marches in March and April 1452. (The story that King Henry forced York's allies to appear naked with nooses round their necks, doing so in atrocious weather, in ice and snow, is a gross exaggeration. But that they were compelled to beg for mercy is true enough, the occasion being less judicial than vengeful, and a bald demonstration of the power of the House of Lancaster in a Yorkist stronghold).

In October there was another perambulation, this time through the principal areas of York's influence south of the Trent. This further exhibition of 'law-giving' occupied the King for a month, and Wiltshire was again among the leading magnates who attended Henry, though not all of the time, or involving himself in all of the trials. But he was closer to the King during what would be Henry's last judicial progress from 3 February 1453 until the opening of the new parliament on 6 March. Again a commission of oyer and terminer, it comprised an impressive selection of the nobles who were sympathetic to the King, Henry being by now clearer as to who were his friends and whom his enemies. Wiltshire superseded York as Lieutenant of Ireland from 5 March 1453.

But being as reluctant to visit his viceroyalty as ever, he stayed on in England, where he undertook the 'guardianship of the seas'[5] – that is, of the English shores – along with the Earl of Salisbury, for a period of three years; for which he received tonnage and poundage to support him in the task. At this period he would also reach the pinnacle of power, as the Lord Treasurer of England; but he held the post only until events again overtook him, and he was ousted.

These events had already been foreshadowed in Wiltshire's earlier career and any astute forecaster could have predicted the outcome. For when the Lancastrians strengthened their grip on England in the spring of 1453, the newly created Earl of Wiltshire displaced the main Lancastrian rival, the Duke of York, as the Crown's representative in Ireland, York disputed the Earl's right to the Lieutenancy. He continued to do this until the situation became confused to the point of it finally being decided hat the sums of money assigned to Ireland should be paid to the Treasurer of England, until it had been legally determined 'who is and who ought to be Lieutenant'.[6] James Butler should have taken more heed of this particular controversy since it prefigured the clashes he would later encounter as an active participant in the struggle for supremacy in England between the houses of York and Lancaster.

In August 1453, the King's hereditary insanity broke out, at which the Duke of York, as next in line, asserted his claim to be regent, in which he succeeded. In April 1454 York – now known as 'Protector of England' during the King's illness – was sufficiently strong to have the dispute about the Irish lieutenancy resolved in his favour and James Butler was again downgraded. It is hard to understand why the Duke of York was so insistent upon the Earl's demotion, since he showed no more inclination to take over his duties in Ireland than did his rival, and nor could he since he was now in full charge of English affairs.

Both men seemed equally reluctant to reside on their Irish estates, and while in York's case this did not especially matter, despite his popularity there, Wiltshire's absence from Ireland was resulting in increasing disorder among the cadet branches of the Butler family as they sought to settle factional disputes. In particular, the Ormonde claim to the manors of Maynooth and Rathmoor against that of the Kildares was being pursued vigorously (and violently) by the Earl's cousins, William and Edmund Butler, about which, in June 1454, the Kildares complained to the Duke of York. The struggle between the two sides over this matter, they reported, had resulted in more destruction in Kilkenny and Meath inside a few years than had been brought about by their Anglo-Irish and Gaelic enemies in half a century. Such was the disorder in the area that many people refused to appear in royal courts, or even to travel to market towns, for fear of being robbed or even killed by the Butler faction. A parliament held by the Earl of Kildare, as York's deputy, in October 1455, was informed that members of the Ormonde family had allied themselves with the MacMurchadha, who had between them burnt and destroyed the county of Wexford over three nights.[7]

The charge of treason against the Butlers, which would be brought by the Yorkists in 1455, revoked in 1458, but reaffirmed in the final session of parliament of July 1460, would exempt Edmond Butler from all culpability, despite his obvious leanings towards the wrong side. But even more amazingly, he would then be recognised as the lawful heir to the barony of Dunboyne, an honour that had been settled upon the third son of the fourth Chief Butler of Ireland, who had been summoned to the Irish parliament in that name in 1274. (He had married the 'Lady of Dunboyne' and so had taken her name). Edmund's elder brother, William, the seventh baron, had been attainted in 1455, dying four years later, and for a time the barony looked to be in danger of expiring with him, but the dignity and estates were restored to Edmund by act of Parliament in 1471. Later he would receive large grants from the Crown for his 'great services in the Irish wars'.[8]

These collateral branches of the Butler family were a strong contrast with the main line, not only because they straddled the York and Lancaster divide, but also in that they had frequently intermarried with Irish families for decades. Edmund's father had married an O'Brien and his son would take as his second wife a daughter of a chief of the Carberry clan. The campaign of 1455 that the Butlers helped to foment revealed the extent of their Gaelicisation as well as their opposition to the Kildares as deputies; and what followed also proclaimed their invulnerability to their Anglo-Norman enemies. Ordered to appear before the Dublin parliament, to answer for their offences 'under pain of being adjudged traitors', the administration had not the strength to compel their attendance. Expressive of an even more open contempt for the legislature, the parliament of 1458 was forced to revoke the sentence of treason against them on the specious grounds that 'they had been *too ill* to appear'[9] to state their case.

But the quarrels between the Butlers and the Kildares, like many similar feuds among the aristocracy in England, were becoming more deeply entangled with that of the wider political conflict between the Lancastrian and Yorkist parties. The Kildares supported the White Rose of York while the Butlers – for the most part – supported the Red Rose of Lancaster, and these were issues that were swiftly reaching crisis point in England.

Queen Margaret had borne a son on 13 October 1453, and although the Duke of York recognised him as heir to the throne, the Queen's fear of him as a continuing rival to the infant Prince of Wales made their enmity inevitable. Yet in February 1454 twenty-eight lords met in the great council chamber (with five notable absentees, among them James Butler) to nominate York as the King's lieutenant, and to allow him the honour of opening and presiding over parliament. The de facto power in the land was the whole council, with York as the main voice within it. On 15 March 1454 the Earl of Wiltshire was among the twenty-two lords (including York) who signed for the creation of the infant Edward as Prince of Wales. At this point York specifically recognised the Lancastrian succession, but he had no use or liking for their adherents, and he made a particular point of rebuffing James Butler.

Later, although the King had recovered from his bout of madness, his indomitable young Queen had taken the government of the realm into her own hands – and various lords were collecting an army under her instructions with the Earl of Wiltshire prominent among them. (This army was created ostensibly to safeguard the King and the infant prince against their Yorkist rivals). In 1454, with the Duke of York again temporarily disempowered, Wiltshire was one of the commissioners appointed to guard the coasts, sanctioned to impress ships and men to serve at sea for the King, his station being the western coast. The appointment was for three years, and tonnage and poundage were officially appropriated to pay for this. In that year, he was again made the Lord High Treasurer of England.

While holding this office he was accused of 'great avarice and extortion',[10] and he was just as rapacious in Ireland, despite being largely absent from that country. When Richard of York toured Kildare in 1454 he was told by the 'true liege people' of these parts that they did not dare to appear in the (Butler) court 'for dread to be slain, taken or spoiled of their goods'.[11] And not only the common people feared the arrogant depredations of the Earl of Wiltshire; he laid waste to the lands of many of his peers with equal zeal; and he even raided his kinsmen, the FitzGeralds, the great lords of Kildare, although they just as regularly expelled his invasions.

In 1454 the Duke of York's position as Lieutenant of Ireland was renewed for ten years, when he immediately made the Earl of Kildare his deputy in preference to Wiltshire, an inevitable snub considering the simmering hatred between the two men. But, partly as a result of York's choice, the local communities, encouraged by the Kildares to give expression to their desire for dependence, created total anarchy outside Dublin; and even within the Pale the royal power was not strong enough to save it from partial destruction. The Anglo-Irish lords, from the cover of their own counties, dominated the parliament in order that it should best serve their interests. (The Earl of Wiltshire and Ormonde was one of the few to take no part in this, but only because he was too well established in England and most of his rule in Ireland was carried out by proxies who followed his loyalist lead).

Perhaps because he had vainly contended York's Irish lieutenancy, Wiltshire was rewarded with the treasurership in 15 March 1455. But once again he would not be long in the office, for in May 1455 York and his ally the Earl of Warwick – afterwards the famous 'Kingmaker' – then in their northern strongholds, recruited a great number of men and marched on London for a confrontation with the royal party. This decision on their part would accidentally lead to the first outright skirmish of the civil war, and would cost James Butler his high office and very nearly his life.

York and his allies stopped short of entering the city of London, coming to a halt in the county of Hertfordshire. York protested that the two men had assembled the 'army' that accompanied them only for their own protection when they attended the council to be held at Leicester, rather than having raised it to take action against the monarch. But the letters that he wrote to Henry VI, explaining their need for this armed force and professing their loyalty to the Crown, were deliberately withheld from the King, and as a result of this the Duke and Warwick were seen to be rallying troops for a more sinister purpose. At St Albans, on 22 May 1455, King Henry and Queen Margaret, marching with a considerable force themselves on their way to the council, found what now appeared to be a hostile army waiting for them outside the town. Or, at least, they took this to be the case, and so the first battle of St Albans came to be fought, by an almost capricious stroke of fate, or by the malicious actions of the King's advisers, among them, naturally, the Earl of Wiltshire.

Yet even then the conflict was deferred for three hours, while the Duke of York tried to get his complaints against his enemies heard by the King, and it was only when he had failed utterly that the battle took place. The ensuing engagement lasted less than an hour, and has been derisively described, but with little exaggeration, as a 'short scuffle in a street'.[12] A contemporary chronicle says of the battle that once the leaders on the royalist side had been slain, the fighting ceased abruptly; but it is equally true to say that the outcome was decided by York's larger numbers, and a surprise flank attack upon the King's men.

The Earl of Wiltshire was said to have borne the King's banner, although there are others who claimed that honour. But he was also said to have been one of the earliest to flee the field, casting his armour into a ditch when he did so, and afterwards making his escape in disguise. On the other hand, he was said to have been extremely active on the battleground, and he would later receive numerous grants from King Henry in reward for his services on the field. Henry himself was wounded in the neck by an arrow, and had clearly lost the day. Yet after the engagement, York and his closest allies knelt before him and asked his forgiveness. The defeated royal party later travelled back to London, almost as the trophies of their vanquisher, and York was rewarded for his triumph by becoming Constable of England.

After the battle of St Albans was fought and lost by the Lancastrians, with Henry VI being taken prisoner and the Duke of York declared protector of the realm, James Butler, having sided with the wrong party, found himself without royal patronage. This was a foretaste of the treatment he could expect to receive should the Yorkist party ever fully triumph, although he seems to have learned nothing from the lesson. The Earl of Warwick, York's main champion took over the captaincy of Calais, whose garrison has been termed 'the largest single force in the King's pay'.[13]

James also lost the lucrative post of Royal Treasurer to one of Richard of York's many brothers-in-law, and his latest commission as Governor of Ireland was naturally taken from him, with the Duke of York being once again declared the Lord Lieutenant (if ruling there by proxy). Literally a fugitive, when he was summoned to Westminster James Butler was only one of the many Lancastrians who thought itadvisable to ignore the order while his safety at Court could not be guaranteed.

Other Butlers, though, were continuing the Lancastrian fight, at least in Ireland. The steward of the Franchise at Wexford wrote to the deputy and lords of the Irish parliament on 18 October 1455, 'truly and faithfully, without any manner of fraud or dissimulation'.[14] to complain of the brutal actions of these men. Their captains – whose names were contained within his letter, along with those of their Irish allies, McMorghowe and Donal Reagh, 'Irish enemy of our sovereign Lord the King' – had, he wrote, 'with banners displayed' ridden throughout the county of Wexford, 'burning and destroying...continually'.[15]

The Butlers listed were Edmund fitzRichard; James 'the son of the said Edmund'; Richard 'the son of the said Edmund (by another name called Iny Glesane)', and Piers fitzJames of the county of Tipperary. Others were Tibbote fitzJames le Botiller of the county of Tipperary, William le Botiller of Dunboyne, Edmund the son of Piers le Botiller, and 'divers others of the *said nation,* whose names were *too long* for us to report'.[16]

'And inasmuch as they be people that will not obey the King's laws, nor may be brought to answer in due process', [the steward ended his letter] we beseech you that due remedy may be provided, and ordained thereupon by the authority of this present parliament. And that our sovereign Lord the King, and his Counsel in England, may be informed thereof by this present parliament. And Jesus have you in his governance.'[17]

In London, York's troops walked the streets in armour and their barges were full of weapons. In October 1455 the King relapsed into madness, and York was again chosen by the lords in parliament to act as Protector; but he took the post this time only on specific conditions: that he had a paid council to assist him, that his salary and all travelling expenses were made over to him directly, and that his tenure of office could not be terminated at the King's pleasure, but only with the consent of his peers in parliament. When, by 14 January 1456, the King made a slight recovery, York, fearing the worst, attended the court at Westminster with a strong retinue. The promises he had received, though, went for nothing, and he was again summarily discharged from his post of Protector but was retained as a chief councillor. The Queen was as strongly opposed to him as ever, and among the lords who took her part was the Earl of Wiltshire.

In 1457 York was summoned to a great council at Coventry where a peace was to be made between the Yorkist lords and the son of the late

Duke of Somerset, who had been slain at St Albans. On 6 March York was again appointed Lieutenant of Ireland, renewed for another 10 years, which meant that the 'English Earl' was once again deprived of any real voice in the Dublin parliament, even had be been moved to cross over to Ireland to put in an appearance.

An engagement that he could not avoid without incurring penalties was the great council that was held at Westminster, with no excuse being accepted for non-attendance. York arrived with 140 horsemen, and his ally, the Earl of Salisbury brought 400 horses, with eighty knights and squires in his company. Their royal enemy, Somerset, arrived later with 200 horses, and when Warwick entered London, having been detained by contrary winds in the Channel, 600 men in livery accompanied him. Yet, in fear of his liberty, the Earl of Wilshire stayed away.

The city would not admit the Lancastrian forces in any case, who they feared meant to 'disturb the peace', and so Somerset was lodged outside the walls. Large bodies of trained bands, employed by the Yorkists, rode about the city daily, and a strong watch against the Lancastrian forces without the city was kept at night. One could say that London was in a state of siege, with the King a prisoner of the besieged. In this situation, conferences were held in an attitude of armed neutrality, but terms of 'peace and friendship' were at last agreed. The day after these terms were settled by all parties a huge procession was made to St Paul's Cathedral, led by the crowned King, followed by the Queen and the Duke of York, with rival lords following in their train, walking together *hand in hand*.

While the peace lasted York was predominant in the King's councils, with the only person of greater influence being the Queen. She was not, however, strong enough to protect all her adherents, and during this period James Butler deliberately avoided prominence at Court. When he did so he was kept mainly in attendance on the King, who had virtually ceased to function as a monarch, although in April 1457 the King and Queen moved temporarily to Hereford, to support a commission of oyer and terminer. This was headed by those peers on whom they could rely, among them the Earl of Wiltshire, but no members of the royal party appear to have learned anything from the previous year's upheavals. Once again the accused were treated very harshly, for there was much unease at court about the loyalty of the shires. James Butler was probably among the magnates chosen to act as a temporary Lord Lieutenant in one of the sixteen counties commissioned to raise a posse to resist and suppress the 'King's rebels'.

But by October 1458 a full court was once again being held in King Henry VI's name, and the old feuds flared up again. An attempt was made to murder the Earl of Warwick as he left the Council Chamber, and it was with difficulty that he managed to escape to the safety of his barge on the Thames. It was rumoured that the Queen had tried to get the King to abdicate in favour of their teenage son, but this plan also failed. York was, however, once more removed from power, and again became a threat to stability. When King Henry called for armed levies to attend him at a council at Leicester on 10 May 1459, no overt act on their part was imputed to the Yorkists that might have called for this expedient. But their leaders thought it advisable to clear their names, writing to the King to say that they had been drive to take up arms only in self-defence.

But it would seem that the King's party – or, more properly, the Queen's – were by now decided upon a final confrontation. King Henry came up with a much larger armed force than was customary when he faced the Yorkists at Ludlow, and he was in a more martial mood than usual. But, hating bloodshed as he did, he also proclaimed that he would pardon all that would lay down their arms within six days (with the exception of those people who had killed the Queen's man in a battle at Blore Heath, whom she had sent to stop Warwick from joining York and Salisbury at Ludlow).

The Yorkists were now deserted by some of their best troops, and seeing that it was useless to fight, York and his second son, the Earl of Rutland, secretly escaped from Ludlow and withdrew into Wales; in fact fleeing ignominiously, breaking down bridges to frustrate pursuit. The Duke's town of Ludlow was sacked by the royal forces, while York himself was again driven into that period of virtual exile in Ireland, during which he would make his curious pact with Wiltshire's father, who had hitherto always been extremely loyal to the Lancastrians.

York's eldest son, Edward of March, fled to the English stronghold of Calais, along with York's leading supporters, the Earls of Salisbury and Warwick. Their estates, and those of their followers, were confiscated to the Crown in a packed and extremely partisan parliament hastily summoned to Coventry in November 1459. York and his associates were subjected to the sentence of attainder, by which they were proclaimed rebels, traitors and outlaws. But the Yorkists were by no means crushed, and York in Ireland was even safer than his eldest son in Calais, for the authority of English writ to arrest traitors in Ireland was disallowed by the Irish parliament.

The Earl of Wiltshire, immediately restored to the post of Lord Treasurer of the Household, then began a systematic exploitation of the jurisdiction of the sheriffs. He did this by creating various offices throughout the shires and then supplying his own choice of men (who were expected to pay for the privilege), without first going through the Exchequer. Whether this distortion of a traditional procedure was the Earl's inspiration, or whether he was acting under orders form the Queen in order to raise money for the continued defence of the royal party, the new system quickly led to a lack of control. And, for whatever reason, it was a clear breach of Wiltshire's remit.

Yet James Butler, castigated as an evil and avaricious counsellor to the King was, despite his dishonesty and greed, singularly honoured in the last years before the Yorkists finally took full control of the country. Whatever his personal defects, he would prove one of the most loyal of Lancastrian courtiers, with never a breach of trust to the royal family. In the next year he was made a Knight of the Garter, and he obtained a grant of the keepership of the forest or park of Pederton in Somerset, then held by the Crown by forfeiture of the disgraced Duke of York, who had now been formally attainted.

Others of the Duke's offices and estates had been distributed among the Queen's friends and supporters, and James Butler also had Cranbourne Chase. Soon after acquiring these new properties (his possession of them would be short-lived), James used his private wealth to fit out five great ships of Genoa, to fight the Earl of Warwick's fleet at sea, and he sailed with his ships to the Netherlands.

Warwick did not immediately use his rival fleet of twenty-six vessels in an immediate attack on England, but instead sailed to Waterford, landing there on 16 March 1460. After meeting up with the Duke of York, and agreeing upon a plan of action for the future, Warwick returned to Calais while York remained in Ireland, which was proving to be his safest stronghold, even though James Butler had again been nominated Lieutenant in his place, and was energetically seeking to undermine York's prestige within the country (admittedly from the safety of England). When attainted by the English parliament in November 1459, all York's offices, including those he held in Ireland, ceased; but this meant nothing to the Irish magnates and the Home Rule Party, who continued to treat the Duke with the deference due to a monarch-in-waiting.

The Desmonds and the Kildares in particular, along with their Gaelic relations, actively espoused the Yorkist cause, and the Irish parliament showed itself ready and eager to protect him. They now had a 'King of their own', and a King who had their interests at heart (or so he led them to believe), and they meant to make good use of him. When York had landed in Ireland in November 1459, he was welcomed 'like a Messiah', and such enthusiasm was at its greatest in Dublin. The fact that he had been charged with treason in England singularly failed to affect Irish fervour for his cause and perhaps even added to it.

York summoned a parliament at Drogheda on 7 February 1460, and it gave him almost sovereign powers as their 'Lieutenant', despite his having been officially superseded. It was said that 'To plot against him was as if to plot against the King',[18] despite the fact that he was now the open enemy of their other King in England. A statute of this parliament enacted that anyone seeking to procure his death or incite rebellion would be held guilty of high treason, and executed accordingly. The Irish parliament refused to accept the authority of the English Privy Seal, and when the Earl of Wiltshire sent over an agent with writs for York's arrest, the emissary found himself attainted and, after being tried before the Duke in person, was hung, drawn and quartered.

The Duke of York clearly enjoyed the support of a great majority of the Anglo-Irish, and from his Irish sanctuary he could prepare for his return to England. (His admirers in Ireland even provided him with a company of archers, to return with him when he left to take up arms against King Henry.) There was, however, a price to pay for Irish championship, and York was forced to acknowledge the independence of the 'land of Ireland', except for the personal link to the English Crown, in return for Irish support. The Duke willingly granted this (for what had he to lose by such a commitment?), and in the summer of 1460 the Earl of Warwick reappeared in Ireland, to concert plans for the overthrow of the Lancastrian regime in England. Ireland remained superficially loyal to the Crown, but by throwing in their lot with the Duke of York the Irish magnates adopted a different allegiance from that still held, however shakily, by their equals in England.

There was a sudden and dramatic reversal of political fortune when, in June 1460, the Earls of Salisbury and Warwick, together with York's eldest son, Edward of March, launched a successful invasion of England from Calais, and soon occupied London. The King, who was then at Coventry, set off to meet them, apparently in sole charge, with his Queen for once taking no part in his course of action. In fact, she was ordered only to come to him if she received a message containing a secret known only to the two of them. Should he fail, she was to make her way to Harlech Castle, to first seek refuge with the King's half-brother, Jasper Tudor, and to go later by sea to seek a more secure protection in Scotland.

All this she had to do when the day was lost for Henry, with his enemies roundly defeating his forces at the battle of Northampton on 10 July. The three earls, occupying a hill from which they could see all that was passing, sent a message to know whether the King would quit the field or fight. To which they received an answer from the Duke of Buckingham (the actual commander of the King's army) that he could not leave without fighting. It would be one more savage clash when, after a morning spent in useless parleying, battle was joined in torrential rain in the early afternoon.

Warwick gave orders not to spare the Lancastrian nobility, knights and squires; all were to be killed or taken prisoner, which duly came about. Buckingham was slain on the field, and the capture of the King in his tent in a nearby meadow was preceded by horrendous slaughter. Yet even so the complete victory of the Yorkists, coming after only thirty minutes' hard fighting, may have been due to the treachery of a King's man, who led the royal vanguard over to the other side. The King was conducted to London with at least an outward show of respect, but the capture of Henry VI enabled the Yorkists to establish a government fully controlled by them; but one run technically in the King's name, and with the 'authority' of their royal prisoner. The Queen and her son reached Jasper Tudor's castle of Harlech with only four attendants, having been robbed by their own servants on the way.

When York returned in triumph to England to stake his claim to the throne, having been recalled by his Yorkist followers, the victors of Northampton, he left the Earl of Kildare as his deputy in Ireland. No greater sign could have been given of his continuing enmity towards James Butler, by now too English in manner and partiality for Irish taste. In fact, the Earl of Wiltshire and Ormonde had more to fear from the Duke of York than had most people, since he had been particularly active in the persecution of the Duke's supporters in England. He had confiscated their property and hung them by the score, in what has been called an interval of 'judicial terrorism'.

He had also introduced an imposition that had never been tried in England before – the French tradition of conscription. This revolutionary process of raising an armed force was first used in London, and was meant initially only to increase the King's personal guard. But it was later extended to include every village, township and hamlet where it was demanded that each place should provide a certain number of able-bodied men and archers, *at the expense of the inhabitants*, for the defence of the country against the Yorkists. It was also rumoured that King Henry, perhaps at Wiltshire's suggestion, had sent letters to the native Irish, encouraging them 'to enter into the conquest of the said land'.[19]

Although he had been made Lord Lieutenant of Ireland in 1459, James Butler never acted as such – at least in the country itself – for more than a few months of the twelve years that he had pledged to serve. Then, all ambition overthrown, in the early part of 1460, 'in fear of the houses of York and Kildare'[20] – a formidable combination in anti-Lancastrian Ireland – the Earl of Wiltshire fled to Flanders, where he took sanctuary at the friary in Utrecht. His flight was made the more imperative after a raid, in which – along with the two other lords, Scales and Hungerford – he had inflicted a series of bloody assizes upon the Duke of York's tenants at Newbury.

York's name is at the head of the manifesto put out by his son and allies, and when he came out of Ireland and into London, he was said to have done so 'with great *bobance*', that is with extreme pomp and ostentation. After the King was brought to London, York sat in judgement in 'divers towns coming homeward' to punish the 'law-breakers'[21] (meaning those who had directly challenged him). He was also accompanied by a body of 1,500 armed men, 'harnessed and arrayed in the manner of war'.[22] Accompanied by trumpeters and clarioners, his banners were emblazoned with the arms of England and his sword borne upright before him, which was the symbol of a victorious king. He entered the palace with a great blast of trumpets, and in the great hall, where parliament were assembled, he laid his hand on the throne, as though about to take possession.

He was popularly rumoured to have beaten down the fixed screens in the Queen's chamber – where the King had taken refuge – upon his arrival in London, 'having no consideration to your highness's presence'; and as before King Henry was made a prisoner of sorts. But this time, in the same way that the French royal dukes had sought to control his mad grandfather, Charles VI of France, York and King Henry's advisers, most notably his uncle, the Duke of Somerset (the only leading Lancastrian at court), fought bitterly to have the mastery of him.

But it was immediately obvious that York intended to claim the crown for himself, as by right, when he laid the particulars of his ancestry before the lords. Descended from Edward III through both his parents, his family would have been the natural successors to the throne but for the deposition of Richard II, when Henry IV had unjustly set aside the Mortimer line. Judges, lawyers and the lords of parliament, however, scotched his claim, while admitting that his title could not be 'defeated'. They were unwilling to dethrone a King to whom they had sworn allegiance, and a compromise was proposed: that York should succeed Henry VI when that King died, thereby setting aside King Henry's son, the Prince of Wales, but that Henry should live out his reign.

York was later proclaimed the true heir apparent and Protector of the Realm; but this arrangement soon ceased to correspond with political reality when the Lancastrians, led by Queen Margaret, quickly mobilised their forces in the north of England. Lord Neville obtained a commission from York to deal with these northern 'rebels', but he betrayed the Duke by carrying the force he had raised into the enemy camp, maltreating the South Yorkshire tenants of York and the Earl of Salisbury.

Richard of York met his end, in fact, by underestimating the strength of his opponents when he left London for the north to deal with these rebels. Attacked by a body of Somerset's men at Worksop, both he and Salisbury sustained great losses, and York was forced to take refuge in his castle of Sandal near Wakefield. There, Somerset, his greatest enemy within the royal family, mustered his men at Pontefract and cut off York's supply lines, thus besieging him. At least 8,000 men were ranged against the Duke of York's forces, and his position became so indefensible that his son, Edward of March, had to come to his rescue.

Before he could reach him, however, the Duke, although advised not to risk a battle, decided to march out and confront the enemy. (The *Annales*, attributed to William Worcester, states that York's men were actually wandering about the countryside in search of food at the time they were attacked by Somerset's troops. It was also alleged that York's men were taken by treachery, against the law of arms, under the protection of a truce).

The Duke of York fell in the brief engagement known as the battle of Wakefield, along with his second son, the Earl of Rutland, and the best of his knights and squires. Altogether about 2,200 of his men died in this action of 30 December 1460; for which James Butler had returned from the continent to take his part in such a decisive encounter, and in which he commanded one wing of the army that finally enclosed the Duke of York's bodyguard. In a brief skirmish, York was despatched, 'oppressed with numbers', and his head, topped with a paper crown, was stuck on the walls of his city, York, along with other 'traitors'. (The Lancastrians were adept at such public mockery).

His death left the Queen and her supporters face to face with York's heir, Edward of March (now, as his father's heir, the new Duke of York). More crucially, they encountered the new Duke's main financial backer, Richard, Earl of Warwick, his cousin and a fine military strategist, as he had already proved. The action that followed determined the future of both royal parties. Edward of March, then at Gloucester, raised a body of 30,000 men from the Mortimer lands on the Welsh borders, planning to face the Queen immediately. But informed that the Earl of Wiltshire, along with Jasper Tudor, Earl of Pembroke, had arrived in Wales by sea, and was ready to fall upon Edward's rearguard, he turned about to give them battle.

He overtook Butler and Tudor leading a body of Irish, Welsh, Breton and French volunteers marching to the assistance of the Queen from Wales. On 2 February 1461 these mercenaries were defeated, with a loss of 3,800 men, at Mortimer's Cross near Ludlow, and were chased as far as Hereford, although both earls managed to make their escape and rejoin the Queen. Just before the battle – 'a happy omen' – the sun had appeared in the sky in a triple image, where the three discs had joined together in one. After the victory, Edward pushed on to London, where he was received as a deliverer.

In Ireland, meanwhile, a ferocious war had broken out between the English of Meath and those of Leinster, during which the greater part of Meath was destroyed. This war between the English appears to have no connection with the struggles then taking place in England, and the only member of the Butler family to make an impact in the Irish affair was MacRichard Butler, who - with an Irish accomplice – took 1,000 horsemen into battle. Heavily armoured, or 'all wearing helmets' as the Four Masters put it, they entered the fray 'without fear or dread'; so contemptuous of their enemies, in fact that they calmly shoed their horses while their foraging parties plundered and burned the countryside around them 'in every direction'.

After the battle of Wakefield the Papal Legate tried to bring the two parties together to patch up some form of truce, but Queen Margaret remained irreconcilable, and then played into Edward's hands. In the mistaken belief that she would be aided in her cause by the French King she marched south to join the victors of Wakefield to confront her enemies, advancing towards London 'with a host of rough northern followers;[24] who ravaged the country on the way. On 17 February 1461, to the surprise of her enemies and allies alike, she vanquished the much-feared Earl of Warwick in the second battle of St Albans. Perhaps this conflict was notable for the Yorkist use of small firearms for the first time in English history; the firearms of this period were of course unreliable.

Warwick had brought King Henry, virtually a prisoner in the hands of the Yorkists, but with their unexpected defeat the King was once more in the hands of his own people. The triumphant Lancastrians took a terrible revenge on the defeated troops, with one instance being particularly appalling. After the victory, the King had made his son a knight on the battlefield, and the Prince, although only eight years old, at the instigation of his mother ordered an enemy knight to be beheaded, which was done while he and the Queen looked on. It was clear to all that no mercy was to be expected, even by those who had played only a minor part in the confrontation. Londoners were divided between fear and hatred, but they were also defiant. When emissaries of the Queen came to demand a contribution of money and provisions for her straitened army, her messengers were denied entrance to the city. The mayor, as ordered, loaded carts with the required supplies but the citizens seized the carts and divided the food and money among themselves.

Margaret may have won this particular battle, but she failed to make her position secure after her unexpected victory, and she would ultimately lose out. For when King Henry, in a rare moment of sanity, begged her not to force her way into London, where her supporters would certainly have run amok, she hesitated for too long. Edward of March, the new Duke of York, took advantage of her irresolution and marched his own troops in the city, to enormous acclaim. The executions carried out by the Queen's men after the battles of Wakefield and St Albans, and the indignity heaped upon their late Duke, had swept away the last inhibitions of the Yorkists. On 4 March 1461 Edward of March seated himself on a throne in Westminster Hall, and was hailed by his supporters and other people present as being king by hereditary right; a proclamation was issued in Edward's name.

Queen Margaret once again retreated north, her people ravaging the countryside as they went, and Edward determined now to pursue her without loss of time. Warwick, too, was bent on regaining his lost esteem, and he left London before Edward, although the main body of Edward's infantry had departed on 11 March. Londoners had gladly contributed a company to the Yorkist army, and the semi-professional force that Edward and Warwick mustered between them was enormous for the time.

Between 13 and 29 March Edward went in search of the Queen's army, and he discovered it in the Yorkshire village of Tadcaster, where the road dipped into a little valley. The Lancastrians had stationed themselves on a small plateau just beyond it at the hamlet of Towton, bound to the right by a brook that was then in flood, and on the left by the high road to Tadcaster. The Lancastrians had broken the bridge and were strongly posted on the other side of the stream, so that Edward's men could only cross by a narrow way, which they had to construct for themselves. But, inspired by their new Duke, or rather 'King', and his champion, Warwick, the Yorkist troops forced a passage 'by the sword' and gave battle on Palm Sunday.

Towton was the most decisive and the bloodiest battle of the Wars of the Roses. It began with the rising of the sun, and it lasted until ten o'clock at night, 'so great was the pertinacity and boldness of the men, who never heeded the possibility of a miserable death'.[25] The sleet and snow that fell almost continuously during the action almost certainly helped to defeat the Lancastrians, being driven into their faces. The chroniclers wrote that the snow was dyed crimson where it lay, and the Wharfe river and its tributaries were also stained with blood. Great numbers were killed on both sides, and of the Lancastrians who fled the field many were drowned in the river because they had themselves broken the bridges 'so that none could pass'. George Neville describes the area for six miles long, and for three broad, as being covered with dead bodies.[26] Heralds were said to have counted some 28,000 men dead, the dying coming from both sides, and they lay unburied for the space of three days.

It was rumoured that King Henry, the Queen, and others of their party had been captured, but they had in fact fled north to Scotland, where the Scottish king gave them temporary residence in a Dominican convent. But their war-party was practically destroyed, having sustained such terrible loss. Among the many prisoners taken by the Yorkists was James Butler, Earl of Wiltshire, who had fallen into the hands of Richard Salkeld, the shield bearer of a knight.

His capture, however, had not been achieved on the battlefield, since he, too, had managed once again to effect his escape (though whether in disguise or not is not recorded). He was taken eventually at Cockermouth in the Lake District, and he, too, was presumably heading for the Scottish border and sanctuary. It is very unlikely that he was hoping to take ship for Ireland from some northern port, for he knew that he would have been as unwelcome there as he was in England. And once captured his death was inevitable, as he had been one of the most consistent of Lancastrian supporters, one of the bitterest opponents of the house of York, and immensely useful to the Queen. In his lifetime he had been regularly described as one of the evil advisers who had estranged the 'lords of the blood' from the King's Council. He was charged with causing King Henry's subjects to be loaded down with taxes, and as a man who had perverted the processes of justice on the grandest scale to serve his own ends.

So as soon as Edward IV reached Newcastle, on 1 May 1461, James Butler was executed 'after the wholesome fashion of those fights'; for the Wars of the Roses were a 'barons' war' on a national scale[27]. (The middle and lower classes stood aside, ready for the most part to let their betters and their followers fight things out. The government, in any case, as a result of the manoeuvres of the opposing faction, ceased to exercise any authority in the country). The bitter struggle was over for one of these contentious lords, though, when James Butler, the 'English' earl, was condemned to be beheaded, and his severed head was sent south to be displayed upon London Bridge.

In the same way that he was more ambitious for political prestige in England than any of his predecessors, James Butler was also more avaricious, displaying a capacity for extortion that was extraordinary even for that predatory age. Married three times, each wife was either immensely rich at the time of the marriage, or potentially so. His first alliance was with Avice, the daughter of John fitsAlan, Earl of Arundel, who was her brother's heir. His second wife, also called Avice, the daughter of Sir Richard Stafford, was an even greater heiress in her own right. His last bride was Eleanor, the sister and one of the co-heirs of Edmund Beaufort, Duke of Somerset. It was this last match that perhaps proved his undoing, as it began a connection that would prove fatal to the main branch of his family, engaging him more deeply in the Lancastrian cause than even he, already a committed royalist, might otherwise have ventured.

He left no issue by any these wives. (The fortune he had amassed through these three marriages alone would have made his heir among the top three richest nobles in Europe. The Beaufort family was the wealthiest in England, with the late Cardinal Beaufort having financed his nephew the King's government from his immense riches throughout his long life.) But fortunate though James was with regard to his 'Midas touch', his wealthy wives were as barren as the gold he had amassed.

The shameful death of the Earl of Wiltshire (as he preferred to call himself, believing an English title – however recent – to be superior to an Irish one – however ancient), would have repercussions for his nearest family members. Both of his brothers, John and Thomas, were also attainted in the English parliament in 1461, with a corresponding loss of property, when ten of the Wiltshire-Ormonde's manors through England were forfeited to the Crown, along with other lands in Essex.

As disastrously, the family would be further attainted in Ireland in 1462, when – for the first time in centuries – the office of Lord High Butler in Ireland was taken away from them. The new king Edward IV, granted this prestigious and lucrative post to Sir William Welles (a relative of the Ormondes by a previous marriage), *for life*. In the volatile circumstances of the period, this meant very little, of course, since Sir William's life was as transitory as any man's of the time; and this honour could, and would, be rescinded. More momentously, the English earldom, which had been so earnestly sought, became immediately extinct with James Butler's death, since he had died without leaving an heir, and – in the eyes of the new royal party – his brothers were as guilty as the attainted earl.

During the first half of the 15th century, the Ormondes had been the favoured Hibernian family, and they had occupied a central position in colonial Ireland and, as such, they were best able to safeguard the interests of the Lancastrian kings in that unmanageable country. But although the 5th Earl had briefly held out against Richard, Duke of York, he had quitted the scene with York's increasing success. His entire life, in fact, can be regarded as a wholly English interlude, and in his long absence from Ireland a cadet branch of his family had managed his estates. Only they, perhaps, truly merit the description of 'Warriors of the Pale' throughout this period, but the Earl of Wiltshire's life is important in that it demonstrates how closely the affairs of England during this volatile period impinged upon those of the English in Ireland.

Wiltshire's failure to concentrate on his Irish heritage had one important outcome in that country, in that it opened up new possibilities for the minor members of the Butler family. At least one of these younger branches, the Butlers of Polestown (or Poolestown) in County Kilkenny, was vigorously expanded under Edmund MacRichard, a grandson of the 3rd Earl. This family more than any other took every advantage of their absentee lord's wilful neglect of his duty to his Irish tenants, particularly after 1454 when the Duke of York secured a new ratification of his original ten-year appointment as Lieutenant of Ireland, when nothing more was heard of Wiltshire's claim to the office, and he lost all influence in the Dublin parliament. Edmund MacRichard Butler was frequently in charge of the earldom, acting as proxy, and he travelled incessantly, either staying in his own castles or in those of the Earl.

Edmund MacRichard's rejection of the Norman fitz (or 'fils') and his adoption of the Gaelic 'Mac' is one of the earliest signs of that side of the Butler family's long-postponed surrender to the seduction of their host country. The Gaelicisation would come to play a great part in the story of their immediate future, and these 'Celtic' cousins, beginning with Richard, would marry Irish wives in defiance of the Statute of Kilkenny, in the process becoming great patrons of Irish culture.

Edmund was a prime example of this cross-cultural propagation, notably as a patron of literature. He was on intimate terms with his scribes, who lived with him, sharing his family life and literary preoccupations, driving them hard, often on Sundays and even Good Friday, having them write by candlelight. Through their good-humoured railing against him (in the inscriptions they inserted into the books they wrote for him), we can follow his journeying around the Earl's estates as he went about

Ormond's business; from the castles to the court at Kilkenny, and other – as the scribes complained – 'desolate places'. The work of Edmund's scribes, however, falls far short of that done a century earlier for the White Earl. (Ormonde libraries in Kilkenny or at Carrick-on-Suir were well stocked with foreign books; as was that of Edmund at his most important castle at Pottlewrath).

A younger brother of Richard of Polestown, James 'Gallda', described as being 'base in blood' (possibly illegitimate), would found the dynasty of Caher.[28] '…in this way did the branchings of the established Normans cover the land.'[29] Their imposing and picturesque castle at Caher, the great tower of which commands the gate and dominates the town, dates from the 13th century, and was in Butler hands from 1375. Perched on an island in the Suir river, it occupied a strategic position at the edge of Ormonde and Desmond lands.

In 1455 a parliament held by the Earl of Kildare, as York's deputy, was informed in October that various members of the Butler families of Polestown, Dunboyne and Tipperary had allied themselves with Donnchadh MacMuchadha, the King of Leinster since 1417. Together they had burned and destroyed the countryside around Wexford for four days and nights, and the campaign of this year reveals the extent of their Gaelicisation as well as the family's long-established opposition to Kildare as deputy. (They did not have to take a lead from Wiltshire, deprived of the lord lieutenancy, in this; they were more than willing to act in their own right.) Edmund's granddaughter Joan would later marry the grandson of Donnchadh MacMurchadha, who would inherit the 'kingdom'.

This would be a continuation of an established marital practice, for in about 1460, Saiv, the daughter of an Irish chieftain, Donald Reagh, had married Sir James Butler, the son of Edmund MacRichard Butler, a joining that had made allies of the two families. More importantly – since Reagh was a leading member of the MacMurrough clan – it also revived the King of Leinster's power. Donald Reagh lived in great state at Enniscorthy Castle, and his style can only be described as 'royal'. As late as 1522 Reach's son would still call himself the King of Leinster, and he would always regard himself (and be regarded by many of the Irish) as the leader of Leinstermen. Donald Reagh would become an ancestor of the main Butler family, with the elevation of his grandson to the earldom. But this was in the distant future, and would only follow after the failures of the next two Earls of Ormonde.

# Notes

1. The 'Dual Monarchy' was a fiction of the English by which they maintained that England and France were to be united under the same King. Henry VI was actually crowned in Paris, two years after his London coronation of 1429.
2. 'Trier of Petitions': a person who evaluates formal applications to a royal court.
3. Jack Cade. (?–1450).
4. *Dictionary of National Biography*, Richard, Duke of York.
5. Carte, *Life of the Duke of Ormonde.*
6. Ibid.
7. The Four Masters, *Annals of the Kingdom of Ireland.*
8. *Calendar of State Papers, Ireland.*
9. Ibid.
10. Carte, op. cit.
11. The Four Masters, op. cit.
12. *Dictionary of National Biography*, Richard, Duke of York.
13. Carte, op. cit.
14. *Calendar of State Papers, Ireland.*
15. I am unable to explain the numerals 'iiij'.
16. *Calendar of State Papers, Ireland.*
17. Ibid.
18. *Dictionary of National Biography*, Richard, Duke of York.
19. *Calendar of State Papers, England.*
20. Carte, op. cit.
21. *Dictionary of National Biography*, Richard, Duke of York.
22. Ibid.
23. D. Ross, *Edward IV*.
24. Ibid.
25. Ibid.
26. George Neville (1433–1476). Bishop, Archbishop and Chancellor of England. His letter was written to a papal legate in Flanders.
27. That is, in that the royal participants depended almost entirely upon the varying loyalties of their chief subjects.
28. The Earldom of Caher is now extinct.
29. Carte, op. cit.

# CHAPTER VIII

## *Attainders and Pardons*

The Butlers had fought on the losing side, and they would be swiftly punished for it. King Edward IV's parliament in November 1461 passed a sweeping Act of Attainder against the entire royal family and their chief Lancastrian adherents, including not only the Earl of Wiltshire but also his brothers. John Butler, who would become the 6th Earl of Ormonde but could not inherit the English title, was attainted on 4 November, since he had been present at the hard-fought battle of Towton. His younger brother Thomas was also to be outlawed, although judgement was not passed upon him until some time later. The Irish parliament, now openly Yorkist, followed suit on 15 October 1462, attainting not only the two Ormonde brothers, but also their cousins: Edmund macRichard; Piers, the son of James Butler, and eight others 'who had adhered to the king's enemies'.[1]

For a time it seemed the whole of the Ormonde family faced social obliteration and the extinction of their rights, on this, their second conviction for 'treason' against the house of York. Wiltshire's heirs were certainly excluded from their territories for long enough to render them incapable of playing a major and positive part in Irish affairs, and in England circumstances compelled them to make themselves as inconspicuous as it was possible for a noble family to be. For any aristocratic family in the later Middle Ages, survival in that turbulent period was itself no mean task, and the Butler family had up to this point been singularly fortunate. Now John and Thomas, having escaped death in battle, escaped the executioner's block for treason and conspiracy, yet their forfeiture and the eclipse of their fortunes could be seen as further evidence of their continuing luck. Neither John nor Thomas was imprisoned for the roles they had played in the Lancastrian struggle against the Yorkists.

Like his elder brother James, as a young man John had served in Normandy and France for one year in 1440, under Edward's father, the Duke of York. An able soldier, he had served the Duke well during a difficult time for the English forces in France, and this may have made him more acceptable to the new King. But, to counter this, it was also to be remembered that he had been made a squire to King Henry VI in 1449, and he had fought as ardently in that King's wars in France.

In August of 1449, when John had been taken prisoner by the French army while in command of Vernon Castle in Normandy, he had tried to raise his own ransom by petitioning King Henry VI to allow him to ship tin and wool into France without the payment of customs. His kinsmen and friends had been willing to give or to lend these goods, since (as a younger brother) he had little money of his own; and because of his elder brother's special standing at Court, the King and Commons had quickly assented to the scheme. As a result, John had been released without too a long delay; though, at the surrender of Rouen by the English, in the following October, he had been once again in the hands of the French, but this time as a hostage.[2]

The raising of his ransom apart, John had not sought other favours from King Henry VI, and he could not, in fact, have been said to have benefitted much from his brother James's prominence at Court. An infinitely more honourable man than Wiltshire, he was never seen to profit from the corrupt schemes by which his elder brother had flourished, and he had been 'honourably' exempted from the first Act of Resumption in 1450 (an act by which the mainly Yorkist parliament revoked all previous grants made by the Crown to Henry's over-privileged Lancastrian subjects). This granting system had always been a source of tremendous contention – particularly among those landowners who could not profit from it – since the royal resources had been systematically pillaged by rapacious courtiers eager to take advantage of its generous terms.

An important consideration for Edward IV, too, was the agreement made by John's father, the 4th Earl of Ormonde, with Edward's father in 1450, in which he had sworn to serve him in Ireland; this could certainly be taken into account. Had that Earl of Ormonde lived, matters would have gone differently for the York dynasty (and that of the Butler's), in England as well as Ireland, perhaps. But John's services on the Lancastrian side, in all the battles between the first at St Albans and the final face-off at Towton could not be overlooked, and they were enough to lead to his inclusion in the Act of Attainder of 1461. Additionally, and an offence that perhaps incriminated him more in Edward's eyes, John had not only fought at the battle of Towton, but had later crossed over to Ireland, where he destroyed the town of Waterford and captured the son of the Earl of Desmond, a Yorkist supporter.

Desmond had, in fact, been forced to unite with his rival, the Earl of Kildare, against a Butler insurrection, led by Ormonde (still Sir John) in 1462, when he had sailed for Ireland to make a bid to reverse his fortunes there. Attainted in England, in disgrace, and almost without money, he had still contrived to arrive in Ireland in the company of 'a great number of Saxons'.[3] Waterford, Kilkenny, New Ross and other towns declared for him, while Edmund MacRichard Butler and the junior members of the family in Kilkenny and Tipperary rose to defend him. At Waterford, not only the son of the Earl of Desmond was taken prisoner, but the city had also been taken.

An army of 5,000 men took the field for Ormonde in Meath, led by their relation, John de Bermyngham, along with others of the 'Old English', reinforced by the troops of O'Connor Faly. In response, Thomas, Earl of Desmond, raised 20,000 men, at his own cost, and wasted the Ormonde countryside for seventeen days, when, as a result, Ormonde agreed to give battle and they came to an engagement. Desmond had reduced the Meath rising, and at Pilltown, near Carrick-on-Suir, he defeated John Butler so decisively, and with such heavy losses, that 'for certaine it might not be known how great a number was slain, and Sir John himself was discomfited and put to flight'.[4] In Ireland, though, the feud – as ever – was not so much between York and Lancaster, as between the Geraldines and the Butlers, and their mutual adherents.

In this battle, Ormonde's cousin, Edmund MacRichard – who was famous as a warrior throughout Ireland – fought for his cousin, the presumptive Earl of Ormonde. But it was actually against his will that MacRichard went out to fight that day, since he believed that his side was out-manned. These misgivings proved to be entirely correct, for although MacRichard commanded 1,000 heavily armed horsemen he was heavily defeated and taken prisoner. According to some accounts, 410 of his men were slain and interred, 'besides the number who were devoured by dogs and birds of prey'.[5]

But although he had lost the day for them, MacRichard was still valuable to the Butlers, who sought to buy him back. Famously, as part of the prisoner's ransom, two great Ormonde manuscripts were traded for his freedom; the 'Book of the White Earl', and another described as 'The Book of Carrick'. This being one of the few occasions in warfare when a man's liberty was worth more in paper than gold, although it was recognised even then that the manuscripts in question were national treasures.[6]

The battle of Pilltown effectively finished the Butler-Lancaster uprising, although it simmered on for the rest of the year, with the Geraldines taking Kilkenny and other towns. Despite the wholesale slaughter of his troops (and his community), the Earl of Ormonde remained with his 'Englishmen' in a fortified town, which proved hard to take. His brother Thomas had crossed over to join him (and while on the Irish Sea was said to have taken four ships, with their crew, belonging to the Earl of Desmond). As a result of their uniting, 'the Butlers acquired great power', at least according to the Four Masters, but it is more likely that the situation remained deadlocked, with any further actions between the two parties proving futile.

While still in the country in 1462, John had appointed his failed champion, Edmund MacRichard Butler, to be his 'deputy in the earldom, and as the principal governor of his lands and lordships in Ireland'.[7] That John

Butler could delegate such an authority while being himself under sentence of outlawry, with his civil rights extinct, is an indication of the political uncertainty of the Irish situation. MacRichard himself had been found guilty without trial, and yet he was allowed to occupy John Butler's place and fulfill his duties without any apparent challenge. He was certainly chosen by the putative Earl because he had taken on these responsibilities before, and proved his competence, but it is astonishing that the situation was allowed to stand by the English authorities.

MacRichard – 'the most illustrious and renowned of the English of Ireland' – would die only two years later, but the deputyship of the absentee Earl then passed to his son and heir, James, and after his death in 1487, to his grandson Piers Roe. Edmund MacRichard appears to have acted out his military life seemingly unaffected by the fact that the mother, the paternal grandmother, and very possibly the paternal great-grandmother of his grandson Piers Roe Butler were all of Gaelic birth. He also ignored the Irish strain that ran through the bloodlines of the other members of his extended family: he was as easily found despoiling the Irish as harassing the English.

A proxy for the estates had been considered absolutely necessary, though, once 'Earl' John fled from the havoc of Ireland to the haven of Portugal, which he did soon after losing out at Pillstown. Little is known of his stay there, apart from his attempts to enlist support for the Lancastrian efforts to reinstate the deposed King Henry, as the Queen was in France for the same purpose. Neither of them seems to have been overly successful at securing aid, although Margaret did manage to reach Northumberland in September 1462, in the company of a sizeable number of French knights (after her fleet was wrecked during a terrifying storm). And it was perhaps a point in John's favour that he played no conspicuous part against Edward's regime when, for the next three years, the Lancastrians fought to recover their supremacy in the north. Throughout all the various uprisings that followed on the Queen's reappearance in England, John Butler appears to have diplomatically absented himself in Portugal.

Despite MacRichard Butler's efforts to hold on to the Ormonde estates in their totality, it was inevitable that – in the early days of their attainder – some parts of the territory would have to be forcibly relinquished by the family. Their great enemy the Earl of Desmond certainly lost no time in claiming what he saw as his due, which was a considerable part of the dishonoured Earl's territory. At the first parliament of the new Justiciar, the Earl of Kildare, in 1463, he was granted the custody of the lordship and lands of Carlow and Ross and the seigneury of Dungarven for the term of sixty years; a reward for his services against the renegade 'John of Ormonde' (whose lordship, for the time being regarded as derelict, lay like a No Man's Land between the Irish chieftains and the 'degenerate English', and was a constant temptation to both). From the point of view of King Edward it was best that the Butler lands should not fall into the hands of those who were still hostile to his rule. But the Earl of Kildare took advantage of their being so vulnerable to attack to add large parts of the border country to his own territory.

This situation only changed to the Ormonde family's advantage when the attainder against the late Earl of Wiltshire was reversed by an act of the Irish parliament of 1465, along with those of his brothers, John and Thomas (a decision made not so much to rehabilitate Wiltshire as to make it possible to reinstate Sir John). But a direct result of this act was that the rightful ownership of two great manors, the main cause of the long-standing feud between the Ormondes and the Kildares, was then settled in favour of the latter; with the properties declared to be an ancient inheritance of the FitzGeralds (a loss that the Butlers were ready to accept, if it meant their reinstatement).

But their circumstances were not yet settled, and they would still be at the mercy of the shifting political turmoil. However, they themselves would pull through without any real harm when, over the next few years, the continuing run of treason charges, scares, arrests and executions implemented by the Yorkists culminated in another rebellion against King Edward IV. Even the 'Kingmaker', the Earl of Warwick, who had begun to lose ground as the young King began to assert his royal authority, turned against his erstwhile protégé and began to plot against him.

In 1461 Warwick had seemed 'to be everything in this kingdom',[8] but by 1464 all this had changed. Warwick, in the midst of negotiations for a peace with France, to be sealed by a match with a French princess, had been astounded to be told that Edward was already married to a woman of no dynastic importance; moreover, the widow of a *Lancastrian*. Over the next five years the rift between the two men widened, and Warwick, seeking allies against his increasingly independent young monarch, found a willing tool in the King's weak younger brother, to whom, in 1469, he married his eldest daughter, against the King's direct orders. Later, Edward would increase Warwick's humiliation when, as the Earl was once more negotiating for an alliance with France, Edward negotiated his own with France's great enemy, Burgundy. In 1470 Edward declared Clarence and Warwick traitors, and they had to flee for their lives to France.

Warwick met Queen Margaret at Angers in July 1470, where she was persuaded to forgive him for his past betrayals and, overcoming her reservations, pledged her son to Warwick's second daughter, Anne Neville, in return for his assistance against Edward IV. She took the prospective bride into her Court, almost as a virtual hostage until the marriage could take place, which was not to be until the kingdom could be recovered for Henry VI. And when that took place, her son was to be made Regent on behalf of his father, whose incompetence to rule was now past dispute. A plan was arranged for the immediate invasion of England.

Warwick sailed with an expedition, landing in Devon on 13 September 1470, and waited for the King to meet him in battle. Edward, who was at Doncaster standing by for reinforcements, was there betrayed by an ally and deserted by some of his troops, and fled across the Wash to Lynn, sailing in October to take refuge in Europe. King Henry VI was then restored to his throne by the man who had played the major part in taking it from him, and since Henry was by now a virtual imbecile and his son too inexperienced to rule, Warwick 'the Kingmaker' was monarch in all but name.

Nevertheless it was thought safe for the Lancastrian supporters to return to England; and among them was John Butler, who had probably been one of the Queen's retinue during her travels in France, attempting once more to raise the money for a new assault upon England. (His younger brother Thomas may have been a permanent fixture in her Court, during her exile.) Sir John was now officially recognised as the 6th Earl of Ormonde, the attainder having been annulled by the restored King Henry VI.

Henry's restoration, however, was only temporary, for Edward of York returned as soon as he had built up a new army (mostly of mercenaries financed by the Duke of Burgundy). This army, however, had been much enlarged by the Englishmen who flocked to his banner in the Midlands, men who were already disenchanted with the new regime. Even his estranged brother Clarence, also unhappy with the way things had gone under Warwick's 'rule', went over to his brother's side, taking with him an army raised in Henry's name.

On the Vigil of Easter, 'out of urgent necessity', King Edward set out to confront Warwick's army at Barnet. Here, to the north of the town, in the misty light of Easter Sunday, 'with the good luck that favours every success-ful general'[9], he slaughtered the enemy in time to make a triumphal return to London that same afternoon. Henry's Queen, who had mysteriously delayed her return to England, landed with her son at Weymouth on 13 April 1471, on the very same day that her new ally Warwick was defeated by Edward, a battle in which the 'Kingmaker' himself had been slain.

Margaret and her son took refuge in Cerne Abbey when they learned of the reverse, but the Duke of Somerset and his friends encouraged them to rely on the loyalty of the western counties, which were, they said, ready to rise on their behalf. The Queen issued orders for a general muster and proceeded with a great force to Bristol. They deceived Edward as to their intentions – he thought that they were heading for either London or Chester – but denied entrance to Gloucester the Queen's party was forced to march to Tewkesbury, where they arrived, totally fatigued, in the afternoon of 3 May. They pitched camp before the town, in a position well secured by 'foul lanes, deep dykes, and many hedges'.[10]

Edward arrived on the following day, and he arranged his army for battle. It opened with ordnance and a shower of arrows, until the Duke of Somerset unwisely carried his men out of a more secure position and brought them by certain bypaths to a hill in front of Edward's vanguard. Here, while engaging Edward's forces at the front, he was suddenly attacked in the flank by a detachment of 200 spears. Somerset's men were thrown into confusion, and very soon the rest of the Lancastrian forces broke and were put to flight.

The 18-year–old Edward, Prince of Wales, had been put in nominal command of the 'middle ward' of the Queen's army, although he acted under the advice of two experienced fighters. So when Somerset moved out from his safe position, he seems to have expected to be followed by at least one of the Prince's men. But when they failed to do so, the Duke came galloping back to dash out the brains of one of the Prince's aides with a battle-axe, believing that he had acted treacherously. The other man fled to take refuge; and the Prince of Wales, also turning tail, galloped to Tewkesbury, where he appealed for protection, but was instead taken prisoner by a Yorkist knight, who delivered him up to King Edward IV. (He had been encouraged by a proclamation issued before the battle, which stated that whoever brought the prince to the King alive should have an annuity of 100*l*, and the Prince's life would be spared.)

The battle of Tewkesbury, which followed, put an end to all legitimate Lancastrian claims, after Prince Edward, the only legal heir to throne, was taken by the Yorkists and hacked to death by them after he had quarrelled with their King. (The Prince, as a *favour*, was allowed an 'honorable' funeral, before his father was given the *coup de grace*.[11]) King Henry VI was violently murdered in the Tower of London, a crime that might have been the work of Richard, Duke of Gloucester, who was the principal man in the Tower at that time. But with father and son both dead, Edward of York was now indisputably the next in line, and he crowned himself King once more. John Butler, by having accepted the restored King Henry's reversal of his attainder, faced being convicted of treason for a second time and the extinction of his rights now seemed a certainty.

He could have feared the worst, for Edward IV – who was normally a lenient man (for the times) – now acted with tremendous vindictiveness against the defeated side. The Queen, for example, humiliatingly conveyed to London in a workman's dray, escaped death only because she had more value as a ransom. But if the King could forgive the treachery of his own brother, Clarence, he could certainly overlook that of a lesser subject. The restored King, to the astonishment of many, again pardoned John Butler, and not only pardoned him, but also gave him full recognition as the rightful Earl of Ormonde. In gratitude for the King's act of extraordinary magnanimity, and – since there were no further *legitimate* Lancastrian claimants to the throne, which undeniably left Edward as the undisputed King of England – the new Earl indented to serve him in

Normandy and France for a year, supplying sixteen archers for the company that he raised.

But the attainder by the Irish parliament at Dublin was not to be so easily repealed. Granted by the King in the second year of his reign, it would not be formally rescinded in Ireland for another fourteen years. A seal of statute made in the 16th year of Edward IV, at Dublin, annuls the former attainder of Sir John of Ormonde, in a parliament held at Dublin before the Bishop of Meath. By this decree, the former acts of attainder against both brothers were annulled, and John was restored to his hereditary lands, with 'name and dignity as by right and title of his ancestors'.[12] The exemplification was made on 17 June 1477, and attested by the Common Bench at Dublin.

That John Butler was called 'Sir John' in the official document was not an empty courtesy, since it was an honour that he had fully earned in his youth. Known from his earliest years as an extraordinarily brave and honourable man, he had been knighted by the Duke of Bedford, King Henry VI's uncle, for the strength of his uncommon loyalty to that King, and his undoubted valour in the field. John Butler's high-minded qualities would stay with him throughout his life, and even King Edward IV, who had the least cause to trust him, would say of him that he was 'the goodliest knight he ever beheld, and the finest gentleman in Christendom'.[13] Adding that 'if good breeding, nurture, and liberal qualities were lost in the world, they might be found in John, Earl of Ormonde'.

Whether John Butler served the King in his French campaign, is not known. The force assembled by Edward IV in 1475 was large by the standards of the time, with over forty thousand men attached to the royal party alone, but there is no evidence to show that the 6th Earl of Ormonde mustered men-at-arms and archers, as did other peers. Edward had a more important role for him to play, perhaps, as a mediator rather than a warrior, for John had a thorough mastery of all the languages of Europe, and 'there was scarce a court of it to which the Prince [Edward IV] did not send him as ambassador'.[14]

He may, in fact, have turned his back on warfare altogether, and become not only an exemplary diplomat but also something of a religious zealot. According to family tradition, he died in the Holy Land, during a pilgrimage to Jerusalem, 'in a fit of devotion', sometime before 1478. Since he was unmarried and died without issue, the earldom passed to his brother Thomas.

But however monastically inclined in his later life, John had been unchaste enough in his early years to father an illegitimate son, by an Irishwoman, Reynalda O'Brien, in defiance of the statutes. This son, known as James *Dubh*, or Black James, would afterwards play some part in the dramatic developments in Ireland in the next two reigns, but at John's death in 1478 the Polestown Butlers would become the real heads and protectors of his father's great Irish lordship.

They, too, interbred and indeed intermarried with the Irish; and James, the son of Edmund MacRichard Butler, had by Sair Kavanaugh, three sons: Esmond, Theobald and Piers Roe. The first two were declared legitimate in the Dublin parliament of 1467, as being born 'in affiance between the two – Edmund and Sair – before espousals'.[15] A royal patent also freed Sair and her issue by James, 'those already born and those to be begotten, from all Irish servitude', enabling both her and them to enjoy English laws, 'in the same manner as Englishmen within the said lands'.[16] Sair and her sons had also the powers to acquire and purchase lands, and to 'answer and be answered at the King's courts'.

Their sons and grandsons would all become famous as warriors, with MacPierce Butler (the son of Piers) notably slaying a son of the great Owny O'More in 1478. In the same year, Richard, a son of Edmund MacRichard, would be murdered by an Irish assassin in the doorway of the church of St Canice, the cathedral church of Kilkenny. But their story more properly belongs to a later age.

Thomas, who succeeded his brother John, had also spent the greater part of his life in England. It is possible that he also fought at Towton field, as in 1462 he took refuge at the Scottish court with the royal family, and he crossed with Queen Margaret to Sluys in Belgium in the following April. He was reported to have fought at the battle of Tewkesbury, and been taken prisoner there; but if this is true he made a mysterious escape, perhaps, like his eldest brother James at the battle of St Albans, in disguise.

Confusingly, judgement against him was passed upon him under the name of Thomas Ormonde, *alias* Botiller, knight, although at that time he had not been invested with this rank, and he would make odd use of this when seeking a pardon from the new King. As Thomas Ormonde, *squire*, he petitioned at a parliament held in the twelfth year of Edward's reign, and in this petition it was ingenuously argued that the attainder had been made of *Sir* Thomas Ormonde, with all the examinations taken under a false name. This, it was argued, rendered the attainder invalid: 'By which inquisitions it was supposed Thomas Ormonde, *squire*, to be attainted (who yet was never attainted), and divers manors of the petitioner had thereupon been seized into the King's hands.'[17]

The case came before the judges, and all the stress of the pleadings ran upon his being styled 'knight', a style to which he was not entitled at that time. Since he had no other possible defence, by using this specious argument, with its suggestion that the wrong man had been outlawed, Thomas Botiller 'prayed for an act to revoke the act of attainder and forfeiture'.[18] Astonishingly, this act was eventually passed in his favour, and it was a good time for him to take any further advantages the law could furnish; yet Thomas cagily never insisted upon pressing his claims beyond the reversal of the attainder.

Neither did he make any particular use of the name of Ormonde, although it was the custom in those days for younger sons to take their father's titles for a surname, and it was agreeable to the law. Besides which, he was empowered to use the Ormonde title because he enjoyed a legacy from it, and had been given a huge estate under that name, by the settlement and will of his wealthy grandmother, the 'opulent' Lady Bergaveny.

A general pardon was granted him in 1471, though, and most of his estates and honours were restored to him. (However, in Ireland, even if Edward IV's authority to dictate to the Dublin parliament was not questioned, the Justiciar, the Earl of Kildare, as a confirmed enemy, tried to delay Thomas's restoration to his Irish estates.) Yet although he had been reluctant to use the name of Ormonde in his early years, Thomas Butler lost no time in styling himself as 'Earl' after news of his brother's death reached England from Palestine.

He would also protest strongly, three years later, at the official legitimisation of James *Dubh*, his brother John's bastard son, in fear that James would afterwards claim the earldom (a spectre that would, in fact, take shape within a few years). On this occasion, 'Earl' Thomas's formal complaint was accepted, and he was allowed to retain the title; but exactly how much of the Ormonde estate remained in his hands at this precarious moment in the family's fortunes is unclear. A number of forfeited estates had been placed under the control of receivers and special auditors at the beginning of Edward's reign, among them those belonging to the Earl of Wiltshire. The King had already let some of these lost lands 'out to farm' to private persons, and since these forfeited estates produced a considerable income, it is unlikely that he let the more profitable of them back into the hands of his former enemies. King Edward IV was always keen to profit by his battles, and his victories were invariably followed by a fresh wave of property confiscation.

In view of the significant role that his elder brother had played at the Court of Henry VI (and of his reputation for rapacity whilst holding office), it is unlikely that Thomas Butler was given any part in the new royal household. Neither was he known to have been included in the preparations that were being made for the war against France, for which King Edward IV had long been readying himself. Perhaps Thomas never offered his services, arguing like his brother John that he had seen enough of the battlefield to want to avoid it. Although he had not, like the chivalrous John, religious reasons for avoiding conflict.

If anything, Thomas's main concern appears to have been to keep free of any kind of commitment during the Yorkist years of triumph. He also kept in the background in the months following Edward IV's death (arguably of a stroke) at the untimely age of 41, since Edward's death created a new dynastic upheaval. Although Edward's son, then a boy of twelve, was proclaimed as King Edward V, Thomas appears to have taken no sides when

Richard, Duke of York, set the boy aside and made his own bid for the Crown, declaring both the young King and his brother to be bastards.

The 7th Earl of Ormonde was certainly not in Ireland during the months that followed Edward IV's death; but, wisely, he seems not have been in London either. For these were dangerous times, when Richard brought his still uncrowned nephew to London with a guard of 500 of his own men from his northern stronghold, thus making the young King his prisoner. Later, Richard would use these same troops to surround Westminster Abbey, where the Queen Mother, Elizabeth Woodville, had taken sanctuary (and where he frightened her into giving up her second son, the Duke of York into his 'protection').

Like most of his peers, Thomas must have been aware of the sinister rumours that were already spreading about Richard's intentions; rumours that became a reality when Richard's closest ally, Lord Hastings, was seized on 20 June 1483 by armed assassins. These men, placed behind the arras in the council room in the Tower of London, had then carried Hastings off to Tower Hill, to be beheaded without any semblance of a trial. 'Treason' (or more properly conspiracy against the 'Protector', Richard) was given as the excuse for this summary killing. (The danger of a general uprising in the city, as the news seeped out, was only held in check by reports that more of Richard's men 'from the North' were approaching the capital.) But Thomas Butler must have reasoned that if Hastings could die – killed not by his enemies, but by the friend whom he had never doubted and had served so faithfully – were men like him not in even greater danger? Why should the power-hungry Prince have faith in the loyalty of a man who had, until twelve years ago, been an open enemy?

Was Thomas among the assembly of lords who, on 25 June, mindful of Hasting's fate, decided to accept Richard as King, doing so largely out of fear? Richard was, after all, supported by a multitude of troops. Thomas Butler, like most of his peers, must have decided that pusillanimity was preferable to valour, with the result that Richard could honestly say that he had been ordained King 'by the concord assent of the Lords and Commons of this Royaume'. At Westminster Hall, where he went to formally assume the throne, he was attended 'by well near all the lords spiritual and temporal of this realm'.[19] Was Thomas Butler among those present?

From 11 April 1483, when King Edward IV died, to 16 June, when Richard of York was acclaimed as King, Thomas Butler steered clear of the ominous changes then unfolding. Indeed, after two decades of trimming, Thomas preferred perhaps to avoid the dangerous game of power politics altogether. He skillfully made no move of any kind regarding the Protector, although he did attend the Duke of York's expensive and elaborate coronation as Richard III. But afterwards, Thomas played no noticeable part in the government of that King's brief reign. Yet, amazingly, he never took the obvious measure of removing himself to the comparative safety of his estates in Ireland.

The Duke of Clarence's son, the young Earl of Warwick had also been taken into Richard's care, to be 'looked after' by his wife, and he did not end his days in the Tower of London until the next reign. But the popular report was that the two young sons of Edward IV, the eldest having already been proclaimed King, had been murdered in the month of Richard's coronation, and any other claimants to the Crown, by this time, were also in 'safe hands'. All except one, who would become the last hope of the Lancastrian party: Henry Tudor, Earl of Richmond, one of the illegitimate descendents of John of Gaunt. A pretender to the throne who had even less right to it than the man he dislodged, but who was the natural leader of the alliance against Richard III.

From the autumn of 1483, there was a plan to put Henry Tudor on the throne, said to have been conceived by Elizabeth Woodville, once she was convinced that her sons were no longer alive, and this plan may have involved the Earl of Ormonde, if only peripherally. There were many suggestions that members of the old Lancastrian houses were involved in this plot, 'eagerly sniffing out the air of unrest',[20] although it hardly seems credible that they could have considered the Earl of Richmond as the likely heir.

It is not known if Richard III ever personally pardoned Thomas Butler after he seized the Crown, or if the Earl had accepted such a grace from his hands (as many other former enemies had refused to do). But, even if Thomas had renewed the pardon granted by King Edward IV, men like him, with their old allegiances, could never have been regarded as entirely dependable by the usurper as long as the threat of a Tudor invasion persisted. For the rest of Richard III's reign, Thomas remained as politically inactive as diplomacy would allow. This was easy enough to do, perhaps, for although he now possessed much of his family's lost wealth, he had also lost most of their influence, and Richard III clearly thought that his political support was not worth buying. It is not even certain that Thomas attended Richard's first and only parliament on 23 January 1484, postponed because of a rebellion; little is known of the composition of this assembly, although it was packed with members loyal to the 'King'.

The brief reign of Richard III, though, posed an altogether new set of problems for the Ormonde family on their home ground, since the new King had been popular with the Irish from his days as the Duke of York, when he had spent some time in Ireland. Richard was never looked upon as a tyrant in that country, where the house of York remained perennially popular. Now, of course, with Richard acknowledged as King of England, this popularity would no longer be a matter of simple choice for the Irish, it was also one of necessity. Had he lived, King Richard III might have come to be seen to be as much of a tyrant in Ireland as he was in England.

A long-established problem for the English government had been whether to rely upon the lieutenants they sent over to Ireland from England, or to depend upon the more problematic services of the Anglo-Irish nobility *in situ*, and this was answered by Richard III in a spirit of compromise. He made the English Earl of Lincoln Lieutenant of Ireland, but made the very Irish Earl of Kildare his Deputy, and he also did his best to conciliate the flamboyantly Hibernian Earl of Desmond. It has to be said that, in Richard's brief reign, Ireland was uniquely quiet, and the frequent rebellions that took place there in the first (Lancastrian) Tudor's reign show that the house of York still had a great hold over the Irish people.

Nor do we have evidence of Thomas Butler being among the 'men of substance' who had promised to supply a specified number of men to King Richard III, 'sufficiently horsed, harnessed and arrayed',[21] to help him keep his throne. But equally he was not listed as being among Henry Tudor's associates, those 'murderers, adulterers and extortionists';[22] Tudor had, in fact, few aristocratic supporters.

Yet like most members of his immediate family Thomas was always a Lancastrian at heart, and however cunningly he dealt with the dangers that surrounded him during Richard's notorious reign, he must never have been happy with a Yorkist monarchy. Though whether he was among the 'many others who were revolting from King Richard',[23] and who turned up to join Henry, Earl of Richmond, when he invaded England, 'with a choice band of armed men', is not known. Nor was his presence recorded at the Battle of Bosworth on 22 August 1485, which does not mean that he was not there, to stand on the sidelines, like most of the aristocracy present, taking no part in the action until they could see who would be the victor.

Twenty thousand men met in a fierce, clumsy combat, and the day ended in the surprising but decisive defeat of the stronger army. Its leader, King Richard III, was killed while fighting heroically, and his men saw his naked corpse slung across his horse's back and borne away to an obscure grave. His captains were dead, captured or in flight, but the Earl of Ormonde was not listed among them. He had, perhaps, like most people, grown weary of the 'Wars of the Roses', where 'he who lost the day lost the kingdom also'.[24]

But whether he remained neutral or not during the battle, or whether he was even present at it, what is absolutely certain is that, with Henry Tudor victorious and very soon afterwards crowned King, Thomas Butler immediately threw himself upon his mercy. Seeking to retain the rights that had been granted to him by Edward IV, he pleaded, like many of the men who had been similarly pardoned, that he and his late brother had been coerced into acting against their individual inclinations. Wasting no time, he exhibited his petition in the first parliament held by Henry VII, seeking for a reversal of his attainder; and 'to be restored to all such dignities as he had, the name only of the Earl of Wiltshire except.'[25] This, too, was passed into an act.

The reason for the exception was that the earldom of Wiltshire was then held by the son and heir of John Stafford, who had been 'advanced to the honour' by Edward IV in the ninth year of his reign. As the Earl had died without issue five years later, the title had now become extinct, but neither King Edward IV nor King Henry VII wished to revive it (although Henry VIII would later do so).

Even more than the late King Edward and King Richard, Henry VII needed every friend he could find, and from whatever quarter, since he claimed the right to rule England 'not so much by right of blood as of conquest and victory in warfare'. Even the most devoted Lancastrian could not defend the view that Henry sat upon his throne by divine right, any more than had the late usurper. There was at least one descendant of King Edward III with a greater right to the crown than Richard III still living at his coronation, and there were many more between Henry and his claim. But now, recognising that the Earl of Ormonde had always remained 'a friend in heart' to the Lancasters, Thomas was received into the new king's favour. Henry VII quickly pardoned him for his homage to the Yorkist kings, and once the attainder was reversed Thomas was able to take possession of all the estates his brothers had enjoyed in England.

But once accepted his stock soon rose, and in the very first year of his reign Henry VII made him one of his privy councillors. For the King already knew that most of his Irish 'subjects' had always been drawn to the Yorkist cause, most of them were still faithful to their memory, and Ireland was a seeding ground for those who would try to unseat him from the throne. He also knew how dependent he was upon those Irish nobles who had been loyal to the Lancastrians, however far they may have been forced to stray, if he was to retain any influence over the Irish.

When Henry came to the throne in 1485, the Kildares were the greatest potential threat to him in Ireland, and the Butlers were considered the best people to deal with that particular menace. But it had been the Yorkist conspirators who had opened King Henry's eyes to the dangers threatening the new absolute monarchy of England from the move for Home Rule in Yorkist Ireland. Clearly an immediate necessity was to secure a Tudor bridgehead in Ireland, and to nullify the colonial parliament.

So, from the first years of his reign, the new king – regarded by many throughout the whole of his reign as a usurper – recognised the peculiar value of a family that had so steadfastly adhered to the Lancastrian line during its most insecure period. An Ormonde once again asserting influence in their Irish territories could be very useful, if only to act as a counterweight to the over-mighty Kildares. Henry VII realised the peculiar strength of the Butler position in Ireland, and he tried to encourage the new Earl to maintain even closer links with his estates there. But, however encouraged by the King's interest, Thomas Butler's ambitions, like those of his elder brother James, the beheaded Earl of Wiltshire, always lay closer to the English Court.

In the same year that he became a Privy Councillor, Thomas became a Chamberlain to the Queen, Elizabeth of York, and he would also accept the same position with her daughter-in-law, Catherine of Aragon. Also, from being almost destitute in the years of his disgrace, Thomas was now one of the King's richest subjects, even having only inherited a fraction of his eldest brother's fortune. (After James's death, he had found above 40,000 in sterling hidden in one of his houses at Blackfriars, besides much plate, all of which he carried over with him to Ireland.)

It was not long before revolts broke out against Henry Tudor's usurpation, which were quickly suppressed, but in May 1487, an altogether new kind of threat appeared, with the emergence of the 'pretenders to the throne'. It had long been popularly rumoured that Henry VII had done away with his strongest rival, the Earl of Warwick, by having him murdered in the Tower of London (he was actually still incarcerated there), but a Yorkist imposter now showed up, claiming to be the young Earl. He appeared on the scene with a fantastic story of how he had managed his escape.

The imposter, Lambert Simnel, although only the son of an Oxford tradesman, made a convincing royal claimant, since he bore some resemblance to the Plantagenets and had been taught courtly manners, with this imposture in mind. Once prepared, his sponsors swiftly whisked him away to Ireland, where 2,000 German mercenaries were enrolled in his cause. In Ireland, Simnel's promoters appealed for help, and their story was readily believed by most of the nobles there, since they were by conviction already opposed to Henry Tudor.

Thomas FitzGerald, King Henry's own Chancellor in Ireland, was among the first to entertain the boy as if he was true royalty, and he began to give him his support. The imposture took off, to the point where Simnel was actually named as 'King Edward VI' on 24 May 1487; but was crowned only with a coronet (actually a golden circlet taken from a statue of the Virgin Mary in the cathedral at Dublin).

The Home Rule lords now had a King to their own liking, and a new government was instituted 'which did keep courts, parliaments, and made styles and processes in the lad's name'.[26] Within the Pale, only Waterford still stood out boldly for King Henry VII, and was besieged for six weeks in July and August by a brother of the Earl of Desmond. The Butlers and the Butler towns of Kilkenny, Callan, Clonmel and Fethard, upon a message from Thomas, Earl of Ormonde, took up arms for the Tudor King.

The Yorkist cause, though dominant in Ireland, had to stand the test of battle in England if they were to uproot the usurper, and not simply be some diversion in the Emerald Isle. So having secured the blessing of the boy's supposed aunt, the dowager Duchess of Burgundy, the 'Great Earl of Kildare' then sent an army of mercenaries to invade England, to put the claimant on the throne. Kildare's own Irish army reinforced that of the invasion army, which landed in Lancashire early in June 1487; but even this combined force was a ragged affair, said to have been composed of 'the destitute', and they were inadequately armed.

This was an anxious time for the Butlers, whose position in both countries once again depended upon the outcome. But the Irish force was defeated in a hard-fought battle at Stoke, near Newark, with the Earl of Lincoln 'slain in that place, which they took alive in fighting [sic]', and Simnel was captured. This time, the Butlers had come through, and with most of their Irish opposition humiliated in this defeat they were once more firmly established as a premier force in Ireland, despite the fact that there was still a considerable groundswell of public feeling there for the defeated 'Prince', (whom, because young Simnel was seen to have been the cat's-paw of others, Henry allowed to live, giving him menial tasks in the royal kitchen. The real Earl of Warwick remained a prisoner in the Tower.) But eventually, all support for the pretender foundered, and the Pope issued a bull in January 1488 against the Irish bishops who had crowned him in Dublin.

Then, against all expectation, and greatly to Thomas Butler's disquiet, Henry VII pardoned the Earl of Kildare for his part in the uprising, in the hope that he would remain loyal in future; and he even left him in the Deputyship. Kildare himself felt secure enough of the King to go to England early in 1489, along with a number of other Lords of the Pale. They were royally entertained at Greenwich Palace, where the Earl of Ormonde joined them at dinner with the King. (Henry Tudor had an ironic turn of mind, and a conspicuous feature of the banquet was the humiliation of the Irish by having their former 'King', Master Simnel, wait on them at table.)

Yet despite the victory at Stoke, the unrest continued, and rumours of other true claimants persisted. In December 1489 an abbot was implicated in a plot to set the young Earl of Warwick free from the Tower, and was executed for it, but even then the conspiracies went on, with ships and gold being promised from France and Burgundy.

A different Yorkist plot would enter its active phase in Ireland, when another royal claimant arrived at Kildare's castle in 1491, looking for backers. This was a handsome, 17-year-old Fleming, then staying in Cork, who been persuaded to impersonate the younger of Edward IV's two murdered sons; who, 'by divine intervention', like the previous challenger, had escaped the fate that had been planned for him. The Fleming was Perkin Warbeck, and in contrast to Lambert Simnel he had obtained substantial support from abroad, which made him a more serious threat to the King. For the next six years he was a notorious figure, and a dangerous embarrassment to Henry VII.

Ireland had twice now been the breeding-ground for plots involving challengers to Henry's throne; but for many years, the King had too much on his hands in England to concern himself overmuch with matters over the Irish Sea, and for a time he let things drift. After the Simnel debacle, he had replaced the Earl of Lincoln as Lord Lieutenant with his uncle Jasper Tudor, Duke of Bedford, but had inexplicably kept on Kildare as Deputy; and in this role, the Earl remained the all-but-King of Ireland until 1492. This was dangerous not only for King Henry, but also for the Ormondes.

Yet despite their ancient enmity, it was obvious policy for Kildare to conciliate the Irish Butlers, whom the new royal dynasty – now better established, and set to rule for generations to come – would definitely favour. Kildare therefore effected a marriage between his daughter and Sir Piers Roe, who looked likely to be the next Earl of Ormonde in view of the fact that Earl Thomas had so far produced only female heirs. This compromise also suited Kildare because Sir Piers had an Irish mother, and the Earl himself leaned always towards the Gaelic life. Kildare's daughter Margaret, 'the Great Countess' as she would come to be called 'for her noble spirit and masculine gifts',[27] would live until 1542 and would see the ruin of her house.

In 1491 Perkin Warbeck – masquerading as the 'Duke of York' – made his alleged escape from the Tower of London and arrived in Cork (it was said from Portugal), accompanied by Yorkist agents. For a time, it looked as though there might well be another popular rising within The Pale for the so-called Prince, and John Butler's son, the illegitimate James *Dubh*, was sent over to secure the Irish midlands and the south for King Henry and the Earl of Ormonde.

Black James, who had spent a long time in England, was said to have been his Uncle Thomas's favourite representative in Ireland after 1485. He was also reputed to have played an active part against Lambert Simnel, but there is no record of his presence in Ireland before 1491, when he is described as one of the Esquires of the King's Body. In company with a professional soldier, Thomas Garth, he was ordered to withdraw Kilkenny and Tipperary from the Deputy's control. James Butler, with his noble father and his Irish mother, had strong family connections in Ireland. He was able to call upon them to help him dominate the other Butler relations, especially those of Sir Piers Roe, and they also helped him to remove Kildare's supporters away from Ormonde lands. Garth's forces operated with those of James in the midlands, and they also protected Waterford.

Their prime function was to drive a wedge between the Desmonds and the Kildares, and so prevent any cooperation in favour of the Yorkists. In February, the royal ship *Margaret* was sent to patrol the Irish coast, and Garth and Butler were empowered to supersede the King, as and when they found it necessary. (This authority appears to have been the origin of the title of 'Governor of Ireland' which James *Dubh* retained long after the emergency was past.) Possibly due to the energy with which Butler and Garth pursued their mission, support for Kildare seems to have dissipated by the following spring.

In 1492 Thomas, the 7th Earl of Ormonde, in high favour with Henry VII, was sent on an embassy to France. But in June of that year Henry VII again removed the Earl of Kildare from the office of Lord Deputy, since he was suspected of new plots against the Crown. In the same month the King sent over James *Dubh* for a second time, but this time as Treasurer of Ireland. Going over at harvest time in June 1492 with a small band of soldiers, Butler brought his Irish army into Dublin, where there were fights between them and some of the King's men around the city. It was inevitable that he would also quarrel with Kildare, and a skirmish took place, which was the start of a fresh feud between the Butlers and the Geraldines. Black James made a number of converts among the Irish, and he quickly allied himself to Chilleag Fionn, one of the few Irish chieftains to fully accept King Henry VII, James *Dubh* expressly backing him in his quarrels with Fionn's great rivals, the Kildares.

In June 1492 the Earl of Kildare, furious at James *Dubh's* success, wrote to the Earl of Ormonde, warning him that:

> Your cousin [sic], James Ormonde, publishes in all places that he has 'your interest and title' in all your lands here. For which reason he has brought into your countries, Kilkenny and Tipperary, the Obrenes [relatives of Black James] and other Irish enemies, and they have destroyed the King's subjects and spare no churches or religious places.[28]

Kildare said that he had 'suffered him to do so in fear of the King's displeasure, since he claims the King's authority' – and that of Ormonde's, too, 'or so Sir James said'. Kildare assured the Earl that he would do what he could 'for reformation' when he was 'certified' of Ormonde's mind.

In company with an ally, O'Brien, and O'Brien's kinsmen, Black James led an army deeper into enemy country, where they compelled the people to give the King pledges of their submission. The Irish chieftains of Leinster were taken prisoner, and Sir James's army ravaged the county of Meath. The Earl of Kildare, impatient for Thomas Butler's reply, which inevitably took its time to reach him, took matters into his own hands and astonishingly concluded a peace between himself and James, which contained two conditions: firstly, that each of them should have 'their own father's place'; by which is meant that James Butler should be officially recognised as the successor to the Ormonde earldom, and chief of the Butlers. The second condition was that the 'Deputyship of Ireland' – i.e. the Sword of

State and everything that was connected with it – should be transferred to the Archbishop of Dublin until the King should settle all disputes and 'set them to rights'.

The peace between the Earl of Kildare and James Butler did not, could not, last; and the Earl resigned his office and withdrew his assistance from the English of Meath, excusing his callous desertion of them by stating that they had not assisted him against Sir James. The English throughout Meath would suffer many abuses as a result of this, for as soon as Kildare and Butler abandoned them, they were 'plundered and burned from every quarter by the Irish'; who had been suppressed by Kildare and James Butler equally.

Black James not only ravaged Kildare's lands; he also quarrelled with Sir Piers Roe Butler, to the extent of keeping him out of the Ormonde estates by force. For the present Earl had appointed Sir James to be guardian of his Irish lands, and had charged him with working up the Butler and royalist cause in Ireland. This decision caused an even greater rift in the Ormonde family, for Sir Piers Roe, who had held the hereditary deputyship of the earldom from James *Dubh's* father, had an inherent resentment of this brash newcomer. It is hard, in fact, to see exactly why Earl Thomas dispossessed Piers, after the Polestown branch had been trusted for so long, and had shown that they were worthy of that trust. As a result of this snub, Piers swung over to the FitzGeralds, that is, to the opposition. (The story of other Butlers submitting to Black James as the chief of their clan is not mentioned in any of the published histories of Ireland.)

James *Dubh*, however, proved a notable enemy, showing great courage and tenacity in the Tudor cause, bringing in his Kavanagh and O'Brien allies against Sir Piers and the Geraldines. On his part, though, he acted carelessly in not keeping on good terms with the hereditary enemies of his house, whose power and influence he erroneously conceived to be on the wane. The mutual pride and animosity of all these competitors had burst into flame on James's arrival in Ireland, without regard to the authority of any government, and their 'petty broil' had not only confused the English subjects, it had also encouraged the Irish insurgents.

Casual betrayal being the recurring strain in the relationships of most men in Ireland at this time, Sir James Butler was extremely active against the Irish also, despite having made alliances with some of the septs. Murtough, O'Brien's son, died in Thomond of wounds he had received 'on the hosting of the son [Black James] of the Earl of Ormonde'.[29] (This mention of him in the *Annals of Ireland* is perhaps the result of an attempt by his Irish champions to establish James in the earldom, contrary to the English law of succession, which did not admit the rights of illegitimate heirs, *except when they laid claim to the throne*.)

The chief citizen of Waterford wrote to the Earl of Ormonde in August 1492, complaining of the 'great pain that is caused to him and other dwellers in Ormonde's lordships'[30] by the Earl's continued absence. Ormonde was losing income, his towns were being destroyed (often in his name!), and the condition of the people was so dire that a few of them were actually reduced to living in the churchyard. They also complained about James *Dubh's* actions against them, in the name of their overlord.

Sir James himself, as a matter of record, also kept Ormonde informed of the state of affairs, writing to him on 25 February 1495, for example, after the parliamentary Act of Resumption. He warned him that the Treasurer, Sir Hugh Conway, was 'not his friend', and that his prise wines were under threat. But, having informed him of the situation, James wanted written authority from the Earl before he would make any move against their enemies. This authority was granted to him by Ormonde in June, with Sir James being given the custody to rule all of the Earl's dependants, and with as full a power as if the Earl himself were in Ireland. Since this authority was also given in the King's name, James *Dubh* soon became the most dominant figure in Ireland. Full approval was his in August 1496, but he had already assumed the title of the 'Guardian and Protector' of Ormonde's lands and tenants between June 1492 and June 1494.

By the end of 1493, James Butler's successes had made it possible to withdraw all but 100 of the English soldiers, and Kildare and a representative group of Anglo-Irish clerics and lawyers were forcibly sent to England for a prolonged discussion with the King. These talks continued long into 1494, the object of which was to establish a more secure regime in Ireland, with the reconciliation of Kildare and James *Dubh* being the most essential factor. This solution was not to Kildare's taste, but nothing that he or his associates could say against Sir James changed either King Henry's or Ormonde's golden opinions of their champion. While back in Ireland James *Dubh's* continued triumphs sustained their judgement. By 1494 Butler was able to report that many Gaelic Irish had given up their lands to the King 'voluntarily', and that members of their families had also been given up as pledges of peace (while those who did not comply had their lands harried and destroyed).

In the north, three Irish lords came out in favour of Perkin Warbeck, but without taking any offensive against the English forces, the alignment being political rather than military, although two of the Irish chieftains held the northern approaches to the Pale for Sir Edward Poynings, the King's Deputy.[31] The Earl of Desmond and a number of other Munster magnates also declared for Warbeck. Desmond even raised forces to blockade Waterford, and he sent raiding parties into Butler territory.

The siege began in June 1495, and a fleet under Warbeck's command joined in the blockade from the seaward side. Poynings had already been reinforced with men from England, and in August he marched south with the 'gentry of the Pale, and the citizens of Dublin';[32] and the Butler followers went in full strength. Their artillery train enabled the blockading forces to be dispersed, and a number of enemy ships were taken. The

Earl of Desmond, retreating from Waterford to the security of his own territories, also conveyed Warbeck to safety, with the pretender reaching Scotland and the protection of James IV. After that, Poynings engaged in an effective mopping up operation, so that by November King Henry could decide that the external threat had been fully dissipated.

But throughout this period, there had been major opposition beyond the Pale to Poynings, the King's man, who was forced – against his will – to rely upon Sir James Butler. The deputy took a force into Armagh, where James *Dubh*'s men carried out a devastating trail of fire into the country, after which the Irish soon submitted, and sons were handed over as hostages. By 1495 the deputy was in even greater conflict with a large section of the Anglo-Irish of the Pale, and this forced him again to rely too much upon Black James, who, in April of that year, undertook the siege of Carlow. Although after it was taken, it was then put into Irish care, perhaps as a pledge of their sincerity. There had been no general rising or even a major protest at the downfall of Kildare.

The Bishop of Bangor succeeded Poynings in January 1496, but he could only rely on a force of 330 English soldiers and one hundred hired kerns. James Butler shared command of about half this force, and Kildare's brother, still in the field, was able to raise various alarms within the Pale in the early months of 1496, but his support was gradually cut away; by June, he was suing for a pardon. On Kildare's return to Ireland in 1496, he cooperated closely with the absentee Earl Thomas, Sir Piers Butler, the Earl of Desmond and the city of Waterford, with only James Butler presenting a problem. Although he agreed to renounce his hostility to the Earl of Kildare in a tripartite agreement made between himself, Kildare and the Earl of Ormonde, on 6 August 1496, he had little intention of keeping his word.

The situation was an uneasy one. Black James had accumulated by royal grant the assistance of English money, which paid for Garth's troops between 1491 and 1496, and by the force of these arms he was a considerable power in the land. But he had also made alliances with the Irish lords of Connacht which bordered on being treasonable. Now, faced with the return of Kildare to a position of authority in Dublin and to the prospect of the Earl's certain hostility, James adopted an independent and aggressive attitude. He was soon a predominant force in the area, and he put increased pressure on Sir Piers Butler and other branches of the family to submit to his authority. Piers, since James had the upper hand, complied for the present, but with ill grace.

Kildare and Piers Roe Butler joined together to alarm King Henry VII with their reports about his representative's high-handed treatment of the King's most important subjects in Ireland. Two letters were consequently sent to Black James from the King, early in 1497, ordering him to return to England, but he ignored the summons. By this disregard for the royal command, and by other imperious actions, he now put himself outside the certainty of the King's protection, although he may not formally have been declared a traitor. In a further attempt to lower James Butler's standing with the King, Piers Roe accused James, rightly or wrongly, of inciting Perkin Warbeck to return to Ireland, and Warbeck did, in fact, arrive off Waterford in July 1497. But whether by an arrangement with James Butler or not there is no evidence, and we shall never know the answer, for by the time Warbeck arrived, James *Dubh* was dead.

What is undoubted is that James Butler used any method to achieve his extravagant ambitions. From his arrival in the country, he had seen that Anglo-Ireland lacked a leading magnate who would be wholly acceptable to both the Irish and to King Henry VII, and so he had taken every opportunity to build up his own power, since he believed that he filled that requirement. What he lacked, of course, was a title and the lands that went to support such an honour, and yet this was, he felt, also within his grasp. From as early as 1493, Kildare had warned the Earl of Ormonde that Black James was setting himself up to be his successor, and Sir Piers Roe also reported that James claimed – despite his bastardy – to be the rightful heir to his father, the 6th Earl. (The purpose of their letters being to thoroughly alarm Earl Thomas, in the hope that it would sting him into returning to Ireland to protect his interests. These efforts were in vain, though, for nothing would move Thomas from England, except those commissions from the King to attend various European Courts.)

An able but unsupported adventurer, it seems true enough that James *had* planned to become the next Earl of Ormonde, or even to supplant his uncle, who had no male heirs. He might, indeed, well have succeeded in this ambition, if Piers Roe had not attacked and killed him in a chance encounter between Dunmore and Kilkenny, on 17 July 1497, in what might charitably at best be called a 'duel'. The meeting, which flared into the to-be-expected quarrel, resulted in James being 'pierced through with a dart'.

Sir Piers Roe appears to have felt no guilt in seeing off his rival, and actually wrote a frank account of the killing to the Earl of Ormonde, of which he seemed proud. Earl Thomas, despite his earlier championship of his nephew, seems now to have felt no great regret at the removal of this increasingly dangerous opponent; and with James out of the way, Piers Roe Butler offered again to take over the deputyship of the Ormonde lands. But although the Earl appears to have remained on friendly and cooperative terms with him, he preferred to manage his Irish properties for some years through a number of different agents. Only very occasionally did he make the effort to travel to Ireland to oversee his estates in person. As for the matter of the murder, Kildare, as lord lieutenant in 1498, acquitted Piers Roe of the killing of a man he had himself sought to see dead, and he issued a comprehensive pardon.

The situation in the south remained interesting. In 1493, as part of the machinery for strengthening Sir James Butler's hand, a legal commission had been set up to enforce the law in Kilkenny and Waterford, and this was now revised, with one of Earl Thomas's correspondents being made a special Justice for Kilkenny in 1499. Kildare, too, had very substantial interests in the Butler areas since the Earl of Ormonde, as an absentee landlord, had paid two thirds of his revenue to him whenever he had been Lord Deputy. It was, therefore, always in Kildare's interests to maintain peace and order throughout the Butler territories, despite the mayhem he created elsewhere in Ireland. As we shall see, Piers Roe – whose interests, since he was now undisputed heir to the earldom, were even closer than those of Kildare – also sought to uphold the law in these areas.

But having been bitterly piqued by his demotion from deputy of Ireland, and his subsequent humiliation by the bastard James *Dubh*, the Earl of Kildare now sided openly with the cause of 'the French lad', Perkin Warbeck, and even plotted to bring the Scots into the intrigue.

Henry VII's response to this new challenge to his rule had been to send knights with carefully picked troops to guard the coast and the ports, and to suppress any hint of possible revolt in Ireland. To do this, he sent Sir Edward Poynings over in 1494, to bring the country into a 'whole and perfect obedience'. In Ireland, Poynings equally harried those who had supported Warbeck along with the 'wild Irish', or 'wild men of the woods', who had been joined by other enemies of the King, that they 'might together defend themselves'.

The Irish nobles, however, did not give Poynings the aid they had promised him, so he was unable to make much progress against the 'natives'; men whom he was unable to bring to battle in any one place, 'because they confined themselves to wandering among the marshes and forests on account of their lack of soldiers'.[33] Poynings also blamed his lack of success on Gerald, Earl of Kildare, and so had him arrested and taken over to England. There, Kildare was charged with many offences, but he so brilliantly defended himself that the King sent him back with honour, and he resumed the governorship. 'As all Ireland could not rule Kildare, Henry thought him meet to rule all Ireland', as the *Book of Howth* put it. When Kildare landed in Ireland in 1496, he had been bound to King Henry by many gifts and honours, one of them his being allowed to take a kinswoman of the King's in marriage.

During Poynings stay in Ireland, a number of acts were passed which created a more formal boundary between The Pale and the rest of the country; with the use of Irish customs and laws being proscribed, and Irish dress and manners discouraged within those borders (much as the Hanoverian government did in Scotland, after the suppression of the Jacobites). Poynings, relieved to be disencumbered of Sir James Butler, now called upon the family of Sir Piers Roe for their aid in his efforts to bring the Irish to order and, having agreed to work with him, they quelled a number of disturbances. The Butlers were, once more, the dominant 'Guardians of The Pale'.

But Thomas himself played no major role in these actions while he continued to spend the greater part of his time in England, except for when the King sent him on various embassies. He may have been in the country when Perkin Warbeck invaded England in 1496; but if he was his loyalty was not called into question, since the expedition was an immediate failure. The Scots advanced little more than four miles across the border, to retire in panic-stricken disorder within a few days. When Warbeck tried another invasion, by sea to Cornwall, with three small ships and about 120 men 'or fewer' (he attracted, in all, no more than 3,000 men), he was again beaten, and this time was forced to surrender. He would be executed within two years of his capture, along with the *real* Earl of Warwick, whom Henry had kept alive in the Tower, in order to produce as and when another challenger appeared. But the survival of both men had caused the King immense difficulties, since they were a continuing focus of attention for those who plotted to oust him, and only their death would put a stop to such intrigues.

Earl Thomas continued in the King's service, and was sent as ambassador to the Dukedom of Burgundy in 1497 (which was one of his most delicate embassies, since the Duchess, as Edward IV's sister, was one of King Henry Tudor's most unrelenting enemies). Meanwhile, he sat in all the parliaments from the time of his first summons until the sixth year of Henry VIII's reign.

In the journal of that year he is mentioned as *dominus Ormonde* in the list of the lords present. To enjoy the extravagant lifestyle that he enjoyed in England and on the Continent, Thomas was forced to put his Irish lands into the care of his most trustworthy relations there, if he was to live comfortably off his rents. But the experience with his illegitimate nephew James *Dubh* had shown him the dangers of handing over near-absolute power to ambitious upstarts. It would not be until some years after the murder of Sir James Butler that he would be confident enough to place his faith in his murderer, and put the running of his estates back into the capable hands of the Polestown branch of his dynasty.

The Butlers of Polestown were the foremost strain in the minor Butler bloodline, the undisputed heirs to the title. Yet they were only one of the Butler families that had come into prominence in the period after 1460, when the Ormonde territories were left without effective leadership. By taking advantage of the hiatus created by the fall of the major house in England, all three of the leading cadet branches of the family had managed to extend their influence in Ireland. Not only the Polestown Butlers, but also the Butler barons of Cahir in the south and Dunboyne in the east now came into prominence. Despite the fact that they, too, had largely sided with the losing royal house, all three families had achieved positions of considerable strength by the time of the restoration of Earl Thomas in 1477.

But the Butlers of Cahir had long been enemies of the other two major branches, and little love was lost between the Polestown Butlers and those of Dunboyne. In view of this, the Earl Thomas, while remaining an absentee, had managed very skillfully to play off one cadet branch against another, so that none became dominant. He contrived to obtain substantial income from his lands, using each of them, as and when he chose, as his agents.

The years between Black James's death and Sir Piers Roe Butler's restitution as Ormonde's deputy were stirring times for the Irish branch of the family. In 1500 the O'Briens of Thomond defeated them at Moyaliff in County Tipperary, and a year later Turlough O'Brien raided Limerick County and burned the city. In 1502 appalling weather and disease in cattle led to famine and plague, and their troubles had been added to by the return of Kildare from England. For the 'Great Earl' had returned with his son Gerald, who had been in the King's custody, and by the following year Gerald had been appointed Lord High Treasurer. The outbreak of plague continued into 1505, but that would be nothing compared to the ruin the Kildares would bring to pass during this period. Throughout this time, Piers Roe Butler had shown himself to be the most prominent man among the Anglo-Irish after Garret More, the Earl of Desmond, who had dominated Irish politics with subtle skill for seventeen years. By 1505 Piers had won back the high regard of Earl Thomas, and was acknowledged by him as the deputy and protector of Ormonde interests in Ireland. (His father James, the son of MacRichard Butler, had died in 1486; a cousin, Thomas, had been slain by another cousin, John.) Sir Piers Roe was Seneschal of the Liberty of Tipperary, and Governor of the Earl's lordship in that county and in Kilkenny. From this time on, apart from lacking the title, Piers Roe was the dominant personality in south-east Ireland.

Indeed, the Earl rarely took any real interest in his Irish properties, and even the most desperate entreaties from his increasingly neglected and wretched country went unheeded. In April 1508 the Chief Baron of the Dublin Exchequer wrote to Ormonde 'concerning the commonwealth of this land of Ireland', pleading for financial relief, especially in Dublin and the town of Drogheda, 'which be right sore decayed'. There was, he wrote, 'daily war in the defence of the King's subjects here'.[34]

There were times, though, when the unresponsive Earl was forced to act, if only in his own interests. For instance, when the Earl of Kildare arranged a marriage between Lord Slane's daughter and Sellinger, a grandson of one of Ormonde's own daughters, since if this had gone ahead, it would have affected Ormonde's status in Ireland. If such a close relative had gone to live there as a permanent resident the Earl's rights would have been touched, since his grandson would have been eligible for tax, and those taxes would have been paid out of Ormonde's rents. 'My Lord shall lose the two parts of all the advantages, which will amount to a right sum in a few years'.[35] And not only Ormonde's interests would be disturbed; those of Sir Piers Butler, his chief representative in Ireland, would be also, and the Earl could not afford to lose the goodwill of Sir Piers and his wife, 'by reason of the said marriage'. In June 1507 Ormonde sent his servant, 'John of Devonshire', with instructions to have the wedding stopped, but again ignored all attempts to get him to go to Ireland in person.

Kildare, too, was proving a greater menace than ever. Confirmed in his appointment as Lord Deputy in 1510, he had received a royal patent granting him a limited interest in all the possessions he could recover from any rebel in Ireland. As a result of this open invitation to strip even innocent men of their possessions, he enthusiastically took to campaigning in Munster, where he not only took two castles from the 'Irish enemy' but also mopped up properties belonging to the Butlers, on which, he claimed, these 'rebels' lived.

The tenants of Rush and Fingal petitioned the Earl in April 1511. Their towns were so deteriorated, they wrote, that they were unable to live in 'your inhabitacions, but must remove elsewhere'.[36] They had complained to the present steward time after time without effect; but they were more concerned that Edmund Golding, who wished to be Ormonde's new steward – and was in constant touch with the Earl in England – wanted to take over the estates completely. 'We know him [to be] of such cruel demeanour that if he have any rule upon us we must well avoid your lands, for we shall not agree with his conditions, and would not be in jurisdiction or danger in any wise.'[37] The townspeople had joined together to pay for this letter to be written by a notary, so concerned were they about a possible change of stewardship. But, as usual, the Earl did nothing for them.

Thomas Butler died in August 1515, in London, where he was buried in the church of St Thomas de Heres. Among the other estates restored to him had been Rochford in Essex, and the title of Lord Rochford was given to him by writ in 12 Henry VII, which English title permitted him to attend the House of Peers. He took his place there, next to the Prior of St John of Jerusalem, and he sat, somewhat surprisingly, as the first *Baron* of England. This was either a compliment made to him by the other barons, out of regard to his superior (though Irish, and therefore 'foreign') title, or as a particular favour to the King. (It was a part of the prerogative of the Crown, until Henry VIII changed the guidelines, to give precedence according to royal pleasure.)

Thomas Butler had married Anne, a daughter of Sir Richard Hankford and Anne, the eldest daughter of the 3rd Earl of Salisbury. By her, Thomas had two daughters, but no son. The eldest daughter, Anne, married Sir James St Leger, from whom a famous Devonshire family descended, and her sister Margaret married Sir William Boleyn, a Knight of the Bath. Of the two daughters, Margaret made the more dazzling match in historical terms, since her granddaughter Anne would reign briefly as a Queen of England, and her great-granddaughter would be the glorious Elizabeth I.

Thomas Butler made his will on 31 July 1515, which was proved in the next month. In it, he left to his grandson, Sir Thomas Boleyn, and his issues male, a curious relic.

> A white horn of ivory, garnished at both ends with gold, and a tyret of gold thereupon, which (says he) was myn ancestors at the first time they were called to the honour, and hath sythen continually remained in the same blode; for which cause my lord and father commanded me upon his blessing, that I should do my devoir to cause it to continue still in my blode, as for furth as might lie in me done to the honour of the same blode.[38]

This drinking vessel – although possibly only a token of the office of cup-bearer – was generally believed to be the horn from which Thomas Becket, the martyred Archbishop of Canterbury, had drunk, and it was kept very religiously in the family for centuries. Indeed, so anxious was Thomas to keep this precious relic within his own bloodline, that he laid down express instructions for its being handed on to his own descendants. As Thomas had failed to provide the dynasty with a male heir, the relic was to pass to the children of his daughters, and if Sir Thomas Boleyn died without issue, it was to go to Sir George St Leger, and his issue male. Only if both these men should fail to produce the necessary males was it to go out of the direct line; to the next 'issue male' of his grandfather, James, the 3rd Earl of Ormonde.

This saintly relic was, in fact, passed down through the St Leger family, until its whereabouts are not now known. It would not return to the Ormonde line, whose title, for the first time in its history, was about to pass from the direct succession.

## Notes.

1. *Calendar of State Papers, Ireland.*
2. *Dictionary of National Biography*, (under Henry VI).
3. The Four Masters, *Annals of the Kingdom of Ireland.*
4. Ibid.
5. Ibid.
6. The manuscripts were most likely illuminated, probably by Irish monks. Edmund MacRichard Butler was a noted patron of Irish literature, apart from being a famous warrior.
7. Carte, *The Life of the Duke of Ormonde.*

8. Ibid.
9. D. Ross, *Edward IV*.
10. Ibid.
11. Ibid.
12. Ibid.
13. Carte, op. cit.
14. Ibid.
15. Ibid.
16. Ibid.
17. Ibid.
18. Ibid.
19. P.M. Kendall, *Richard III*.
20. Ibid.
21. Ibid.
22. His forces were overwhelmingly made up of French mercenaries.
23. P.M. Kendall, op. cit.
24. Ibid.
25. *Calendar of State Papers, England.*
26. R.L. Storey, *The Reign of Henry VII*.
27. Carte, op. cit.
28. Ibid.
29. The Four Masters, op. cit.
30. Carte, op. cit.
31. Sir Edward Poynings (1459–1521), in Leland's *History of Ireland*.
32. R.L. Storey, op. cit.
33. Ibid.
34. Carte, op. cit.
35. Curtis, *Calendar of Ormonde Papers*.
36. Carte, op. cit.
37. Ibid
38. Ibid.

# CHAPTER IX

# A Break in the Line

A new problem was presented to the Lord Justice of Ireland, the Earl of Kildare, at the end of 1515, when he was instructed to facilitate the transfer of the Butler lands to the heirs general of Earl Thomas, his daughters Anne St Leger and Margaret Boleyn. All of the English estates (except for a small part around Deptford in Kent) had already been ceded to them, but the Irish territories were another matter, for they went with the honour, and so must pass to the heirs male. For the first time in 300 years they could not descend to the direct line, and they were to be transferred to a descendant of Sir Richard Botiller, the second son of James, 3rd Earl of Ormonde, who had died over one hundred years before.

Sir Thomas Boleyn, Margaret's son, was already influential enough at court to obtain the aid of Cardinal Wolsey, the Lord Chancellor, and even that of King Henry VIII himself. But Kildare was by now on very good terms with his brother-in-law, Sir Piers Butler, the new claimant, and neither wished to see the lands go into what they saw as 'foreign' hands; Thomas Butler had done damage enough, simply by being an absentee landlord. The result was that the Earl of Kildare delayed judgement for as long as he could, informing the King that he was doing his best to get Piers to appear in Dublin, to arrange for the transfer of the estates to the English heirs. Complaining that Piers – who was by then calling himself the Earl of Ormonde – had failed to come before the Chancellor, sending numerous excuses for his non-appearance.

It was, perhaps, because of King Henry VIII's personal interest in the matter that the illegal transfer of the English estates to the two sisters was not challenged by the Irish heirs, but they insisted that primogeniture rights must be preserved in Ireland. Guardianship of English property in Ireland, and with it The Pale, must pass to the male line. The Butlers of Polestown at once maintained that they were the true and only heirs for the Irish title and estates if the premier stock should expire, or end in females, as had happened. This successor was Sir Piers Roe Butler, the great-great-great grandson of the 3rd Earl; yet the right to succeed to the Irish property after Thomas's death would be fought out ruthlessly over the next ten years. Thomas's daughters tried to dispossess the new Earl of his Irish estates, and Henry VIII only prevented them by getting all their rights invested in himself, by use of the Act of Absentees. He then conveyed the deeds to Piers and his heirs male, to whom they were further secured by an act of Parliament.

Judging by the ease with which the St Leger and Boleyn families squandered their English heritage, it was a matter of some importance for the Irish lands to remain under the capable control of the Polestown Butlers. Indeed, had they maintained charge of the English property also, it would have been more advantageous for the clan as a whole, since the English estates that went to the English co-heiresses amounted to seventy-two manors, (thirty-six to each), besides other lesser properties. (It has been argued the first three Earls of Ormonde had each entailed these lands upon heirs male only, and left ample documentation to that effect, but that Earl Thomas suppressed these deeds in favour of his daughters.)

As it was, the English estates failed to prosper in the hands of those who acquired them, 'notwithstanding the largeness of it, and the vast sums of money left to the heiresses'.[1] By the end of Elizabeth's reign, Margaret Boleyn's family would have very little left of their share, and Sir John St Leger not only sold his portion but even his own inheritance, '...so that he had not a foot of land left in England, all the manors being fallen into the hands of strangers.'[2] The Boleyn family was, of course, almost extinct by the end of the 16th century.

The new Earl's paternal grandfather was Edmund Butler, the grandson of the 3rd Earl of Ormonde. Commonly called 'MacRichard', he had built the castle and the bridge of Carrick-on-Suir, and been buried, at his death in 1464, at the Greyfriars at Kilkenny. Edmond left three sons: James (whom we have already met), Walter and John. James had taken the side of the Lancastrians against Edward IV, for which he was penalised in that King's time, 'repeating all attainders, judgements and outlawries against the said James Butler, fitzEdmund, fitzRichard, on account of siding with [King] Henry VI'.[3] But, as with his Ormonde cousins, his lack of political judgement had been overlooked by Edward IV in the King's need of knowledgeable men in Ireland, and the apparent treachery would be later wiped out by the many services that James later rendered him. For it was in consideration of this that the King, in the eighth year of his reign, granted him the manor of Callan, and the advowson of its church, for life.

As we have seen, the relationship between James and John, 6th Earl of Ormonde, would seem to have been close, and that Earl certainly trusted his cousin in a manner he did not show to his brother Thomas (perceptively, where it came to the protection of his Irish properties, as the 7th Earl's life shows). The most extreme example of John's confidence in James had been when the 6th Earl, upon setting out on his fatal journey to the Holy Land, had appointed James as his attorney and deputy, in all causes concerning the Earl in his lands and jurisdiction in Ireland. During his cousin's pilgrimage, James had worked diligently, having 'established certain orders for the good government of Carrick-Magriffin, and building the castle of Nehom, near Carrick'.[4]

Dying on 16 April 1487, James Butler was buried in the priory of the Augustine hermits at Callan, which he had founded. He had married Sawe Kavanagh, a daughter of MacMurrough, 'prince of his nation', and a descendant of the old King of Leinster who had caused such grief to the English a century before. Because of her ancestry, Sawe had, on the occasion of her marriage, a patent of denisation; which, by its nature, is worth setting down in full (the italics are mine). It was granted to Sawe, as the wife of 'James fitzEdmund, fitzRichard Butler'[5] that:

> ...she, and all the issues between them, begotten and to be begotten, be of a *free* state and condition, and that they be free of and acquitted from all Irish servitude; and that they may use and *enjoy the English lawes* in the same manner as Englishmen within the said land do use and enjoy the same; and that they answer and be answer'd unto in all courts whatsoever of us, our heirs and successors, and may acquire and purchase lands, enjoy the same, be *promoted to ecclesiastical benefices*, and enjoy the same in the said lands do, have and enjoy them, notwithstanding any *Irish condition or custom*, or any statutes, acts, ordinances or privileges to the contrary thereof in *former times* had or used.[6]

This extraordinary document, with its intriguing insight into the English attitude to the Irish, some four hundred years after the takeover of their country, was witnessed by the Earl of Desmond, then Deputy, and by George, Duke of Clarence, the King's brother. It was signed at Trim, on 20 May in the seventh year of Edward IV's reign. This James had two sons whom he recognised: Sir Piers Butler and Thomas Butler, gentleman.

It was Sir Piers, or Peter – the first half-Irish Butler – who might well expect the title, and he openly took it on Earl Thomas's death, without sons, in 1515, despite being opposed by Thomas's grandsons, George St Leger and Thomas Boleyn. Having assumed the title, Piers then did all he could to consolidate his position and hold on to the lands, especially those that had been entailed by the 4th Earl to the heirs male only.

It was not until 1528 that a reluctant Henry VIII would admit his right to be the 8th Earl, and paradoxically only when he granted him the new title of Earl of Ossary in place of the older one of Ormonde, which he wished to award to another. For, among other complications, the claims of Earl Thomas had passed to his daughter Margaret, who had married Sir Thomas Boleyn, and this would create a problem for the King when he became embroiled in the Ormonde/Boleyn dispute over the lands and title. It would not be until 1537 that Henry finally accepted Piers as the rightful Earl of Ormonde. Yet the St Legers and the Boleyns were not the only competitors for the Ormonde fortune, for from the outset the title had been fiercely contested, since Piers – known as 'Piers Roe, or Red Piers, from the colour of his hair'[7] – had, in fact, two older brothers then living. Both of these men were born before their parents were married, but were said to own as good a claim to the earldom as that of Piers. Nevertheless, although the elder brothers were legitimised by an act of the Irish parliament, their father, in his last will, referred only to Piers as 'my natural and lawful son, my true heir',[8] and this was taken to mean that Piers had first right to the title. Piers's claim, then, was paper thin, despite the fact that the 7th Earl had also granted him many manors and lands, in recognition of him as his eventual heir. In 1509, for example, Piers had been granted three manors for the rest of his natural life, along with their issues and profits, with the 7th Earl's right, of course, to 'dispute and name at any time afterwards another person, if Piers did not fulfill his obligation'.[9]

But Piers had one tremendous advantage working in his favour, the fact that he was married to a daughter of the 'Great Earl of Kildare'. This extraordinary man 'of great parts' had managed to keep the feud between the Butler and Geraldine clans – 'the Guelphs and Ghibellines of Ireland'[10] – at a manageable level for some years, and he was for most of his life recognised as the leading authority in Ireland. The power and influence of his father-in-law, in his double aspect of English Deputy and hero of the Anglo-Irish, was simply too great for lesser men to oppose, and Kildare had already shown himself to be Piers Butler's champion.

(In 1504 Piers had reached an agreement with his father-in-law by which Kildare should buy from Piers the whole, or part, of his future interests in Ireland. He would further give Kildare – 'in satisfaction of his present receipts' – two thirds of the profits that he derived from the properties of the absentee landlords under the Statute of Absentees, and half of the revenues he drew from their lands. In return, Kildare gave Piers the manor of Cloncorrey, 'for the singular favour, affection and cousinage that he hath unto the said Sir Piers'.[11] He also granted him the minor rights and privileges in Castle Warny.)

It was at Kildare's request that Piers had been pardoned of his crimes against the Crown, and which had been granted by Henry VII in 1498. Kildare's petition (as Lord Deputy), had been sweepingly inclusive of all Piers' crimes against the King's Peace, which had included the giving and selling of horses, arms, victuals, salt, steel and English cloth, to 'Irish enemies and English rebels'. He was also to be cleared of the crimes of 'alterage' and 'gossiping with the Irish enemy' as penalised by the Statutes of Kilkenny, and the fact that he had taken 'coign and livery from the earth-tillers',[12] as well as taking the field against his private enemies and the government. All such 'abominable customs' had been re-condemned in the Statutes of the Poyning's parliament.

Piers would later prove ungrateful to his father-in-law, though, when – in retaliation for Kildare having acted against his interests by arranging a marriage between two people who might have kept Piers from his inheritance – he would be a prime mover in the overthrow of the Kildares. His rivals for the Ormonde treasure, the Boleyns, had even assisted Piers in this act of retribution, for a time, since their interests had also been equally endangered.

Yet by acting in this way, Piers was not simply doing so out of revenge, but was also pursuing a political course with consistency, once Kildare had served his purpose. In many ways, in the political climate of the time, it was essential for him to dissociate himself from his in-laws, since they 'played on a dangerous string', in that they continued to support the Yorkist line. The Butlers preferred to play the safer line, by remaining loyal to the Lancaster-Tudor dynasty.

When, on 3 September 1513, the Lord Deputy Kildare died at Athy from gunshot wounds, his son Gerald Oge was appointed to the same office, on roughly the same terms as his father. Within two years, he would be setting off for London to answer allegations of corruption before the King's Council; yet he would be back in Ireland by September 1515 with his Lord Deputyship confirmed. This despite the fact that earlier, in June, Sir William Darcy had submitted papers to the English council suggesting a need for political reform in Ireland, and strongly indicting Kildare's form of government.

Another factor in Piers's favour, though, even with his father-in-law no longer able to sustain him, was that at a difficult stage in his reign King Henry VIII needed a man such as Piers as much as Piers needed the King. For Henry – just as his father had done before him – recognised that he was a man of outstanding military ability, and the King had a strong need of such men. Piers had already distinguished himself in the service of the Crown, in particular by suppressing the insurrections of his mother's countrymen, at which he had been extremely successful, and for which he was highly regarded at the Tudor court.

Such men as Piers Butler were especially needed by King Henry, since in 1519 the King decided to 'do something' about Ireland, even though he had other, greater, issues to concern him. (In the first twenty years of his reign, Henry VIII was to fight two wars with France, one with the Holy Roman Emperor, and one with Scotland. This last, the tremendous victory at Flodden Field in 1513, had great consequences for Ireland since it saved the country from again being invaded by the Scots, with the death of the Scottish king – along with all his chivalry – at their spectacular defeat.)

But King Henry was determined to tackle the problem of his most troublesome outpost; his first move being to summon the Earl of Kildare to court, to answer charges of maladministration. Kildare left for England, having appointed his kinsman, Sir Thomas FitzGerald of Laccagh, as deputy in his absence. In London, he was kept hanging about for some months by the Lord Chancellor, Cardinal Wolsey, and upon first meeting, both men took an instant dislike to each other, with Wolsey losing no time in depriving the Earl of his post, and even ordered him to remain at court. (Where, to the Cardinal's vexation, Kildare made a great impression, acquitting himself with notable elan at the Field of the Cloth of Gold, Henry's most extravagant act of self-promotion.[13])

Someone had to take Kildare's place in Ireland, and the obvious choice was Piers Butler. But Piers was now his brother-in-law FitzGerald's most bitter rival, and it was in view of this that it was decided not to raise him to the office, since Wolsey reasoned that it would only refuel clan conflict. Instead Thomas Howard, Earl of Surrey, was given the post of Lord Lieutenant.[14] He arrived in Ireland at the head of 1,000 soldiers on 20 May 1520.

Like many Englishmen before him, Howard must have asked himself if this honour was a promotion of sorts, or else a peculiar form of exile. Sent to Dublin with a brief to employ a firm hand in establishing an efficient (and profitable) administration, Surrey undoubtedly believed that he had drawn the short straw when offered this government appointment. For Ireland – by the end of the 14th century – was seen as the Ultima Thule of English domestic affairs, and the truth was that it was an unpopular job with Englishmen, and one that none of the King's other generals wanted.

Surrey could expect no support from the relatives and cronies of the deposed Earl of Kildare, and they even plotted to frustrate his endeavours. Kildare's Irish son-in-law, Con O'Neill, was exceptionally hostile to the King's policy of anglicisation, and on the arrival of the Earl of Surrey he immediately invaded The Pale. He was unsuccessful, owing to the support that Piers Roe Butler rendered to the new Viceroy, and O'Neill submitted before long.

Kildare himself, from his detention in London, certainly urged his fellow peers to create so much havoc that his deputy, at least, would have to be recalled. But when Surrey reported his suspicions to Wolsey and the King, nothing was done about them. Instead, King Henry sought to make O'Neill an ally by knighting him, and he also tried to get him to live in England; Surrey floundered deeper into a political morass. The unpalatable truth was that Kildare and Piers Roe were the only men ever likely to maintain any kind of firm rule in Ireland; and, realising this, Henry did all he could to bind Kildare to the house of Tudor, even allowing him to marry into the King's own family. And this, despite the fact that Kildare had already shown himself unreliable time and time again.

King Henry VIII, unlike most of his predecessors, seems to have woken up to the disorder of the Irish situation, and saw it as his imperial duty to ensure an effective and orderly government in the country. But this was only to be achieved, he instructed Surrey, by 'sober ways, politic drifts and amiable persuasions, found in law and reason'; certainly not, he insisted, by 'rigorous dealing...by strength or violence...'[15]

Quite how Surrey was to achieve this was never divulged, but it was accepted that 'to bring the Irishry into an appearance only of obeisance' would be 'a thing of little policy, less advantage and no effect'.[16]

Surrey had a number of early successes; and by July and August he had forced the submission of the O'Carrolls in Leinster and the O'Neills in Ulster. A year later he avenged a confederation against The Pale by the O'Connors, O'Mores and O'Carrolls of the midlands, but he could only achieve this by a scorched-earth policy. He was, as an Englishman, hampered by his complete ignorance of the clan rivalries that formed the basis of Irish politics; and he was, as ever, inadequately resourced.

Like most other English monarchs before him, King Henry VIII insisted upon his deputies carrying out the necessary reforms, and paying their staff and soldiers, out of Irish revenues; and Surrey had soon discovered that taxes could only be extracted when backed up by a large and intimidating force. Without men and money to back him he could not raise the necessary funds, and without funds he could not raise the men; most revenue was gobbled up by the costs of military action. Within weeks of his arrival in Ireland, Surrey was writing to the King for larger funding; appeals that would be repeated several times without result.

But King Henry *had* taken the first steps towards the eventual conquest of Ireland, beginning with the termination of the policy of separation between the Anglo-Irish and the Gaelic Irish; while, at the same time, forcefully – peaceful expedients being soon abandoned – putting down any independent Anglo-Irish leaders and Gaelic chiefs. What Henry wanted to create was a more homogenous population, but one which was based on English customs, dress and manner: in fact, the Ireland that had been pre-figured in the Statute of Kilkenny, but this time with modern overtones.

In pursuit of this Henry ruthlessly put down a rebellion by the son of the 9th Earl of Kildare, and the success of this counterstroke broke the last remaining Irish claim on self-governance in his lifetime. The Butlers would afterwards be active in helping the King to carry out the policy he then installed: of a governing council, led by a Viceroy who was directly answerable to the Crown. As a policy this would be largely successful, though brought about more by brute force than the 'amiable persuasions' King Henry had originally desired.

Sir Piers Roe had been recognised, if unofficially, as the 8th Earl of Ormonde, and he campaigned with Kildare against the O'Carrolls, destroying Garrycastle. In fact, despite being passed over for the Lord Lieutenancy, Piers's achievements were outstanding in the service of the Crown, and he actively supported the new Lord Lieutenant. By 1520 Surrey had also won over the new Earl's most influential allies with shows of strength to the south-west and north, and he achieved truces with other clans. But it was rapidly made clear to the Englishman that the wily Irish lords were using him as a counter in their own power games, and in December he reported to Cardinal Wolsey in desperation, 'This land will never be brought to due obedience but only with compulsion and conquest'.[17]

Long before Surrey completed his first year in Ireland, he realised that he was wasting his time, money, reputation and health, and achieving nothing, either for himself or his master; and forced marches and days and nights passed in campaign tents were not the thing for a 50-year-old man. Yet he could hardly claim that his many failures were not actually his own fault, since Henry would not listen to such 'excuses'. Surrey was caught between the Irish lords, who made and broke pledges with equal ease, and a home government that steadfastly refused to give him the tools for the job. In these circumstances, it was impossible to achieve anything, but he was, of course, blamed for the failure; the discredit was on his head.

This was in contrast to Piers Roe, who by 1521 had been declared the 'true and lawful heir' to the late Earl of Ormonde by Act of Parliament, and whose stock with the King and Wolsey was constantly rising. He had proved invaluable to the Earl of Surrey, helping him to force the submission of the O'Carrolls in Leinster and of the O'Neills in Ulster. He had also been on hand when Surrey avenged the confederation against The Pale, the success of their campaign in the midlands being largely achieved by a scorched earth policy. But Piers's victories were so many that, when the Earl of Surrey left the country in 1521, it was not so much by Surrey's friendship (they were intimate friends) as by the King's orders that Piers was left as deputy in his stead. On 26 March 1522 the new Earl of Ormonde was sworn in as Lord Deputy.

His task of controlling Ireland, though, was made all the more difficult because he had a greatly depleted force with which to do so, as the Earl of Surrey had carried back to England all the forces that he had originally brought with him. This weakened the army at a time when there was reason to expect another invasion by the Scots, which in turn would lead to an even graver defection of the Irish. (In August 1522 the Irish Privy Council appealed to Wolsey for six ships of war to cruise between Ireland and Scotland, to stem the tide of a Scottish invasion of Ulster. Only four were sent.)

But, in the process of securing his own power base in Dublin, Piers Roe brilliantly recreated the domination by the Butlers of the Irish political arena which would last for some years to come, and his own past peccadilloes were long forgotten. (For example, his having accepted an appointment as High Sheriff of Kilkenny by the imposter Lambert Simnel during his brief 'reign', a misdeed that was put down to youthful irresponsibility, since he had been a minor at the time.) 'Red Piers' had in fact received a pardon for 'all crimes committed by him in Ireland'[18], before being knighted by King Henry VII in 1497, but that he was now fully exonerated is shown by the unusual trust that Henry VIII put in him. (The likeliest explanation for Piers having supported the Yorkist pretender to the Crown lies in his relationship with his late father-in-law, since the Kildares were, and would remain, fervent Yorkists.)

In a sense Piers's marriage, although it proved a very happy union, had brought him a double burden, for in one sense it compromised him with the Tudors, and yet it had not extinguished the feud between the two households (despite the fact that an indenture between the Butlers and the FitzGeralds 'to keep the peace' was signed in July 1524). The Butlers were, throughout this period, in a state of constant contention with their recent allies but ancient enemies – who now sought to undermine their newly found authority in whatever way they could. Piers's brother-in-law, who had previously held the position of Chief Governor until being replaced after a number of complaints against his rule, deeply resented Piers being made Lord Treasurer in 1524.

When Robert Talbot, a great favourite of Ormonde's, went to keep Christmas with him, and was set upon and murdered by the young James FitzGerald's servants, Piers Roe – exasperated beyond measure – sent to England an impeachment against James's father, the Earl of Kildare. But this rebounded against him, since Kildare's new father-in-law, the Marquis of Dorset, had greater influence than he did at court, being a member of the royal family. Dorset prevailed to have a set of commissioners sent over to Dublin to examine the matter – and as they were extremely partial to the Marquis, they inevitably found in Kildare's favour.

The Butler lands and interests were much divided between Munster and Leinster, but Piers Roe's activities were always directed towards The Pale and the south-east. His links with Waterford and Wexford were close, but they had always to meet the rivalry of the Kildares, who once they had consolidated a foothold in Carlow were anxious to retain their control of the river valleys that led down to Waterford harbour. As a result, they would inevitably side with Butler enemies.

For example, when Piers Roe was in conflict with the O'Briens on the borders of Tipperary throughout the 1520s, the Kildares aided them against him, at least to begin with, only relinquishing their support in November 1523. But, equally, the Butlers were as quick to side with Kildare's opponents when it suited their purpose, with Piers Roe intervening in affairs outside his territory; as when the Earl of Desmond was in controversy with the FitzGeralds over their refusal to accept the Earl's gallowglasses around the same time. On this occasion, Desmond was besieged in Dungarvan Castle by a force including Piers Butler, and Desmond had escaped only with difficulty by sea.

But it was a considerable blow to Piers's prestige when, to make an unacceptable situation even worse, the Irish commissioners removed him in 1524, and appointed Kildare's son Gerald deputy in his stead. On 13 May, the Earl of Kildare himself was re-appointed Viceroy, even as three commissioners from England arrived to investigate further complaints against him. Fortunately for Kildare, they found for him, and he was confirmed in office. His installation was a uniquely splendid affair at which Con O'Neill carried the sword of state.

The King, though, to show that Ormonde's removal from office was in no way connected to his personal displeasure (and not wishing to lose so valuable a servant), made Piers the Lord Treasurer of Ireland, and Piers's place in Henry's esteem seemed assured. But during these wild times, other relatives of the Butlers were also acting provocatively, and some of them were openly in league with the hereditary enemy. The Earl of Desmond, a distant cousin, 'meditating a rebellion', had sent to the French for aid, and was charged with high treason for entering into a treaty with the King of France. Orders were sent to Kildare, who was also a near relation of the rebellious Desmond, to seize him when he refused to attend the court convened to answer these charges. But although Kildare made token forays into Munster, he never actually confronted the forces of his defiant cousin, partially armed by the French. (Instead he gave them private notice of his own intention to create an uprising against the English Crown.)

For this projected insurrection, he had engaged the equally anti-English Byrnes clan to join him, and by a letter sent on 18 July 1526, he also invited the Desmonds to meet him at Ossary, with the obvious intention of raising a force against the Crown forces. When this letter was intercepted, Kildare was once more arrested and sent to England, ostensibly to answer charges arising out of his failure to arrest Desmond. In London, he was impeached, imprisoned in the Tower, and examined by the Council, but was then, for some reason, 'enlarged' upon bail. (That is, he had in some way made amends for his crime, possibly by the payment of a colossal fine. It was said that several influential dukes had stood bail for him, and afterwards helped to restore him to royal favour.) In the event, the charges against him, if not exactly dropped, were never pressed.

But that Kildare did have seditious plans is borne out, shortly before his arrest, by a meeting of the principal men of Ireland, which had been held in Dublin, and over which he had presided. Earls, barons, knights and other eminent men intended to 'form a league', and to reconfirm their peace in the presence of the Lord Justice. That such men, long at odds with each other, should decide to unite can only be explained by their allegiance to the Kildare cause. Fortunately for the English government, even after the conspirators had debated and argued upon every covenant that had ever been entered into between them 'until that time', it was still found impossible for them to be reconciled to each other. 'They returned to their homes, and strife of war between them was renewed.'[19]

Some members of the Butler family were inevitably involved in these conflicts – since their clan loyalties were by now inextricably divided between English and Irish interests – which often led to confrontations between themselves. In spite of Lord James Butler's efforts to hold them together, they were riven by internal dissension. An example of this is the defeat given by the son of MacPierce Butler to the sons of Edmund, a natural son of Earl Thomas, in 1526. That this battle was a sizeable affair is shown by the huge number of chieftains and cavalry killed in that defeat, along with many mercenaries.

In the two years from 1526 to 1528 both King Henry and Cardinal Wolsey showed an astonishing disregard for the interests of the Irish lordship, despite the fact that the English government had plenty of evidence that The Pale was almost uniquely weak and defenceless. Its administration, in the absence of the only two men with the power to sustain it in some measure, was vulnerable to every minor attack from outside, if no possible help was at hand. Yet not a single soldier was dispatched in keeping The Pale, and the reputation of the Dublin administration with it, intact. Consequently, these were the years when the authority of the Irish government reached its lowest point, and it was only the forbearance of the greater Irish chieftains, men such as O'Neill and O'Brian, that allowed it to survive, shattered though it was by the raids of the minor Irish commanders.

Sir Thomas FitzGerald appeared to assist the officials in Dublin in an attempt to organise The Pale for defence during 1526, but he felt that he had not the full support of the other members of the Council, and he resigned his office before 14 September 1527. During the Earl of Kildare's detention in England, O'Neill and his allies did all they could to obstruct the government of Piers Roe, and it was made apparent that a stronger hand than his was needed; Sir William Skeffington was sent to take over the Deputyship. FitzGerald's failure is probably due to the fact that the lesser Meath magnates were now, as they had attempted to do in the past, trying to shake themselves loose from FitzGerald dominance, to which they had submitted from 1496.

They would have made a better showing if they had been given English money with which to hire troops. But the new Deputy had no financial help, since Irish revenues had run out, and he was therefore forced to oppress the people of The Pale even more than his predecessor had done, in the sheer effort to keep his management alive. He was in fact so desperate for money that he stopped paying the 'black rent' that had long been paid to Irish chieftains to dissuade them from raiding English territory. The final straw came when the Deputy Governor was ambushed and taken hostage, the price of his release being the return of Kildare to Ireland.

Lord James Butler, who was with the government party during this surprise attack, was allowed to go free, having a safe conduct, despite the fact that he was a known enemy (Sir Thomas FitzGerald had been involved in the kidnapping). Officials stressed to the Duke of Norfolk that The Pale was 'destitute of good capitaynes'[20]. So the English government had little choice than to bring back Sir Thomas FitzGerald, this time as 'a generall captaine for these parties'[21], as by this time the Butlers were too far away, and too preoccupied. James Butler stressed that the whole affair had been inspired by 'the Erll of Kildare, his counsaillours and band'[22], and he appears to have been correct in this assumption, with Sir Thomas FitzGerald's restoration being 'a symbol of its success'.

By 1528, though, the Butler family was deeply involved in a more private form of warfare, one in which the officers were lawyers, as they settled a dynastic quarrel of their own.

As long ago as May 1510, Anne St Leger and George, her son, had appointed Sir James Boleyn to act for them, and to receive all issues of their lands in Ireland. For the next eighteen years, Anne and her sister would contest the fate of the Irish lands, even after they had been confirmed to the heir male, Piers Butler, in 1516. (When King Henry had also appeared to recognise Piers's right to the title, Irish lands, and to the traditional prisage of wines in Ireland. The Irish patent of recognition on 6 April 1516 and the decision of the Court of the Exchequer were entered on Memoranda Rolls 7–8 Henry VIII. This had been something of a challenge by Kildare to the authority of the King, and it may not ever have been formally communicated to him for fear of reprisals!) But the heirs general would not abandon their claim, and the King left the final disposition of the earldom in suspense.

James Boleyn was again chosen to conduct the case for their restitution, and he was able to assemble the documents that were formerly in the possession of the 7th Earl of Ormonde (the 7th Earl's papers coming into the hands of the Crown through the Boleyn family.) But now, the continual affronts to the Polestown Butlers – who, whatever their faults, had proved to be more loyal to the Lancastrians than were many other nobles now accepted by the Tudors – were to be further added to by the inconsiderate actions of King Henry VIII.

For the King, having for so long wavered over the full acceptance of Piers as the Earl of Ormonde, (although when appointing Piers to the office of Treasurer of Ireland in May 1524 he had been described as such), now asked Piers to make a complete sacrifice of the title. For this was the time of Anne Boleyn's sexual ascendancy over Henry VIII, who had already created her father Viscount Rochford in 1525, as his daughter rose higher in royal favour; and now Henry wanted the Ormonde earldom to give as a gift to Rochford. In 1527, while Piers was visiting England, a 'friendly' compromise was reached by which he surrendered his title and claims, after it had been explained to him that Sir Thomas Boleyn 'was very desirous of the title', and the besotted King wished to honour his future father-in-law with it. The reason behind this being that it was the one title regarded as the most appropriate for him, as the grandson of the 7th Earl.

King Henry was never a man 'to disoblige with safety', and Sir Piers, while loathe to relinquish the title, but ill-at-ease in Henry's court and 'dreading his displeasure', chose to resign it rather than draw upon himself King Henry's resentment. For the loss of his ancient honour, he received a fee of creation of 10*l* a year out of the farm of Waterford. A tripartite indenture to settle all claims was drafted on 18 February 1528, between the King, Sir George St Leger, Sir Thomas Boleyn, Piers Butler and his son James:

> Summary witness whereas contentions have arisen between Dame Anne etc and Sir Piers and James to the title of Earl of Ormonde, and the castles etc., etc., belonging thereto; the two parties by mediation of Thomas, Cardinal Archbishop of York [Wolsey] agreed upon the following:
> 1. That the title, etc., of the Earl of Ormonde and annuity of 10*l* shall be at the deposit of the King.
> 2. That Piers and James shall renounce all right to the title and annuity, and agree to do any acts required by the King for further exclusion from the title, etc.
> 3. And Dame Anne, etc shall surrender the title and annuity to the King, which he accepts.[23]

Piers Butler was allowed two manors, which had been the gift of Edward III, while Anne held on to the castles of Carrickfergus. Kilkenny Castle went to Piers, along with the manor of Gowran, perhaps because these two important residences were seen as essential to the safeguarding of the country. He also had land to the west part of the Barrow River, except for certain manors that he could only hold for thirty years, and for which he was to recompense Anne. The lease was to be determined 'at the King's pleasure'.

Each party could claim in court by written evidence that the claimant had the true title, the matter to be attested before the Lord Chancellor, 'whose opinion being declared into the parties by writing, the said parties shall obey such opinions as a final judgement'.[24] After thirty years had elapsed, every person to the two-party agreement was to be excluded from making claim against any other party; providing that neither party made any claim to the title of Ormonde or the annuity of 10*l*.

As compensation, in the nineteenth year of his reign, the King created Piers Earl of Ossary, 'with great pomp at Windsor', and he assigned him a creation annuity of 20*l* a year out of the manor of Newcastle, in County Dublin. On the passing of a new Irish Absentee Act by the Irish Parliament in May 1536, the Ormonde title, and the greater part of the Ormonde lands, reverted to the Crown, since the newly created Earl of Ormonde was resident only in England. Because of this, the arrangement of 1528 was terminated, and the earldom was, for a time, extinguished.

Henry VIII, to further induce Piers to surrender the title of Ormonde, had, by letters patent granted him, and his wife Margaret, four manors, castles, rents, along with the chief rent of Downmoyan in County Kilkenny. With these properties went two other places in Tipperary, by service of one knight's fee, but these were never enough for Piers Butler. On Anne Boleyn's death in 1536, he would petition to have the whole of the Ormonde property in Ireland returned to him, as the male heir of the 7th Earl.

There was great opposition to this from Lord Grey (a distant relative), and the Irish Council, who urged that King Henry should take the opportunity created by this break in the lineage to have the entire palatinate of Tipperary abolished. But the King, who had never failed to appreciate the Irishman's unique value to his cause in Ireland, once more acknowledged Piers' claim, and granted to him, and also to his son Lord James, certain manors that had been comprised in the former Butler lordship, along with other grants. In the next year, Piers had the family title fully restored and confirmed to him, and he recovered the palatinate power of most of the Irish lands.

But for a brief and extraordinary period the title had passed out of the Butler family, though their forfeiture lasted no longer than it took for Anne Boleyn to reign as Queen, and by the time Piers regained the older title, he was in possession of another. For when Henry restored the Ormonde earldom to him Piers was also allowed to keep that of Ossary, with a grant of all the property of that earldom. (But for which the newly recreated Earl and his heir were forced to fight the Desmonds, who owned one of the Ossary castles, at Dungarven.)

Piers Butler was by then regarded as the most experienced warrior in Ireland, and was famous for his 'mighty English heart' (having, it would seem, largely repudiated his mother's Irish blood). King Henry had restored his title largely in consideration of Piers' eminent services, 'lately performed in the wars of Ireland. Even for spilling his blood in his Majesty's wars against the Geraldines and others'.[25]

For back in 1528, in the same year that he surrendered the Ormonde earldom, Piers Butler had returned from England and been sworn in – under his new title of Earl of Ossory – as the Lord Deputy of Ireland, one of the main signs of his success at King Henry's court. Granted the deputyship in August 1528, Piers made his way to his political headquarters by way of his southern possessions, and he did not bother to reach Dublin until October. The snub to these Anglo-Irish citizens may have been deliberate, repaying them for their lack of enthusiasm for his earlier efforts, but

Ossary was also trying to emphasise that The Pale must now learn to live with its Gaelic neighbours if it was to avoid being ruined by them.

On arrival in Dublin, to his distress, and to that of his newly-formed government, he learned that the Earl of Kildare had once again turned against him, employing his daughter Lady Slane to stir up the O'Neills and O'Connors, encouraging them to ravage the new Earl's lands. Which 'they readily did, committing great waste there, upon which all pensions formerly granted to Ireland were suppressed'.[26]

Piers Roe, who had hitherto been on good terms with both Earls of Kildare, firstly his father-in-law and then with his wife's brother, now found – ironically enough, in view of his recognition by the Great Earl – that the Kildares were intolerant rivals. Although perhaps a major cause of the strife was that Piers refused to compensate his brother-in-law for the two thirds of the income lost to them from the Butler properties, which the Kildares had enjoyed while the title was held by the absentee Thomas of Ormonde.

Relations were made no easier by the fact that Kildare had lands of his own in Kilkenny and Tipperary. Or that one of the men that Kildare had dismissed from his employment was a certain Robert Cowley, who now put his legal talents and an able and vindictive pen at Piers Roe's service. The new Earl now proved as willing to carry complaints against the Earl of Kildare to the English Court, as Kildare had been to carry complaints against his last great rival, James *Dubh*. (In doing this, Piers may have initially been more encouraged to do so in the hope that English recognition of his earlier title would follow as a result of this further display of 'loyalty'.)

Lord James Butler became deeply involved in border warfare with Desmond in the south, while his father spent several months in putting The Pale's defences into some order; and it is a testament to Piers' loyalty to the Crown that he continued in this thankless task. Indeed, he may not have thought too highly of the deputyship granted to him, since the King's new concessions to him as the Earl of Ossary now involved him heavily in the midlands and the south, if he was to safeguard his new possessions effectively.

The situation in Munster was again serious since the Earl of Desmond, in carrying on his campaign of attrition against the southernmost Butler lands, was able to find an ally, and a surprising one, in Pier's illegitimate son, Edmund Butler, Archbishop of Cashel. Edmund, who had studied at Oxford, was a member of the Privy Council in Ireland, and had held an important provincial synod at Limerick in 1529. Now, he joined up with his cousin, James, Baron of Dunboyne, who was married to Joan, Piers's daughter, and the two of them supported Desmond against father and father-in-law.

Desmond, who had sought an alliance with France, had seen it come to nothing as a result of the French defeats of 1525. Now he sought a compact with the Holy Roman Emperor, the uncle of Catherine of Aragon, since Henry VIII had become embroiled with him in his efforts to set his first wife aside. With him, Desmond attempted to negotiate a pact that would give him arms and assistance against the English King – or, more particularly – against the Earl of Ossary and his son James. Lord James showed himself to be an astute politician when challenged, mobilising a number of influential local people in a makeshift army (among them being Desmond's uncle, Sir Thomas FitzGerald, who was his heir to the earldom). The fighting that followed seems to have concentrated largely in County Waterford, where Richard Poer, Desmond's other ally, was routed, leaving the way to Dungarvan open to the Butlers. (This explains the grant of Dungarvan to the new Earl of Ossary in 1528: for if he were able to install himself in that particular fortress, he would have a powerful bulwark against Desmond in the all-important south.)

The Butlers made good headway in 1528, and their eventual defeat of Desmond forced him to flee for a time to seek shelter in Thomond. Although he made something of a comeback in 1529, his death on 18 June removed one of the main obstacles to Butler dominance in the south. However, although the Desmond question may have been temporarily settled, they were then faced with a new problem when Sir William Skeffington was sent to Ireland to report on the military situation there. Sir Thomas More was also one of those recommended to go to Ireland as a deputy, in order to relieve Ossary of his commitments in The Pale. After assessing the Irish situation, it was decided – an unprecedented step – to put the chief governorship into the commission of a 'secret council', which was set up to represent the 'authority of the King's deputy here'.[27] Ossary, relieved of a position he had not really prized, was made one of the Justices of the Peace for his own territory, in Kilkenny, Tipperary and Ormond. He was to administer these areas in the King's name, and this was a solution that must have been to his ultimate satisfaction.

He was to cooperate closely with the new (and more amenable) Earl of Desmond, his wife's nephew, although any disputes with him were to be submitted to arbitration, should the old rivalry between the two houses flare up. Ossary was in this way left to take best care of his new gains and to consolidate his somewhat impaired position in the Butler heartland. His removal from the deputyship had implied no disgrace, he was at no time considered to have failed in his duty. The new decision simply recognised that his primary concerns, for the time being at least, were with the midlands and the south.

The Duke of Richmond and Somerset, the natural son of Henry VIII, was appointed Lord Lieutenant of Ireland in 1530;[28] but even before that decision Piers Roe had lost the office of Lord Deputy, through the machinations of Archbishop Alen and others. Sir William Skeffington had come over in 1529 to be the King's special commissioner in Ireland, and at the

Duke of Richmond's return he was left as Lord Deputy, but Sir William soon lost his place to the Earl of Kildare, who had returned to Ireland with him. In 1530 Skeffington and Kildare combined to attack the O'Mores throughout the midlands, and in 1531 Skeffington laid waste much of Ulster. But Kildare, once he was in possession of the supreme power, used it also to invade Kilkenny with his government-backed forces, and there he destroyed all that he could belonging to Piers Butler and his friends.

In fact, throughout this entire period, the newly won prestige of the Ormonde Butlers was under threat from various quarters, including that of the clergy. But Piers Roe may have earned the enmity of the Archbishop of Dublin not so much by his own actions as by those of his own illegitimate son, the Archbishop of Cashel, who had convened a synod at Limerick where it was decreed that ecclesiastics could be arrested for debt. This ruling was certainly unpopular with the lower clergy, who considered it a breach of their ecclesiastic privileges; and Archbishop Alen who, like most highly placed churchmen resented any secular interference in church law, may have believed that this essentially doctrinal decision had been influenced by Piers. He certainly sympathised with the lower clergy, and he revenged them by seeking Piers's dismissal. Alen himself, following his friend Thomas Wolsey's fall from power in October 1529, had been forced to plead for a pardon, since he was Wolsey's choice for commissioner; and he was afterwards replaced as Lord Chancellor by the Archbishop of Armagh, but this came too late to save Piers Roe.

In 1532 Piers's second son, Thomas, was killed by Dermot fitzPatrick, who was the displaced heir to the earldom of Ossary, the murder being in retaliation for the loss of his title. (King Henry's offhand bestowal of an existing earldom upon a man with no real claim on it had understandably created fresh hostility towards the Butler family. Piers should perhaps have held out for a defunct earldom rather than an existing one; although there had never been any question of him giving up an ancient title in return for a newly created one, since there was no distinction in that.) Yet the power of the Butlers prevailed, and not long after the murder, Dermot was personally delivered up to Piers Roe by his own brother in order to stave off reprisals against the fitzPatricks. Incarcerated in a Butler dungeon, Dermot lived out the rest of his short life in fetters, 'in revenge for his son, and of every other misdeed which Dermot had committed against him up to that time'.[29]

The restoration of Kildare in 1532 established things on an old footing, and the people of The Pale were soon complaining about their kinsman Con O'Neill's actions against them, since he seemed able to plunder them at will. To support himself by force in his post of Lord Lieutenant, and to carry out his measures more effectively, Kildare had married off two of his daughters to Irish chieftains who were the most obstinate enemies of the English Crown. Others had followed his lead; and in this way the whole

country was becoming 'in a manner entirely Irish', with the English tenants and other inhabitants being expelled. This naturally led to an outcry,
with Piers Butler, Skeffington and others of the Irish Council, employing
the Master of the Rolls to prosecute their affairs at Court. The King sent
for Kildare to attend him in England, to explain his conduct, but Kildare
naturally sought every pretext not to cross the sea. None of his excuses
were accepted, and the delays made him ever more suspect to the English
government, for it was now obvious that Kildare was playing for total
control of Ireland.

The first half of the 1530s was eventful for both England and Ireland.
In October 1529 Cardinal Wolsey had been dismissed as Chancellor of
England for his failure to effect a divorce between the King and Catherine
of Aragon. On 11 February 1531 Henry VIII had been recognised by the
convocation of Canterbury as 'Supreme Head of the Church of England',
and in January 1533 the King – after an 'Anglican' divorce – had married the cousin of the Butlers, Anne Boleyn, (who is said to have born in
Ireland, in an Ormonde castle).

On 11 July the Pope excommunicated Henry VIII, and the stage was
set for the total reform of ecclesiastical life in England, and even more
catastrophically in Ireland also. In that year, too, Kildare had made his
own changes in the Church of Ireland, when, after convening a special
parliament, he had confirmed the supremacy of the archiepiscopal see of
Armagh over that of Dublin. In September, following furious representa-
tions from the Irish Council to the King over this scandal, Kildare was
summoned to England, and the Earl cynically replied by sending his *wife*
to answer the charges.

But Kildare knew that he could not avoid the King's wrath for much
longer. Once he had furnished all his castles – particularly Maynooth and
Ley –with ammunition and arms (from the King's store), and having also
liberally supplied the 'Irish enemy' with the same, he sailed for England
in November 1526. He could not, however, have left a worse substitute in
his place, for his young son, Lord Offaly – known to his many enemies
as 'Silken' Thomas – was a 'forward, rash youth, scarce twenty-one years
old'.[30] To aggravate matters further, young Thomas was always supported
in his recklessness by the English-hating Con O'Neill, his brother-in-law.

On his arrival in London, the Earl of Kildare was arrested on the King's
orders, and 'lodged' in the Tower. In May the appointment of Sir Patrick
Finglas as Chief Justice of the King's Bench in Ireland over Kildare's vehement protests signalled a new direction of constitutional reform 'across
the water'. (Thomas Cromwell had replaced Cardinal Wolsey as Lord
Chancellor and was then drafting most of the Reformation legislation.)
That these reforms in Ireland also took in the new religion is borne out
by the rapidity with which Piers and James Butler, now charged with the
government of Kilkenny, Waterford and Tipperary, adopted the Protestant

faith. Pledged to resist 'the abuse and usurped jurisdiction of the Bishop of Rome',[31] they sought to secure its passage through the Irish Parliament.

A report having been spread in Ireland that Kildare had been beheaded at London, his son, 'goaded into rebellion' by this rumour without waiting to discover the truth of the report, went on the warpath. The impetuous Silken Thomas had already declared against the 'Protestant' King. 'He rendered up the Lord Deputy's Sword [of State] in a rage [upon hearing of King Henry's renunciation of the Catholic Church], having denounced the King as a heretic.' Now he renounced all obedience to the King, and after raising an insurrection, he besieged the castle at Dublin.

He entered the city at the head of 140 horse and a thousand men, and the terrified Archbishop of Dublin attempted to flee to England without success; after being driven ashore by contrary winds at Clontarfe, he was murdered by Silken Thomas's followers. The young hothead had by this time assembled all the forces that he could, raising a 'numerous army of English and Irish', with all his troops enraged by the new religious edicts. After encamping for a while within the English Pale, and forcing an oath of confederacy from the 'prime gentlemen of the country', he left a party of men to continue the encirclement of Dublin Castle, and then marched to invade the country of his main enemy, the Earl of Ossary, a decision that was as inevitable, considering their ancient enmity, as it was foolish.

But Piers and James Butler had forces in readiness, 'to oppose his violence', and any anticipated success was prevented by the combined vigilance of father and son, who always worked well together. As they did now, on every occasion that Thomas challenged them on his forays into their territory, until FitzGerald, 'becoming doubtful of the outcome',[32] in view of the strong measures they had taken to prevent him gaining a victory, sought to buy them off. He sent the two men 'divers messages and letters' containing various proposals; and in one in particular, to Lord James Butler, he put forward the idea of dividing the kingdom between the FitzGeralds and the Butlers, letting James have half of it, if he would join him in the enterprise. James's reply was masterly:

> Taking pen in hand to write you my absolute answer, I muse in the first line by what name to call you, my *lord* or my *cousin*, seeing your notorious treason hath impeached your loyalty and honour, and your desperate lewdness hath shamed your kindred. You are by your expressions so liberal in parting stakes with me, that a man would weene you had no right to the game; and so importunate for my company, as if you would perswade me to hang with you for good fellowship. And think you that James is so mad as to gape for gudgeons, or so ungracious as to sell his truth and loyalty for a piece of Ireland? Were it so, (it cannot be), that the chickens you reckon were both hatch'd and feather'd; yet be thou sure, I had rather in

this quarrel dye thine enemy, than live thy partner. For the kindness you proffer me of good will in the end of your letter, the best way I can propose to requite you, that is, in advising you, though you have fetch'd your fence, yet to look well before you ever leap over [it]. Ignorance, error, and a mistake of duty hath carried you unawares to this folly, not yet so rank, but that it may be cured. The King is a vessel of mercy and bounty: your words against his Majesty shall not be counted malicious, but only bulked out of heat and impotency, except yourself, by heaping of offences, discover a mischievous and wilful meaning. Farewell.[33]

'Nettled by this answer', Offaly, assisted by O'Neill and other Irish chieftains, ravaged all the county of Kilkenny as far as Thomastown, dangerously close to the core of Butler domination. In fact, FitzGerald almost pulled off a coup quite early in their skirmishing, when, advancing with a small party to Jerpoint, Lord James was suddenly attacked by a strong body of the enemy's cavalry. Although several of these horsemen were killed in this action, the Butler troops were eventually overpowered, and they dispersed. James himself was wounded in the fighting, and he rode from the field to his house at Dunmore, near Kilkenny. He stayed there until his wounds were cured, and it was discovered that not as many of his men as he feared had been killed in the action, so that he could re-form to face the enemy again.

His father – alarmed by this unexpected setback – now assembled a greater force and advanced against the rebels to engage them in battle. Surprisingly, his opponents were easily crushed, with FitzGerald almost immediately quitting the territory, despite the fact that he had held – temporarily, at least – the upper hand. But intent upon creating as much havoc as it was possible to wreak, he marched back towards the English Pale, committing all the outrages that an undisciplined army could upon 'the King's subjects in those parts';[34] especially upon the citizens of Dublin, who had declared against him, and had set upon the party he had left to besiege the castle. Retaliating, FitzGerald forced the inhabitants of The Pale to join his army, and he again surrounded the capital with all his military strength.

But Sir William Skeffington, Master of Ordnance, and again Lord Deputy, landed soon after, with supplies from England, to raise the siege. He arrived in October 1534, with an army of 2,300 troops, and marching to the relief of Drogheda he proclaimed Silken Thomas a traitor. From this time on, FitzGerald's triumphs on the battlefield grew fewer, and in the next year he lost his 'impregnable' castle of Maynooth, and others fell to the English soon after. The fight for Maynooth Castle is the first recorded uses of siege guns in Ireland, and it was taken after less than a week's bombardment. In the cynically named 'Pardon of Maynooth', Skeffington put the entire garrison to the sword, explaining scornfully that 'We thought it expedient to put them to execution as an example to others'[35].

Thomas FitzGerald was roundly defeated in a general engagement with the Deputy's forces, although he was given a fleeting respite when Sir William Skeffington fell sick, dying at Kilmainham. Yet he managed, in fact, to hold out until 26 July 1535, when he finally submitted, with Con O'Neill among his troop, to Lord Grey at Drogheda. Lord Grey was then Lord Deputy, arriving in July as Marshal of the Army, his sole aim being to suppress the rebellion.

But if FitzGerald had hoped to cut a deal with the King, from a comparative position of strength still, since even though broken he yet wielded much influence among his father's people, he had gravely erred. Grey sent him, along with five of his uncles, to London – where all were executed, as common criminals, on the gallows at Tyburn, a humiliating end to a proud life. His father, the Earl of Kildare, had not lived to witness this particular humiliation, since he had died some months before in the Tower of London, of grief, it was said, for his son's 'extravagances'.

These 'extravagances' had ultimately worked to the Butler family's advantage, since they inevitably benefitted – not only by the removal of their greatest rivals from the political scene – but also materialistically from their rival's downfall. For it was upon the conviction and spectacular forfeiture of the Kildare clan, that King Henry gave the Earl of Ossary, and his son, all the manors, and the other possessions in the county of Catherlogh, that had belonged to them.

With Lord Grey back in England, Piers's son James took over the King's forces in Ireland, and marching to Clonmel, he 'extinguished the remainder of the rebellion'.[37] Kildare's strongest bastions within the sphere of Butler influence fell to him in rapid succession. Dungarven immediately surrendered, and Youghal, Cork, Mallow, Kilmallock and Cashel all submitted after a token resistance. James very rapidly put the country 'into a state of quietness', although this did not last long, for once having seen off the unruly Kildares, the Butlers now had to deal with their other fractious kinsfolk, the Desmonds. When the head of that family died, his heir – a 'turbulent man' – raised new disturbances in Munster.

But he was 'timely opposed' by his cousin, James Butler, who 'wasted his lands in Limerick'; and who also repaired and garrisoned the castle of Lochguir, 'to suppress his sudden excursions'.[38] James, backed up by the new deputy's forces, marched with two armies against this new insurgent, and – having sharply defeated him – accepted his submission. The Earl of Desmond took an oath of fidelity to the King.

Even here the situation was complicated, for the new Lord Deputy was a son of the Marquis of Dorset, and therefore allied to the Desmonds through marriage. So although he had marched against his kinsfolk in the company of James Butler, he still – 'out of pique' – sent part of his army to waste the lands of his ally's father, the Earl of Ossary. (This was a practice common at the time, at least with the government of Ireland. Even when entrusted with the King's service, individual families would still gratify their private passions and resentments, and turn upon those men they were obliged to support.)

But with much of Leinster crushed, and – by a legal fiction – forfeit to the Crown, more active policies directed to the subjugation of the whole of Ireland now seemed at last to be feasible (although the implementation would prove slow, arduous and costly).

The year 1536 was a momentous one for the English of England and Ireland. In April the King forbade any Irish usage and customs, although at first only in Galway, and in May the 'Reformation Parliament' met in London to pass the Act of Supremacy, which made Henry VIII the Supreme Head of the Church of England. On 19 May Anne Boleyn, having failed to produce the desired male heir, was beheaded for crimes which her prosecutors could not prove, and in July the 'Ten Articles', the confession of faith of the Anglican Church, as approved by the King, were published. As importantly for the Butlers, in that same year Parliament attainted the FitzGeralds, and an act resuming to the Crown the land of absentee landlords in Ireland was passed. For the rest of Piers's life, his family would be supreme in his country.

Parliament in England refused to pass taxation bills and bills for the suppression of certain monastic houses in England and Ireland, and Henry VIII demanded that Ireland be made self-supporting, with savings to be made by reducing expenditure on the army. This was always the Crown's answer to the Irish problem, but for a time these economies had little effect on military successes in the country. Lord Grey, having ravaged the territory of the O'Connors in Offaly, took Dungan Castle, County Meath, and the Earl of Desmond, convinced perhaps by the example of the near obliteration of the FitzGerald clan, renewed his offer of loyalty to the King. And to show good will, he attempted to reduce the whole of Munster (ironically much of it still owned by the ever-loyalist Butlers) to obedience to the Crown.

The first step towards the total conquest of Ireland was to give Henry VIII control of the Irish Church, and to provide him with capital by dissolving the monasteries there, as was then being done in England. So the state 'Church of Ireland' was called into being in 1537. From the beginning to today this would be the church of the minority, for Protestantism was something alien, introduced by English officials and planters.

The year 1538 began well for the Butlers, for on 22 February, the Ormonde earldom was irreversibly returned to Piers, Earl of Ossory, and he was now unassailably the Earl of Ormonde. Whether, in his new role of Protestant, he participated in the increasingly punitive measures against the Catholic majority is not recorded. In mid-August 1538 there was a public burning in Christ Church Place, Dublin of religious objects of great antiquity, including the so-called 'staff of Jesus', and the (perhaps) more genuine staff of St Patrick, along with an ancient statue of Our Lady of Trim. In November the Augustinian house of All Hallows was handed over to the King's commissioners, the first religious house in Dublin to be suppressed.

In the following year, a commission was issued to the Dublin government – at which Piers certainly took his place – to take the surrender of, and to suppress, all the monasteries, and to destroy all images that were objects of popular idolisation and pilgrimage. Proclamations ordered the clergy to instruct the laity in the 'right use and effect' of religious ceremonies; that is in the duller forms of Protestant worship. As not only Irish peasants, but also most of the middling classes, were passionately devout – if wonderfully superstitious – Christians, the papal brief which excommunicated all those who accepted King Henry's religious supremacy in Ireland created huge divisions within their communities.

Since Piers Butler was said to be a man of intense piety (which before Henry's revolution had presumably meant being at least conventionally Catholic), it is hard to see how he accommodated himself to the new religion. For many years it had been his practice, for the last fortnight in Lent, to retire to a room near St Kenny's church in Kilkenny, called *Paradise*.[39] There he prayed, contemplated and gave alms, only returning to his castle on Easter Eve. As a pious Catholic but also a loyal royalist, his personal reaction to the 'heresy and new error' of Henry's church reforms, which reached Ireland in 1537, must have been extreme. The Irish considered that they had 'sprung up in England through pride, vainglory, avarice and lust, and through many strange sciences',[40] a conclusion that was conceded by many intellectuals of the time. It must have been as equally clear to even the most backward of Ormonde's tenants, and been even clearer to himself. So, at best, Piers' hasty change of religion may only have been a temporary measure.

Fortunately for Piers, his loyalty to the new monarchy or the Old Church was never put to the question, since he died within two years of this fresh calamity for Ireland. But the enigma remains; he was regarded in his own lifetime as a man of great honour and sincerity, and yet he had swiftly cast off his religious beliefs in what must seem a cynical act of self-preservation, perhaps largely because he shared at least three of King Henry's declared imperfections: pride, vainglory and avarice. He was said to have been infinitely good-natured, and he was also described as a plain man, kind and loving, familiar and liberal to his friends, but a great scourge to his enemies.

His wife Margaret, the daughter of Gerald FitzGerald, Earl of Kildare, was in many ways even more remarkable than her husband, regarded as 'a person of great wisdom and courage, uncommon in her sex'.[41] Despite the bad blood between their two families, Piers and Margaret were seen to live very happily together, and 'with great regularity'. Their marriage was a singular success, and fairly unique for the times in that it was a more or less equal partnership. They did much to improve the local economy within all their widespread holdings, bringing skilled craftsmen and manufacturers from Flanders, whom they employed at Kilkenny, 'in working tapestries, diapers, Turkey carpets, cushions, etc'.[42] The whole province benefitted from the introduction of these workers in luxury goods.

The Anglo-French civilisation that had died out in the rest of the colony continued to flourish throughout the Butler territories, particularly around Kilkenny, the capital of the Ormonde earldom. It is probable that, even from earliest times, the Butlers had spoken Gaelic, but they were still considered to be the most English of the 'first families'. Piers Roe Butler, through his grandfather, Edmund MacRichard, was certainly an enthusiast for all things Irish, and his mother was a princely Kavanagh, but he still clung resolutely to the English traditions. Having founded a grammar school at Kilkenny, he welcomed the period of comparative peace in his last years as a further opportunity to bring in foreign refinements, and in these endeavours he was always inspired by his wife, the 'Great Countess'. But unhappily, later troubles would not allow the colony they created to survive.

Piers died in Kilkenny on 26 August 1539, at the age of 72, and he was buried in the chancel of St Kenny's church. His widow later built a schoolhouse in his memory, near the churchyard, 'where many famous men were afterwards educated'.[43] (Indeed, the list of 'old boys' is a roll call of the Irish arts and sciences.)

They had two sons and six daughters. The sons were James, who succeeded his father, and Sir Richard Butler, 'a goodly personage, and as comely a man as could be seen. A very honorable and worldly gentleman, who did great service for the Crown'.[44] For which usefulness he was, on 23 October 1550, in the fourth year of Edward VI's reign, created Viscount Mountgarret in the peerage of Ireland.[45] Sir Richard's first wife would also be a near-relative, Eleanor, a daughter of Theobald Butler of Neigham, County Kilkenny.

Piers had not always been faithful to his wife, however, despite the unusual bond between them. As we have seen, he had at least one natural son: Edmund Butler, who became the Archbishop of Cashel in 1527, and was, not long after this, made one of the Privy Council to Henry VIII.

# *Notes*

1. Curtis, *Calendar of Ormonde Deeds*.
2. Ibid.
3. Ibid.
4. Carte, *Life of the Duke of Ormonde*.
5. Ibid.
6. Ibid.
7. Ibid.
8. Ibid.
9. Ibid.
10. Guelph and Ghibelline; the two political factions that supported either the Pope or the German Emperor during the Middle Ages.
11. Curtis, op. cit.
12. *Calendar of Patent Rolls*.
13. Kildare's behaviour at the Field of the Cloth of Gold is no more insincere than that of Henry VIII or Francis I. Even as they were making separate treaties with other interested parties, Kildare was entering into negotiations with the 'Wild Irish' to invade The Pale.
14. Thomas Howard, 2nd Earl of Surrey (1473–1554), *Dictionary of National Biography*.
15. Ibid.
16. Ibid.
17. Ibid.
18. *Calendar of Patent Rolls*.
19. *Annals of Loch Ce*.
20. *Calendar of Patent Rolls*.
21. Ibid.
22. Curtis, op. cit.
23. Ibid.
24. Ibid.
25. Carte, op. cit.
26. The Four Masters, *Annals of the Kingdom of Ireland*.
27. *Calendar of Patent Rolls, Ireland*.
28. The Duke of Richmond and Somerset: born to Elizabeth Blount, ten years after Henry VIII married Catherine of Aragon. Henry had, at one time, planned to legitimise this son, and make him King.
29. Curtis, op. cit.
30. Carte, op. cit.
31. Ibid.
32. Ibid.
33. Curtis, op. cit.
34. The Four Masters, op. cit.
35. Curtis, *History of Medieval Ireland*

36. Another version has it that upon hearing of Thomas's actions, Kildare did not care to blame him, but only wished that he had 'a little more age and experience'. The Earl is buried in St. Peter's Church within the Tower.
37. Carte, op. cit.
38. Ibid.
39. This room is still much as it was, but is not available for viewing.
40. The Four Masters, op. cit.
41. Margaret Butler, the Countess of Ormonde, had a vehement animosity towards her brother.
42. *Dictionary of National Biography,* under *Sir Piers* (or *Pierce*) Butler.
43. Among others, they included Congreve.
44. The Four Masters, op. cit.
45. The Mountgarrets would become the second line of the Butler dynasty.

# CHAPTER X

# *The Last of the Warriors*

The death of Earl Thomas in 1515 severed an almost unbroken line, for the Ormondes are fairly unique among British aristocrats in that the title was kept within the premier family for some ten generations. But his death also pre-shadowed another change, since it marked the waning of the Middle Ages and the rise of the modern world; he died during the High Renaissance in Europe. If we date the beginning of the new age from 1500 – or even from 1492, the year, the year in which the New World was discovered – this is the turning point of the revolution.

Piers Roe Butler had also lived through another revolution, the religious upheaval brought about by Henry VIII, when huge numbers of Irish, under Kildare, revolted against the King's damnable new Church and its English liturgy. The Anglican religion would remain that of a minority in Ireland from that time until today, although – as politics and government were largely the business of this minority – it would influence life throughout the island for centuries to come. Since Piers Roe died in 1539, only six years after the marriage of King Henry to his kinswoman Anne Boleyn and the Act of Supremacy, he would play no great part in the English Reformation. Yet there is a strong connection between this break with the Catholic religion, with its cross-currents of politics, economics and theology, the dawning of the Renaissance, and the ending of the guardianship of the Pale. The years that followed on from Piers Butler's death were an important period in the history of his family.

For it was during this time of great change that Tudor military enterprise, under the vigorous initiative of Henry VIII, began to make English rule in Ireland effective for the first time since the original invasion. The first conquest had by general admission failed, with the collapse most fully attested in the Poynings Statutes. English rule in Ireland had for generations been more theoretical than effective, and the links between the Irish aristocracy and England had grown much looser than had, for example, those of the Welsh nobility. The indigenous Irish were now virtually free from government control, and the Anglo-Irish upper classes were more tempted to align themselves with their Irish neighbours than with the English over the sea.

Henry had been repeatedly forced to send an army to Ireland to quell any number of disturbances, and it had become apparent that the Irish could not be subdued until the *whole* of their country was under English control. With the Desmond and FitzGerald clans in disarray – the heir to the earldom of Kildare had been taken in disguise to France, *en route* to Rome – the Butlers, were once more, the 'Guardians of the Pale'. But the Pale itself was no longer viable, and its defensive walls were about to collapse – but to collapse outwards from the pressure within, rather than from attack from without.

The new conquest of Ireland was largely accomplished under the Tudors, in the lifetimes of Red Piers's son and grandson. James, the 9th Earl, was called 'the Lame'; born about 1504, he was brought up at the court of Henry VIII, who made him an esquire of the body in 1527. James could easily have settled in England, and become as English as the 7th Earl, but he would go on to play a great part in Irish politics. Despite being a cripple, James was personally a very brave man, as he had proved in the long running battle with 'Silken James' FitzGerald. Severely wounded in Thomastown, County Kilkenny in 1534, he had later distinguished himself against the Irish rebels in 1535, '36 and '39. A man of great political skill, he was appointed Admiral of Ireland in 1535, and he was also a Privy Councillor during his father's lifetime. In 1539 he was appointed General of the Irish Forces, to serve in Scotland under Lennox.

Along with his father, James had opted to side with the new religion, and he may have been a great deal more sincere in this volte-face than his father had been. He almost certainly benefited financially from his decision to become a Protestant. After 1540, when the last of the 34 monastic communities were voluntarily suppressed, and leases were granted on their dissolved estates, James Butler was in receipt of many of them. But that he was sincere in his change of heart is borne out by his many attempts to win over his fellow peers. On 1 March 1540, when the Protestant faith was officially established as the religion of Ireland, James was on hand to explain this matter to the Dublin parliament.[1] At this important assembly, Irish chieftains were allowed to attend proceedings for the first time, and this life-changing manifesto had to be translated for their benefit.

In 1544 James went to Canricard to assist an Irish kinsman, William Burke, then under attack from his dependants, who firmly rejected the new religion; but their party was defeated, with more than forty of Ormonde's troops slain in the gateway of the town wall of Athenry. This kinsman, like many Catholic Irishmen who recognised King Henry VIII as King of Ireland and Supreme Head of the Church, had also been granted an earldom. There were a number of such; and at least one, the Earl of Tyrone, was admitted to the Irish Privy Council, which was overwhelmingly Protestant by this time.

In 1545 James was involved in a dispute with the Lord Justice, and both men sailed for England to settle the argument before the King, with both having sworn that only *one of them* should return to Ireland. And only one of them did, the Tudor era being the hazardous period that it was: Earl James died from drinking poison, taken at a supper at Ely House, London, in October 1546. Whether by accident or design has never been decided, for the poisoner was not identified, and nor was the motive for the murder ever revealed; although because of his support for the new and detested faith it may have been religious in origin.

James was much mourned by the court, but he was buried in Ireland, where it was said that he 'would have been lamented, were it not that he had greatly injured the church by his advice to the heretics'.[2] He had been an invaluable aid to the 'King of Ireland; (an enactment of 1541 had formally declared Henry VIII to be King, instead of the customary Lord, and it was now high treason to impeach this new title). Beyond all other uses, James had made himself the government's interpreter, since all English legislation had to be translated, as most of his fellow noblemen, even those who still clung to Norman surnames and English customs, could now no longer speak the language of their fathers. Like his forebears, and unlike most of his peers, James had always retained his sense of being English.

Perhaps the most remarkable detail in James Butler's life was that he had once almost been engaged to his distant cousin, Anne Boleyn. In 1519 the Earl of Surrey, then Lord Deputy, having made a close acquaintance with them, had been deeply impressed with the Irish Butlers. Seeking for a solution in the dispute over the earldom of Ormonde, he had suggested an arrangement that would satisfactorily tie up several loose ends. The King should recognise Piers Roe's title, and at the same time his son James should be betrothed to Sir Thomas Boleyn's 13-year-old daughter, Anne, which would keep the matter within the family.

Surrey had pushed the plan vigorously for seven months, receiving the backing of both King Henry and Wolsey. Henry was content to support Piers as a workable alternative to Kildare, and Wolsey was prepared to regard him as a back-up candidate if he could win the King's support for FitzGerald. That James was, in fact, one of the King's wards and a member of his household only helped matters. If he were to be married to the daughter of King Henry's friend, and *kept at court*, the government would have a permanent hold over Piers Roe while he lived. These negotiations had stumbled on for several months, but the proposal had come to nothing in the end, perhaps because of some reluctance on Piers's part to have his hands tied in this way.

This failed liaison was actually fraught with significance, for it was in anticipation of her marriage to James Butler that Anne Boleyn was brought from France to make her appearance at the Tudor court. Had this marriage taken place, the entire history of Britain would have had to be rewritten, for there would have been no possibility of *two* divorces being allowed. Henry would have had to seek a brood-mare from another stable, and the English Church might never have materialised.

James, in fact, married an even closer kinswoman, his cousin Lady Joan FitzGerald, and this marriage was, perhaps, also an attempt to keep their differences within the family. This, too, was doomed to failure, for Joan was heiress of the Earl of Desmond, and her later bid to claim the Desmond estates after her father's death, far from creating a new accord between the two families, only stirred up more discord.[3] The Butlers would be embroiled in this fight for the Desmond fortune for decades to come.

The Earl of Desmond had been only one of the many Anglo-Irish, and even native Irish, who had made their peace with King Henry VIII, or 'come into acknowledge their duties towards us', a policy known as 'surrender and regrant'.[4] James FitzGerald, the 13th Earl, had submitted to the Lord Deputy at Cahir in 1541, but almost the whole of Ireland, by the time of James the Lame's death, had been brought into complete subjection, with most Irish chieftains having made their formal submission to 'Great Harry', some of them in England, in the King's presence.

The 10th Earl, Thomas – called 'Black Tom' or 'Tom Duffe', from the darkness of this complexion – was brought up as a Protestant at the English court, and he was the first of the family to formally adopt the new religion; he was 14 years of age at this father's death. As a companion to Edward, Price of Wales, he was knighted at the boy-king's coronation in 1547, and despite his immaturity he was said to have taken part in the battle of Musselburgh a year later.[5]

From boyhood he had been a cause of controversy; and none more so than in 1553, at King Edward VI's death, when priests spread a false report in Ireland that he was also dead, having been murdered in England. The young Earl's Irish tenantry rose up in revolt against the English officials who then managed his estates, believing them to be in some way responsible. This revolt was ruthlessly put down; but a year later, when Thomas set foot in Ireland for the first time in his young life, he did so 'amid great rejoicing on the part of the native population'.

If the young Earl's English upbringing had been designed to estrange him from his Irish background it had singularly failed, since from his first days in Ireland he made it clear that he was open to this new experience, and had a great love for all things Irish. He attempted, even at a very young age, to mediate between his people and their English rulers, and he may even have been secretly sympathetic to their old religion, restored to them briefly by the Catholic Queen Mary I.

He was, in fact, as theologically ambiguous as his distant relative, the Princess Elizabeth, but what is certain is that his loyalty towards the *ideal* of the crown always outweighed any doctrinal scruples. Despite being reared in the new religion, tutored in fact by the same divines who taught Prince Edward, Black Tom proved himself to be surprisingly adaptable in the unstable period that followed the young King's death, when Mary Tudor sought to re-impose papistry on the country. In 1554 he even served as a lieutenant of horse against Sir Thomas Wyatt, during his uprising against the marriage of Queen Mary to Philip of Spain. In Ireland, in 1556, he accompanied the Earl of Sussex into Ulster against the Scots, but most astonishingly – in view of his religious upbringing – he was made a Privy Councillor to the Catholic Mary, in her brief reign. But without, as far as one can ascertain, being asked to conform to the Queen's dogmatic faith.

(By 1556 the Lord Deputy of Ireland had firm instructions from the Queen to advance the Catholic religion, and to punish heretics. More importantly, in the long view, he had also been ordered to create plantations in Leix and Offaly, on which new immigrants from England were to be settled. Conversely, this fresh transfusion of English blood would help to accelerate the spread of Anglicanism in the next reign rather than the Catholicism that she so wished to impose, a complete reversal of Queen Mary's intentions. Her government may have wished only to introduce an English stock into the character of the country, but that strain would be largely Protestant.)

In 1559, after the accession of Elizabeth I, Thomas Butler, who had kept up very friendly relations with the Lord Deputy in Ireland, took an oath as Privy Councillor to the new Queen, acting in the same capacity to Elizabeth as he had to her sister. He also, at the age of 27, became the Lord Treasurer of Ireland, a positioning which his actions were always 'unhappily fettered',[6] but which he would hold for the rest of his life.

Elizabeth I had confirmed Gerald FitzGerald, the 15th Earl of Desmond, in his Irish holdings, and he was soon in dispute with the Earl of Ormonde, whose 'conciliatory disposition' failed to remove the ancient grudge between the two families. The cause of their first dispute was the ownership of three manors, and this was made the pretext for a military demonstration in Tipperary in 1560, when the retainers of both their houses set about each other; but the affair proved abortive, and nothing was achieved. The English government tried to bring their implacable rivalry to an end by a judicial award of the disputed territory, in this particular case to the Earl of Desmond, but any permanent settlement was out of the question.

The 10th Earl of Ormonde opening avowed his Irish sympathies, but at the same time – true to his English upbringing – he was resolved to introduce a respect for the English concept of law and order into the country. From January to February, a session of parliament restored the spiritual supremacy of the Crown, and demanded from all ecclesiastics, judges and all other temporal officers an oath of recognition. The Act of Uniformity demanded attendance at the parish church on a fine of 12*d*

– the recusancy fine – and provided for the use of the Book of Common Prayer. The laws against heresy were repealed, and the Queen's title to the Crown of Ireland was recognised. In June an 'Act for uniformitie of common prayer and service in the Church, and the administration of the sacraments' came into force.

In 1562 Thomas Butler sought to extract from Shane O'Neill, who was by now virtually an independent ruler of Ulster, an acknowledgement of the supremacy of the English Crown and a promise to abstain from further aggression against Ulster chieftains. O'Neill treated Ormonde with 'unusual consideration' and responded to him in ways that he had hitherto not shown – having so far resisted all attempts to reduce him 'to his duty'. He agreed to visit England, but only in Thomas's company (presumably as a security), to come to some settlement with the Queen herself. O'Neill was also willing to submit all his differences to a board of arbitration, at which he desired the Earl to take a seat.

The Elizabethans mostly regarded the native inhabitants of Ireland as a sub-human species, and they were in general appalled by their 'outlandish' appearance, little changed since the time of King John. O'Neill's arrival at court, surrounded by a ferocious-looking guard of axe-men, created a sensation, for they seemed as barbaric to the courtiers as any pagan. When O'Neill confessed to his crime and rebellion 'with howling' (a ritualised keening), this was seen as further evidence of the savage state of his countrymen. The only good thing to come out of Ireland, the Elizabethans believed, was whiskey, 'the best in the world of that kind'. But even here they were shocked by the vast amounts the Irish drank of it.

For the formidable Irishman to visit the English court had been a diplomatic *coup* for Black Tom. But in 1563 O'Neill broke the vague promises he had made, in the tradition of most Irish chiefs, and renewed his attacks on his main rivals in Ulster. Even so, it was with great reluctance that Ormonde – who appears to have genuinely admired O'Neill – aided the Earl of Sussex, then Lord Deputy, in seeking to repress the powerful leader.

Meanwhile, his own quarrel with Desmond grew fiercer, and Munster, where the chief estates of either house lay, was in constant turmoil as a result. Both peers had been summoned to London at the close of 1561, but little had come of their interview with Elizabeth I. For a while, Ormonde tried hard to keep the peace in the face of his enemy's constant aggressions, and late in 1563 he formally complained to Sussex that Desmond was repeatedly harassing his relatives and tenants, and it was 'only fair' he should retaliate. That he should have shown such forbearance towards Desmond is all the more remarkable in that he was a man of explosive temper himself. Given to brawling in the London streets like any common thug, he was committed to the Fleet Prison as late as 1565 for such offences.

He was always to stand high in Elizabeth's favour, though, and he and the Queen appear to have had a special affection for each other. This is borne out by Elizabeth's mysterious nickname for him 'my dark husband', and the fact that he was allowed to take extraordinary liberties in her presence, and – like her chief favourite, the Earl of Leicester – spent many hours with her in private. In turn, he was fanatically loyal to the Queen, who also called him her 'chief pillar in Ireland'.[7]

But not even he could prevent the younger members of this family from taking the field against her, since many of his kinsmen rejected the new Protestant religion, and were prepared to take up arms to defend their own. Tudor attempts anglicise Ireland for the most part failed, and most of Ireland outside the crumbling Pale would remain stubbornly devoted to the old faith. Indeed, in their mutual desire to retain their innate Catholicism, the Anglo-Irish and the native Irish were completely united. Many throughout the Butler clan were also forced to weigh their faith against that of the new religion. Identifying both with the emergent Protestant ascendancy and their 'popish' Irish tenants, they were caught in a pincer-grip.

On 1 July 1564 Ormonde issued a notable proclamation, in which he forbade the exaction of Irish customs within his territories; a decision made in the interests of his poorer dependents. He was contemplating other reforms when an attack by Desmond on his kinsman, Sir Maurice FitzGerald, who promptly sought Ormonde's aid, led to a pitched battle between the supporters of the two earls at Affane, County Waterford, on 1 February 1565. Desmond was wounded by Sir Edmund Butler, Ormonde's brother, and taken prisoner.

Elizabeth, angered by this renewed act of private war, summoned both men again to her presence; but her counsellors were divided as to the degrees of guilt attaching to the offenders, and court factions further aggravated the struggle. The Earl of Sussex insisted that Ormonde was guiltless, while Sussex's rival, Sir Henry Sidney, denied that Desmond had shown disloyalty to the English cause in Ireland. In the end, it was decided that both men should enter into their recognisances in 20,000*l*, to abide by such orders as the Queen might prescribe. Elizabeth, as ever, sympathised with her Butler cousin and the particular attentions she paid him at this time gave rise to some scandalous rumours. But Ormonde felt sufficiently rewarded by her interest to remain at court for the next five years.

Sir Henry Sidney succeeded Sussex as Lord Deputy in January 1566, and was always inclined to favour Desmond, but the Queen invariably insisted that Ormonde's claims in whatever conflict arose 'deserved a higher consideration'. Early in 1567 even the long-suffering Sidney was forced to accept that Desmond's actions verged on the treasonous and he took him prisoner at Kilmallock, County Limerick, sending him to the Tower of London in December of that year. He had visited Munster in June, reporting that the territory was absolutely uncontrolled, and 'as turbulent as it well could be', with Desmond ravaging the area in Black Thomas's absence.

In that same month a commission had been established to enquire into the causes of the differences between the two families, and another was nominated in October to determine the truth of Ormonde's allegations that he had suffered from the Earl of Desmond's aggressions. This time, Sidney could not come to Desmond's defence, and an award was made in Ormonde's favour, with Desmond mulcted in the phenomenal sum of 20,894*l*, 12*s*, 8*d*.

With his main rival Desmond, along with a brother, incarcerated in the Tower, Black Thomas was in the ascendant, in England and at home – even though he (in Sidney's words), 'politickly kept himself in England'. But his continued absence from Ireland began to make him unpopular there, since Edward and Sir Edmund, Ormonde's younger brothers, used their power as his representatives in Munster 'with the utmost cruelty and injustice'.[8] In June 1569 Sir Edmund – who had a personal hatred of Sir Henry Sidney – broke into revolt against the Lord Deputy, invading the barony of Idron, which had been claimed by an 'English adventurer', Sir Peter Carewe. (Sir Edmund worked in temporary concert with certain members of the hereditary enemy, the Desmonds). Sidney asserted that Ormonde's presence was indispensable to the peace of southern Ireland, and the Earl returned home with the Queen's permission, landing at Waterford in July 1569.

There he found Munster in the throes of a virtual civil war, in which his brother Sir Edmund was matched against the adventurer Carewe. Ormonde earnestly tried to arbitrate between the combatants, but Sidney clearly regarded him at the time with deep suspicion, and Ormonde had other, more pressing, worries on his mind. For in October 1569 the Earl of Kildare and his family had been 'restored in blood' by a repeal of the act of attainder of Henry VIII, and Black Tom feared their renewed influence in Ireland, which was by now *his* country.

He had good reason to fear their reappearance on the Irish stage, and his fears were soon justified, since within a few months of their restitution Sir James FitzMaurice, along with his Ulster allies, was planning a new rebellion. Conor O'Brien, Earl of Thomond, 'one of the Munster malcontents', rose up against the Crown, encouraged by the Kildares, protesting at the inclusion of Thomond into the province of Connacht; although he submitted to Thomas Butler a few weeks later.

These outbreaks, savage in the ferocity they unleashed, were dealt with by equally ghastly repression, which took a terrible toll on the civilian population, always the ones to suffer most. In 1569 Sir Humphrey Gilbert 'killed man, woman and child, and spoiled, wasted and burned by the ground all he might, when he was sent to repress the fitzMaurice rebellion'.[9] It was his ghoulish practice to decapitate the corpses of rebel soldiers and set up their heads outside his tent, so that all that came to see him had to pass through a line of these grisly trophies. As an English soldier commented (with approval), 'It did bring great terror to the people when they saw the heads of their dead fathers, brothers, children, kinsfolk and friends lie on the ground before their faces'.[10]

Early in 1570 Ormonde wrote to Sir William Cecil, Queen Elizabeth's Secretary, saying that he and Sir Henry Sidney were now reconciled, and that his crushing of Thomond's rebellion had been a proof of his goodwill towards Elizabeth's English government. By now Black Tom had also been order to 'parly [with], protect or prosecute' Sir James fitzMaurice who, with his Munster allies, was also planning a rebellion.

For some reason, Thomas ignored this order, although it may have been caused by the anger he felt at having his three brothers, Edmund, Edward and Piers, attainted because of their actions against Sir Henry Sidney. Ormonde passionately protested against 'this indignity', but his pleas fell on deaf ears, and the Butler brothers were not pardoned until 1573; and even then – although they became loyal enough subjects – they were not, through some legal error, restored in blood.

Throughout 1571 Black Thomas was busily engaged in repressing further tumults in Munster, which the Desmond influence continued to foment. At the beginning of 1572 Sir William FitzWilliam, the new Lord Deputy, wrote to Cecil that 'the South was always the ticklish part of Ireland, and that Ormonde alone could manage it'. Yet a year later Ormonde was back in London, where he spent several months enjoying the pleasures of the capital. He visited his old rival, the Earl of Desmond, who was still in confinement, and Desmond begged him to use his influence with the Queen to secure his release. Ormonde probably recommended the course, which was soon after adopted, of letting Desmond return to Ireland under guarantees of good behaviour. If this was the case, then his old adversary soon betrayed him, once he had spied a weakness in Ormonde's position; that is, in the increasing turbulence throughout the Earl's own territory, due to his absence. Even his own family was up in arms, with the Lord Deputy facing defeat by a Butler force of gallowglasses near Kilkenny. The Earl of Desmond – seeing this, and scorning all his promises – resolved on striking one last desperate blow at English rule in southern Ireland. A prisoner in England since 1567, and immediately re-arrested on his return to his own country, he had escaped from Dublin, and while affirming his loyalty to Elizabeth, refused unconditionally to give himself up. By July 1573 he had entered into a confederacy with other rebellious Irish leaders and Ormonde entreated him in vain to abandon his threatening designs.

In August 1573 the 1st Earl of Essex landed at Carrickfergus with an army, under instructions to crush Turlough O'Neill as 'the principal maintainer of rebellion'. The elderly Turlough's age and ill health meant that death was always near, which somewhat curtailed his activities, and he in fact submitted by the end of April 1574. But his ally, the Earl of Desmond, then refused terms, holding out until September, when he surrendered to the Lord Deputy, making over his lands to his nearest relatives in a bid to escape their seizure by the Crown. In October 200 Irish soldiers were treacherously killed at the command of the Earl of Essex, when they responded to his invitation to attend a banquet at Belfast. There were other such incidents, though none so infamous; and by the following February, James FitzGerald had sailed for the continent, to seek aid from the Pope and from European monarchs in bid to uphold the Catholic religion in Ireland.

On 22 May 1578 the Queen informed Essex that his scheme for Ulster was ended, and she ordered him to evacuate the country. By June, though, Essex had made a treaty between himself and Turlough O'Neill, and a month later he ordered the massacre of an entire family on Rathlin Island, where they had been placed for safe-keeping. Sir Henry Sidney was brought back as Lord Deputy, while Essex was appointed the Earl Marshal of Ireland. Another Irish family was massacred while meeting with the English under a pledge of safety, and pattern of treachery and betrayal was being set that would last for centuries to come.

While Ormonde was on another visit to London in 1579, news reached Elizabeth of a rising by the Desmond faction in Munster, this time aided by papal envoys who had brought with them foreign soldiers. On 18 July FitzGerald returned to Ireland, mooring in the harbour at Smerwick, County Kerry, establishing a base at Dun an Oir with a Spanish-Italian Force. He carried letters from the Pope to the Irish lords, absolving them from all allegiance to Elizabeth I and calling on them to rise in support of Holy Mother Church. But in August FitzGerald was killed in a skirmish, and the leadership of the rebellion fell to Sir John FitzGerald, a brother of the Earl of Desmond. He almost immediately defeated an English force near Lough Gur.

Ormonde was straightaway appointed the Military Governor of the province, with a commission 'to banish and vanquish those cankered Desmonds';[11] and he arrived back in Ireland on 3 October 1579. The Earl of Desmond was proclaimed a traitor when he took over command of the Munster rebel forces after his brother had been defeated in County Limerick, and his entire clan was made renegade by association. This meant that they were at the mercy of the Queen's new troops, drafted in specifically to deal with the situation, and on 6 December Ormonde began a policy of scorched earth in their country. In February 1580 he and Sir William Pelham, the Lord Justiciar, met at Rathkeale to arrange a further extension of that policy.

In March 1580 the English fleet was instructed to search the Irish coast for Spanish ships, and Ormonde himself marched from Kilkenny to Kerry, 'ravaging the country with fire and sword'.[12] In the mountains of Kerry he captured many of the rebel leaders; and in a report of his services, drawn up in July 1580, he claimed to have put to the sword (within three months), forty-six captains, 800 'notorious traitors and malefactors', and 4,000 'other persons'.

In August Sir James FitzGerald, a brother of the Earl, was captured, and promptly hanged, drawn and quartered. In September the rebels were encouraged to renew the struggle by the arrival of a second detachment of 600 papal troops at Smerwick. (The arrival of their eight ships of the coast of Kerry had been duly reported, though no action seems to have been taken to stop them from landing.) Ormonde himself was said to have shown a lack of interest in their pursuit, and was perceived as being curiously inactive, although he still maintained a large army and generally supported the movements of the government.

By November Ormonde's men – aided by Sir Walter Raleigh – had massacred the entire Spanish-Italian force that was mustered at Smerwick, but again Tom Duffe's strangely listless handling of the situation gave rise in England to some groundless suspicions of his loyalty. It is obvious that he had an increasing distaste for his duties, and it could simply have been that he was suffering from battle fatigue. For in April 1581, when the Desmond faction had been practically annihilated and all immediate danger had passed, he declared himself weary of killing, and he induced Elizabeth to proclaim private pardons for all of the rebels, save Desmond and his brothers.

However in 1582 the country was still disturbed. 'They seek', Sir Henry Wallop wrote of the native Irish, 'to have the government among themselves', which could have come as no surprise to even the most blinkered obscurant. The English answer was to attempt to conciliate the Irish by appointing Ormonde as Lord Deputy. But Wallop and other English officials, jealous of Tom Duffe's influence, both at the English court and in Ireland, protested that 'Ormonde is too great for Ireland already', and as a result he was merely confirmed as the Military Governor of Munster, where plague and famine raged. There were reports that indicated '30,000 dead of famine in half a year, besides numbers that are hanged and killed'.[13]

Desmond was still at large in the mountains of Kerry, and a few of his supporters maintained the old warfare. Ormonde, who arrived back in Waterford in January 1583, was inclined to treat the enemy leniently for the moment, since the Earl of Desmond had been almost totally deserted by his followers. But in May he concluded that now was the time to attack, which he did with all his former vigour, once he had cast off his former lethargy. Desmond, already attainted, had a price set upon his head, and in October the rebellious Earl was captured and killed by a servant of the O'Moriartys near Tralee, County Kerry, where he had been hiding in a cave.

His put an emphatic end to the Desmond rebellion, and Ormonde was at last given an opportunity to pacify Munster, in November insisting upon an indemnity being granted to all those who had taken part in the revolt. In letters to Sir William Cecil, then Lord High Treasurer and the Queen's chief adviser, he wrote indignantly of those English officers who had advocated further rigorous measures against the Irish. They were men, he wrote, who wished him to break faith with the penitent rebels he had taken under his protection.

Throughout the next five years, in some part due to Ormonde's efforts, Ireland entered into an uneasy peace, and plans were made for the plantation of Munster, which progressed during this period of relative calm. For Elizabeth, events in England were of greater concern, when the great Spanish armada appeared off her south-west coastline, although this also held a threat for English interests in Ireland. In fact, after the partial defeat of the Spanish in the Channel by the English fleet, and after their almost-complete destruction by storms in the Hebrides, seven ships of the Armada managed to anchor in the Shannon estuary. They left, though, when refused aid by the locals, whose fear of English reprisals outweighed their desire to help their allies.

A Spanish ship was driven aground in Blacksod Bay, and another was wrecked off Doonbeg, County Clare. But here again the Irish, in fear of the English, reacted with surprising savagery. Of the 300 men who swam ashore to safety, sixty were slaughtered on the beach by followers of the O'Briens, who then plundered the wrick, while the rest were 'officially' executed. All in all, sixteen Spanish ships from this disastrous expedition were wrecked on the coast of Ireland, with 5,394 men drowned, killed or taken. The Lord Deputy ordered the execution of all Spaniards found in the country, and Black Tom was among those who helped to capture and kill the refugees. For his efforts in this enterprise, little more than an exercise in wrecking, he was – perhaps even to his own astonishment – made a Knight of the Garter.

The administration of Ireland during Elizabeth's reign was particularly grim, since – so far as the Queen had an Irish policy to speak of – it resolved itself into one fixed idea, to which she clung with more than her usual tenacity of purpose. Ireland was to be assimilated in *all* respects to England, especially in law and religion, and the country must be made to pay for its own expenses, and if possible to contribute to the English exchequer.

During her reign, deputy after deputy was sent over, only to be swiftly returned to England, more often than not in disgrace. The ancient Brehon law was done away with, although the ancient religion stubbornly remained. It was a continuing story of treachery, bloodshed, wholesale massacres and ferocity on one side or the other, of a hideous monotony, but far greater in intensity than anything that had preceded it. The sole monument to English rule in Ireland to reflect with honour upon the Queen is the creation of the University of Dublin, which opened its doors on 9 January 1594.

In that year Hugh O'Neill, Earl of Tyrone, appeared in Dublin to fulfil a kind of truce, a promise he had made to Ormonde. Yet at that time, Spanish gold was current in Tyrone's land, and rumours were rife of Spanish invasion. The English deemed an act on Tyrone to be essential, and he was proclaimed a traitor in England, and at Dundalk in Ireland. As a result there was plenty of skirmishing and a considerable loss of life, but the English failed to bring Tyrone to an engagement.

However a year later the Ulster rebellion broke out, and for half a decade Ireland would again be ravaged and plundered by one side or another, with a barbarity that no other overthrown people in English history had previously endured. In 1596 King Philip of Spain got together a force of 100 ships and 10,000 men for the support of this new rebellion, but this second Armada achieved even less than its predecessor, being dispersed by a gale as soon as it set out from Spain. A second attempt a year later would fare no better. However, the rebellion made progress without Philip's help when in June 1595 the Earl of Tyrone emerged as a natural leader, defeating the English forces, which were saved from rout only by O'Neill's lack of ammunition. In July 1596 Tyrone called upon the Munster chieftains to rise and 'assist the Catholic religion, and join in confederacy and make war with us'.[14]

On 29 October 1597 Black Thomas was appointed Military Commander of the entire 'army in Ireland', which was composed of Irish recruits backing up a hard core of English troops. It was believed that Tyrone would seize the opportunity to overrun The Pale, which he could easily have done, 'even to the gates of Dublin'. But to the astonishment of all, he submitted himself to Ormonde at Dundalk, 'and upon the knees of his heart professed most hearty repentance for his disloyalty, and especially his foul relapses thereinto'.[15] Ormonde promised to transmit his grievances and petitions to England, to Elizabeth, in which 'free liberty of conscience for all the inhabitants of Ireland' held the foremost place.

Black Tom had agreed a truce of eight weeks with Tyrone, in talks near Dundalk – later extended to 7 June 1598 – but by August 1598 matters came to a second crisis point. Hugh O'Neill, feeling the demands of the crown, if fully met, would utterly destroy his authority over his *urraghs*, had a change of mind. Taking advantage of the expiry of the truce, he laid siege to Blackwatertown, a stronghold of some importance, well garrisoned and stubbornly defended, situated about five miles from Armagh. He then failed to capture the town, but the lack of provisions reduced the garrison to dire extremities. A strong force under Sir Hugh Bagnell, Marshal of the Queen's Army in Ireland, hurried to the relief of the fort, with nearly 4,000 men. But to the general astonishment, Tyrone turned upon these troops, and this time cut the English to pieces, with Bagnell himself, along with a large number of his officers and more than 700 of his men, butchered. The completeness and the disgrace of the defeat made a profound impression on both Irish and English alike, and it is considered to be one of the major battles in Irish history.

After this triumph, Tyrone might well have marched directly upon Dublin, but he again showed no ability to profit by his successes, allowing the remnants of Bagnell's troops to retire to Newry. However as a result of his unexpected victory, smouldering elements of discontent burst everywhere into open activity. Nowhere was the effect more visible than in Munster, which, in the expressive language of the Irish annalists, again became 'a trembling sod'.

Three months passed, though, before Tyrone sent a strong force into Munster, provoking an outbreak of rebellion in Ormonde's own territory, in October 1598. Black Tom could expect little help from England, for it was said that Tyrone was held in such esteem by Philip II of Spain, that the king 'stayed all Irish ships that had not the earl's pass' and Elizabeth did not come to Thomas's aid on this occasion either. James FitzThomas FitzGerald had assumed the title of Earl of Desmond, and finding himself at the head of 8,000 clansmen, he led the rebellion in person against the plantation in Munster.

This time the O'Mores of Queen's County defeated the Ormonde forces, and to add to his problems, Black Tom's distant kinsmen, Viscount Mountgarret and Lord Cahir, joined in Tyrone's rebellion. (Throughout his Munster estates, the English planters had fled without striking a blow.) Any prospective settlement between Ormonde and his enemies 'vanished like the unsubstantial fabric of a vision'.[16] Unfortunately, Tyrone lacked the qualities of a good general, and months of precious time were lost during which he might have made himself master of Ireland, since he was now in a position to weld together all the scattered elements of hostility towards England.

In London it is possible that Thomas's own loyalty again came under question, on the evidence of his inability to put down this upsurge of Irish defiance. Yet if this was so, Elizabeth's government made a huge mistake when, on 15 April 1599 – in a move, perhaps, to keep Black Thomas mindful of his allegiance – the 2nd Earl of Essex was sworn in as Lord Lieutenant, and Governor-General of Ireland. Ormonde, jealous of his rivals at any time, had never had good relationships with any of the Queen's favourites, and he was certainly not on friendly terms with the last of them, Robert Devereux, the 33-year-old Earl of Essex.

Scornful of the military tyro's plan of securing Munster, Leinster and Connacht, it was harshly criticised by Ormonde, although it was the manner of its execution rather than the scheme itself that was responsible for Essex's failure. The fruitless expedition to Munster returned to Dublin in July 1599 with it forces 'weary, sick and incredibly diminished',[17] and from soon after his arrival, Black Tom was complaining to the council in London that the Earl was not earnestly striving to crush Tyrone. (This was hardly true, for Essex had succeeded, at least, in obtaining the submissions of Cahir and Mountgarret by May 1599, which Black Tom had singularly failed to do). Indeed Essex might have expected some shred of gratitude from his rival on this account, since these were the very men whose actions had placed Ormonde in his previously invidious position. Receiving no thanks, Essex retaliated against the older man's charge of slackness by renewing the Court's earlier suspicions of Thomas's own loyalty. The Queen, though, enamoured as she was by the Adonis-like Essex, favoured Ormonde, as she had always done.

She was also anxious to keep Essex away from London – where he had become the focus of movement against her – and she forbade him to leave his post in Ireland, instructing him to proceed once more against the insurgents. Her orders came at a point where it was obvious to all that it would be wise to postpone further operations for that year, but Essex still left Dublin, with a wholly inadequate force of some 2,500 men. There was some general skirmishing between the Essex and Tyrone outposts, but no direct engagement, and Essex would outrage Black Tom, and also the Queen, when he decided to parley with the enemy. The gist of O'Neill's demands on this occasion appeared in a document called 'Tyrone's Prepositions'.[18]

Keen as the Queen was to keep him in Ireland, Essex was by now very anxious to leave a country where his policies were visibly failing (at a cost to England of 1,000*l* a day). The young Earl, the darling of the 'men of [political] action' by now entertained governmental ambitions and even the hope of acting as a 'king-maker' for the Scottish James VI, seen by some as the natural heir to Elizabeth's throne, as the queen declined towards death. Every day that he spent away from Court increased the risks of him being superseded by others, particularly by Robert Cecil, who had obtained both his Council seat and his Secretary's seal while Essex was out seeking military glory. When his campaign in Ireland yielded him no laurels, in his last weeks there the Earl decided upon an action that would be practically a *coup d'état* against the Queen. In this – with the aid of his young admirers – he would make a secret return to London, to challenge Elizabeth in a personal confrontation, by which he would contrive to restore his fortunes and overthrow the Cecil party. If this failed, another part of the design was to capture and imprison the Queen until she met his demands.

On 6 September 1599 the smooth-talking Tyrone and the headstrong Essex met on opposite sides of the Lagan river, and in their half-hour parley, a truce was agreed between them. Essex certainly failed to persuade the rebel Earl to alter his terms for a settlement (which fell little short of a demand that England should abdicate from all power in Ireland), but at that stage perhaps he had lost interest in the matter of Ireland. Abdication was precisely what Essex had in mind for the aged Queen herself and he left Dublin for England on 24 September 1599 in direct defiance of Elizabeth's express command. Four days later, he burst in upon an astonished Queen and her ladies at Nonsuch Palace in Surrey to face the Queen alone. The outraged monarch handled a delicate situation with the sureness of touch she had always displayed throughout her reign when confounding her enemies, and having persuaded the headstrong young man to abandon his designs, she committed her wayward favourite to the custody of a friendly councillor. Later, avoiding a worse punishment, he was dismissed form all offices of state and became a house-prisoner 'at the Queen's pleasure'.

Essex's defection from duty had actually been the best thing for the English in Ireland, where the brash self-seeking hopeful was superseded by an older and more experienced man, Charles Blount, the eighth Lord Mountjoy. A far better soldier than the man he supplanted, Mountjoy was sworn in as Lord Deputy, with an army of 20,000, raised specifically to suppress the insurrection. He would eventually succeed brilliantly where Essex had so deplorably failed, although success would be some time in coming. Black Thomas, who must also have rejoiced at his young rival's ruin, had himself worse luck at this juncture; captured by Owney O'More in April 1600, while parleying with the enemy at Ballraggett, he was not released until June. (Owney O'More would later die in a confrontation with Mountjoy.)

On 21 September 1601 the long-awaited Spanish invasion of Ireland began with the arrival of 3,500 Spanish troops at Kinsale, County Cork, which they then fortified. Five days later, Mountjoy reached Kinsale from Kilkenny, reconnoitring the town on the 29th. His full troop of 15,000, of whom half were Irish, assembled for combat; but hunger and disease effectively reduced it to 6,600 within an astonishingly short space time. On 21 November, having earlier repulsed a Spanish attack, Mountjoy opened fire on Kinsale, but failed to take it. The Spanish sent reinforcements from the Continent, which landed near the Kinsale fort, and they then took three ports while Mountjoy still failed to storm a breach at Kinsale.

For a time it looked as though nothing would go well for him. An English fleet was repulsed in an attack on Berehaven, Tyrone was closing in on his troops, and the Spanish beat off yet another attempted breach on the town. Then, in a brilliant reversal, Tyrone – supremely overconfident of his supremacy in the circumstances – rashly attacked the English troops, and was defeated by Mountjoy in an engagement that lasted for less than three hours.

Tyrone's great mistake had been to place too much trust in his 'modernised' army, which was still no match for the better-organised English troops.[19] Mountjoy's previous attempt to force his way into Ulster by the Moyry Pass had well demonstrated the Irish talent for setting an ambush and their brilliance at skirmishing. However once put in a defensive position, they quickly showed that they were unable to cope with a well-planned frontal assault as they had ever been. Crushed and humiliated, Tyrone began a retreat to Ulster, and the Spanish commander surrendered on terms to Mountjoy. His troops were sent home (at the victors' cost), sailing from Kinsale on 16 March 1602.

It was the nature of Elizabethan warfare to take a peculiarly horrid toll of civilians, always well above that of the death rate of soldiers, in order to deprive the Irish of food, succour and possible recruits. In the year of his greatest triumph, Lord Mountjoy began a scorched-earth policy around Ulster in June, strikingly described by the poet Edmund Spenser:

> ...brought to such wretchedness as that any stony heart would have rued the same. Out of every corner of the woods and glens they came, creeping forth upon their hands, for their legs would not bear them. They looked like anatomies of death; they spake like ghosts crying out of their graves, they did eat of the dead carrions. Yea and another soon after, in so much as the very carcasses they spared not to scrape out of their graves.

This inhuman method of destroying everything that could be useful to the enemy, especially by fire, was Spenser's preferred form of warfare. (Spenser was secretary to Lord Deputy Grey at that time.[20]) It had been advocated in Ireland since the massacres of 1530, but the methods used by Lord Grey and the Earl of Essex in the last year of Elizabeth's reign were probably some sort of innovation, and the system grew increasingly horrendous. Grey was even censured by his contemporaries for his wanton brutality.

Not that the lives of the Irish – soldier or civilian, male or female, young or old – was held to much account by the new invaders. Mountjoy was thought by many to be a humane man, but the descriptions of his devastation of Ulster, his policy of forced starvation and the cannibalism that resulted from it, make unbearable reading. The only strategy was spoliation, for it was thought by most of the English legislators that 'when ploughing and the breeding of cattle shall cease, then will the rebellion end'.[21]

The official view continued to stress that this present was not one of 'conquest', for how could it be when the country was already defeated and 'mostly loyal'? No, it was simply that a few 'unnatural and barbarous rebels' needed to be 'rooted out'. Yet it had been suggested in 1599 that the *entire* Irish population should be deported to England, to provide a new class of serfs; a radical new approach that was in direct contradiction to a proclamation issued in England in 1594, which ordered the removal from the kingdom of certain Irish peasants 'who cannot be identified as having good cause for their presence in England'.[22]

To the end of her life, Elizabeth I remained mindful of the words of her first viceroy in Ireland,[23] who had told her in 1560 that she must give the highest priority to seeing that the country was secure. 'Not so much for the care I have of Ireland, which I have often wished to be sunk into the sea', he reported, but because it would be catastrophic for the Queen if one of her enemies gained possession of it. The country was an ideal base from which to launch an attack upon England, and it was this constant fear of seeing it occupied by a hostile power that made the English so fiercely determined never to relinquish control of it.

It was partly in consequence of this that the Queen had always treasured her cousin Ormonde her 'dark husband', which she did until the end of her life; in 1602 granting him many of the lands she had confiscated in Munster. But there would be little more of her largesse for the Queen had only a few months left to live. She last long enough to hear that the Irish rebellion had been brought to an end; but the formal submission of Tyrone came too late, having been drawn from him six days after her death. It was made to her successor, James I, who was proclaimed 'King of Ireland' in Dublin on 5 April 1603.

Black Tom's active life, too, was all but ended, even though he outlived the Queen by eleven years. He would hold only one honour under the new King, when he was made Vice-Admiral of Ireland in 1612, although the office had now changed radically and his duties would be far different from those that he had carried out in Elizabeth's reign. His main concern now was no longer to protect Ireland's shores from Spanish attack, but to simply repress piracy.

Tom Duffe had served the Queen well, having been Treasurer of Ireland from 1559, a position he was allowed to hold until his death, but it was evident to all that his glory days were far behind him. When, on 11 April 1603, Cork City refused to acknowledge the new King as monarch and mounted an insurrection it was Mountjoy, not Ormonde, who put it down. Yet the Earl had been made Lieutenant General of Her Majesty's Forces in Ireland in 1597, and King James had renewed his commission on coming to the throne, a position that he would also hold for the rest of his life.

The unavoidable fact was that his last military post was for the most part an anachronism: after the classic defeat at Kinsale, Irish resistance had largely collapsed, and Mountjoy had successfully forced the submission of the chiefs in other Irish territories. Between that time and Ormonde's death, any further outbreaks were spasmodic and largely futile, and with the 'Flight of the Earls' – Tyrone and Tyrconnell – for the Continent in 1607, the main contenders were effectively removed from the scene.[24]

The only flare-up of any importance was the burning of Derry in April 1608, with the death of the governor as the main casualty, but this rising was soon put down when its leader was shot dead in July, with his head being sent to Dublin for public display. There was simply no longer any need for a man of Ormonde's experience, however distinguished his successful operations against the Irish rebels throughout the 1580s had been. Besides which, of course, Black Thomas was simply, however zealous he remained, too old for any further service. He died in 1614, at the great age of 83, having, in fact, been blind for some years. Yet his health and physical vigour had been the wonder of all who knew him.

Thomas Butler can be said to have been the last of the Warriors of the Pale, a man who had rarely met defeat, though a man whose triumphs had never made him popular with either his officers or men. A perennial favourite of the Queen, he would always remain as unpopular with her courtiers as he did with his troops. But with him passed a remarkable renaissance that had coincided with the downfall of the Butler family's most enduring rivals, the Desmonds and the Kildares, leaving the Ormondes in unchallenged possession of the field.

Ormonde was married three times. His first wife was the daughter of Thomas, tenth Lord Berkeley, but the marriage was without issue. His second wife was Elizabeth, a daughter of the ninth Lord Sheffield, by whom he had two sons, James and Thomas, and a daughter Elizabeth. His third wife, Helen, a daughter of the Viscount Buttevant, also produced no heirs.

In fact Ormonde's hopes of continuing the dynasty were doomed to failure within his own life-span; for despite his three marriages the title would pass from his line when both of his sons died before him, without either having provided successors, and when his third wife proved barren. Thomas's second brother James, left an only son who also died childless, and so the title passed to Walter, son of his youngest brother, Sir John Butler of Kilcash.[25]

Walter Butler's title to the earldom was incontestable, but Sir Robert Preston, who had married the only daughter of Earl Thomas, claimed a large portion of the Ormonde estates in right of his wife. After much time and money spent in litigation, King James I made an award to Preston, to which Earl Walter refused to submit. In 1617 he was committed to the Fleet Prison, where he remained for eight years in great want, with no rents reaching him from his estates. The King, meanwhile, brought out a writ of *quo warranto* against him for the County palatinate of Tipperary, vested in the Butler family for nearly 400 years. No answer was made to the writ (since none could be made with Walter in prison), and James took the palatinate into his own hands. It would not be restored to the Ormondes until 1663.

Earl Walter was set at liberty in 1625, with a large part of his estates restored to him. He lived for a time in Drury Lane, London, but eventually retired to his estates in Ireland. In the tradition of this property-building family, Walter's grandson married his distant cousin, Elizabeth Preston,

Earl Thomas's granddaughter, and he was granted wardship of her lands by letters patent. After their marriage, he were recognised as the proper heir to her grandfather's lands, bringing them into the new line of the Ormonde dynasty.

Perhaps the bitterest blow to Earl Thomas had been that he could not leave the title to his third – but illegitimate – son (the maternal side of whose parentage is one of the great mysteries of the Elizabethan age, although many of his descendants have long believed they possess the answer). This son, Piers fitzThomas, born out of wedlock about 1576, was knighted when an infant by Queen Elizabeth, and given vast tracts of former monastic lands by that notoriously parsimonious monarch. His birth was both romantic and mysterious, since his mother – presumably a great lady at Court – was never named.

Piers himself was smuggled into Ireland while still in swaddling clothes, and grew up quietly as a landed gentleman, and very rich in right of the Queen's magnificent settlement upon him. His father, too, executed a deed of conveyance in 1597 (when Piers had reached his majority). This consisted of certain church lands, originally granted by the Queen to Thomas's brother, which reverted to the Earl at the death of his brother's son.

Piers could not inherit the Ormonde title, even though his father had managed to have him legitimised; but he, too, would go on to produce a notable line. After marrying Katherine, a daughter of Lord Stone, his son Sir Edward Butler would be created the first Viscount Galmoy being raised to the peerage by Charles I in May 1646, during the early stages of the English Civil War. His son Piers would fall at the battle of Worcester in 1650 and Piers was succeeded by his grandson, whose own son Richard was captain of the royal guards.

The Galmoys would go on to make a further mark upon Irish history; with the third Viscount Galmoy, a supporter of James II, being present at the siege of Londonderry (where the Protestants accused him of great barbarity and treachery). Considered by his own kind to be a distinguished officer, he fought at the Boyne in 1690, and also at Aughrim in Galloway, for which he was outlawed by the English government. For his adherence to King James II, who had created him Earl of Newcastle, his English estates were forfeited, and he was attainted in 1697, when he followed the exiled King into France. His son, who had previously been a colonel in King James's army somehow managed to ingratiate himself with the new Stuart monarchy and served under the Duke of Marlborough in the War of the Spanish Succession, losing his life at Malplaquet.

Many of Black Thomas's descendants would serve in the Irish Brigade, and many would be prominent during the catastrophic reign of James II, siding not only with the Stuarts but also with the Catholics. There was, in fact, only one notable exception, the son of a dragoon in King James II's army, who himself served as a dragoon in the army of George II, and conformed to the Protestant faith in 1719. This line would officially expire in 1861, although there are still some claimants who assert their right to be the genuine descendants of the 10th Earl of Ormonde, the last of the 'Warriors of the Pale', by the mystery bastard of the unknown but 'purebred' woman.

Other Butlers, away from the major branch, would create new dynasties in particular the Caher, Dunboyne and Mountgarret lines, who would play a significant part in both Irish and English history. Within a century of Black Tom's death, the members of these families would no longer be as anglicised as they had once been, even as Ireland itself came more under the control of the English. They could, in fact, be said to have faced two ways: one towards Dublin and London, and on the other to their friendly or hostile neighbours, in whose shifting alliances and recurring wars they would be ever more closely involved.

It would be too simple to suggest that the ever-extending family of the Butlers, because of their longer connections with England, had retained a greater measure of English law and custom than had their Anglo-Irish peers. And neither were they any more likely to wholly subordinate their own or their kinsfolk's interest to that of the administration at Dublin, or even to that of the monarch of the day. The decisive factors were always survival, family self-interest and tradition, and their lives would run like a blood-red thread through Ireland's future history, although none of them would feature as boldly in it as had their forebears.

None, certainly, would need to guard the Pale, that narrow fringe of England on the edge of Gaelic Ireland; since by the end of the 17th century it would have largely vanished, absorbed into the newly formed nation of the Protestant Ascendancy. The Palesmen, predominant among them the Butlers, both heroes and villains of this hugely disturbing period, a true 'dark-ages' for the embattled people of Ireland in their long struggle against the invader, now seem as remote to us as the immortals of Celtic mythology. For the most part having been loyal to their rulers' interests, they had seen themselves as the upholders of English values in an alien culture, and in this way they had tragically helped to widen, not narrow, the gap between Gaelic majority and the Anglo-Irish. In many respects their history had been a foretaste of England's ever-increasing and progressively doomed involvement in the greater Irish story of the centuries to follow.

For long after the fortifications of the 'Land of Peace' were dismantled, and the Pale itself had been absorbed into Gaelic Ireland, the idea of the Pale would endure, if only as a state of mind, where those considered unfortunate enough to live 'beyond the pale', of whatever nationality, would be implacably condemned as existing outside the bounds of civilised society.

## Notes

1. There were some six Irish earls in this parliament.
2. Carte, *Life of the Duke of Ormonde*.
3. James Butler's wife, as the only daughter of the Earl of Desmond, believed that her father's inheritance was hers by right.
4. Once a renegade had formally surrendered to King Henry's 'pleasure', he was willing enough to regrant the property taken from them.
5. In East Lothian, on the Firth of Forth. The battle there in the 16th century probably took place on what is now the racecourse.
6. He was 'unhappily fettered' by the habitual parsimony of the English government towards Irish finances.
7. Carte, op. cit.
8. The Four Masters, *Annals of the Kingdom of Ireland*.
9. *Dictionary of National Biography*, see: Sir Humphrey Gilbert (1539–83). Gilbert was convinced that 'no conquered nation could be ruled with gentleness'.
10. Ibid.
11. *Calendar of State Papers, Elizabeth I.*
12. Carte, op. cit.
13. The Four Masters, op. cit.
14. Carte, op. cit.
15. Ibid.
16. Curtis, *Calendar of Ormonde Papers*.
17. Carte, op. cit.
18. Tyrone's letters are regal in style. He sent them to six chieftains, appointing a meeting at 'Holy Cross' in Tipperary, 'to learn the intentions of the gentlemen of Munster with regard to the great question of the nation, liberty and religion'.
19. Tyrone's army could still not match the improvements made to that of the English.
20. Spenser wrote flatteringly of the Earl of Ormonde in some lines of his poem, 'The Faerie Queen' (an equally fawning tribute to Elizabeth I).
21. Doherty and Hickey, *A Chronology of Irish History since 1500*.
22. *Calendar of State Papers, Ireland.*
23. 3rd Earl of Surrey.
24. Teague O'Keenan, a famous bard of that time, wrote an account of the flight of the Earls. Both died in Rome, as dependants of the Pope.
25. An ancestor of Queen Elizabeth II, through the late Queen Mother.

# Conclusion

## Towards Total Conquest

The policy of creating plantations in Ireland, started in Queen Mary Tudor's time, had resulted by the end of King James I's reign in a remoulding of the Irish landscape: so much so that many parts of the country began to resemble England in its orderliness. Lordly mansions, surrounded by a well-stocked deer-park, fruit orchards, fishponds and stud farms had begun to spring up in the areas taken over by the new planters. Though beyond these illusory English enclaves, the nature of the original land remained, intractable as ever.

A constant tension between the Gaelic lordships and the Pale had existed since the time of Henry II, although in later centuries the edginess felt by the English within the confines of the Pale itself had extended towards the Anglo-Irish also. Henry VIII's policy of re-granting 'English' lands, (within, or near) the Pale, to Irish chieftains, on English tenures and English terms, had put a whole new strain upon relations between the two nations. Although, since Irish lords entered in and out of treaties as easily with the King of England as they did with their Irish overlords, (or come to that, with each other) these new arrangements had only ever been tentative. Yet Henry's policy had left the Anglo-Irish with the uneasy sensation of being penetrated by the enemy, and exposed to their Irish ways; although even within the Pale itself certain ancient patterns of the Gaelic lifestyle had always survived, at least among the lower orders.

By 1600, faced with the most serious resistance the English forces had encountered in many centuries, its officials had come to conceive of the Pale as an ever-moving colonial frontier, which – if only to preserve it – should be pressed remorselessly outwards. What remained to be conquered, though, was nothing short of the Irish way of life, a culture that was always baffling to the English. Elizabethans were the first people to actually define the Irish as a 'barbaric' nation, and the first to decide to intentionally eliminate their national character. The men that Elizabeth sent out to master Ireland indeed brought a new kind of reality to this ambition.

245

But, first, the people would have to be completely subjugated, and even after the devastating triumph of Kinsale, that would be no easy task. In some ways, Irish forces were better adapted for the new circumstances than were their enemies, being now not only equipped with fast, lightly-armed horsemen, but also still possessing their unrivalled knowledge of their territory. The professional expertise of the Scots-Irish gallowglasses and the mobile 'kerns' they had begun to employ was impressive, and by 1600 their soldiers had become proficient with firearms. O'Neill had modified Irish warfare by using the ancient Gaelic practice of military service to an overlord to build up a trained militia. Yet despite these new developments in martial strategy, and the ease with which they mastered them, the Irish could still not adapt to campaigns waged by sieges and assaults on fortresses, as 1601 had demonstrated, with the disastrous Spanish intervention at Kinsale.

The centuries–old English-held 'Pale' was an outmoded concept by 1600, when even the word itself sounds anachronistic. By 1623 there would be a strong distinction between the English-Irish and the solely Irish Gentlemen of the English Pale, whereas the 'English of Irish birth' had remained the general term up to this time. But now the old English were, Janus-like, forced to face in two directions at once, and their position was more insecure than it had ever been, for authority within the Pale was so fragmented that they could not achieve a fully defined status within this new Ireland. By 1600, the hardening and institutionalising of religious differences had also, of course, heightened their alienation.

To an outsider, the disloyalty of a grandee such as the Earl of Desmond may have seemed scandalous, but to an insider it had also been inevitable, for it was evident that the beguiling customs of the country had corrupted the old settler stock from which he had been bred. And he was only one of many such; for generations, a number of parents within the Pale had been so divided in their allegiance that, while they sent their children to be educated in England they also sent them to be 'fostered' with Gaelic families.

Their position was indeed betwixt and between, since they were considered to be 'Irish' in England but almost entirely English in their homeland. Yet by now, the typical Anglo-Irishman was not some great lord or a landed gentleman of Norman ancestry, but a man of more modest background. And while he and his like might have considered themselves to be professional gentry within the Pale – having cornered the commercial market, dominated the legal offices, and sent their sons to be educated in London, Oxford and Cambridge – outside the Pale their status was questioned on all sides.

The idea that they were in some way debased by their intermediate position in English society, an accusation that was levelled at them by their critics from both sides of the divide, is at odds with their actual situation. For the truth was that they were engrossed by the 'civilised' – i.e. English

– values of the Pale. (Despite having travelled a long way from the days when 'the humblest colonial resident in the English province would not give his daughter in marriage to even the most noble of Irish chieftains'.)

Many English families were by now completely Gaelicised, and not only outside the Pale. The religious polarisation that had come with the Reformation, and the difficult relations with increasing waves of Tudor settlers had seen to that. Because they clung to their faith, families that were still loyal to the Crown were now driven, however unwillingly, towards an uneasy alliance with their fellow Catholics, even when they were native Irish of the underclass. With many, the religious impulse would override their fealty to the King.

Between the 16th and 17th centuries, the Old English in Ireland moved from a position of lacking the will to determine their future to one in which they actively planned to do so. In this, they even managed to achieve a coherent outlook, based on the unifying force of their embattled religion, as they rallied against the aggressive spirit of Protestantism. This was not an immediately apparent response, nor was the progression simple or even clearly recognisable; the way in which the Old English were detached from their 'English' identity was gradual and halting. What finally helped to harden their resolve was that, after 1603, the reins of government in Ireland were returned to local hands, but were offered to the Protestants only.

It rankled also that these Protestants were almost entirely composed of the new colonists introduced by the Tudors on their ventures at plantation. Plans to install them on lands forfeited by the Church (or by the FitzGeralds) had been mooted from the 1520s, but started under Queen Mary in the counties renamed for her and Philip of Spain, 'Queen's' and 'King's Counties'. Frequent schemes of centralisation had circulated throughout the 16th century, the idea being to transplant English ways across the sea, and the settlement of Munster had been a huge undertaking, involving a major population displacement. By 1622, probably 12,000 settlers had colonised Munster lands. More settlers would come throughout the 17th century, but a sizeable number of Protestant farmers, small holders, and artisans were already in place. Their presence explains much of the force of change in the next two centuries.

The Irish countryside, then, had ceased to look as it had done throughout the medieval period: with its village dwellings of wood and mud, wattle and thatch, and the landscape dominated by the tall, narrow castles of the invaders. In some of the larger towns, there had always been some stone buildings of substance, but large houses in the English style were few and far between.

The Butler mansion at Carrick, officially dated 1565 (but perhaps not finished until forty years later) resembled – like their castle at Nenagh – no other home in Ireland; but even though it stands out as a magnificent house, it is still attached to a massive and pre-existing castle.[1] Only from the 1600s is there to be found a discernibly Irish style of country house; castles would take another hundred years to become simple dwelling-places. Even today, there are modest farmhouses grafted on to the shell of a late medieval keep.

The vast majority of people were still rustic, despite the changes to the countryside, and even the most sizeable town had something rustic about it. They may have been protected by a complex system of walls, yet thatched cottages were still to be found within their bastions. The country at large was still fortified throughout its length and breadth; ports had quays guarded by moles and castles, and even in the newest plantations, settlements such as Philipstown and Maryborough,[2] intended as market towns, were essentially garrisons.

Dublin, still for the most part a timber-built city, had extensive sub-urbs, but the wealthy preferred to live within its protective walls. The city was the focus of a coastal communications system, and despite its barred harbour – the larger ships unloaded at Ringsend – it was strong, well defended and populous. Described as 'royal', its great days were still to come, as the threat of perpetual assault slowly receded. Kilkenny, the 'capital' of the Butler domain, was the only important inland city, for all the others were located on coastal sites. Rich and powerful Kilkenny, though, while remaining an Ormonde preserve, was in fact run by a small oligarchy of merchant families.

The political theory under which Ireland operated as a Tudor kingdom and where English law was to apply to the whole island was little more than a fiction, maintained only by the government in Dublin. The country was far from being a political entity, and the extent of the conquest itself remained too shifting and uncertain, though there was no doubt that the conquest was expanding.

Old bad habits died hard. For example, a Lord Deputy remained at the head of the administration, but – as had been the case for centuries – the deputy never stayed long enough at his post to do any real good. Indeed most, particularly if the deputy was greedy, did great harm:

> For magistrates often changed, like hungry flies suck more blood. And as the devil rageth more because his time is short, so these magistrates, fearing soon to be recalled, are not so much bent to reform the commonwealth, the fruit whereof should be reaped by the successor, as they are vigilant to enrich them-selves and their followers. Neither indeed can that crafty and subtle nation [the Irish] be well known to any governor by few years' experience.[3]

The deputy now presided over a Privy Council formed by a chancellor and law officers, called the 'Common Council', with the addition of some great magnates to bulk it out.[4] A 'Great Council' (contrarily with less effective powers) was effectively made up of the same groupings as the parliament, but all these members were drawn only from within the Pale. Following the Geraldine rebellion of the 1530s, Henry VIII's officials had done what they could, through the reformation and anglicisation of policies, but guidelines changed frequently; and provincial councils and presidencies, while often attempted, never really took root. (In his later life, the autocratic Earl of Ormonde had often been in serious contention with the 'democratically' elected President of Munster.)

Local factions inevitably remained dominant and the ensuing calculations and manipulations may go a long way to explain such upheavals as the great Desmond rebellion. In turn, the English government in Ireland (backed by such men as Black Tom) often used local power struggles 'to lend a rough and ready stability to Irish politics, somewhat akin to the untidy but relatively efficient two-party system of modern democracies'. For this reason, to contemporary commentators, it seemed that Ireland was not being governed as a conquered country, and the policy of encouraging one chief to act against another was highly criticised at the time. The country was, after all, nominally subject to English law, law officers had been established, parliamentary representation arranged. Ireland was a 'sovereign kingdom', and this, along with the policy of surrender and re-grants of Gaelic lands was intended to create stability.

The Act of 1541, whereby the King of England was also to be known as the King of Ireland, was actually an initiative taken by the Irish Council and was not particularly due to Henry's ambitions. The hope was that the mercurial local alliances would now be directed enduringly towards the Crown and its favours, but the truth was that, by 1600, the local authorities were resurgent, and the end of the war would see the resumption of authority by central government. So the situation bore little resemblance to the blueprints of the constitutional reforms of sixty years before.

In 1600 the Catholic Old English started to use the Poyning's law of 1495 to protect their position against a very antagonistic Lord Deputy, who was trying to rush through legislation that was inimical to their interests. With the spread of the Reformation, the adherence of the Old English to the Roman religion was a key factor of 16th–century Irish politics, since it meant that there was always potential opposition to royal policy within the parliament. After 1613, however, the Irish parliament was tightly packed with Protestants, to the exclusion of the Old Catholic members, due to the creation of the plantation boroughs.

Government policies were nevertheless largely an irrelevance to the greater part of Ireland; for although the parliamentary bills – legal, administrative, fiscal and private – were meant to apply to *all* Ireland, they really only affected the Pale. Besides which, in 1600, no parliament had been convened for fourteen years, and it would be another thirteen before one was summoned again. Although in 1603, Sir John Davies, the Irish Solicitor-General,[5] had proposed summoning a parliament that would show that the English conquest of Ireland *had been completed*, and which would promise 'a new era of just and orderly rule'. Such a step was also, of course, intended to symbolise the final extirpation of the Gaelic social and political system. No such assembly was called, and in many ways matters remained much as they had been.

The perception of the Ireland that lay beyond the Pale by those within it remained as inaccurate as always, and the distinction between that uneasy enclave and Greater Ireland similarly held good for matters such as finance. Government receipts and profits were largely restricted to the Pale, and their customs and tax collectors often alienated the local authorities elsewhere. These fiscal wrangles were a three-way problem, too, for Dublin was often as much at odds with London as with the native provinces. As for the judiciary, although judges enforced laws on their circuits, it is doubtful how far their writ ran outside the counties bordering Dublin.

After 1603, the English legal system spread more easily, with the assizes reaching into the north and west. But the old Gaelic observances of the ancient Brehon law[6] continued to have some influence, despite a theoretical condemnation of it by the English authorities. The Irish Court of Chancery had even enforced some Brehon judgements in the 16th century, and local custom had been found to have the force of law. Courts occasionally made awards and fines for homicide in the Gaelic tradition, even as late as 1600; established English practice such as 'trial by jury' was made nonsense of in Ireland, due to the fact that kinship links made the securing of an impartial jury almost impossible. There, as elsewhere, the intractable Irish identity of old remained beneath the English imposition – sometimes working with it, but more often counteracting it. To the increasing irritation of the authorities in England, who could not account for the Irish adherence to a way of life that was clearly impractical, outmoded, and undesirable.

So the Irish continued to cling to their Catholicism, and Protestantism was 'not much noticed'.[7] The priests, by now driven underground, preached that it was no sin to break faith with England, and some Irish Protestants also believed that to be the case. The Irish tradition of asceticism, monasticism, and an exaggerated respect for the clergy, allowed them to maintain the archaic structure of the old faith. Under the Tudors the Reformed Church was inseparably connected with the efforts to make Ireland English in outlook and form, but Protestantism never really took root; Ireland was too extreme a case, and religious resistance, in the end, became a form of patriotic duty.

In 1604, Sir John Davies wrote, '...the churches are ruined and fallen down to the ground in all parts of the kingdom. There is no divine service, no christening of children, no receiving of the sacrament, no Christian meeting or assembly, no, not once a year; in a word no more demonstrations of religion than among Tartars or cannibals!'[8] Ireland was about to become a different sort of battleground: with the native Irish using guerrilla tactics in their religious defiance, in their own version of the Counter-Reformation.

In 1596, Ulster chiefs had petitioned for 'liberty of conscience, or at least immunity from harassment for their clergy',[9] but this was denied them, since freedom of religious choice could not be an inseparable part of the whole package. The English loosely understood that Gaelic identity went with a lax and archaic Catholicism, but what was more worrying to them was that, by the 1600s, it was growing increasingly clear that too many of the Old English were also going to cling to the detested Roman faith.

With religion, so with the language in which it was expressed. The Irish had a decided aversion to speaking 'clattering English', even when they were proficient in it; they would punish their own people for speaking the hated foreign language, and Irish people of both sexes had been killed for not adhering to 'the old tongue'. To cleave to Gaelic was taken as a deliberate statement of the refusal to conform, and even the parliament of 1613–15 contained some members who could not – or would not – speak English. The children of newly arrived settlers were often forced to interpret among their neighbours for the benefit of their non-Gaelic speaking parents. Irish place names were only transposed when it came to writing them down in English documents. Even Trinity College, a bastion of English Puritanism, was forced to allow its tutors to deliver their lessons in Irish. By and large the Gaelic tongue was associated with Irish resistance, a peculiarly apt form of counter-action for a nation so obsessed with the magic of words.

In the Gaelic Ireland of the 1600s, two things had been established which would keep Catholicism alive in Ireland. First was the practice of studying for the priesthood abroad – between 1592 and 1605, Irish colleges had been founded at Salamanca, Lisbon, Douai, Louvain and Paris – and second was the growing number of Catholic schoolteachers who roamed the land, teaching in secret. This underground education system not only reinforced the old patterns of learning and – even more importantly – worship, it also managed to drive the wedge between English and Irish understanding even deeper.

Language itself became a vehicle for insurrection, and the Irish love of verbal exaggeration, their bizarre usage, and their deliberate pleasure in paradox and wit only served to madden their conquerors further; particular the leaden-tongued Puritans. As a result, the conceptions of Ireland were different between the two nations, the Irish appearing to dwell in a different world altogether, one that grew increasingly more abstract and hazy, and increasingly more infuriating to the stolid English.

Although this may have long been the case; the Irish 'fool' that Mountjoy kept for his amusement was said to have had 'the craft of humouring every man to attain his own ends', and he was only one among thousands with the same ability. By the mid-1600s the cultural gulf between the regularity of English life and the volatile ways of the Irish imagination seemed too wide to be bridged. But all the same, the Gaelic world was doomed, with the Irish helpless to withstand the modernising influence that came with the Reformation. By 1600, the Irish bards were lamenting the passing of the old Gaelic order, and by the middle of the century, when England was itself in the throes of civil war, Irish history would be again rewritten, as the country was caught up in the English conflict.

Another Butler, James, the 11th Earl, a convinced royalist in the Butler tradition, would play his part in this. In 1642, during an Irish rebellion, he was commissioned to command the army in the absence of the English-born Lord Lieutenant, (who never left England). And Ormonde would act ferociously towards the Irish during his time in Ireland, beginning with the burning of Newcastle and marching on Naas, County Kildare, which was abandoned, leaving his troops to loot the surrounding area. Having laid waste to the Boyne valley, and later, having wasted County Kildare, he would do battle against his own kinsman, Viscount Mountgarrett, at Kilrush near Athy, with James Butler the victor. By the end of the year he would be made Lieutenant General under the Crown.

When the English parliament met in the autumn of 1641, a rebellion had broken out in Ireland, with the native Irish rising in Ulster, and the revolt spreading throughout the land. It brought in its wake so many cruelties against the English as to earn it the name, among the Puritans, of the 'great massacre'. By that year the parliamentary party in England was beginning to enjoy a number of successes against King Charles I in their disputes of over their respective prerogatives, but all the same the Commons dared not place an army to suppress the rebellion in Ireland under royal command. The King, it was supposed, might be tempted to use such an army against his ministers, and it was decided that any war against the Irish must only be managed by parliamentary officers.

In the wake of parliament's proposal to take command of the army away from King Charles I, the wildest rumours swept through Westminster, which swiftly blew across the Irish Sea. Foremost among these rumours was a belief that the 'papists' were rising in England as well as Ireland to destroy the Protestant religion. In an atmosphere of increasing political hysteria, the ground was set for civil war in both kingdoms.

In Ireland, Ormonde, now a Marquess, working on behalf of the King, had managed to build a coalition of sorts out of disparate and even hostile elements. Not only the Anglo-Irish royalists, but native Irish, and even some of the Scots of Ulster had rallied beneath his flag. For a time they were so successful that it seemed as though they would be able to dislodge the slight parliamentary hold on Ireland and send over an expedition to Wales as well.

In April 1643, Ormonde defeated the Confederate Thomas Preston at Old Ross, and – under the orders of King Charles I – he negotiated for the cessation of arms with the Confederates,[10] signing a truce for one year on 13 September. A truce that was, as always in Ireland, inevitably broken. In November, he was appointed Lord Lieutenant, and by October the next year the English parliament, now in sole command in London, with King Charles I fighting for his very survival, had accepted that war in Ireland would have to be a charge on the public purse.

In September 1643, a Solemn League and Covenant had been agreed between the English parliament and the Scots, which was then ordered by the English Puritans to be carried throughout the whole of Ireland. When Scottish officers took the Covenant at Carrickfergus, it spread into Ulster by April 1644. As Lord Lieutenant, Ormonde condemned the Covenant, but by May the city of Belfast had fallen to the Scots. Perhaps because of this, and certainly because of his failure to keep his negotiations with the Confederacy open, Ormonde tendered his resignation, which was refused by the King.

In 1646, the Earl had concluded a peace with the Confederation on 28 March; a peace which was condemned by the papal nuncio,[11] who declared all who had adhered to it to be perjured, announcing their excommunication on 1 September. A year later, at the seventh meeting of the General Assembly of the Confederation of Kilkenny (by now dominated by the pope's representative), the Confederation declared against the Ormonde peace treaty. More alarmingly for the Earl, a parliamentary army of 2,000, commanded by Colonel Michael Jones, landed near Dublin, and soon proved their strength. Although Ormonde negotiated a treaty with the parliamentary commission, he agreed to surrender Dublin and the sword of state, and to leave the country, which he did by 1648, having seemingly failed in his mission.

But he was back by September 1649, and again concluded a peace with the Confederates on 17 January. But to little avail for the royalists, since King Charles I, captured by the Scots and sold to the parliamentarians, was executed only thirteen days later. By 17 February, the uncrowned King, Charles II, declared Ormonde to be Lord Lieutenant of Ireland from his place of exile, which proved a futile gesture. For on 29 March, Oliver Cromwell accepted command of the Parliamentary Army in Ireland, and when, on June 28, he was also commissioned as Governor-General of Ireland, with civil and military authority, the true conquest of Ireland had begun.

Colonel Michael Jones, commanding a parliamentary force, defeated

Ormonde at Rathmines, Dublin, creating a bridgehead for Cromwell and his well-equipped veteran army, which allowed him to concentrate rapidly on Dublin, and thence move swiftly north or south with his forces, supported from the sea against the Irish royalists. James Butler did not again take the field, and his battle against the parliamentary army would, in fact, be the last fought in Dublin until Easter 1916.

Within weeks of Cromwell landing at Ringsend, Dublin on 15 August 1649, and with the arrival of Henry Ireton and his army, the onslaught had begun. Drogheda, a seaport into which many of the finest troops in the Irish coalition had been thrown, was besieged, and the garrison and the inhabitants massacred in one of the most brutal of all Anglo-Irish encounters, with Cromwell justifying his action on two grounds. Firstly, that 'this was a righteous judgement of God upon those barbarous wretches who have imbrued their hands in so much innocent blood' [the massacres in the uprising of 1641] and, secondly, that 'it would prevent the effusion of blood for the future'.[12] This was an argument that would be obscenely belied by the methods of waging war that he himself continued to use thereafter. Belfast was also besieged, and Wexford fell to Cromwell, with another barbaric massacre of the entire garrison, and the larger part of the civilian population. The royalist garrison holding Cork, trying to save their troops from a similar nemesis, deserted to Cromwell in a body on 19 October; driving the Irish out of the town before them.

The royalists, supposedly under Ormonde, fought back, but with rapidly depleting forces. When New Ross surrendered to the parliament army on 20 October 1649, Ormonde (still the Lord Lieutenant, if only in name) entered into a treaty with the Confederate Owen Roe O' Neill, only to have him die on him sixteen days after they agreed to act in concert. It is indicative of the fluctuating loyalties of the Irish during this momentous year that O Neill had previously entered into an armistice with the Parliamentarians. Cromwell raised the siege of Waterford after only a few days and he set up his winter quarters in the town, with his troops for the most part having to shift for themselves.

In December, the Roman Catholic bishops held a synod at Clonmacnoise, where they called for unity between Catholics and King Charles II against Cromwell. The Marquess of Ormonde met with the bishops at Limerick, receiving their loyalty on 28 March 1650. (The day before Cromwell had taken the Ormonde ancestral seat of Kilkenny.)

Then, perhaps to the surprise of all involved, having accepted the almost bloodless surrender of Cashel, County Tipperary, Cromwell met the heaviest resistance of his entire campaign at Clonmel, which was vigorously defended by Hugh O'Neill. The town surrendered, on favourable terms, only when O'Neill had left. This would be Cromwell's last engagement in Ireland, and on 26 May 1650, he left for England, leaving Ireton in command.

The slaughter continued, though, with Athlone taken and Carlow surrendering to Ireton, along with Waterford. On 4 October 1650, the English parliament, perceiving the war to be over, appointed four commissioners for the civil administration of Ireland; and the country was, according to them, was – like England – now under new management. The Irish were to find the experience even grimmer than the English, during the doleful period between the death of Charles I and the restoration of his son. The Marquess of Ormonde, recognising defeat, sailed for Brittany on 11 December 1650, (losing the vessel that contained his personal effects *en route*.[13])

In England, on 3 September 1651, in the last pitched battle of the Civil War, Cromwell decisively defeated Charles II at Worcester and Charles fled to seek refuge with his cousin, the King of France.[14] Limerick surrendered to Ireton as plague raged the city, with a Catholic bishop among those hanged by the occupying forces. In November the royalist offices of Lord Lieutenant and Lord Deputy were abolished by the English parliament. Henceforth, commissioners were to receive full responsibility for military as well as for civilian administration.

Despite the death of Henry Ireton of the plague in late November, the subjugation of Ireland proceeded. Galway and Roscommon surrendered, articles of agreement were made between the Confederate forces and the parliamentarians, and the Leinster Confederate Army surrendered under the terms known as the 'Articles of Kilkenny'.[15]

By 12 August 1652, an 'Act for the Settling of Ireland' had divided the whole population into six categories, according to 'purported guilt', and which set out the treatment applicable to those who would not be pardoned. In 1653, the first plans were made for the transportation of 8,000 Irish to the 'Tobacco Islands',[16] and an order to the Commissioners for the Relief of the Poor directed them to hand over 'incorrigible vagrants' for shipment to white slavery in the Caribbean.[17] A new and more ferocious attempt was made to enforce the expulsion of those Jesuits and seminary priests who were holding the line for the Old faith in secret.

On 14 February 1653, Inishbofin, the only military stronghold in the British Isles where the royalist flag still flew, had surrendered to Parliamentary soldiers, and on 27 April, the Irish at Cloughoughter laid down their arms; the last formal surrender of the Irish Civil war. On 26 September, the 'Act of Satisfaction' claimed the rebellion in Ireland to be at an end. It stated that the counties of Waterford, Limerick, Tipperary, Queen's County, King's County, Meath, Westmeath, Armagh, Down and Louth were to answer all claims of the adventurers and arrears of the army since 5 June 1649. The Commissioners in Ireland estimated the war had created debts of 1,750,000 pounds sterling, but as the amount of land to be sold to meet them amounted to only 800,000, the remainder would have to be repaid from some other source than Irish landholdings.

It is difficult to estimate the exact Irish population of the 1650s, but it had certainly dropped dramatically, which was immediately obvious. 34,000 Irish soldiers in arms had emigrated, and others were either conscripted or sold into slavery abroad. (Slave hunts throughout Ireland were definitely a feature of the period, although they may have been much exaggerated.) Only the 'inferior sort of rebel' was to be pardoned at once, yet there were some 12,000 Irish of both sexes in the West Indies by the 1660s. The government policy was not to hold drumhead court-martials, although there was widespread sentencing in the makeshift courts that were convened.

Men who had not been deprived of their life or their liberty were to be categorically dispossessed. Their property was taken from them initially as a punishment for their insurgency, but there was also a more ambitious and far-reaching aim: the total remodelling of land ownership. For a decade the English parliament allotted Irish land to English investors, as well as offering land to soldiers in lieu of pay, and using it as security for loans raised to prosecute the war. The acts of 1652, in fact, were prompted solely by the necessity to make sure there were enough funds to meet such obligations. The situation was naturally volatile, with a constant fear that the land would run out, which created an unrelenting pressure to accomplish matters swiftly. And the result was the wholesale confiscation of land without a real understanding of the nature of the country, and with the measurement of these forfeit acres being purely conjectural.

The early ideas of a total population clearance, though, were abandoned; not for reasons of humanity so much as because of the difficulty of attracting enough English freeholders to replace the uprooted peasants. By this time, the lands of the greater majority of those landowners who remained faithful to the old religion had been taken into public use, although many of these former estate-owners were later resettled in smaller holdings. They were to remain the 'representatives of the old aristocracy and minor gentry', and among them were many 'lords and ladies of the Pale'.

Paradoxically, the dwindling members of the Catholic upper classes still held on to odd pockets of land within the 'Old Pale': which had, by now, virtually ceased to exist. Only the counties to the extreme west of Ireland – Sligo, Mayo, Roscommon, Galway and Clare – could be said to be still truly Irish, and even there English soldiers and sailors guarded the land along coastal strips and on the banks of major rivers. The rest of the country, from Donegal in the north to Cork in the south, had been wholly confiscated by the English parliament and reallocated. The counties of Dublin, Kildare and Carlow were now a government reservation, and all five provinces bordering the Pale had been assigned to English Protestant adventurers and ex-Cromwellian soldiers. Their settlement was a complex matter, for the men were often unwilling to make their home there. In fact the plan to establish English freemen and Protestant military veterans was one of the first to be thwarted.

The Ormondes' once great palatinate of Tipperary was one of the main counties to be divided up.[18] With 77% of land in the hands of settlers, by 1655 it was reported that not a single 'inhabitant of the Irish nation that knows the country' was left in one Tipperary barony, and only the labouring community remained in much of the rest. As with Tipperary, so with Kilkenny, where 58% of the land had been assigned to English troops.[19]

At the restoration to the throne of King Charles II in 1660, the first Marquess of Ormonde returned as the royalist Viceroy, but now with a ducal title. He would be forced to grapple for many months with the competing claims of the incumbents and the dispossessed, not to mention having to deal with the forcible reclamation of his own domain. The 11th Earl, 1st Marquess and 1st Duke of Ormonde, had proved himself to be a great survivor during his long exile from Ireland. His wife, too, left behind during James Butler's wanderings with the outcast Charles II, had become a heroine to the Irish, after aiding them in their struggles against the Puritans.[20] But the couple, for all their formidable energies, would find the new English hard to dislodge, not only from their estates but also from the land allotted to them by the government of the Interregnum.

That, however, is another story. The new duke – one of the few dukedoms created by Charles II for *political* services – would play a significant role in Charles II's new regime, and his grandson would take the wrong side in the Jacobite rebellion, bringing complete ruin to his line, and a premature end to the dukedom. Other Butlers, too, away from the major line, would create new dynasties, and their lives would run like a bloody thread through Ireland's future history: though none of them would feature as boldly in the pages of Irish history as had their forebears.

None, certainly, would need to guard the Pale, that narrow fringe of England on the edge of Gaelic Ireland; by the end of the 17th century it had vanished, absorbed into the newly formed Ireland of the Protestant Ascendancy.

# Notes

1. Carte, *Life of the Duke of Ormonde*.
2. King's and Queen's County; both named for Mary Tudor and Philip II of Spain.
3. Fynes Moryson, *Itinary*; quoted in P.F. Foster's *Modern Ireland*.
4. Cox & Leland, *Histories of Ireland*.
5. Sir John Davies (1569-1626.)
6. The Old Irish law, by now largely superseded.
7. Quoted in P.H. Foster's *Modern Ireland*.
8. Sir John Davies, writing to William Cecil.
9. Harassment for their clergy. This was part of Tyrone's attempt to draw the Irish together in defence of their Catholicism.
10. The Irish Confederacy was more of a conspiracy of diverse units, both Catholic and Anglican, held together only by their mutual hatred of the Parliamentarians.
11. The papal nuncio largely excommunicated the Confederates on the grounds that many of them were not true Catholics. The papacy hoped to make the Confederacy a purely Catholic undertaking.
12. Cromwell explained himself thus to parliament. *DNB*.
13. He would spend long years in exile, supporting the uncrowned Charles II 'in his wandering'. Ormonde was not, however, ever as poor as his king, due to the heroic efforts of his wife to raise money in Ireland, and to smuggle it out to him in France and Holland.
14. Where he was joined by Ormonde.
15. Which bore some resemblance to the earlier Articles of Kilkenny, in that they were as punitive.
16. The Tobacco Islands are more likely native to tropical America. The Parliamentary Party early seized on tobacco as a profitable commercial enterprise.
17. Again, whole families stripped of their property, and not necessarily vagabonds in the modern sense. More likely people of no settled abode due to the pressures of conquest.
18. Carte, *Life of the Duke of Ormonde*.
19. This is a fairly accurate assessment. Other landowners were similarly dispossessed, but Ormonde was one of the most heavily despoiled.
20. The Duchess of Ormonde was regarded as a saint by many in Ireland, due to the work she did for those who fell foul of the English invaders. She was one of the few individuals ever to stand up to Oliver Cromwell. *D.N.B.*

# Bibliography

*Acts of Privy Council of England*, London, 1890, 34 vols.

Archdall (ed.), *Lodge's Peerage of Ireland*, Dublin, 1789.

Blackall, Sir Henry, *The Butlers of County Clare*, North Munster, vol. VI, 1952.

Boylen, H., *A Dictionary of Irish Biography*, Dublin, 1988.

Brewer, J.S. and W. Bullen., *Calendar of Carew Manuscripts* (London, 1867–73).

Burtchaell, G.D., *The Butlers of Daugan & Spidogue* (RSAI, 1869).

Butler, W., *Some Account of the Late Duke of Ormonde*, London 1716.

Butler, W.F.T., *Confiscation in Irish History* (Dublin, 1917).

Butler, W.F.T., *Gleanings from Irish History* (London, 1925).

Butler, W.F.T., *The Descendants of James, 9th Earl of Ormonde* (RSAI, 1929).

Butler, W.F.T., *An Irish Legend of the Origins of the Barons of Cahir*, (RSAI, 1925).

*Calendar of Close Rolls*, (Record Commission, 1835).

*Calendar of Fine Rolls*, (PRO, HMSO).

*Calendar of Patent Rolls, Elizabeth I*, (HMSO, London).

*Calendar of State Papers, 1385–1618*, (London, 1912*)*.

*Calendar of State Papers Relating to Ireland, 1509–1670*, (London, 1860–1908).

Carte, Thomas, *History of the Life of James, Duke of Ormonde* (OUP: Oxford, 1857).

*Chronicles & Memoirs of Great Britain and Ireland* (London, 1870).

Clare, Rev. Wallace, *Testamentary Records* (Peterborough, 1932).

Comerford, M., *Collections* (Dublin, 1883).

Comerford, Thomas, *History of Ireland from Earliest Accounts of Time until the Invasion of the English under King Henry II* (Dublin, 1751).

Cosgrave, Art (ed.), *History of Medieval Ireland* (Clarendon Press: Oxford, 1987).

Creton (ed. J. Webb), *History of King Richard II*, Society of Antiquaries, 1770 (vol. 20).

Curtis E. (ed.), *Calendar of Ormonde Deeds, 1172–1603* (Dublin, 1932–43).

Curtis E., *History of Medieval Ireland* (London, 1950).

Curtis E., *Original Documents Relating to the Butler Lordship* (1931–33).

De Burgh, U.H.H., *The Landowners of Ireland* (Dublin, 1878).

De Paor, *The People of Ireland* (London, 1986).

Docherty and Hickey, *A Chronology of Irish History since 1500* (Gill & MacMillan: Dublin, 1989).

Donovan, John (ed.), *Annals by the Four Masters* (Dublin, 1851).

Foster R.F., *Modern Ireland* (Allen Lane, 1998).

Foster R.F., *The Irish Story* (Allen Lane, 2001).

Froissart, Sir John (ed. Thomas Johnes), *Chronique* (London, 1803–5).

F.A. Gasquet, 'An Article' in *Dublin Review, 3rd Series.*

Gilbert, J.T., *Ormonde Manuscripts*, History Mss. Comm. 8th report

Gill (ed.), *History of Ireland* (Dublin, 1972).

Giraldus Cambrensis, (ed. Brewer), *Expurgantio Hiberniae*
    [as quoted in various articles in *DNB*]

Glyn, John & Thady Dowling (eds.), *Annals of Ireland – to 1600*
    (Dublin, 1849).

Grace, Jacobi (ed. R. Butler), *Annals Hiberniae, 1074–1504*
    (Irish Archaeological Society: Dublin, 1842).

Griffith, P.J., *The Butlers of Poulakerry & Kilcash*, 'Waterford, vol. XV', 1912.

Gwynn, A. and R.N. Hadcock, *Medieval Religious Houses in Ireland*
    (London, 1970).

Harris (ed.), *Ware's Bishops* (Dublin, 1744).

Hennessy, W.M. (ed.), *Annals of Loch Ce, 1014–1590* (Dublin, 1939).

Holt, J.C., *Magna Carta* (CUP: Cambridge, 1965).

Hook, Rev. W.F., *Lives of the Archbishops of Canterbury* (London, 1860–76).

Hoveden, Roger de (ed. Stubbs), *Rolls Series up to 1201*
    [As quoted in various articles in *DNB*]

Hughes, Rev. James, *The Butlers of Duiske Abbey* (RSAI, 1869).

Hunt, J., *Irish Medieval Figure Sculptures* (Dublin & London, 1974).

Kendall, P.M., *Richard III* (London, 1955).

Killanin, Lord, and Michael V. Duignan, *Shell Guide to Ireland*
    (Macmillan, 1962).

Kyngeston (ed.), *Expenses Rolls* (Camden Society).

Leask, H.G., *Irish Churches & Castellated Buildings* (Dundalk, 1964).

Ledwick, Rev. Edward, *The Antiquities of Ireland* (Dublin, 1790).

Leland, Thomas, *The History of Ireland from the Invasion of Henry II*
    (Dublin, 1773).

*Liberate Rolls* (Record Commission, 1835).

Mac Airt, Sean (ed.), *Annals of Innisfallen, AD 433–1320* (Dublin, 1951).

MacLysaght, Edward, *Surnames of Ireland* (Irish Academic Press: Dublin,
    1957–97).

MacLysaght, Edward, *Irish Families* (Alan Figgis & Co Ltd: Dublin, 1957).

Meehan, Rev. C.P., *The Confederation of Kilkenny* (Dublin, 1846).

Mills A.D., *British Place Names* (OUP: Oxford, 1971).

Morrin, Edward J. (ed), *Patent Calendar of the Close Rolls of Chancery In Ireland*
    (Dublin, 1861–62).

Norgate K. (ed), *England Under the Angevin Kings* (Oxford, 1887).

O'Keefe, Tadhg, *Medieval Ireland: An Archaeology*, (Tempus Publishing Ltd,
    Stroud, 2000).

O'Neill, T.P., *Life and Tradition in Rural Ireland* (London, 1977).

Orpen, G.H., *Ireland under the Normans* (Oxford, 1911–20).

Plucknett, T.F.T., *The Legislation of Edward I* (Oxford, 1949).

Reaney P.H., *A Dictionary of British Surnames* (OUP: Oxford, 1995).

Deputy Keeper of Public Records in Ireland, *Fiants of Henry VIII, Edward VI,*
  *Philip and Mary, and Elizabeth* (Public Records in Ireland, 1874–89).
Ross, D., *Edward IV* (London, 1973).
Ryan, M. (ed), *Treasures of Ireland* (Dublin, 1983).
Stafford, Thomas (ed), *History of the Wars in Ireland, in the Reign*
  *of Queen Elizabeth* (Standish O'Grady: London, 1896).
Stephen, Sir Leslie and Sir Sidney Lee, *Dictionary of National Biography* (Oxford:
  OUP, 1917).
Storey, R.L., *Reign of Henry VII* (London, 1968).
Stubbs, *Gesta Henrici II* (London, 1887) [as quoted in *DNB*].
Vicars, Sir Arthur (ed.), *Index of Prerogative Wills of Ireland, 1536–1810*
  (Dublin, 1897).
Warren W.L., *King John* (London, 1961).

Illustrations are from the author's collection except nos 2, 26, 27, 28, Library
of Congress and nos 1 and 25, courtesy of Tadhg O'Keefe from his excellent
book, *Medieval Ireland: An Archaeology*, Tempus Publishing, 2000.

# Index